The publisher and the University of California Press Foundation gratefully acknowledge the generous support of the Roth Family Foundation Imprint in Music, established by a major gift from Sukey and Gil Garcetti and Michael P. Roth.

Experiencing Latin American Music

EXPERIENCING LATIN AMERICAN MUSIC

Carol A. Hess

UNIVERSITY OF CALIFORNIA PRESS

University of California Press, one of the most distinguished university presses in the United States, enriches lives around the world
by advancing scholarship in the humanities, social sciences, and
natural sciences. Its activities are supported by the UC Press Foundation and by philanthropic contributions from individuals and
institutions. For more information, visit www.ucpress.edu.

University of California Press
Oakland, California

Library of Congress Cataloging-in-Publication Data

Names: Hess, Carol A., author.
Title: Experiencing Latin American music / Carol A. Hess.
Description: Oakland, California : University of California Press,
    [2018] | Includes bibliographical references and index. |
Identifiers: LCCN 2018000777 (print) | LCCN 2018002205 (ebook) |
    ISBN 9780520961005 (Ebook) | ISBN 9780520285583
    (pbk. : alk. paper)
Subjects: LCSH: Music—Latin America—History and criticism. |
    Music—Latin America—Analysis, appreciation. | Music—Social
    aspects—Latin America.
Classification: LCC ML199 (ebook) | LCC ML199 .H44 2018 (print) |
    DDC 780.98—dc23
LC record available at https://lccn.loc.gov/2018000777

27 26 25 24 23 22 21 20 19 18
10 9 8 7 6 5 4 3 2 1

To my students
past, present, and future

Contents

Audio Selections

Audio Files that accompany this book may be found on the UC Press website. See Note on the Text, p. xix

CHAPTER 3: EXPERIENCING MUSICAL CONCEPTS: FOCUS ON LATIN AMERICA

Sound Link 3.1. *Guitarrón.*

Sound Link 3.2. *Vihuela.*

Sound Link 3.3. *Charango.* "Alegría," by Quechua musicians. *Instruments and Music of Indians of Bolivia* (Smithsonian Folkways, FW 01412, 1962, 2004).

Sound Link 3.4. *Berimbau.* Various artists. *The Music of Capoeira: Mestre Acordeon* (Smithsonian Folkways, FW04332, 1985, 2004).

Sound Link 3.5. *Conch shell trumpets.* Q'eros authorities. *Mountain Music of Peru,* vol. 1 (Smithsonian Folkways, SFW40020, 1991).

Sound Link 3.6. *Siku.* Aymara musicians. *Instruments and Music of Indians of Bolivia* (Smithsonian Folkways, FW 01412, 1962, 2004).

Sound Link 3.7. *Agogô.*

Sound Link 3.8. Cowbell.

Sound Link 3.9. *Pandeiro.*

Sound Link 3.10. *Caxixi.*

Sound Link 3.11. *Güiro.*

Sound Link 3.12. *Maracas.*

Sound Link 3.13. *Bongos.*

Sound Link 3.14a. *Conga.*

Sound Link 3.14b. Conga in *guaguancó.*

Sound Link 3.15. *Timbales.*

Sound Link 3.16. *Claves.*

Sound Link 3.17. Major scale, played on the piano.

Sound Link 3.18. Minor scale, played on the piano.

Sound Link 3.19. Chromatic scale, played on the piano.

Sound Link 3.20a. Andalusian-Phrygian scale, played on the guitar.

Sound Link 3.20b. Another Andalusian-Phrygian scale, played on the guitar.

Sound Link 3.20c. Andalusian-Phrygian sonority, played on the guitar.

Sound Link 3.21. Pentatonic scale, played on the piano.

Sound Link 3.22. Tritonic scale, children's taunt.

Sound Link 3.23. Major scale and a I chord, played on the guitar.

Sound Link 3.24. Minor scale and a i chord, played on the piano.

Sound Link 3.25. Major scale and a IV chord, played on the guitar.

Sound Link 3.26. V chord, in a major scale, played on the guitar.

Sound Link 3.27a. I-IV-V-I chord progression, basic strum, played on the guitar.

Sound Link 3.27b. I-IV-V-I chord progression, alternative strum, played on the guitar.

Sound Link 3.27c. I-IV-V-I chord progression, broken chords, played on the guitar.

Sound Link 3.27d. I-IV-V-I chord progression, played on the piano.

Sound Link 3.28. I-V-I-V-I chord progression, played on the piano.

Sound Link 3.29. Authentic cadence, played on the piano.

Sound Link 3.30. Half cadence, played on the piano.

Sound Link 3.31. Deceptive cadence, played on the piano in a familiar song.

Sound Link 3.32. Sequence, played on the piano.

Sound Link 3.33. A familiar triple-meter song, played on the piano.

Sound Link 3.34. The same familiar song in duple meter, played on the piano. Arr. David Gregory Byrne.

Sound Link 3.35. The same familiar song, syncopated, played on the piano. Arr. David Gregory Byrne.

Sound Link 3.36. The same familiar song with some improvisation, played on the piano. Arr. David Gregory Byrne.

Sound Link 3.37. The same familiar song with more improvisation, played on the piano. Arr. David Gregory Byrne.

Performers: guitarrón, Jesús Rico; vihuela, Robert Blake; percussion, Chris Froh (with Stephen Bingen in Sound Link 3.14b); guitar, Jonathan Favero; piano, Carol A. Hess.

CHAPTER 4: EXPERIENCING LATIN AMERICAN RELIGIOUS MUSIC

4.1. "Babalú Ayé: Oru para Todos los Santos," part 2. San Cristóbal de Regla Gourd Ensemble. *Sacred Rhythms of Cuban Santería* (Smithsonian Folkways SF 40419, 1995).

4.2. "Salve Regina." Edmundite Novices. *Gregorian Chants Sung by the Edmundite Novices* (Smithsonian Folkways FR 8954 1961, 2007).

4.3. "Music and Song for Sheep." Domingo Chompi and Luisa Sera Chompi. *Mountain Music of Peru*, vol. 1 (Smithsonian Folkways SF40020; 1966, 1991).

4.4. "Credo," from *Missa Ave Regina Caelorum*. The Sixteen, director Harry Christophers. *Streams of Tears* (The Voices of the Classic, 2008).

4.5. Shaman Chant no. 11. Lola Kiepja. *Selk'nam Chants of Tierra del Fuego, Argentina* (Smithsonian Folkways FE 4176 1972, 2007).

4.6. "Kol nidrei." Cantor Abraham Brun. *Cantorials for the High Holidays* (Smithsonian Folkways Archival FW 6940 1956, 2006).

CHAPTER 5: EXPERIENCING LATIN AMERICAN MUSIC AND IDENTITY

5.1. "Sin ti." *¡Ayombe! The Heart of Colombia's Música Vallenata*. Ivo Díaz, singer, and ensemble (Smithsonian Folkways Recordings SFW CD 40546, 2008).

5.2. "Cholo orgulloso." La Pallasquinita, singer, and ensemble. *Huayno Music of Peru*, vol. 1 (Arhoolie Records CD 320, 1989).

5.3. Cordon: Candombe lento. Various artists. *Uruguay: Tambores del Candombe* (Musique du Monde, Buda Records 92745–2, 1999).

5.4. "Piririta." Alejo Benítez. *Maiteí América: Harps of Paraguay* (Smithsonian Folkways SFW CD 40549, 2009).

5.5. "Los trece." Marimba Chapinlandia. *Chapinlandia: Marimba Music of Guatemala* (Smithsonian Folkways SFW CD 40542, 2007).

5.6. "Ahora sí." Tito Matos and Viento de agua. *Viento de Agua Unplugged: Materia prima.* (Smithsonian Folkways SFW CD 40513, 2004).

5.7. "Malambo," from *Estancia*. Gustavo Dudamel and Simón Bolívar Venezuelan Youth Symphony. *¡Fiesta!* (Deutsche Grammophon 0289 477 7457 0 GH, 2008).

5.8. "Aquarela do Brasil." Francisco Alves (singer), ensemble. *Ary Barroso: Aquarelas,* vol. 1 (historic recording, reissued by Instituto Cultural Cravo Albin).

5.9. "¡No!" Willie Colón (singer) and ensemble. *Willie Colón: Mis Favoritas* (Sony US Latin CD 8869 770886 2, 2010).

5.10. "Las abajeñas." Mariachi Cobre. *Mariachi Cobre* (Kuckuck Schallplatten CD 11105–2, 1995).

5.11. "Llanero, sí soy llanero." *Joropo Music from the Orinoco Plains of Colombia* (Smithsonian Folkways CD 40515, 2004).

CHAPTER 6: EXPERIENCING LATIN AMERICAN MUSIC THROUGH THE BODY

6.1. Ladainha: Rei Zumbi dos Palmares; Chula: Rei Zumbi dos Palmares; Rei Zumbi dos Palmares: Santa Barbara. Grupo de Capoeira Angola Pelourinho; *Capoeira Angola Pelourinho* (Smithsonian Folkways SFW40465, 1995).

6.2a. "El choclo." Sexteto Mayor. *50 Best Tangos* (EMI, 2011).

6.2b. "Adios muchachos." Carlos Gardel, singer. *Carlos Gardel: Sus 40 Tangos Más Famosos* (Suramusic S.R.L. FK 026, 2003).

6.3. Yaqui Deer Dance. Male Yaqui singers and ensemble. *Indian Music of Mexico* (Smithsonian Folkways FE 4413 1952, 2006).

6.4. Cueca. Olga Guzmán, singer, harp. *Chile: Hispano-Chilean Métisse: Traditional Music* (Smithsonian Folkways Archival UNES 08001, 2014).

6.5. Vals venezolano no. 1. Elliot Frank, guitar. *Elliot Frank: South American Guitar Music* (ACA Digital Recordings 20049, 2006).

6.6. "Así lo grita Totó." Los Gaiteros de San Jacinto. *Un fuego de sangre pura* (Smithsonian Folkways Recordings CD 40531, 2006).

6.7. "La bamba." José Gutiérrez y Los Hermanos Ochoa. *La Bamba: Sones Jarochos from Veracruz* (Smithsonian Folkways CD 40505, 2003).

6.8. "America," from *West Side Story. West Side Story: Original Motion Picture Soundtrack* (Sony Master-works, 1965).

CHAPTER 7: EXPERIENCING LATIN AMERICAN MUSIC AND POLITICS

7.1a. "Guantanamera." Pete Seeger, singer and guitarist. *Headlines and Footnotes: A Collection of Topical Songs* (Smithsonian Folkways Recordings CD 40111, 1995).

7.1b. "Guantanamera." Pete Seeger, singer and guitarist. *The Essential Pete Seeger* (Sony Legacy 475 1598, 2005). Note that there is no online audio guide for this selection; rather, it is a complement to selection 7.1a.

7.2. "Tragedia de la Plaza de Tres Culturas." Judith Reyes, singer, guitars. *Mexico: Days of Struggle* (Smithsonian Folkways Archives CD PAR01012, 2006).

7.3. "Zelão." Zelia Barbosa, singer, and ensemble. *Brazil: Songs of Protest* (Smithsonian Folkways MFS 717, 2006).

7.4. "Aquí me quedo." Víctor Jara, singer and guitarist. *Manifiesto* (Wea International CD 87610, 2003).

7.5. *Sensemayá.* Mexico City Philharmonic; Fernando Lozano, director. *Mexico City Philharmonic Orchestra and Fernando Lozano* (Forlane, 2009).

CHAPTER 8: BUT IS IT ART? EXPERIENCING LATIN AMERICAN CLASSICAL MUSIC

8.1. "Venus en los montes." Judith Malafronte (Venus), Andrew Lawrence-King (harp). *La púrpura de la rosa* (Deutsche Harmonia Mundi 05472 77355–2, 1999).

8.2. "Le Printemps." Clara Rodríguez, pianist. *Music of Teresa Carreño* (Nimbus NI6103, 2009).

8.3. *Sinfonía India.* London Symphony Orchestra, Eduardo Mata, director; *Carlos Chávez: The Complete Symphonies* (Vox CDX 5061, 1992).

8.4. *Bachianas brasileiras* no. 5, mvt. 1. Kiri Te Kanawa, singer; cello ensemble. *Kiri Te Kanawa: Canteloube, Songs of the Auvergne/Villa-Lobos, Bachianas brasileiras no. 5* (Decca 411–730 1DH, 1995).

8.5a. Epilogue, movement 4 of *Canciones de Jara.* Roberto Díaz, violist; Symphony in C, Stillian Kirov, director [permission of the composer, Ricardo Lorenz].

8.5b. "Canción del Minero." Víctor Jara, singer and guitarist. *Habla y canta* (Sucesión Víctor Jara, B01FFB7DYY, 1972, 2016). Note that there is no online audio guide for this selection; rather, it is a complement to selection 5a.

8.6. *Nic Quetza Tohuehueuh.* UC Davis Early Music Ensemble, Will Cooper, director, 2014 [permission of the composer, Gabriel Bolaños].

Acknowledgments

After many years of experimentation in the classroom, I am delighted that this book is seeing the light of day. I have aimed to keep it at a manageable length and therefore do not address music in the French, English, or Dutch Caribbean. (Other fine textbooks do so and can be used as supplements if desired.) I have also tried to design the book as a springboard for independent research and critical thinking beyond the topics it introduces.

I describe my approach, which differs from existing textbooks, in some detail in the instructor's packet. Here I have the pleasant task of thanking the many people who helped me to realize it. First on my list is Mary Francis, formerly executive editor for Music, Cinema, and Media Studies of the University of California Press, who initially floated the idea of my writing this book, gently prodding me to go through with the project and shepherding it in its early stages. Her successor at the press, Raina Polivka, has consistently provided that artful blend of encouragement and firm guidance any author welcomes. Editorial assistant Zuha Khan, also formerly of the press, is technologically nimble and resourceful, as is her successor, Maeve Cornell-Taylor; I have greatly appreciated the support of Kim Robinson, editorial director at the Press.

I also thank the three anonymous ethnomusicologists who reviewed the manuscript, and did so much to sharpen its focus. My colleague at the University of California, Davis, the ethnomusicologist Henry Spiller, was especially generous with his advice. Thank you, Henry, for giving me a new perspective on the overlaps and also the points of contention between ethnomusicology and historical musicology, the discipline in which I was trained, and for refreshing my thinking on Latin American music. Over the course of this project, I have more than once recalled extended conversations with my former professor Lester Monts, who introduced me to ethnomusicology back in 1989 when I was trying to figure out if a classically trained pianist could ever hope to make a career as a historical musicologist specializing in the musics of Latin America and Spain. Lester encouraged me in ways I have never forgotten. Of course, any mistakes remaining in the book are my own.

I am thankful that so many colleagues and students responded to my seemingly infinite questions on a wide variety of topics. They include Steven Cornelius, Elainie Lillios, Víctor Márquez Barrios, Marie Labonville, Alfredo Colman, Trinidad Alcalá-Arcos, Doc Watson (a capoeirista in the Sacramento area who takes the famous guitarist as his namesake), and Lauron Kehrer. Above all, I thank composer Ricardo Lorenz of Michigan State University, whose insights into Latin American music have enlivened my thinking on the subject ever since we became acquainted over ten years ago.

I have also prevailed upon colleagues and friends for help with translations, whether from Yaqui, various registers of Spanish, a dialect of Quechua, or Portuguese. Here I thank Juan Avila, Renzo Aroni and Vicente Torres Lezama, Sergio Díaz-Luna, Víctor Márquez Barrios,

Milton Azevedo, Edgardo Raul Salinas, and especially Leo Bernucci. Myra Appel, Zoila Mendoza, and Jessica Bissett Perea facilitated several of these connections. Many are colleagues at the University of California, Davis. Others from my home institution include the composer Pablo Ortiz, who shared his insights and opinions on several Latin American genres (especially Argentine tango) and the ethnomusicologist Juan Diego Díaz, whose exhaustive knowledge of capoeira informs his activities as both scholar and practioner. I have also gained new admiration for two percussionists on our faculty. Chris Froh and Brian Rice had long dazzled me with their stunning performances but it was only when I began working on this project that I became aware of their uncanny ability to communicate scholarly and practical knowledge. These skills inform the performances by Chris in the sound links and Brian's extensive work on the percussion-dominant listening guides, which render an often complex array of timbres and techniques in a form intelligible to the student reader. Each of these artists has opened up a new world to me, and I am as grateful to them as I am to Jonathan Nadel, who shared with me his expertise in cantorial singing; Sarah Messbauer, for her knowledge of hip hop and rap; Esther Delozier, for her expertise in Venezuelan popular music; and Rhio Barnhart, Amelia Triest, and Phebe Craig, for their nuanced understanding of early music performance. It has also been a pleasure to include a piece by the US-Nicaraguan composer Gabriel Bolaños, a talented UC Davis graduate. Robert Blake and Jesús Rico, of the UC Davis Mariachi Cielito Lindo, show in both their weekly rehearsals and their ambitious performance schedule just what a group of devoted music-lovers can do, and I am delighted to include their performances on the vihuela and guitarrón, respectively, in the sound links, just as I am pleased to acknowledge Jonathan Favero's artistry in the guitar examples. Stephen Bingen, the Music Department's audio and recording engineer, helped coordinate our several recording sessions with good humor and flexibility. Karen Nofziger and the departmental staff facilitated several logistical matters. Other UC Davis colleagues, less directly involved with this book, provided encouragement without even trying to do so, especially Jessie Ann Owens, Kurt Rohde, Christopher Reynolds, Beth Levy, Pierpaolo Polzonetti, Laurie San Martin, Sam Nichols, D. Kern Holoman, and Katherine Lee (now of UCLA). In fact, all Music Department faculty collectively create a special esprit de corps that makes coming to work each day a pleasure. A sense of humor in the workplace is a great boon, all more so when the occasional wisecrack prevents an author from taking herself too seriously.

I have been blessed with fine teachers. Even those not associated with Latin America have given me food for thought on how to communicate musical knowledge on that subject. I especially thank my piano teachers Aiko Onishi, the late Raymond Hanson, and the late Anne Koscielny. Immanuel Willheim, my first musicological role model, made it clear to me early on that every type of music has its human dimension. It has been my privilege to stay in touch with these inspiring individuals for decades. My own students have allowed me to test my ideas in the classroom over the years. I especially thank those from UC Davis who enrolled in my Latin American music class during fall quarter 2016. They gave me their honest feedback on the manuscript before it went to press, making it a better book. Sandra Arias, Mirelle Sandoval, Daniela López, Jessica Nuñez, Jeanatan ("JC") Hall, and Trinidad Alcalá-Arcos were especially generous with their constructive criticism and encouragement.

Many of the colleagues just mentioned are also my friends, a fact at which I marvel daily.

Another friend, Dorothy Weicker, has been a source of support over many years, as has Amelie Mel de Fontenay. I am equally grateful for more recent friendships. Long walks with Rachelle Trerice are stimulating and relaxing whereas my Davis "sisters," Gail Finney, Juliana Schiesari, and Xiaomei Chen, are always ready to lend a willing ear—or just have a good time.

My biological family is the foundation of whatever I have attempted in my work. In this project, I collaborated with my nephew, the composer David Gregory Byrne, who critiqued the chapter on film music and wrote the musical arrangements for the sound links. Both he and I were fortunate to be raised in families where no one ever completely grew up. Just as his genera-tion did, my sisters and I played outlandish games of make-believe when we were little girls (many instigated by my sister Judy Byrne), an experience that shaped our outlook on the world and our place in it. I hope that a fraction of the imagination and sheer fun of such esca-pades have found their way into some of the assignments detailed in the instructor's packet, which takes as its premise the idea that learning should be enjoyable. Through them, I hope to awaken the creative impulse and natural curios-ity I believe all our students possess. Our ongoing quest to identify and then channel their innate gifts is what makes our work as instructors—collaborators in learning—so very rewarding.

Note on the Text

In the case of diacritical marks in proper names, I have chosen what seems to be the preference of the individual involved (Ray Suarez rather than Suárez, Leonor Xochitl Perez rather than Pérez). All translations are my own unless otherwise indicated. Because the book contains so many foreign-language terms, I use italics on first mention but then revert to roman font. All italicized musical terms appear in the glossary. In addition to Instructor's Resources, supplementary materials for the text include the following online resources for students: customized Spotify playlist, online audio guides, audio sound links to reinforce musical concepts, and activities for solo and group work. These materials can be found on the UC Press website: www.ucpress.edu/9780520285583.

Experiencing Latin American Music: An Introduction

F ew human beings are indifferent to music. Indeed, responsiveness to music is intrinsic to the human condition (Sacks 2007). When Congresswoman Gabrielle Giffords was shot by an assailant in early 2011, wounds to the left side of her brain prevented her from speaking. Yet during her long rehabilitation, she was able to sing before she regained her ability to speak. Alzheimer's patients immersed in the gray fog of forgetfulness will suddenly "look alive" when they hear music that is special to them, such as a popular song from their youth.

How do most of us relate to the phenomenon of music, which weaves itself into so many aspects of our lives? Many people consider music an accompaniment to another activity, such as dancing or studying. Others attend concerts of what is usually labeled "classical" music, at which listening is the sole activity. Others listen to music for emotional satisfaction or relief from stress. Listening to music can be a solitary activity or a shared one.

Clearly each of us experiences music in a personal way. As you will discover in Activity 1.1 (below), it can be difficult to pinpoint exactly what it is about a particular musical creation that moves us. Indeed, many people who

ACTIVITY 1.1

List three musical selections that mean (or once meant) a great deal to you. These can be from anywhere in the world, not necessarily Latin America. Choose one selection from your list and ask yourself the following:

- What were the circumstances of my life when I first began listening to this music? What was my psychological state and why was this music important?
- Which aspects of this music seemed to speak most directly to my circumstances? The melody? The rhythm? Instruments used? Vocal style? The way the lyrics fit the music or vice versa? Some general quality that is more difficult to put into words?
- If I decide to listen to this music years after these life circumstances have passed, how am I likely to react?
- How might other people in my community react to this music? What might it mean to people other than myself? To people outside my community?

Sum up your reflections in a short statement. If you like, do the same for the other two musical selections. You do not need to show this writing to your instructor (or anyone else for that matter). If you do not have a deep connection to music, write about that.

listen to music propose that if language could describe the musical experience then music itself would be unnecessary. For this reason, music has sometimes been relegated to the realm of the emotions, earning second-class status in Western philosophy, which has long privileged the mind above the emotions and the body (Claxton 2015). As a result, it has only been relatively recently that music has been considered worthy of serious study, despite its compelling qualities.

This book will broaden your understanding of music by focusing on Latin America, a region rich in musical practices and traditions. Besides learning musical concepts, you'll reflect on musical *meaning*, the ways in which music interacts with societies, environments, and cultural values throughout Latin America. To that end, we'll consider Latin American history, the events and the stories told about them that have informed the lives of Latin Americans over time. All these factors, in combination with musical sound, create a web of associations and meanings for listeners both in Latin America and worldwide.

Figure 1.1 Enthusiastic crowd at a summer music festival.
Phmelis/Shutterstock.com.

MUSIC IN LATIN AMERICA: A GENERAL VIEW

One premise of this book is that we cannot know the culture of a region or country without knowing its music. Unfortunately, many people in the industrialized world do just that. They wrongly suppose that if they can't read music, they are automatically disqualified, unaware, perhaps, that most of the world's music is neither written down nor made by people who read music. Consequently, college students learning Spanish or Portuguese or majoring in Latin American studies may know Latin American literature, painting, and film quite well but not music. In this book, you will enrich your understanding of Latin America by studying a variety of Latin America musics. (Note the plural form of "music," which suggests something other than a monolithic category.) Because music is connected to human experience, it offers us a lens through which to understand Latin America while also affecting us powerfully in and of itself. It is one thing to learn about historical developments or social practices in Latin America from textbooks, lectures, and discussion, all valuable, time-tested approaches. By also letting the soundtrack to these phenomena speak to us, we discover that experiencing Latin American music—reacting to it and reflecting on its multiple meanings—is one more way of understanding Latin America.

Like most large agglomerations of countries, regions, and peoples, Latin America abounds in contrasts. Especially noteworthy is the region's

Figure 1.2 Afrocuban musicians playing on the street in the UNESCO (United Nations Educational, Scientific, and Cultural Organization) World Heritage old town of Trinidad, Cuba.
Gabor Kovacs/Shutterstock.com.

geographical variety, which encompasses the rain forest of the Amazon, the peaks of the Andes, the beaches of the Caribbean, and the vast, fertile plains of Argentina known as the *pampas*. Besides these natural phenomena, we find world-class museums and theaters alongside areas of extreme poverty, urban and rural. The human landscape is equally varied, stemming from indigenous, African, and European populations and considerable mixing among them (*mestizaje* in Spanish; *mestiçagem* in Portuguese). Mestizaje has been common since the sixteenth century, the era of colonial expansion when Spain and Portugal ruled much of the world, subjugating indigenous populations and imposing slavery in their dominions by forcibly importing thousands of Africans. People from the Middle East, East Asia, and Central Europe have also made Latin America their home, all contributing to this diverse panorama.

Another element of contrast is language. Spanish and Portuguese are spoken today, as are indigenous languages such as Nahuatl, Quechua, Aymara, and hundreds more. Although Spanish is the most widely spoken language in Latin America, it is by no means uniform. An Argentine does not pronounce Spanish the way a Colombian does, for example, and a simple word such as the equivalent of "blanket" will differ from one country to another.

Although numerous ethnic and language groups can coexist within the borders of a given Latin American country, some individuals identify more

ACTIVITY 1.2

Do an internet search on the Mexican singer Lila Downs. Find out:

- the basic facts of her biography
- some of the languages in which she sings
- the kinds of songs she sings (traditional, hip hop, etc.)

Then, listen to some of her songs in indigenous languages, such as "Yucu yucu ninu" or "Icnocuicatl" and prepare to discuss your reactions to them in class.

strongly with their region than with a nation-state. For the rural people of the plains *(llanos)* of the Orinoco River basin, "home" is a territory that encompasses both Colombia and Venezuela, such that *llanero* identity may be more meaningful than citizenship of either country. Does this mean that the political borders found on the map are artificial? Does Latin America as a concept even exist? These are questions on which music can comment.

As we'll also see, Latin American music has something to say about the region's powerful neighbor to the north, the United States. At various points in history, the United States and Latin America have been at odds, whether due to territory grabs during the US-Mexican War in the mid-nineteenth century, US business's exploitation of cheap Latin American labor and abundant natural resources, or military interventions by the United States in Latin America, especially during the last century. Some Latin Americans also complain that US citizens remain ignorant of Latin American history and culture; indeed, a famous journalist once wisecracked that people in the United States will "do anything for Latin America except read about it" (Hamilton 2009: 126). In addition, racism has reared its ugly head: just as anti-Latino sentiment has a long history in the United States, the Indian, African, and mixed-race populations of Latin America have been stigmatized north and south.

To be sure, at various points in history, prominent Latin Americans have admired the United States, and Latin Americans have cultivated bonds with it, feeling a sense of belonging to the American continent. A prime example of this spirit was the 1930s and 1940s, the so-called Good Neighbor period, when the administration of US president Franklin D. Roosevelt (1882–1945) crafted a series of policies to unite the hemisphere against European fascism and Nazism, effectively seeing the Americas as one. This period, however, was short lived, and nowadays, especially in the ongoing political turmoil over immigration in the United States, it is all too easy to overlook the historical concepts of "Greater America" and the "American continent" (i.e., all of the Americas).

These structures of thought have also affected education. Until nearly the end of the last century in the United States, for example, primary- and secondary-school teachers would begin their study of American history with the New England colonies. In doing so, they bypassed the fact that within the territory now known as the United States, the Spanish predated the Pilgrims and Puritans by roughly a century. Since the Latino population in the United States is projected to reach 29 percent by 2050, many people are reconsidering their conception of America (Pew Research Center, cited in "The Hispanicisation of America" 2010: 35). As the Latino journalist Ray Suarez declares, "You won't be able to understand the America that's just over the horizon if you don't know Latino history. Latino history is your history. Latino history is *our* history" (Suarez 2013: xi).

Consequently, the term "America" can be problematic. When, in everyday English, we refer to "American interests," "American character," or "American music," we generally mean "of the United States." Yet Panamanians or Colombians may well object that they too are Americans since they reside in the Americas. One challenge is that whereas in Spanish and Portuguese it is possible to denote "of the United States" *(estadounidense, estadunidense),* English lacks an adjective that differentiates a US citizen from other inhabitants of the Americas. For the sake of clarity, in this book we'll use the term "US" as an adjective when referring to something or someone from the United States.

A first step is learning current borders. Central America, with Mexico to the northwest and Colombia to the south, consists of seven countries (Belize, Costa Rica, El Salvador, Guatemala, Honduras, Nicaragua, Panama) and South America consists of twelve (Argentina, Bolivia, Brazil, Chile, Colombia, Ecuador, Guyana, Paraguay, Peru, Suriname, Uruguay, Venezuela). (French Guiana is an overseas territory.) Several areas of the Caribbean are also considered part of Latin America, such as Cuba, Puerto Rico, and the Dominican Republic. Note that in this book we will not address the music of the French, English, or Dutch Caribbean.

ACTIVITY 1.3

Download blank maps of North, Central, and South America. Fill in each. If you don't know a country or city, look it up. Make sure to include

- the names of the various countries
- the names of capital cities
- the Amazon and Orinoco rivers and the Andes mountains

Commit the maps to memory by mastering the basics of three countries a day.

LATIN AMERICA IN THE WORLD

The United States, Canada, Western Europe, and parts of Asia constitute what scholars call the *Global North*, that is, those "developed" countries that are part of the industrialized world and that have similar economic systems. (Although not geographically in the north, Australia and New Zealand are also considered part of the Global North for their economies.) The *Global South* encompasses Africa, parts of Asia, the Middle East, and Latin America and is, in general, a poorer region in that food, shelter, and other basics are far less abundant than in the Global North. Over history, the Global South has been subject to several labels conceived by the Global North. These include "the orient, the primitive world, the third world, the underdeveloped world, the developing world, . . . a place of parochial wisdom, of antiquarian traditions, of exotic ways and means" (Comaroff and Comaroff 2014: 1). It pays to ask, as we will do throughout this book, how helpful these either-or denominations really are, especially in an increasingly globalized world. As you study global inequality, you may also see two additional either-or terms to distinguish these regions: *center* and *periphery.* The technological innovation, economic structures, and political and cultural clout of the center (the Global North) are generally presented to stand in contrast to the hardships of life in the periphery (the Global South). These terms apply to Latin American music insofar as Latin American musicians see themselves in relation to the center, often wearing their peripheral status proudly to defy the *hegemony* (dominance) of the center and performing music of resistance.

One contradiction: Latin America is not "Latin." The term arose in France in the nineteenth century to designate those regions of the Americas in which a Latin-based (Romance) language such as Spanish or Portuguese was spoken, a locution that would presumably distinguish "Latin" peoples from Anglo-Saxons. It falls short in several ways. It does not, for example, include the indigenous languages just mentioned. Nor is "Latin America" normally understood to encompass French-speaking Québec. (Indeed, despite the fact that Canada is part of North America, it has seldom figured in the debates among politicians and historians over what sort of relationships should exist among the Americas.) The imperialist overtones of the term "Latin America" are summed up by one scholar, who has declared that "the idea of Latin America was an *invention* forged in the process of European colonial history and the consolidation and expansion of the Western world view and institutions" (Mignolo 2005: 2, emphasis original).

Still, despite geographical contrasts, ethnic and racial diversity, regional affiliations, and the plethora of languages, many Latin Americans see themselves as unified. Over history, they not only have recognized their relationships to their own countries but have professed allegiance to *pan–Latin Americanism,* an idea tested by the Venezuelan "liberator" Simón Bolívar in the early

Reflect on the following idea: "Latin America: Label of convenience."

- Who proposed this label?
- Why was "Latin" seen as a desirable term?
- What are the principal Romance (Latin-based) languages spoken in Latin America?
- In what country is Portuguese spoken?
- What are the main population groups in Latin America? Does the label "Latin America" accurately represent them?
- How does the concept of Latin America relate to the rest of the Americas?

nineteenth century. Pan–Latin Americanism implies an essential bond among the Latin American republics.

MUSIC IN LATIN AMERICAN CULTURE: SELF AND OTHER

Music is a cultural phenomenon, one that we can "use" to learn a great deal about other cultures, just as we do when we read historical documents, analyze sociological data, or study the literature, painting, or monuments that a given community has produced. Often (and perhaps instinctively) we compare these cultural productions to our own values and patterns of existence, which we may wrongly consider culturally normative.

Of course, *culture* has meant different things over time. In the sixteenth century, it referred to the development of the mind, body, and spirit in human beings. (What we nowadays call "exercise" was once known as "physical culture.") In the nineteenth and early twentieth centuries, when people referred to a "cultured" individual, they meant that the person in question was broadly educated and conversant with art, literature, and classical music. Nowadays we are likelier to adopt the usage common among sociologists, anthropologists, and other scholars who research the workings of societies worldwide. One dictionary defines culture in this sense, calling it "the sum of attitudes, customs, and beliefs

Team up with three or four classmates and discuss your understanding of the term "culture." Ask each member of your work-group to give an example of various ways in which he or she has heard the term used. Discuss each one.

that distinguishes one group of people from another," and adding that "culture is transmitted, through language, material objects, ritual, institutions, and art, from one generation to the next" (*American Heritage Dictionary of Cultural Literacy*, 3rd ed., 2005). Included here are everyday behaviors. As one scholar puts it, "culture is [knowing] . . . when to smile, what it means to cheat on the subway fare, and whether one talks about politics at dinner" (Griffin 2009: 266). A sociologist explains that culture is "the order of life in which human beings construct meaning through symbolic representation" (Tomlinson 1999: 18). Clearly this definition relates to music, which awakens so many visceral responses and often arises in specific communities but whose actual meaning is often open to debate.

When we use the term "culture" in this book, we'll do so from a sociological-anthropological standpoint, in each instance bearing in mind the often complicated relationship between self and other mentioned above. Our selves are shaped by the culture we know. Even if we resist the temptation to consider our own culture as normative, as we study unfamiliar music, we may nonetheless experience a vague feeling of tension between self and other. One day in class my students were discussing a musical example in this book, one from a culture distant from theirs and that contained sounds completely unfamiliar to them. When a young man confessed, "it creeps me out," some members of the class laughed, a bit nervously, I thought. But in the end, all seemed to recognize that this individual had simply acknowledged the tensions that challenging the self may provoke. Certainly he could have chosen his words more carefully. But his reaction was perhaps the first step in a process of constant monitoring and reflection. Scrutinizing the relationship between self and other is no either-or proposition but, rather, a path that leads inevitably to a thought-provoking paradox: recognizing the self is the first step in decentering it and subsequently opening our selves to the unfamiliar other.

How is it possible to "read" a culture through music? Music's meanings both mirror and create societal relations and are thus inscribed in patterns of social interactions. Consider the ways in which you have just reflected on your own experience as a listener (activity 1.1). Multiply that experience by an entire region, people, or nation. Listeners, composers, agents, critics, sound engineers, publicists, performers, and everyday people who make music spontaneously may be involved. When we study musical activity within a group or a society—a culture—we discover a great deal about the values of that culture. In this sense, music becomes a way of *knowing*.

ACTIVITY 1.6

Now with different classmates than the group with which you collaborated in Activity 1.5, speculate on ways in which music and culture can relate. Then, arrive at a working definition of "culture." Write it down and present it to the class.

In studying Latin America, it is also essential to consider *cultural appropriation.* In music, cultural appropriation involves incorporating or adapting the characteristics of a particular culture's music into one's own. Sometimes such borrowing can take the form of an homage, a gesture of respect. But cultural appropriation per se is problematic, especially when a powerful entity such as the music industry avails itself of the musical expressions of the less powerful, since performers of the appropriated music may well receive handsome royalties while its original practitioners go unrecognized and uncompensated. In music, these matters are complicated by the fact that tracing the definitive source of a rhythm or a melody is by no means straightforward, since any number of communities and individuals may draw upon musical sounds that are strikingly similar.

Figure 1.3 In the early twentieth century, many architects in the United States took what they believed to be Mayan style to design theaters, skyscrapers, house of worship, and private residences. Popularly known as Mayan Revival, this style was considered authentic to the Americas. This view from Miami, Florida, shows a decorative Mayan motif.

Walter Smalling Junior/Library of Congress, Prints and Photographs Online Catalogue.

Beyond issues of copyright and intellectual property, the question of *ownership* takes on a profound psychological dimension. When a given community identifies, often quite adamantly, with a particular kind of music, tensions between self and other can rise to the fore. In part, frictions brought about by cultural appropriation are also linked to the phenomenon of musical change, a central theme of this book. As we'll see, Latin American music changes over time, just as economic, societal, political, and aesthetic values change. Couple this musical reality with an increasingly globalized world, in which the term "Latin America" has become increasingly nebulous, and it is clear that music once associated with a particular country or region may nowadays be so nomadic and mobile that it is reshaped in different parts of the world. Will this reality necessarily dilute the strong feelings of identity many feel toward "their" music? Many times over the course of this book we will ask the question of who "owns" a given musical style. As we probe for answers, we will come to recognize that no music is ever frozen in time and that whatever identification we feel with a particular style of music can be enhanced rather than diminished once we know more about the often circuitous patterns of transmission and reformulation it undergoes as it circulates throughout the world.

TALKING ABOUT MUSIC

Music is often defined in terms of sound. A sound (or combination of sounds) cuts through silence and enters our awareness through our sense of hearing. Beyond that initial entry point, music acquires meaning. Meaning can be conferred when an individual or a community associates something nonmusical, such as national pride, religious observance, or political rituals, with musical sounds. Meaning can also arise when music triggers the memory of an individual, community, or event (see activity 1.1). In addition, meaning can correspond directly to bodily movement, which is intimately linked to musical patterns.

If you peruse some of sources listed at the end of this chapter, you'll find several studies that discuss the nature of music (see also chapter 3). The vast literature on music represents another paradox—namely, although music speaks to us on a deep, nonverbal level, many people want to talk about it and have fashioned a technical vocabulary to do so. One way of introducing this technical language to students, common in music textbooks, is to identify certain *elements* of music, the various components or building blocks in any music. When you listen to an unfamiliar piece, you'll likely notice some of these basic musical attributes right away. Is the musical sound high or low? Loud or soft? How long does it last? Be aware that such perceptions are conditioned by your own listening habits and by your culture. What sounds "high-pitched" to a listener in the Global North may sound entirely normal to other listeners.

When people in the Global North talk about music, they tend to rely on a range of labels such as rock, hip hop, reggae, country, pop, or the all-embracing "world" music, a marketing category fashioned in the late twentieth century. Such labels depend not only on musical characteristics but may also relate to the following factors:

- who listens
- who plays
- how the music is created
- how the music is made available to others (i.e., diffused)
- the main use to which the music is put

Popular Music

Popular music is generally written down by a *composer,* an individual with specialized musical training. The music is created for consumption by the mass public and is mediated, mass produced, and widely diffused through established distribution channels, often with high financial stakes. Popular music is generally nonparticipatory or *presentational* in that a professional artist performs for a ticket-buying public that is separated from the artists on stage. (To be sure, the public may react by dancing, movement, or even singing.) Despite a good many exceptions, popular music is often considered ephemeral in that its composers and lyricists seek to capture the tastes and interests of the moment, ensuring that last year's songs will be "old." For some listeners, this is part of popular music's appeal. Of course, recordings, along with the sheet music industry, make it possible to listen to popular music from many eras.

One caveat on studying Latin American popular music: the word "popular" has more than one meaning in Spanish and Portuguese. As in English, it can mean "well-liked" but it can also be translated as "of the people." We use the term here in its customary English sense.

ACTIVITY 1.7

What does the term "popular music" mean to you? Collaborate with a classmate or two and devise a broad definition of one or two sentences. Apply the criteria in the list above (who listens, who plays, etc.). Then make a list of the music you've listened to in the past forty-eight hours. (It does not have to be from Latin America.) Would you call it popular music? Why or why not?

Figure 1.4 Whether indicating "Sold out," "Boletos agotados" (Spanish), or "Bilhetes esgotados" (Portuguese), signs such as these affirm the widespread appeal of popular music.

MaxyM/Shutterstock.com.

ACTIVITY 1.8

What does the term "classical music" mean to you? Collaborate with a classmate or two and devise a broad definition of one or two sentences. Apply the criteria in the list above (who listens, who plays, etc.). Here, however, consider geographical origins. Also, consider any points in common with popular music.

Classical Music

Another broad label is "classical." Many classical music traditions exist worldwide, as in the Indian subcontinent, for example. In the Global North, the term "classical music" refers to that of Western Europe, where it was generally written down by a composer. The resulting music, called a *piece*, is often performed in concerts, where listening is the sole focus of activity, as noted above. Like composers, performers have special training, many having studied classical music since childhood. Be advised of certain overlaps between classical and popular music. As we've just seen, both types of music are written by composers and a division exists between performer and public. On a more technical level, much classical and popular music of the Global North is saturated with a system of melodic patterns and chords that prevailed for centuries in Western Europe. This system, called *tonality*, depends upon a *tonal center*, a note that serves as a point of reference. Given the presence of tonality in much Latin American music, we'll explore this phenomenon in further detail in chapters 2 and 3.

Figure 1.5 The world-famous Venezuelan classical conductor Gustavo Dudamel (born 1981 and known affectionately in some circles as "The Dude") in June 2016.
s_bukley/Shutterstock.com.

Why all this emphasis on Western Europe? The reason is that this region wielded a powerful hold on Latin America during the colonial period and in the ensuing centuries. Indeed, throughout the world, Western European influence has been so strong in any number of arenas that a dichotomy arose between "the West" and elsewhere—"the West and the Rest," as some people quip. Expressions still in use today, such as "Western civilization," "Western Judeo-Christian heritage," and "Western music," reflect this influence. The United States, a world power as of about 1900, was eager to receive European culture, which it considered a mark of prestige. Further, as a dominating global force, the United States is considered part of the West.

What about Latin America? Is it "the West" or "the rest"? As explored throughout this book, the indigenous peoples of the region sustained their musical traditions for centuries before—and after—being conquered by Europeans. Likewise, the African presence remains strong in many kinds of Latin American music. Yet classical music and popular music in Latin America have been shaped both by these traditions and practices and also those of Western Europe, with many composers considering Western European standards a mark of refinement and professionalism and others preferring to develop a uniquely Latin American musical voice. In short, when it comes to "the West and the rest," Latin America is both a meeting ground and a site of contestation.

Traditional Music

One meeting ground between Latin America and the West is traditional music. During the colonial period, the Spanish and Portuguese brought with them their songs and dances and in succeeding generations, Latin Americans with European backgrounds themselves (usually Spanish or Portuguese) continued to make European-inflected music. Although their music shared certain traits with Western European classical music, it also absorbed many characteristics from its new environment, which distinguish it from European models. You will often see the label "folk" for much of this kind of music.

But an extremely important and enduring dimension of Latin American traditional music is the hundreds, if not thousands, of musics associated with indigenous communities. Some of these communities, such as the Pu'répecha of Michoacán (Mexico), lack a direct translation of the English word "music" in their language. In others, such as the Q'eros of southeastern Peru, music is always part of a ritual and not considered a phenomenon unto itself. In one Andean community, music and dance are so intertwined that the musicians who play it refer to their music-making as "dancing." As with any type of music, meaning depends on the culture in which it is played, sung, listened to, or danced to. The same can be said for the traditional music of Africans. These enslaved peoples brought with them not only their languages and religions but their musical sensibilities and practices. Remarkably, African music survived both the abuses of the colonial period and the discriminatory racial policies that followed abolition in the nineteenth century and that continue into the present. Today, many African practices flourish, some of which influence popular and classical music, and which can be a symbol of resistance.

Like most of the world's music, traditional music is often not written down, although it may be. It is often participatory, without the dividing line that

ACTIVITY 1.9

What does the term "traditional music" mean to you? Note that some kinds of traditional music are often labeled "folk music." Again, collaborate with a classmate or two and devise a broad definition of one or two sentences. Apply the criteria in the list above (who listens, who plays, etc.).

Figure 1.6 A shaman (spiritual healer) from an indigenous Indian tribe in the Venezuelan Amazon playing a panpipe.
Wikimedia.com.

classical and much popular music imposes between performer and public. As one scholar remarks, it's "music for *doing* rather than *listening*" (Turino 2008: 21, emphasis original). As in any kind of collaboration, this "doing" involves a variety of participants, each either playing, singing, or dancing. As we'll see in the chapters that follow, African, indigenous, and European traditional musics often blend, ensuring a variegated mixing of sounds and meanings.

WHAT'S IN A NAME?

Mastering labels, classifications, and terminology can be tedious. Yet the Global North, whether in the music industry or academia, is immensely fond of categorization despite the overlaps, inconsistencies, and imprecisions that invariably arise in discussing a topic as complex as music. As we explore these complexities, a few caveats are in order that, once clarified, will enable us to proceed with the musical conversations in the rest of this book.

One imprecision lies in the term "classical." Properly speaking, "classical" refers to a style of music composed in the late eighteenth century, rather than the centuries-long tradition of composition classical music aficionados enjoy. For this reason, some scholars use the term "Western European art music." But do we really want to suggest that jazz, rock, popular, and other kinds of music are something other than art? This position seems unfair to listeners who enjoy an opera as much as they do a rap song or salsa music. Another alternative term for classical music is "concert music," which is not particularly useful either, since rock music is widely performed in concerts, as is jazz and other kinds of music. As for the fact that listening is the sole focus in classical music, it's worth noting that progressive rock artists such as Jethro Tull, the Beatles, and Frank Zappa all wrote music for listening.

Despite such imprecisions, the three labels discussed above at least indicate certain overriding traits for each type of music. They also reflect ordinary usage: over many decades, enough people have accepted them and conferred meaning on them so as to furnish a degree of convenience and provide a common vocabulary, necessary for discussing any topic whatsoever. Another necessary term is *genre,* which is simply a category of music that refers to the instruments or voices used (symphony) or denotes generally consistent parameters of how musical characteristics are combined *(salsa).* Subgenres exist as well, such as *salsa dura* and *salsa romántica,* for example. It is not always possible to assign genre labels to all the music found within the broad types of music (popular, classical, traditional) just discussed. Ultimately, these terminological quirks and norms invite us to reflect on the nature and meaning of music in manifold ways.

SEARCHING FOR MEANING: WHO DOES WHAT

Among those who think about musical meaning for a living are scholars, ordinarily employed in universities and colleges. *Ethnomusicologists* research traditional and popular music and are often trained in anthropology. They study music from all over the world, sometimes through *fieldwork,* which involves going to the actual place where a certain type of music is performed (the field), learning how to play this music from local teachers, and interviewing performers and listeners. Ethnomusicologists also make recordings (field recordings) of music they encounter, some of which we'll listen to in this book. In seeking to discern what certain musical practices mean to a given community, ethnomusicologists who do fieldwork are both participants and observers in that they work from an insider's perspective but remain mindful of their own outside frame of reference. Consequently, fieldwork reveals the complicated relationship between self and other as few other experiences can.

The work of ethnomusicologists complements that of *historical musicologists* who mainly study Western European classical music. Until recently, historical musicologists (or simply "musicologists") have recovered manuscripts, often centuries old, from archives or monasteries, sometimes having to decipher older forms of musical notation. Other activities for musicologists include writing biographies of classical composers or studying in depth a particular style or period of classical music. Traditionally they worked with print sources rather than through interviews or fieldwork, although in recent years, as musicologists have begun studying present-day trends, they may well interview musicians and listeners. The divisions that once separated the two disciplines are far less evident than they were, say, thirty years ago. Whereas popular music was once strictly the purview of ethnomusicologists, nowadays musicologists study it too; likewise, on the premise that "the past is a foreign country," musicologists often explore distant historical periods in terms of cultural context, searching for meaning beyond the score or manuscript. In turn, ethnomusicologists might study classical music from an anthropological perspective or incorporate historical methods when studying the music of West Africa or of karaoke bars in the Midwestern United States.

ACTIVITY 1.10

Interview a musicologist or ethnomusicologist (or both) at your college or university.

- Prepare for your interview by looking up this individual's area of research. You can find this information on your university's webpage.
- Read the section "Interviewing Strategies" at the end of chapter 9 (p. 339), which contains basic suggestions and tips for outside reading from the ethnomusicological literature on interviewing.
- Ask your subject a few questions about his or her experience in the discipline. Some of your questions can be quite basic, such as "how did you become interested in ethnomusicology?" or "what do you do every day as a professional musicologist?"
- Ask additional questions on your subject's area of research. What new information or point of view has your subject brought to light?
- Ask additional questions on how your subject understands his or her role in the discipline as a whole. Inquire, for example, how this individual's research corresponds to the discipline's broader goals and trends. Don't be surprised if he or she has to stop and think for a moment.
- Above all, listen. As discussed in greater detail below, listening is the interviewer's principal task.

EXPERIENCING LATIN AMERICAN MUSIC:
HOW TO USE THIS BOOK

In this introductory course, we can sample only a small portion of Latin American music and the ways in which it relates to the questions posed above. Throughout, we will experience music by becoming conscious of our selves, along with our own reactions to music, while seeking to grasp as fully as possible its meaning in Latin America.

Before we can experience music, we must first notice it. How often do you simply connect to your Pandora playlist without really being aware of what you're listening to? Have you ever been in some environment and noticed music playing only when someone pointed it out? One especially enjoyable way to become sensitized to music is through the study of film. In the next chapter, we'll "listen to" two films produced and directed in Latin America, *Como agua para chocolate* (Like Water for Chocolate, dir. Alonso Arau) and *La historia oficial* (The Official Story, dir. Luis Puenzo). Both films are set in Latin America (the first in Mexico, the second in Argentina) and both draw on the talents of Latin American composers: Leo Brouwer of Cuba wrote the music for *Como agua para chocolate* and Atilio Stampone and María Elena Walsh of Argentina for *La historia oficial.* Besides the music of these composers, each film features music or instruments associated with Latin America. We discover that music is just as significant as plot, dialogue, or character and, along the way, also introduce some basic musical concepts, which we'll revisit throughout the rest of the book.

Chapter 3 delves into indigenous and African-influenced Latin American musics, with emphasis on the aural experience of selected Latin American instruments. While exploring broad musical categories—the nature of musical sound, how music is laid out in time, how different sections of music can be arranged, how musical sound is generated—we'll also introduce topics such as gender, performance contexts, and musical production, all of which relate to the music discussed in chapters 4 through 8, the book's core chapters. Over the course of these chapters, we'll study several genres (nearly fifty in all), putting human experience front and center. We consider ways in which music heightens religious observance (chapter 4), how it complements and negotiates the human need for identity (chapter 5), how it connects with the human body (chapter 6), how it can accompany political activity (chapter 7), and how it may come to acquire the label "classical" (chapter 8). The six to ten audio selections in each chapter are accompanied by online audio guides; also, each genre is considered in relation to musical change (the "Over Time" sections), underscoring the point that music is not a fixed value but rather a fluid, dynamic force.

Of course, we can discuss practically any musical genre from multiple perspectives. If we dance salsa, for example, we may be engaging our bodies, making a political statement, and expressing identity all at once. If a woman performs in a mariachi ensemble, she is likely to be keenly aware of mariachi's importance as a symbol of Mexican identity even as she is subverting gender norms. Religious music may satisfy spiritual urges but also speak deeply to a community's sense of identity. The fact that we focus on one experience per genre in the chapters that follow is simply a matter of practicality. It can stimulate you to listen to music beyond this class from as many perspectives as possible.

In fact, you'll do just that in chapter 9, which concludes this book. In it, we reflect on Latin American music specifically from the standpoint of globalization, recognizing that although Latin American music has always crossed national, ethnic, regional, spiritual, and psychological borders, this phenomenon has intensified since the turn of the present century. In lieu of the audio examples that I've chosen for the core chapters, chapter 9 proposes that *you* select those genres, artists, or ensembles that most interest you. Using the tools and musical vocabulary you've mastered in the rest of this book, you and your classmates will effectively generate your own text.

Every chapter in this book spans many years, often centuries. For each genre studied, we take a snapshot of it at a particular place and time, with historical background given as necessary. We'll connect Latin American music to general history, literature (fiction) by Latin American authors, and the visual arts, all covered in inserts throughout the text. While each genre has its own story, these connections show that music is hardly an isolated phenomenon reserved for the specially talented but rather touches on multiple aspects of the human experience. This approach, which will likely feel incremental, is simply a variant on the phenomenon known as "chunking," which psychologists have recognized for years. My hope is that you'll create your own connections between and among these "chunks," a fundamental element of creativity and characteristic of the "ravenous brain," as one neuroscientist calls it (Bor 2012). As the late Steve Jobs reportedly said, "creativity is just connecting things."

Your instructor may assign additional activities beyond those in the text to encourage you to reflect further on some of these broader questions. Another component of this book that your instructor may assign is simulations, exercises in which you step out of yourself and assume the role of another character, whether a firsthand witness to some musical phenomenon, a historical figure, a film director, or a college student in another time and place. Simulations reinforce the fact that history is acted out by human beings who confer meaning on it. More than once, whether through activities or simulations, this book will urge you to pursue history in another way: by talking to the older people you know to glean their stories of experiencing Latin American music. These projects can be powerful. One student of mine interviewed her grandmother on the music she listened to just after immigrating to Northern California from El Salvador, and reported to me, "It's the best conversation I ever had with *mi abuela*." History comes alive when you realize that you, your family, and your community are part of it.

SUGGESTIONS FOR SUCCESS: THE LISTENING JOURNAL

Since listening is the backbone of any music class, I recommend that you keep a listening journal to track your impressions of the music you hear. Try the following approach for each audio selection:

- Listen to the audio selections to be covered in class once or twice beforehand.
- Jot down your immediate reaction, in incomplete sentences if you like. Set forth your gut feeling about the music. How does it make you feel? Relaxed? Irritated? Uplifted? Does the music remind you of anything? What might the music mean? Don't hold back—write down whatever comes to mind.
- Read the corresponding material in the textbook and listen to the audio selection again, now following the online guide provided.
- Write down a few words on how the music "works." You will be able to do this because you will have studied certain musical concepts, as well as the description of the music in the text. Listen to the selection several more times.
- Listen a few times without the guide. You'll be amazed at how musically sensitized you've become.
- Reread your initial reactions and see if they have changed. If so, how? If not, why not? How did your classmates react?
- Write a few lines on what this music may mean to the community with which it's associated. Here, you'll likely rely on the textbook and on class notes.

Remember that to master the audio selections you cannot multitask. Follow the procedure just outlined without outside distractions. Once you know the music well, you may wish to listen to it as "background," although be aware this is not the same thing as concentrated listening. Consider also the role of emotion, which music constantly awakens. As some neurologists have been asserting since the 1990s, emotion plays an essential role in intellectual and cognitive development, a fact we intuitively accept and for which we now have scientific evidence. No matter how knowledgeable you become about music, never lose sight of your emotional response to it. These responses are among the things that make music meaningful and that make us want to pursue ever more avidly this enduring form of human expression. Because you will be able to apply the listening skills you develop in this class to any piece of music, you might find yourself keeping listening journals for years to come. You won't regret this, as it will enable you to come to know yourself as a listener.

With regard to this class, however, you'll find that if you write in your listening journal, keep up with the reading, and do activities and simulations as assigned, you can look forward to

- understanding some of the intersections between Latin American music, society, and culture

- reflecting on a variety of musical genres and their significance to certain communities
- experiencing on a deep level the music you study in this book—through the ear, the mind, and the body
- laying a skill-based foundation for future musical experience

In comparison with some other disciplines, music may seem to yield few definite answers, opening us up instead to emotional or visceral reactions that elude verbal description. Yet music stimulates us to *interpret,* and studying it affords fresh habits of mind and new perspectives, a glimpse into cultures past and present, a disciplined analytical framework, and an opportunity to think beyond the merely literal. This orientation is well worth cultivating and complements other academic pursuits. As college and university students, you and your classmates face some daunting challenges upon graduation. There is every chance that you will work in jobs that have yet to be invented. Consequently, it will be increasingly necessary that you leave college not just with the tools you've honed in your major field of study but with an array of other perspectives. Developing musical sensibilities and understanding music as a human experience endowed with meaning by different communities can only complement the cognitive skills you develop in your major. I hope you enjoy pursuing these goals—not just while you're enrolled in this class, but for the rest of your life. Such is the power of music.

STUDY GUIDE

Key Terms
culture

mestizaje, mesiçagem

Global North, Global South

cultural appropriation

aesthetics

Nahautl, Quechua, Aymara

musicologist

ethnomusicologist

fieldwork

pan–Latin Americanism

classical, traditional, popular music

presentational versus participatory

genre

For Further Study

Blacking, John. *The Anthropology of the Body.* London: Academic, 1977.

Bor, Daniel. *The Ravenous Brain: How the New Science of Consciousness Explains Our Insatiable Search for Meaning.* New York: Basic, 2012.

Brill, Mark. *Music of Latin America and the Caribbean.* Boston, Columbus: Pearson/Prentice Hall, 2011.

Cardoso, Fernando Enrique, and Enzo Faletto. *Dependency and Development in Latin America: Dependencia y desarrollo en América Latina.* Expanded and emended ed. Translated by Marjory Mattingly Urquidi. Berkeley, Los Angeles, and London: University of California Press, 1979. Originally published in 1971.

Clarke, David, and Eric Clarke. *Music and Consciousness: Philosophical, Psychological, and Cultural Perspectives.* Oxford: Oxford University Press, 2011.

Claxton, Guy. *Intelligence in the Flesh: Why Your Mind Needs Your Body Much More Than It Thinks.* New Haven and London: Yale University Press, 2015.

Comaroff, Jean, and John L. Comaroff. *Theory from the South: How Euro-America Is Evolving Toward Africa.* Stellenbosch, South Africa: Sun, 2014.

Damásio, Antonio. *The Feeling of What Happens: Body and Emotion in the Making of Consciousness.* New York: Harcourt, 1999.

Edelman, Gerald. *Wider Than the Sky: The Phenomenal Gift of Consciousness.* New Haven, CT: Yale University Press, 2004.

Fernández-Armesto, Felipe. *Our America: A Hispanic History of the United States.* New York: Norton, 2014.

Fuentes, Carlos. *The Buried Mirror: Reflections on Spain and the New World.* Boston and New York: Houghton Mifflin, 1992.

Gibson, James Jerome. *The Senses Considered as Perceptual Systems.* Westport, CT: Greenwood, 1983.

Griffin, Martin. "Narrative, Culture, and Diplomacy." *Journal of Arts Management, Law, and Society* 38, no. 4 (2009) 258–69.

Hamilton, John Maxwell, *Journalism's Roving Eye: A History of American Foreign Reporting.* Baton Rouge: Louisiana State University Press, 2009.

"The Hispanicisation of America: The Law of Large Numbers." *Economist* 396, no. 8699 (September 11–17, 2010): 35–36.

Holden, Robert H., and Eric Zolov, eds. *Latin America and the United States: A Documentary History.* New York: Oxford University Press, 2000.

Kuss, Malena. *Music of Latin America and the Caribbean: An Encyclopedic History.* Austin: University of Texas Press, 2004.

Levitin, Daniel. *This Is Your Brain on Music.* New York: Dutton Penguin, 2006.

Mignolo, Walter. *The Idea of Latin America.* Malden, MA: Blackwell, 2005.

Moore, Robin D., and Walter A. Clark, eds. *Musics of Latin America.* New York: Norton, 2012.

Nettl, Bruno. *The Study of Ethnomusicology: Thirty-One Issues and Concepts.* Urbana: University of Illinois Press, 2005.

Nettl, Bruno, and Ruth Stone, Timothy Rice, and James Porter, eds. *The Garland Encyclopedia of World Music.* New York: Garland, 1998–2002; *Garland Encyclopedia of World Music Online.* Alexandria, VA: Alexander Street, 2008.

Noë, Alva. *Out of Our Heads: Why You Are Not Your Brain, and Other Lessons from the Biology of Consciousness.* New York: Hill and Wang, 2009.

Olsen, Dale A., and Daniel E. Sheehy, eds. *The Garland Encyclopedia of World Music: South America, Mexico, Central America, and the Caribbean.* New York and London: Garland Publishing, 1998.

———, eds. *The Garland Handbook of Latin American Music.* 2nd ed. New York and London: Routledge, 2008.

Raymont, Henry. *Troubled Neighbors: The Story of U.S.–Latin American Relations from FDR to the Present.* Boulder: Westview, 2005.

Rizzolatti, Giacomo, and Corrado Sinigaglia. *Mirrors in the Brain: How Our Minds Share Actions and Emotions.* New York: Oxford University Press, 2008.

Rothman, Joshua. "The Meaning of Culture." *New Yorker,* December 26, 2014.

Sacks, Oliver. *Musicophilia.* New York: Knopf, 2007.

Schechter, John, ed. *Music in Latin American Culture: Regional Traditions.* New York: Schirmer-Thomson, 1999.

Shepherd, John, ed. *Continuum Encyclopedia of Popular Music of the World.* London: Continuum, 2003.

Skidmore, Thomas E., and Peter H. Smith. *Modern Latin America.* 5th ed. New York and Oxford: Oxford University Press, 2001.

Suarez, Ray. *Latino-Americans: The 500-Year Legacy That Shaped a Nation.* New York: Penguin, 2013.

Tomlinson, John. *Globalization and Culture.* Chicago: University of Chicago Press, 1999.

Turino, Thomas. *Music in the Andes.* Experiencing Music, Expressing Culture. New York: Oxford University Press, 2008.

Williams, Alistair. *Constructing Musicology.* New York and London: Routledge, 2001.

Young, James O. *Cultural Appropriation and the Arts.* Sussex: Wiley, 2008.

Experiencing Latin American Film Music

COMO AGUA PARA CHOCOLATE (LIKE WATER FOR CHOCOLATE)

It's a fine day on Doña Elena's ranch near Piedras Negras, Mexico, close to the US border. A handsome young man named Pedro has just presented a bouquet of roses to Tita, Dona Elena's youngest daughter, who is about sixteen. Tita is not only pretty but an artist in the kitchen, blessed with a keen sense for balancing flavors and ingredients. On the pretext of celebrating her first anniversary as head cook on the ranch, Pedro hands Tita the roses, gazing at her adoringly. She is thrilled at his gesture.

As you know, this scene is from the film *Como agua para chocolate* (Like Water for Chocolate), released in 1992. As you also know, the action commences in 1895, the year Tita is born. Doña Elena, a widow of a strong traditionalist persuasion, runs the ranch with an iron hand, supervising two of her three daughters and a few servants, including Nacha, an older indigenous woman who is a mother figure to Tita. Toward the middle of the film, the Mexican Revolution begins and life on the ranch is forever changed.

The director of *Como agua para chocolate* is Alfonso Arau (b. 1932). Born in Mexico City, the multitalented Arau has worked not only as a director but as an actor, producer, and writer, coming of age during the so-called Golden Age of Mexican cinema. Thanks to enviable levels of production and an especially strong talent pool between the mid-1930s and the 1960s, Mexican films became known around the world, with several earning the status of blockbusters, such as *Allá en el rancho grande* (Out on the Big Ranch) of 1935, and others winning prestigious prizes, such as *María Candelaria* of 1943. One of Arau's more recent films is *Zapata: El sueño de un héroe* (Zapata: The Dream of a Hero), made in 2004, when he was seventy-two years old.

For a time, Arau was married to the Mexican author Laura Esquivel (b. 1950), who wrote the best-selling, eponymous novel on which *Como agua para*

Figure 2.1 Dolores del Río (1904–83) was one of the most important female figures of the Golden Age of Mexican cinema. Immortalized in this Hollywood mural by Alfredo de Batuc, del Río starred in *María Candelaria,* the first Mexican film to win a prize at the prestigious Cannes Film Festival.

meunierd/Shutterstock.com.

ACTIVITY 2.1

Research the history of Mexican cinema. What are some of its high points and who are some of its central protagonists? Choose two films by Mexican directors to watch and make notes on the music.

chocolate is based. It's an example of magical realism, a flexible, imaginative style in which authors insert elements of fantasy into otherwise realistic plots. Magical realism is widely associated with Latin American authors of the mid- to late twentieth century, among them Jorge Luis Borges (1899–1986) of Argentina, Gabriel García Márquez (1927–2014) of Colombia, and Isabel Allende (b. 1942), of Chilean descent but resident in the United States. Esquivel wrote the *screenplay* for the film, the script that includes staging and instructions to the actors.

How does music enhance *Como agua para chocolate?* The composer for the film is Leo Brouwer of Cuba (b. 1939), who was raised in Havana, where he enjoyed the advantages a musical family can offer. His great uncle, Ernesto Lecuona (1895–1963), was one of Cuba's best-known composers, and several women in the family distinguished themselves musically, including Brouwer's grandmother, the pianist and composer Ernestina Lecuona y Casado (1882–1951), and his second cousin Margarita Lecuona (1910–81), who wrote a hit song. At first, Brouwer learned the guitar. Then, as a teenager, he began composing, and for a while studied in the United States to augment his early training. After returning to Cuba, Brouwer composed not only film music but many other kinds of pieces, including several works for guitar. We'll launch our study of his music for *Como agua para chocolate* by delving into the scene just described. First, however, we'll consider some of duties a film composer is expected to fulfill.

FILM MUSIC: BASIC PRINCIPLES

Generally, the music the film composer creates is notated (unless it was written with a sequencing program on a computer) and the resulting document is called a *film score.* Most films involve a music team that collaborates with the principal composer. For example, the team might research music of whatever period corresponds to the story or take on the responsibility of *orchestration,* that is, deciding which instruments best complement the composer's musical ideas, all of which relate to the action onscreen. Occasionally an individual without much musical training arrives at an idea for a score but must dictate it to a scribe. In the film music world, greatly influenced by Western European classical music, composers who have to rely too much on others for such tasks are called *hummers.* The term is not a compliment. Whatever the division of labor, the principal composer and the music team must be extremely careful about timing: each musical sound must adhere to the time allotted—often to the second—by the director and the production team. Within these limitations, the music team represents musical characters, mood, and action.

To see how these principles apply, we'll study three moments of *Como agua para chocolate* that are especially important from a musical standpoint. Each takes place at a different *plot point,* or significant event in the story. The first is the scene with the roses just discussed. It occurs twenty-six minutes and five seconds into the film (26:05, as timings in this chapter will be shown). What is special about this scene? Pedro's conduct is perfectly normal, except for one thing—he's already married. Not only that, but his wife is Tita's sister, the disagreeable Rosaura. He can't marry Tita, whom he loves, because of an obscure family custom according to which the youngest daughter may not marry but must remain at home to take care of her mother. Whereas some mothers might make this obligation at least tolerable, the sharp-tongued Doña Elena makes it unbearable. Even after learning of this senseless tradition, Pedro cannot stop loving Tita, and married Rosaura only because he wants to live on the family ranch and be near his true love. Doña Elena, well aware of the feelings between Pedro and Tita, orders Tita to throw the flowers away. But on advice from Nacha, Tita outsmarts her mother by making a delicious rose-petal sauce out of the bouquet, and when the family eats the sauce at dinner that evening, a magical mood overwhelms the room. Clearly love is in the air.

In the second plot point (1:15:57), years have passed and Pedro is still unhappily married to Rosaura. But since Doña Elena is dead, he and Tita are less cautious about showing their love for each other, and for a time, Tita even believes she is pregnant with Pedro's child. She worries that Pedro may be angry (after all, he is still married to Rosaura) but to her immense relief, Pedro is delighted by her news. Eventually Tita discovers that she isn't pregnant after all.

The third plot point occurs at the very end of the film (1:37:34). Rosaura has died and Tita and Pedro can finally be together. Like a young groom, he carries her across the threshold of a small cottage near the main house, where they make love amid the glow of multiple candles. Pedro is so overcome with passion, however, that he dies. Suddenly Tita remembers something she learned from a wise character earlier in the film: inside every human being is the equivalent of a match, which each individual must discover how to light. The resulting illumination forms a "radiant tunnel," which occasions the death of our physical bodies while marking a path that leads us back to our divine origins. When all the matches are lit at once, the experience can prove too much for the human system and the radiant tunnel—death—beckons prematurely. This is what happens in this final scene, first to Pedro and then to Tita, who decides to join her beloved. The ending may seem strangely bleak but in fact it's part of a long-standing literary tradition, according to which lovers feel so deeply for each other that their feelings cannot be contained on this Earth. Instead, their emotions are transcended in what became known as a "love-death" and they are forever united.

These three scenes encompass many years and various stages in the characters' lives. Yet they all have something in common: in each, we hear the same music. As a result, the three plot points are linked in the mind (and ears) of the viewers. Did you notice that the music was the same? If not, don't be discouraged, for film music presents a great paradox. Many people are so intent on the visual elements, dialogue, and dramatic action that they are completely unaware of the music, with its ongoing commentary meticulously crafted by the music team. We can nonetheless suppose that film music reaches even the most indifferent viewer on a subliminal level, or awareness beneath the normal threshold of consciousness. You can demonstrate this phenomenon by watching a scene that has music but no dialogue and turning down the volume. Right away, you'll sense that something is profoundly absent. We'll now analyze some aspects of music that combine to create this strong but mysterious expressive force, with specific reference to *Como agua para chocolate.*

Timbre

Listen again to the first of these three scenes. As Pedro hands Tita the bouquet, we hear an orchestra consisting solely of stringed instruments—violins, violas, cellos, and string basses. Each member of the string family has its own *timbre,* or sound quality, which depends on a combination of acoustical factors. How can we describe the timbre of the string ensemble? Is it warm? Intimate? Dusky? Be advised that describing the timbre of any instrument is an elusive business, rather like trying to put your finger on some delicious flavor. Musicians themselves often rely on fanciful descriptors such as "dark" or "bright," and sometimes use the terms *timbre* and *tone color* interchangeably. In subsequent chapters, we'll explore the fact that these descriptors are culturally conditioned. For now, try to cultivate sensitivity to the timbres in *Como agua para chocolate.*

Performing Forces

In choosing timbres to fit a certain mood, the film composer must make appropriate decisions about *performing forces.* Which instruments will do justice to the mood the composer wants to create and how many instruments are needed? (Of course, such questions are often dictated by budget.) In deciding to use stringed instruments for this scene, Brouwer and his team opted for their distinctive timbre, which some people compare to the human voice. In the scene with the roses (26:05), for example, the string timbre surfaces out of nowhere, perhaps surprising even the most attentive viewer as it highlights the sudden rush of intimacy between Pedro and Tita.

Melody

Besides timbre and performing forces, notice also the *melody* here. The simplest definition of melody is "tune." Listen to the scene with the roses again and hum along, to get the melody into your ear. As you hum through the scene (more than once if necessary), be mindful of the string timbre. Think also about the actions and feelings of the characters. Are you now beginning to associate this melody with a certain mood, even if perhaps you were not initially conscious of having done so? Jot down your impressions in your listening journal.

Pitch

A melody is a series of *pitches*. Pitches, also called *notes* or *tones*, are either high or low depending on *frequency*, the number of vibrations per second in the sound wave. In a film score, the composer writes down a series of pitches according to his or her taste and expressive aims, resulting in a melody.

As mentioned, we hear this melody in each of these three plot points in *Como agua para chocolate*. (We actually hear it one additional time but we'll get to that later.) Each time, the melody appears in a slightly different guise, however. In the scene with the roses, an orchestra of stringed instruments plays it. When Pedro tenderly greets the news of Tita's pregnancy, however, we hear a solo violin play the melody, complementing an individual reaction, a man digesting the life-changing revelation his soul mate has just confided. Play this scene (1:15:57) several times as well, again, humming along with the melody and noticing the difference in performing forces.

The next time we hear the melody, it highlights the greatest mystery of the human condition, death. As Tita and Pedro begin to consummate their love, after years of pent-up passion and frustration, the string orchestra returns in full force. Again, watch the scene and hum along, taking note of the performing forces.

Musical Form

As you hum along with the love-death scene, you may notice that this time Brouwer briefly inserts another melody, which contrasts with the main melody. As you see in online audio guide 2.1, we can label such contrasting sections of music with letters, a shorthand that helps avoid interminable verbal explanations. In this case, we'll call the main melody "A" and the contrasting melody "B." (Here, the second A is at a higher pitch, although the melody is still recognizable as A.) After B, the main melody, A, returns at its original pitch.

The procedure just described is one example of musical *form* or structure, the way sections of music unfold in time. Listen again and be aware of the contrast between A and B. Then listen to the entire scene, in which you'll hear Pedro shout, "¡Te amo!" (I love you), no longer having to hide his feelings. You may also notice several precisely timed moments of silence. In music, such moments are called *rests*, which some might compare to sighing, at least in this scene. After "the matches are all lit at once," the radiant tunnel opens. When Pedro enters it—when he dies—Tita at first despairs, and covers his lifeless body with a blanket. But when she decides to join him, the music surges as flames engulf the ranch, the site of repression, joy, fate, and desire for so many decades.

THEMES AND MOTIVES: HOW FILM COMPOSERS INVITE US TO REMEMBER

A *theme* is an extended musical idea, often a melody, which a composer takes as a point of departure for further extension or development. A theme usually consists of several short sections or *phrases,* which can be compared to clauses in a sentence. In film music, a composer can write a theme to represent a character, a mood, a physical object, or a feeling. The music outlined in online audio guide 2.1 can properly be described as a theme.

Now that we've studied the music of these three plot points, go back and listen to the very beginning of *Como agua para chocolate.* As you'll immediately hear, the love-death theme figures in the *opening credits,* the part before the film proper begins and in which members of the creative team are acknowledged. In other words, before we have any idea of what will transpire, this theme sets the tone—literally—for the entire film. Clearly it was this transcendent music that the team believed best captured the essence of *Como agua para chocolate,* a tale of memory, loss, and the enduring power of love. Each time we hear a theme in a film, no matter whether the composer changes the instrumentation or otherwise adjusts it, we are invited to remember the action, dialogue, or sentiment connected with the first time we heard it. Further, whenever the theme returns, it accumulates new meaning while simultaneously reminding us of a past event, mood, or character. Our memory of these past events blends in with the action of the present, a rich web of associations enhanced by *thematic recall,* the procedure just described.

A *motive,* on the other hand, is shorter than a theme. Lacking a full melodic profile, it generally consists of just a few notes. We can compare a theme to a complete sentence and a motive to a phrase. Just as a well-written sentence will make us want to read on, a theme will often lead to a related or contrasting theme (as we heard in the love-death scene) whereas a motive arrests our attention only momentarily. The effect of a motive can be just as powerful, however. After outlining a few other concepts, we'll discuss a motive in *Como agua para chocolate.*

OTHER STRATEGIES IN FILM MUSIC

Here are two other points related to film music:

- **Diegetic music.** In the three scenes just discussed, we analyzed music that comes "from without," that is, music of which the characters are unaware. Sometimes, however, music is part of the plot. For example, a character may listen to music on the radio, or the cast of characters may include musicians who perform. Such music is called *diegetic,* meaning that its source (the radio, the performing musicians) is part of the action of the film. Additionally, we can refer to *diegetic sound,* such as traffic noise or a dog barking. Listen again to the love-death scene of *Como agua para chocolate* and notice the diegetic sound of thunder.

- **Preexisting music.** Some film music is not newly composed but *preexisting music.* Often such music is in the *public domain,* a legal category that indicates that the intellectual property rights of its creators have expired and that enables the studio to use it with any fee. Music not yet in the public domain can also appear in films but the studio must pay fees to the copyright holder, either the composer or the composer's estate. Using preexisting music does not necessarily mean that the film composer was lazy or short on ideas. Rather, a particular song may be rich in associations and thus able to communicate with viewers on a gut level, perfectly encapsulating the action onscreen and expressing meanings that would otherwise require many lines of dialogue.

We now explore some of these strategies in *Como agua para chocolate.* Consider the *sequence* (series of scenes) at 1:30:32, in which the camera zooms in on several pairs of hands engaged in the traditional work of the ranch. The hands are either sewing, laboriously removing seeds from chiles, addressing a letter by hand, or waving an envelope in the air to dry the ink. Thanks to other images, such as an indoor bathroom, a refrigerator door opening and closing, and a radio, the viewer understands that many years have passed.

The diegetic music in this sequence (the radio provides it) reinforces the passage of time. The song is "Mi viejo carro Ford" (My Old Ford Car), in which the singer complains that his car has broken down. Whereas at the beginning of the film, radios, indoor plumbing, refrigeration, and automobiles were foreign to families such as Tita's, these amenities now not only are commonplace but can be "old." Without verbal explanation, diegetic music, in tandem with these images, tells us that modernity has overtaken daily life at a dizzying pace. Perhaps they even hint at an underlying question—namely, might the arbitrary custom that binds the youngest daughter to her aging mother also recede into the past? As you know from having watched the entire film, Rosaura unsuccessfully attempts to impose this practice on her own daughter.

Another instance of diegetic music is "Ave Maria," a religious song by the Austrian classical composer Franz Schubert (1797–1828). The Latin title means "Hail Mary," a reference to the mother of Jesus Christ, according to Christian belief. When we hear "Ave Maria" sung at Rosaura and Pedro's wedding (17:02) we can imagine Doña Elena smugly approving of this selection, which, after all, marks the wedding as worthy of "una familia decente" (an upstanding family) whose good taste the rest of the community admires. Yet to listeners more musically sensitive than Doña Elena, the singer's untrained voice, along with the halting organ playing, signals the rural family's isolation and lack of sophistication. Not only that, but the head-splitting performance underlines Tita's despair.

ACTIVITY 2.2

Listen to a recording by a professional singer of Schubert's "Ave Maria." (You can find a translation of the text on the internet.) How does it compare to the rendering of this famous song in *Como agua para chocolate*? Then listen to Beyoncé's "Ave Maria." What characteristics does it share with the original? Evaluate your reactions to the three performances in a few sentences.

Following the ceremony is the wedding feast, which Doña Elena has forced Tita to prepare with Nacha. In making the wedding cake the night before, Tita cried so profusely into the batter that Nacha sent her to bed for fear of ruining the cake. Too late: the tear-drenched batter goes into the oven and the cake is filled with sadness. At the banquet, as the camera pans the guests seated at the long tables outdoors, we hear the song "Paso del norte" (Passage to the North) played by a small ensemble hired for the celebration (19:17). They play string bass and instruments in the guitar family, including the guitarrón, a large guitar-like instrument that is tuned lower than the standard guitar. (The suffix—"ón"—in Spanish means "big" or "outsized.") "Paso del norte" is a *ranchera*, a Mexican song that often expresses nostalgia, either for a distant beloved or for one's faraway homeland. The composer of "Paso del norte," Felipe Valdes Leal (1899–1988), probably knew something of this nostalgia, since he moved north from his native Mexico to Los Angeles in the 1920s. In *Como agua para chocolate*, the singers, who are all men, bemoan their fate, feeling nothing more than a profound desire to "sit down and cry" (Ay que destino, para sentarme a llorar). Certainly it seems a strange selection for a wedding celebration.

In fact, as the guests eat Tita's cake, they too are overcome with nostalgia. Even the hard-hearted Doña Elena remembers a past love affair and begins to weep. The song also anticipates the geographical separation the family will shortly experience, since some members will eventually cross the US-Mexico border. In the end, sorrow proves too much. Deeply affected by the tear-drenched batter—viscerally affected, we might say—family and guests all make their way to the river and collectively vomit, including Rosaura in her wedding dress. It is as if they are unable to discharge their pent-up feelings in any other way.

Other diegetic music centers on the middle sister, Gertrudis. Unlike Tita and Rosaura, who grudgingly obey their mother, Gertrudis follows her own instincts. As she grew into womanhood, her sexual appetites were so great that she left home to work as a prostitute. (Not surprisingly, Doña Elena promptly disowned her.) Eventually, Gertrudis marries and becomes a *soldadera*, one of the many women who took up arms in the Mexican Revolution. She has even risen to the rank of *generala* (general), barking orders at her subordinates and sporting a *bandolera*, a leather strap worn crosswise over the chest that holds cartridges.

Figure 2.2 The guitarrón, to be studied in more detail in chapter 3, is a staple of Mexican mariachi music.

funkyplayer/Shutterstock.com.

The Mexican Revolution

Along with the war of independence from Spain (1810–21) and the US-Mexican War (1846–48), the Revolution was among the most significant events in Mexican history. Lasting from 1910 to 1921, the Revolution brought down the thirty-five-year regime of strongman Porfirio Díaz (1830–1915), ending the span of decades known as the *porfiriato,* a period characterized by internal peace and economic growth—for the wealthy. In 1911, Díaz was ousted due to a struggle over the presidential succession and a series of battles and assassinations ensued, with complex alliances forming on either side. Some of the better-known figures in the Revolution were Pancho Villa (1878–1923), a general in the revolutionary army, and Emiliano Zapata (1897–1919), the leader of an armed group that fought on behalf of land reform. The period of armed conflict ended in 1920 with the election of President Álvaro Obregón (1880–1928).

After Doña Elena dies, Gertrudis makes a surprise visit home with her husband, Juan Alejandrez. The two do a *polca* (polka), a lively dance of European origin, which came to Mexico in the nineteenth century when Germans, Poles, and Czechs immigrated there, many to build the railroad connecting Texas and Mexico. Since the polca is part of the action, it is diegetic music. It is also preexisting, titled "Jesusita en Chihuahua" (Jesusita in Chichuahua) and composed by Quirino Mendoza y Cortés (1862–1957), who also wrote the well-known Mexican song "Cielito lindo." Like Gertrudis, he served in the Mexican army during the revolution. Indeed, the music team for *Como agua para chocolate* clearly did its homework: although the viewer does not hear the words to "Jesusita en Chichuahua" (no one is singing), the song is about *soldaderas,* an association that at least some listeners might grasp and that others will appreciate once they become aware of it (1:11:05).

Figure 2.3 This Monument to the Mexican Revolution was actually begun as a triumphal arch during the porfiriato. When Díaz was toppled, work on the monument continued but during the revolution funds were short. It was finally completed in the late 1930s, during the administration of President Lázaro Cárdenas.

Felix Lipov/Shutterstock.com.

MUSICAL TIME

As Gertrudis and her husband dance, Rosaura and Tita watch the couple's agile, well-coordinated strides. Enviously, Rosaura comments to Tita that Gertrudis is the only one in the family with any sense of rhythm. What does it mean to have this sense? Is it significant that the free-spirited Gertrudis possesses it rather than Rosaura? The polca exemplifies basic concepts in the Western European system related to musical time. One, *rhythm,* can be defined as the way a given musical creation is organized in time, and is intimately linked to *meter* and *beat.*

A beat or *pulse* is a series of steady, evenly spaced durations or time units, like a regular heartbeat. The polca Gertrudis is dancing is in *duple meter,* which means that we consistently hear the music in patterns of two beats, with a slight emphasis on the first of each two-beat group (**1** 2, **1** 2, **1** 2 . . . etc.). This emphasis, on the first beat of any grouping, is a common feature in Western European music and is called the *downbeat.* Such regularly recurring groupings, marked by downbeats, constitute meter. You can experience meter by listening to the scene in the film (or by finding a version of "Jesusita en Chihuahua" on YouTube) and tapping your foot (**1** 2, **1** 2, **1** 2, **1** 2, etc.). This is the meter. Now play the polca again and, this time, clap or tap along with the pitches of the melody, played in the film by the accordion, a favorite polca instrument. (Notice also the timbre of the accordion.) Whereas your foot tapped the meter, the smaller durations you clapped are the rhythm. If you can, clap the melody (the rhythm) and tap the beat with your foot (the meter) at the same time. Surely your sense of rhythm is as good as Gertrudis's.

Another preexisting song appears more than once in the film and, like the others, is diegetic. We first hear "Ojos de juventud" (Eyes of Youth), by Arturo Tolentino Hernández (1888–1952), at a Christmas party at the ranch, early in the film (6:38). As Pedro, still single, tells Tita rather abruptly that he will love her forever, we hear "Ojos de juventud" played on the harmonium, a reed organ operated by foot pedals and popular in middle-class homes since it was less expensive than a piano. Unlike "Jesusita en Chihuahua," "Ojos de juventud" is in *triple meter* in that we hear three beats or pulses in a regularly recurring pattern. If you tap your foot to it, you'll sense the downbeat (**1** 2 3, **1** 2 3, **1** 2 3, etc.). Having heard "Ojos de Juventud" during the Christmas party, we come to associate it with Pedro's declaration of undying love for Tita. We might even say it is "their" song.

Elsewhere in the film, however, "Ojos de juventud" is treated like a motive in that we hear only a few notes of the song. One morning, after Pedro has finally overcome his revulsion to his wife and consummated their marriage, Rosaura strolls breezily into the kitchen and announces to Tita that she will cook dinner that night, undaunted by the fact that she has never cooked before. Under

Figure 2.4 In an era when many well-appointed homes boasted a piano (or harmonium, as at Doña Elena's ranch), the sheet music industry ensured that popular songs such as "Ojos de juventud" circulated widely.

Enrique Munguía, Mexico City.

her breath she sings the opening phrase of "Ojos de juventud" (24:23), this time with the words. With just a snippet of the song, Rosaura not only takes over Tita and Pedro's song but Tita's territory, the kitchen. In fact, the words to "Ojos de juventud" tell of love but also of betrayal, a wry comment, perhaps, on Pedro's real feelings. As for Rosaura, does she seriously think she can cook better than her sister? In the end, her dinner fails miserably.

INTERPRETATION AND MUSIC

Note that remarks such as those above constitute an *interpretation*. They are not statements of fact. Unless a composer explicitly says so, we cannot be sure that he or she has such associations in mind; in fact, many composers resist explaining too much about their work on the premise that music should speak for itself. On the other hand, many welcome interpretations that never would have occurred to them. In formulating any musical interpretation, we will want to give our imagination free rein but also gather as much concrete information as possible. We can then arrive at an educated judgment by drawing on musical, historical, cultural, or literary considerations.

Further, as we test our musical interpretation, we constantly engage with whatever we hear. What stands out? Timbre? Melody? Some lively rhythm? In nearly all instances, film composers will try to ensure that the soundtrack deepens the viewer's understanding of the characters and their motivations. Ultimately, as we look for meaning, we recognize that interpretation strives not so much to "answer" questions as to illuminate them, often while raising other questions. Interpretation is just one of the many delights and complexities film music affords.

LA HISTORIA OFICIAL (THE OFFICIAL STORY)

La historia oficial also deals with political upheaval and interpersonal conflict but without the whimsy of *Como agua para chocolate.* Grounded in grim reality, the film is set in Argentina in 1983, the final year of a right-wing military regime that took power in 1976. Its director, Luis Puenzo (b. 1946), is a native of Buenos Aires. As in Mexico, cinema in Argentina achieved international status in the twentieth century, with a "golden age" that lasted from around 1930 to 1950 followed by a series of films influenced by French *cinema verité,* including the Oscar-nominated *La tregua* (The Truce), directed by Sergio Renán. (Cinéma verité sought to capture the reality of ordinary life.) By the time of the dictatorship, Puenzo had made several films and worked in television advertising. But once the dictatorship seized power, many directors felt uneasy with the government (some were considered enemies of the state) and he returned to advertising. Puenzo made *La historia oficial* in 1985, bringing to moviegoers

ACTIVITY 2.4

Research the history of Argentine cinema. What are some of its high points and who are some of its central protagonists? Choose two films by Argentine directors to watch and make notes on the music.

worldwide the human dimension of this dark period in Argentina's history. Thanks to its brilliant acting and compelling story, *La historia oficial* received the Oscar for the best foreign-language film from the Academy of Motion Picture Arts and Sciences.

The dictatorship was brutal. Many who opposed the regime were taken prisoner and subject to various forms of torture, including rape. Those who were put to death were known as *los desaparecidos* (the "disappeared" ones) because whenever family members made inquiries about their whereabouts, the authorities claimed they had simply disappeared. Human rights groups calculate that thirty thousand Argentine citizens perished during this period, whereas official figures hover around ten thousand. The exact number may never be known. When the regime undertook a failed military campaign against England over the Falkland Islands (Islas Malvinas) it lost credibility among its initial supporters and collapsed of its own weight.

As you know from watching *La historia oficial,* the film is about an upper-class woman, Alicia, and her search for truth. Alicia is married to Roberto, a successful businessman. With their adopted daughter, five-year-old Gaby, the couple lives a happy, comfortable life in Buenos Aires, a Latin American capital noted for its sophistication. Although Alicia doesn't need the income, she teaches history at a boys' high school. She reminds her class that "history is the memory of the people" and that it consists of indisputable facts—an "official story"—that serve as a point of reference for the entire nation. Some of Alicia's students see history differently, however. Early in the film, one dares to argue that "history was written by murderers," effectively proposing that those in power can eliminate the perspectives of common people simply by eliminating those very people and then writing whatever version of history they like. Alicia squelches any discussion on this point, flatly stating, "This is a history class, not a debate." In doing so, she not only ensures her authority in the classroom but avoids asking unsettling questions about her own life. Only when Ana, Alicia's childhood chum, returns to Buenos Aires after a mysterious absence does Alicia begin to rethink her own behavior. She becomes aware, for example, that among the tortures the dictatorship inflicted was taking babies away from pregnant women who gave birth in prison. She starts to wonder about her adopted daughter, researching Gaby's birth records and other data, and ultimately uncovers disturbing facts that affect the whole family.

Define history. Then look up *historiography* and define that as well. Explain to your classmates the following historiographical models: (1) the Great Man theory, (2) historical materialism, (3) microhistory. Also, read chapter 1 ("Columbus, the Indians, and Human Progress") in *A People's History of the United States* by the late Howard Zinn (see bibliography). Compare these approaches to historiography with the lesson Alicia gives her students in *La historia oficial*.

FILM MUSIC WITH WORDS

How does music help tell this gripping tale? The composer for *La historia oficial* is Atilio Stampone (b. 1926) and, like Puenzo, a native of Buenos Aires. Like so many immigrants to Argentina, his parents came from Italy. Stampone began his career as a pianist, playing in tango ensembles and eventually directing his own orchestra. For many years, he performed on radio and on recordings, often showcasing his own compositions, several of which are for tango ensemble. For a time, he composed for a ballet company.

La historia oficial opens not with Stampone's score, but with preexisting music, used diegetically. After a rough, scratching sound, the Argentine flag emerges through a grayish light, and we hear a recording of a brass band, amplified through loudspeakers. We soon discover that the recording is being used to accompany live singers in the courtyard of a school, teenage boys neatly dressed in blazers and ties—future leaders of society—and their teachers. It is March 14, 1983, the first day of school (autumn in the Southern Hemisphere). Some teachers hold umbrellas against the light drizzle as they sing and several faces appear in the shadows, including Alicia's. Naturally everyone knows the words.

In texted music, the words (text) usually come first. A composer finds a suitable text, often a poem, reads it many times, and then determines what sort of music will best suit its sentiments, a procedure called *text setting*. Both the words and the music to the Argentine national anthem have changed several times. The initial version dates from the period when freedom from Spanish rule was of paramount importance and, consequently, the words expressed some vehemently anti-Spanish sentiments. (Ironically, the first composer of the music, Blas Parera, was Spanish, although he moved to Argentina in 1797, when he was only twenty.) In the years following Argentina's declaration of independence (1816), Spanish immigrants began arriving in vast numbers to Argentina and the anti-Spanish words were eliminated. The music underwent several changes as well; in fact, so many variants arose that at one point, when the national anthem was sung throughout the country, it was unclear exactly how it was supposed to sound. Eventually the Argentine composer Juan Pedro

Esnaola (1808–78) was commissioned to revise Parera's music. Finally, in 1942, the anthem was made official, by government decree.

Complementing the opening scratch of the phonograph needle that opens *La historia oficial* is the diegetic sound of traffic noises. The first *musical* sound is the anthem's long introduction, played by instruments alone. In contrast to the string theme of *Como agua para chocolate,* we hear the timbre of brass instruments, although the sounds are distorted through the inferior recording equipment. The introduction is both long and elaborate, involving several motives. Some of these motives lend themselves to marching, suggesting fanfares, whereas others are more songlike. It almost seems like the sort of introduction we would hear in an opera, a grandiose statement introducing a trained singer about to perform a technically demanding solo.

Tempo

Also figuring in the introduction are changes of *tempo* (speed). After the slow opening, the pace quickens a bit (with some interference by traffic noise), and when the voices enter, the tempo slows again. Although such speeding up and slowing down may be peculiar to this performance, it also seems appropriate to the music's dramatic style. (Note that a slowing down in music is called a *ritard* or *ritardando* whereas a quickening of tempo is called an *accelerando*.) We might even propose that in *La historia oficial* these changes in tempo foreshadow the convulsions of the nation.

Let's also consider the melodic structure of the national anthem. When the voices eventually enter, we hear a new melody, one not heard in the introduction. Indeed, while listening to the whole anthem, we realize that nearly every line of the text is set to a different melody. As mentioned previously, this relationship—between sameness and contrast—is fundamental to musical structure. In laying out their compositions in time, composers frequently wonder about sameness and contrast. Should I repeat a melody for unity? Introduce a new melody, for variety? Recall the relatively simple A-A-B-A structure of the love-death scene in *Como agua para chocolate.* As you can see in online audio guide 2.2, the melodic structure of the Argentine national anthem is rather more complex.

Tonal Center

The Argentine national anthem also involves more than one *tonal center,* a feature of much Western European classical and popular music and an important aspect of *tonality,* as noted in chapter 1. To internalize the concept of a tonal center, think of the song "Do-Re-Mi" (Do, a Deer, a Female Deer) from the film *The Sound of Music,* released in 1965. The basis of this famous number is the *scale*, "do-re-mi-fa-sol-la-ti-do," a pattern of pitches. This scale is only one of many thousands used throughout the world but is likely the one most familiar to you (listen to sound link 3.17, discussed in further detail in chapter 3). "Do, A Deer" begins and ends with "do," which serves as an anchor or tonal center, as do many popular or traditional songs, such as "Cielito lindo"; others, such as "Noche de paz" (Silent Night) begin on a pitch other than "do" but are no less firmly oriented. Although each of these songs uses other pitches besides "do," the feeling of rootedness, of being centered on "do," pervades. Listen to this scene while following online audio guide 2.2. If you can't hear all these things just yet—the elaborate introduction, the multiple melodies that constitute the musical structure, and the shift of tonal center—don't worry. Simply be aware of them and they will gradually sink in to your musical consciousness.

In this scene, also consider the way the students and teachers perform. Despite the inclement weather and the noise of traffic (not to mention the fact that many probably regret that summer vacation has ended) everyone sings this challenging music with assurance. As is common with national anthems, they sing from memory, having internalized the high-flown diction of the nine-teenth-century poetry. As citizens, they realize that the anthem is a musical symbol of their country's values; indeed, they are *performing* these very values. Significantly, the Argentine national anthem is the most complicated music in the entire film.

More Diegetic Music in *La Historia Oficial*

Another scene early in the film takes place in Alicia's well-appointed home. Gaby, who is about to celebrate her fifth birthday, is taking a bubble bath, which Alicia supervises. At one point, Alicia has to go into the next room and, in a light-hearted way, tells Gaby, "sing, so I know you haven't drowned." Gaby plays with the foam and sings "En el país de no me acuerdo" (In the Land of I-Don't-Remember), which tells of someone in a mysterious country of obscure origins who can't remember whether she has stepped forward or backward (or at all). As a result, the singer feels lost (6:00).

In Gaby's little voice, the song sounds as if it might be a fairy tale, perhaps one about a land of make-believe in which a child loses track of ordinary points of reference but is led into a magical kingdom. The song was familiar to Argentine audiences of the 1980s for other reasons, however. Its composer, María Elena Walsh (1930–2011), was born in Buenos Aires province, and by age fifteen was publishing her songs in a mass-circulation magazine; she later became a poet, singer, and author of children's books. Because her work often contained political messages, she sometimes lived outside of Argentina. One such song is "En el país de no me acuerdo." The words are given in their entirety below.

> **En el país de no me acuerdo (In the Land of I-Don't-Remember)**
>
> | | |
> |---|---|
> | En el país de no me acuerdo | In the Land of I-Don't-Remember |
> | doy tres pasitos y me pierdo | I take three steps and I'm lost. |
> | Un pasito por allí | One step over there |
> | no recuerdo si lo dí. | I wonder if I took it. |
> | Un pasito por allá | One step over there |
> | ay, que miedo que me da. | oh, what a big scare. |
> | En el país de no me acuerdo | In the Land of I-Don't-Remember |
> | doy tres pasitos y me pierdo. | I take three steps and get lost. |
> | Un pasito pa' atrás | One step backward |
> | y no doy ninguno más. | and that'll be my last. |
> | Porque ya, ya me olvidé | Because I no longer know |
> | donde puse el otro pie. | where my other foot will go. |

Clearly, questions of memory and selfhood loom. Of course, Gaby is too young to be curious about her own past. She just sings away, amusing herself with the foam in the bathtub. Yet as Gaby concludes her bath, all at once her song blends into a commercial recording of "En el país de no me acuerdo." In this shift to nondiegetic music, we now hear a trained voice with the *accompaniment* (support) of a harp and a flute. We hear a change in musical *texture.*

Texture

When Gaby is first singing, no instrument accompanies her (normal enough for anyone taking a bath), such that her melody stands alone, without other pitches complementing it or sounding in the background. We call this *monophonic texture.* Even if many voices were singing exactly the same pitches as Gaby, not adding any pitches beyond the melody, the texture would still be monophonic. (A term for this kind of singing is *unison.*) When the adult voice enters, the pitches of the melody stay the same as when Gaby was singing. But thanks to the harp and the flute, there is more musical activity. Besides the shift from diegetic to nondiegetic music, besides the change in timbre, additional pitches have been added to enhance the melody, pitches that are not part of the melody itself. (You can hear these pitches most clearly in the harp.) Still, the melody remains paramount and our ear tends to focus on it. This showcasing of a melody against an accompaniment of complementary but ultimately subservient pitches is called *homophonic texture.*

ACTIVITY 2.6

Following the lyrics to "En el país de no me acuerdo" above, listen to this scene again. By taking the online audio guides in this chapter as models, craft your own guide for this song, accounting for as many musical features as you can. Also, research the career of María Elena Walsh and report to the class.

What does this shift of texture mean in *La historia oficial?* As Gaby sings in the bathtub, the very picture of childhood innocence, her monophonic song is as simple as can be, and she has no idea of how the words actually reflect the world around her. When the studio recording blends into the scene, with homophonic texture and new timbres, nondiegetic music suddenly comes "from without," enveloping not just Gaby but everyone in Alicia's cozy home. The household—Alicia, Gaby, and Rosa the maid—goes about its usual business while viewers hear a polished studio recording of this quietly fearful song. Although the Land of I-Don't-Remember hovers nearby, its menace is concealed by the smooth, gentle music. Just as unexpectedly, a flourish on the harp concludes the song and diegetic music yields to diegetic sound, namely, the evening news with its biased account of the Argentine army's exploits.

This is not the only time we hear the song. After Alicia begins to suspect that Gaby was taken from her birth mother, she gazes at the baby clothes Gaby was wearing when she came home from the hospital (52:22). Now a cello accompanies the melody of "En el país de no me acuerdo," joined by several other stringed instruments. As Alicia dreamily fingers Gaby's little garment and sheds a tear, a humming voice is heard, now in monophonic texture. Again, nondiegetic music blends into diegetic sound as we hear the wail of a woman giving birth in a hospital delivery room and the cry of the newborn Gaby, a sound that lives only in Alicia's memory. This memory, combined with the music of not remembering, hints that Alicia is about to venture out of the Land of I-Don't-Remember and enter far riskier territory.

Given the potentially explosive words of this song, we might wonder about the effect of humming rather than articulating them. The film's searing conclusion makes this impact plain. Again, it's Gaby who sings, this time over the telephone to her father, showing the growing distance between Roberto and the rest of the family. He listens helplessly to Gaby's voice, small and tinny. Then we see her all alone, lying in a hammock and singing in the dark, ending on the words "what a big scare" before falling silent. Gaby is still the innocent child. But much has happened since we first heard "En el país de no me acuerdo" in the playful bathtub scene. After a few moments, the humming voice takes over and leads into the *end credits.* Clearly the events depicted in the film are too shattering for words.

FOLLOWING ANA'S THEME

One especially prominent theme is associated with Alicia's friend Ana, who left Argentina seven years earlier but has returned to Buenos Aires. She and Alicia reconnect at a high-school reunion held at a restaurant, and where Ana spontaneously plays the piano before dinner (15:33). Delighted to see her old friend, Alicia goes to the piano and murmurs, in English, "Yesterday," implying, perhaps, that Ana's piano playing conveys some of the nostalgia of the famous Beatles song of that name. (Other than a general mood, the two compositions aren't all that similar.)

Let's identify certain aspects of what we'll call "Ana's Theme" (outlined in the text box below). Listen to its initial occurrence (15:33). Then, in your listening journal account for melody, texture, and meter. (Try not to look at the right-hand column of the text box.) Decide whether the music is diegetic or not. Also, jot down your personal reactions to the music. Don't spend a lot of time thinking about these. Just write whatever spontaneously comes to mind.

One salient aspect of "Ana's Theme" is its consistent rhythmic structure, with its repeated pattern of durations: "short-short-short-LONG." (Note that the second "short" is the downbeat.) Any musical gesture so insistently repeated invites interpretation. Might it relate to memory? As Sigmund Freud pointed out in an essay from 1914, "Remembering, Repeating, and Working-Through," when we have had an unpleasant experience—or, as in Ana's case, a traumatic one—we often continue to repeat it mentally, reliving the experience over and over no matter how much we strive to forget. In other words, rather than fostering the ability to simply remember the trauma and relegate it to the past, we obsessively *repeat* it mentally. As a result, we can never put the past behind us, much less rise above its horrors.

The next time we hear "Ana's Theme," the trauma is no longer below the surface. Alicia has invited Ana over for dinner, and after the meal, Robert retires so that the two friends can catch up. As they laugh and chat about old times, "Ana's Theme" suddenly insinuates itself, nondiegetic music that hints that the lighthearted conversation may take an unexpected turn (22:55). At first, it's

"Ana's Theme": *La historia oficial* (first occurrence)	
performing forces:	piano
Melody:	played by the right hand
Texture:	homophonic, with left-hand accompaniment
Meter:	duple
Diegetic:	yes

played on the piano, just as at the high-school reunion. Alicia asks Ana why she left Buenos Aires so suddenly and it becomes clear that horrible things have happened to Ana. Yet the two women giggle nervously. Perhaps they had too much wine with dinner? As Ana relates the details of her kidnapping, their laughter takes on a desperate, robotic quality, contrasting bizarrely with the music and the subject of their conversation. When Ana begins to detail the torture she underwent in a detention center, a cello takes the melody of her theme while the piano accompanies. Then, when she confesses that she sometimes feels as if she were drowning, the left hand of piano plays low notes in the bass register.

By now, Alicia is troubled. She asks Ana several questions, all of them naïve. She also becomes visibly agitated when Ana mentions the women who gave birth while detained, and the babies taken from them. As Alicia demands, "Why are you telling me this?" the music concludes with a few notes on the piano, which has now returned to round off the scene. A tense silence ensues and the noises of everyday life take over, such that Ana's sad tale is capped by the overwhelmingly ordinary, even banal sounds of people going about their familiar routines.

Foreshadowing

"Ana's Theme" returns once more in *La historia oficial*. By now, Alicia has scrutinized Gaby's birth certificate. She has asked Roberto if he knows anything about Gaby's birth mother but succeeds only in irritating him. She has confessed to her parish priest, telling him, "I always believed whatever anyone told me." He, too, brushes her off and instructs her to obey authority. Finally Alicia makes up her mind. She will defy both her husband and religious strictures and find out the truth about Gaby.

But how will a complacent, upper-class woman with scant aptitude for critical thinking manage this task? How can the authoritarian high-school teacher who insists that history is not a matter of debate get beyond "the official story" she has believed for so long? One day in class, Alicia's students are taking a test. She sits at her desk, indifferent to the rampant cheating going on under her nose. All of a sudden, we hear "Ana's Theme," even though Ana herself is nowhere to be seen (1:01:06). Thanks to a device called *foreshadowing*, this music prepares us for the next scene, in which Ana does appear. Alicia has gone to the high-end clothing store where Ana has managed to find work and asks her friend to help her track down Gaby's origins. Having foreshadowed this scene, "Ana's Theme" now accompanies the tense conversation that takes place between the two women. It also foreshadows the next scene, where we find Alicia visiting the hospital (without Ana, who cannot take any more risks). As Alicia faces the unwieldy bureaucracy of the hospital archives, the deep notes of the cello conclude the theme. Heard amid the bustle of human activity,

"Ana's Theme" no longer symbolizes the trauma of an individual but rather a trauma shared by all.

SARA'S MUSIC AND BANDONEÓN TIMBRE

In the hospital, we meet Sara, an older, working-class woman whose daughter was disappeared. Sara is looking for any clue that will lead her to her daughter's children, Sara's grandchildren. Thinking that Alicia is also looking for a lost child, Sara speaks sympathetically to her and proposes that they help each other. Alicia plays along, never letting on that she is most likely the adoptive mother of a child taken from her real mother. As you know, Sara later makes a strong case that she is Gaby's grandmother.

To represent Sara musically, Stampone scores a theme for the *bandoneón*, an accordion-like instrument in which the player pushes a series of buttons, seventy-one in all, while manipulating the bellows (1:03:12). The instrument was brought to Argentina by German immigrants in the nineteenth century and became so popular that it is much associated with Argentine identity. Although many a composer making a film on Argentina would be tempted to overuse the bandoneón, Stampone saves its plangent timbre for this special moment, in which two Argentine women of different social classes and educational backgrounds, but with the common experience of motherhood, size one another up. Eventually they decide to bond.

Motherhood, Tragedy, and Hope in Argentina

Motherhood is one of the central themes of *La historia oficial* but it was also much in the public consciousness during the dictatorship. The Madres de la Plaza de Mayo (Mothers of May Square), shown in the film, began to demonstrate regularly in the Plaza de Mayo, which is in the heart of Buenos Aires. The Plaza de Mayo was the site of the so-called May Revolution of 1810, which ultimately led to independence from Spain, and is thus a national symbol. Many an Argentine president has greeted crowds in the Plaza from the balcony of the nearby Casa Rosada, the presidential residence. During the dictatorship of 1976–83, the Madres would stand silently in the Plaza holding photos of their disappeared children. Eventually grandmothers *(abuelas)* joined too, all wearing the signature white bandana. Both the madres and the abuelas continue to agitate for social causes today and are a symbol of freedom and persistence to many Argentines.

Figure 2.5 The Madres and Abuelas are a presence in Argentina today. In this photo the Casa Rosada, or presidential residence, is in the background. Gerardo C. Lerner/Shutterstock.com.

Montage and Cadence

We next encounter the bandoneón music when Sara chances to see Alicia picking up Gaby from school one day. Alicia pretends not to notice Sara, but the next day, Sara stations herself at the school and speaks directly to Alicia after Gaby enters the building. They go to a café, where Sara shows Alicia photographs of her daughter, all she has left of her child. By now, Alicia has confirmed Gaby's date of birth, the hospital in which she was born, and an identifying birthmark. As Alicia examines photographs of Sara's daughter when she was the same age as Gaby, both women realize that Sara could be Gaby's grandmother.

Montage, a set of short scenes connected by one piece of music, makes this revelation especially poignant (1:25:23). We first hear the bandoneón theme (accompanied by guitar) several scenes earlier, with Alicia alone in her bedroom the night before, mulling over an unsettling conversation with Roberto. The next morning, the theme continues as Alicia gets Gaby ready for school, braiding her hair just as her own mother did hers; the theme, intensified with stringed instruments, then follows mother and daughter as they walk to Gaby's school. All lead to the encounter with Sara and the visit to the café.

Figure 2.6 The bandoneón produces its signature sound with a combination of bellows, buttons, and the player's skill.

elnavegante/Shutterstock.com.

This sequence is noteworthy for another musical gesture as well. The moment the two women are settled in at their table in the café, the bandoneón theme reaches a *cadence,* a musical gesture that marks the end of a section or composition, providing a point of rest or articulation. Cadences, which are fundamental to Western classical and popular music, are often constructed through patterns of *chords,* several pitches played simultaneously, and are linked to the concept of tonal center discussed above. Many different kinds of cadences exist. For now, it's enough to recognize that, with the cadence heard in this sequence, a section of music comes to a point of rest thanks to the pull of the tonal center. This feeling of rest—culturally conditioned—can be compared to the way a period ends a sentence, securely and without hesitation, a phenomenon that musicians trained in the Western European system call a *resolution.* Here, the impact of the resolution is heightened by the camera work: as the bandoneón theme plays, the viewer observes Alicia and Sara through the window of the café. Then, after the cadence and the brief but electric pause that follows it, we see Sara move closer to Alicia to show her the photos, at which point the camera takes us inside the café. In other words, by coordinating the viewer's perspective with the musical resolution effected by the cadence, Puenzo and Stampone hint at the *dramatic* resolution that will now begin to unfold as the film begins its inexorable progression to its tragic final moments.

ACTIVITY 2.7

Search on the internet for performances of bandoneón music. What are some of the pieces you find? How would you describe the timbre of this instrument?

CONCLUSIONS

You can explore other aspects of these two Latin American films in additional activities and simulations your instructor assigns. For now, simply compare the musical points in common between these two very different films. In both *Como agua para chocolate* and *La historia oficial,* some combination of musical ingredients—timbre, melody, rhythm, meter, performing forces—highlights the dramatic action. In each film the music team takes advantage both of the composer's score and of preexisting music, used diegetically or nondiegetically, to enhance the action. In some instances, music complements the characters' actions, reinforcing their personalities and their motives, but elsewhere it comments on the characters, perhaps conveying information to viewers of which the characters themselves are unaware. All these musical gestures are subject to interpretation. As Rosaura sings a few notes of "Ojos de juventud," is she really conscious of her broken heart? Can little Gaby possibly know the import of "En el país de no me acuerdo"? Clearly, film music can be as powerful as plot, character, setting, or cinematography. Although film audiences may often be only subliminally aware of music, once we bring it to the forefront of our consciousness and analyze its ingredients, we stimulate the creative impulse for music all human beings possess and enrich our experience of any film we choose to watch.

Although the scores for both of these films are by Latin Americans, the music is influenced by Western European classical and popular music. In the next chapter, we'll expand our musical understanding by exploring a host of Latin American musical practices that fall outside of the Western European tradition.

STUDY GUIDE

Key Terms

magical realism	timbre
Mexican Revolution	pitch
film score	melody
plot point	theme, motive
preexisting music	diegetic music
public domain	nondiegetic music
	opening credits

end credits

meter

rhythm

form

tonality

tonal center

foreshadowing

sequence

tempo

montage

bandoneón

text setting

For Further Study

Freud, Sigmund. "Remembering, Repeating, and Working-Through." In *The Standard Edition of the Complete Psychological Works of Sigmund Freud*, edited and translated by James Strachey, vol. 12, 147–56. London: Hogarth, 1958.

Gardner, Nathanial. *Como agua para chocolate: The Novel and Film Version*. Critical Guides to Spanish & Latin American Texts and Films. London: Grant & Cutler, 2009.

Gilly, Adolfo. *The Mexican Revolution*. New Press People's History. New York: New Press, 2006.

Hart, Stephen. *Como agua: A Companion to Latin American Film*. Rochester: Tamesis, 2014.

López-Rodríguez, Miriam. "Cooking Mexicanness: Shaping National Identity in Alfonso Arau's *Como Agua*." In *Reel Food: Essays on Food and Film*, edited by Anne L. Bower, 61–74. London: Routledge, 2004.

Niebylski, Dianna. "Passion or Heartburn? The Uses of Humor in Esquivel's and Arau's *Like Water for Chocolate*." In *Literature and Film: A Guide to the Theory and Practice of Film Adaptation*, edited by Robert Stam and Alessandra Raengo. Oxford: Blackwell, 2005.

Prendergast, Roy M. *Film Music: A Neglected Art*. 2nd ed. New York and London: Norton, 1992.

Timerman, Jacobo. *Prisoner without a Name, Cell without a Number*. Translated by Tony Talbot. New York: Knopf, 1981.

Zinn, Howard. *A People's History of the United States*. New York: HarperCollins, 2003.

Reading for Pleasure

Azuela, Mariano. *The Underdogs: A Novel of the Mexican Revolution*. Translated by Sergio Waisman. New York and London: Penguin, 2008. Original: *Los de abajo* (1915).

Esquivel, Laura. *Like Water for Chocolate*. Translated by Carol Christensen and Thomas Christensen. New York: Doubleday, 1992. Original: *Como agua para chocolate* (1989).

Lisé, Gloria. *Departing at Dawn: A Novel of Argentina's Dirty War*. Translated by Alice Weldon. New York: Feminist Press at the City University of New York, 2009. Original: *Viene clareando* (2005).

Experiencing Musical Concepts: Focus on Latin America

In chapter 2 we analyzed two Latin American film scores and identified several aspects of music that likely sounded familiar to you. We now focus on musical concepts in a wider context, beginning with several Latin American instruments and their timbres. Sound links referred to in this chapter are available on the UC Press website at www.ucpress.edu/9780520285583.

WHAT'S PLAYING? TIMBRE AND PERFORMING FORCES

As we've learned, timbre simply means sound quality. For many listeners, it provokes an immediate reaction. When a certain timbre catches our attention, we may say, "I wonder what instrument is playing" or even "what are the performing forces?" On a higher level of inquiry, we can consider timbre in terms of context: What does the instrument that produces it mean to a given community?

Latin American music offers a vast array of instruments, each with its own timbre. This wealth of instruments can be fruitfully compared to the number of indigenous languages that once existed in Latin America. When Columbus landed in the Americas in 1492, approximately two thousand indigenous languages were spoken in Latin America. If we assume that each language group probably played at least three different musical instruments, we arrive at a total of some six thousand instruments, and when we add those brought by the Spanish, Portuguese, and Africans, the total is closer to seven thousand. Although many instruments fell out of use as indigenous cultures disappeared, the number is nonetheless impressive.

Don't worry—you won't be expected to identify the timbres of thousands of Latin American instruments. But sound links 3.1–3.16 will introduce you to a few that will both orient you and develop your ability to discriminate between one timbre and another, an ability that will transfer to whatever listening you do in the future. Listen to each sound link several times and see how easy or hard it is to tell them apart. Don't be too concerned about naming the instruments, at least not at first. Simply internalize the timbre and be aware that both the materials and the method of construction used to make the instrument affect timbre.

Now, a few words on some of the instruments that produce these timbres (see also images starting on page 53). Along with the guitar, the vihuela and the guitarrón form the harmonic and rhythmic underpinning of the typical *mariachi* ensemble. Other mariachi instruments include trumpets and violins, often playing in harmony. The guitarrón, vihuela, charango, and berimbau are just three among the hundreds of stringed instruments that exist throughout Latin America. Some of these instruments have followed a complicated trajectory. The Brazilian *cavaquinho*, for example, resembles the Hawa'iian ukulele but was actually modeled on an instrument brought to Hawa'ii by immigrants from Portugal. Despite their resemblance, the two instruments are tuned differently and the cavaquinho has wire rather than nylon strings. One final point: prior to the Conquest, there were no stringed instruments in what we now call Latin America.

Both conch shell trumpets and sikus, which rely on the player's breath, were played in Latin America centuries before the Conquest. You've also heard the timbres of several percussion instruments, some of which, like the berimbau, were brought to Latin America by enslaved Africans. As you listen again to sound links 3.13–16, pay particular attention to timbre and be aware that African drummers greatly prize timbral variety, which they achieve by using some of the strategies just described. In addition to the thousands of instruments found in Latin American music, human voices, used in hundreds of ways, possess their own timbres.

Sound Link 3.1. *Guitarrón.*   This stringed instrument, which looks like an over-sized guitar, is featured in *Como agua para chocolate* at Rosaura's ill-fated wedding banquet (revisit figure 2.2). Despite its size, the guitarrón is surprisingly light. Its six strings are tuned lower than those of the standard acoustic guitar and it generally plays the lowest part, often short, repeated melodies that mark out the harmony and that the other instruments weave around.

Sound Link 3.2. *Vihuela.*   Narrower than the standard six-string guitar, the vihuela is smaller than the guitarrón, although it is made of the same kind of wood. Instead of six strings it has five, which are tuned to higher pitches than those of the guitarrón and which go upward for the first three strings and then down for the remaining ones, a format called *reentrant tuning*.

Sound Link 3.3. *Charango.*   Also in the guitar family is the charango, from the Andean region. In its indigenous guise, the charango is often quite small in size. It also varies in materials: the charango in sound link 3.3 is made from an armadillo shell. Most indigenous charangos have ten or twelve thin metal strings whereas the charango associated with mestizo performers has nylon strings, which produce a less penetrating sound.

Figure 3.1 The charango has undergone any number of variants in shape and number of strings over the years, although one unifying factor is its small size.
Grinchenkova Anzhela/Shutterstock.com.

Sound Link 3.4. *Berimbau.*   This Afro-Brazilian instrument consists of a hollowed-out gourd attached to a musical bow made of wood and a single metal string stretched the length of the bow. The sound is produced when the player strikes the string with a stick. Berimbaus come in different sizes and figure prominently in Brazilian capoeira, a martial art that resembles a dance.

Figure 3.2 Berimbau player using a stick and a stone to produce sound.

Gergely Zsolnai/Shutterstock.com.

Sound Link 3.5. *Conch shell trumpet.* As pictorial evidence shows, conch shell trumpets were common in pre-Conquest Mexico. (Other types of trumpets are depicted in murals at Bonampák, the ancient Mayan architectural site in Chiapas state.) The Andean version, called a *qquepa,* could be made of a conch shell, clay, or metal. The instruments heard here, with drums, accompany a pilgrimage.

Sound Link 3.6. *Siku.* "Siku" is the Aymara word for Andean panpipes. (The Quechua word is *antara;* the Spanish is *zampona.*) It consists of a double row of panpipes, made of bamboo or cane. Sikus are generally played in groups of ten to fifteen musicians. Sound link 3.6 features fourteen siku players and five drummers.

Figure 3.3 Siku (panpipe) common in Andean music.
elnavegante/Shutterstock.com.

Sound Link 3.7. *Agogô.* This double bell, made of iron, is used in ensembles that accompany Brazilian samba and other genres. The two bells are connected by a piece of flexible metal. In sound link 3.7, the player strikes them with a wooden stick. Note the timbral variety: one timbre for one bell, one for the other, and a third timbre that is produced when the two bells are squeezed together thanks to the flexible metal that joins them.

Sound Link 3.8. *Cowbell.*   The player holds the metal bell and strikes it with a heavy wood stick, either on the rim of the bell (making an open sound) or on top of the bell using the tip of the stick (making a closed sound).

Sound Link 3.9. *Pandeiro.*   The pandeiro, used in several traditional Brazilian genres, resembles a tambourine. Essentially a shallow drum, it has a wooden frame and metal jingles. The head of the drum can be tuned for higher or lower pitches, which can be regulated by the player. Compare the deeper, open sound produced with the thumb on the head of the instrument, to the closed sound, produced with a slap. All are enhanced by the jingles.

Sound Link 3.10. *Caxixi.*   Also used in Brazilian capoeira, this handheld rattle looks like a small, closed basket. Inside are beans, seeds, or stones, which sound when the basket is shaken. A piece of gourd sewn to the bottom serves as a resonator and permits variety of timbre and volume: if the materials inside hit the gourd, the sound will be louder than if they hit the wicker basket. A player may shake one or more caxixi at a time. (In sound link 3.10, the performer is playing two at once.)

Figure 3.4 Caxixi, used in capoeira. Note that the berimbau player in figure 3.2 is playing a caxixi with his right hand.
GoodMood Photo/Shutterstock.com.

Sound Link 3.11. *Güiro.* The güiro is a dried gourd with a series of notches cut into it, against which the player scrapes a wooden or metal stick. Güiros are common in the Caribbean and in Central America; they can also be found in parts of Mexico. In this recording, the player sweeps a metal comb along the notches.

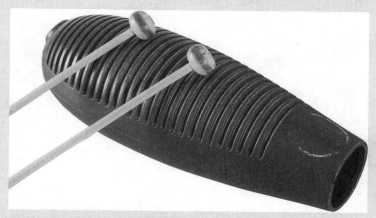

Figure 3.5 Güiro, a percussion instrument found in many kinds of Latin American music.
Baishev/Shutterstock.com.

Sound Link 3.12. *Maracas.* Maracas are rattles made from wood, leather, or small gourds, and contain seeds. They are usually played in pairs and can be found throughout Latin America, especially in Cuba, Mexico, and Puerto Rico. Listen for the higher and lower-pitched sounds produced in sound link 3.12.

Sound Link 3.13. *Bongos.* These small, paired drums are joined by a piece of wood and figure in many kinds of African-influenced music. Bongos have no bottoms and one is usually slightly larger than the other. Notice that in this example, the performer makes two different kinds of sounds on the higher-pitched drum and an open tone on the lower one.

Sound Link 3.14a. *Conga.* Conga drums, used in many Afro-Cuban musical genres, are taller than bongos and have a lower range. Compare the low-pitched sound, produced by striking the drum with the palm of the hand, to the higher-pitched, accented "slap."

Sound Link 3.14b. Conga in *guaguancó*.   One genre that features the conga drum and shows the variety of sounds it affords is *guaguancó,* a Cuban couple dance. In sound link 3.14b, one player performs on a higher-pitched conga and another plays two lower-pitched ones in a guaguancó rhythm, repeating the same pattern or "groove." By listening for all three drums you can cultivate your sensitivity to timbre.

Sound Link 3.15. *Timbales*.   Like bongos, timbales are paired drums and are used in salsa and other Caribbean genres. Unlike bongos, they are arranged on a stand and resemble snare drums such as those in military bands. (In fact, during the colonial period in Cuba such drums were played by black and mixed-race conscripts.) The sticks are thinner than those used for snare drums but otherwise quite similar. The player can strike both the head and the sides of the drum. In sound link 3.15 notice the open sound of each drum along with the characteristic *rim shot,* a sharply accented sound made when the player strikes the head and the rim simultaneously.

Sound Link 3.16. *Claves*.   Claves are wooden dowels that the player strikes together to establish the basic pattern of several African-influenced genres. The wood used may vary, and a clave stick may be hollow. (The claves used in sound link 3.16, both of the same size, are made of rosewood and neither one is hollow.) A clave rhythm consists of a group of three beats followed by a group of two beats or vice versa. For this reason, musicians may refer to the "three side" or the "two side" of the clave. The pattern here is called a 3–2 *son* clave, meaning that the three-beat group comes first. (The Cuban son is a genre we'll study later.) Internalize the rhythm by clapping along.

Figure 3.6 Wooden claves, common in many African-influenced Latin American genres.

Miguel García Saavedra/ Shutterstock.com.

Listen to sounds you might not ordinarily categorize as music. Try sitting in a café, in your student center, or someplace where you can safely observe traffic noises or the sounds of human activity. Spend at least ten minutes, with your recording device turned on. Make notes on those sounds that stand out to you. Can you identify them? Can you comment on their timbre or volume? Then, listen to your recording. Did you actually register all the sounds that surrounded you or were your perceptions selective?

Hearing Timbre

Whenever you hear a timbre, especially an unfamiliar one, it will be useful to study the way you process it. Everyone reacts differently to sound. For example, adjectives may well occur to you, such as "heavy," "bright," or "dark." Be sensitive to the fact that such adjectives are subjective and culturally conditioned. What sounds "dull" or "nasal" to you may prompt an entirely different reaction to someone else, especially someone from another culture.

Also recognize that whenever you express approval or disapproval toward any musical utterance, you are making an *aesthetic* judgment. Aesthetics is the branch of philosophy concerned with evaluating works of art, and aesthetic judgments are also culturally conditioned. In Panamanian traditional music, for example, a good voice is one that is powerful enough to cut through other instruments (including drums), a chorus, or even outside noise. Listeners from another culture might find such a voice strident. It will be helpful to think of musical characteristics as existing along a continuum: some pieces will simply be louder, softer, higher, lower, faster, or slower than others.

As your hearing grows more acute, you'll be able to identify multiple instruments, even when several are playing at once. In other words, you'll hear the performing forces. Likewise, if certain timbres are already familiar to you, you can refine your experience of these. Maybe you play the piano. Can you hear a difference between a concert grand and the dilapidated upright in your campus cafeteria? This is only one kind of aural discrimination that can enhance the musical experience. In the chapters to come, you'll be exposed to many more timbres from Latin America.

ORGANOLOGY

The study of musical instruments is called *organology.* Among other things, it encompasses the histories of instruments and their acoustic properties.

Cultures around the world classify instruments in various ways. In certain communities from West Africa, a region that influenced much Latin American music, instruments fall into one of two categories in that they are either struck or blown into. One taxonomy, used in the Global North since the early twentieth century, initially comprised four categories. Devised by two German scholars, Curt Sachs (1881–1959) and Erich von Hornbostel (1877–1935), the *Sachs-Hornbostel system* encompasses thousands of instruments. It takes as a point of departure the nature of the vibrating medium that produces the sound. In other words, each category identifies the cause or agent of the sound, which is transmitted in waves from a given source (the instrument) and registered in the listener's brain via the eardrum:

- *idiophone.* An idiophone produces sound when shaken or struck. We hear the sound thanks to the resonance of the instrument itself. (The prefix "idio-" means "proper to one" or "one's own.") Some common idiophones are rattles, such as the caxixi.
- *membranophone.* A membranophone produces sound through a membrane stretched over a support, which is then struck. Animal skins traditionally served as membranes but nowadays synthetic materials are used. Drums, such as the conga, are membranophones.
- *chordophone.* A chordophone involves a string stretched over a support. When the string is plucked, bowed, or strummed, it vibrates and generates sound. The stringed instruments heard in chapter 2—violin, string bass, guitarrón—are chordophones, as is the berimbau.
- *aerophone.* An aerophone generates sound through a vibrating column of air. The air may be blown directly into the instrument or through a reed or mouthpiece. Latin American aerophones inlcude panpipes and conch shell trumpets.

In the latter part of the twentieth century, a fifth category arose. Thanks to synthesizers, electric guitars, and other instruments that generate sound via electronics, some ethnomusicologists proposed the category *electrophone.* Another category is the *corpophone,* in which sounds are generated by the human body, as occurs with finger snapping, hand clapping, or thigh slapping. Listen again to the sound links above and reread the descriptions of the various instruments. This time, bear in mind where each fits in the Sachs-Hornbostel classification system.

INSTRUMENTS AND MEANING

Acoustic and material properties aside, an instrument can tell us a great deal about a given community and what that community considers meaningful, whether from a cultural or aesthetic point of view—or both. Some basic parameters here include

- technique
- blended versus differentiated sound
- ensemble relations
- gender roles
- identity
- production

Technique

Technique is the ability to control an instrument or one's vocal cords to produce whatever sound is desired. As such, technique can reinforce the values of a given culture. In Andean ensembles, sikus are played in pairs, with the whole group of ten to fifteen players standing in a circle. The technique involves one individual in each pair playing a pitch followed by the partner, who plays the next pitch, followed by the first player, etc., with each sound overlapping slightly with the preceding one to avoid gaps in the melody. (This interlocking format is also called *hocket*.) The resulting melody is a shared one, reinforcing the communitarian values of Andean culture. Listen again to sound link 3.6 and see if you can hear this technique.

Blended versus Differentiated Sounds

Culture and aesthetics merge when ensembles (groups of musicians) play or sing. Some ensembles involve differentiated (heterogeneous) sounds, such as Afro-Uruguayan candombe studied in chapter 5, which draws on the timbral variety of drums. Other ensembles use similar instruments and cultivate a blended (homogenous) sound, such as the eight cellos in a work by the Brazilian classical composer Heitor Villa-Lobos, studied in chapter 8. These practices can change over time. For example, mariachi ensembles originally consisted solely of stringed instruments, including violin, vihuela, guitarrón, guitar, and harp, resulting in a homogeneous sound. When the harp was eventually eliminated and the trumpet added, the sound became more heterogeneous.

Ensemble Relations

Also important in ensemble are the roles taken by its members. Is there generally a leader, as in capoeira? Or do all the musicians have an equal role, as in much Latin American chamber music influenced by the Western European tradition? Even in communities with a long history of participatory music making, some individuals will likely dance, sing, or play more capably than others. Beginners seek out a skill level appropriate to their abilities while more experienced players assume a leadership position, sometimes guiding those with less experience. This situation prevails in various Andean communities, where musicians play at festival time.

Gender

Such practices can also relate to gender. Gender roles are determined by the cultural norms of a given community, thanks to which behaviors typically understood by that community to be male or female are inculcated. (Sex, on the other hand, is biological, although nowadays, as more people are having sex reassignment surgery, cultural conditioning is in flux in many parts of the world.) In some Quechua and Aymara communities, women don't play musical instruments but do sing, since their voices are preferred to those of men. The indigenous charango heard in sound link 3.3 was traditionally used for courting and played only by young, unmarried men. As one informant explains, "once a man marries, he must put away his . . . *charango*, and if an older married man were to pick up a stringed instrument and play it, it would seem an absurd sight, even laughable, since it would look like the man was trying to 'pick up' a younger girl" (Turino 2008: 53). Besides performance practices, a genre itself may be influenced by gender. Salsa, for example, has traditionally been male dominated, with most songs written by men and many salsa lyrics stereotyping women's bodies or implicitly defending a double standard. To be sure, gender roles have changed in some of these male-dominated Latin American genres. For example, several female salsa artists have challenged the norms described above, just as some Latin American women classical musicians are overcoming gender stereotypes by working as symphony conductors, a job in which men significantly outnumber women.

Instruments themselves can be gendered. In Afro-Venezuelan communities where different-sized maracas are played in pairs, the larger one is considered male because it contains more seeds and has a deeper sound. The smaller one, with fewer seeds and a higher-pitched sound, is considered female. Among the Garífuna of Belize, the drums used in religious music are gendered, with the lead drum considered male (the *primera*) and a bigger drum *(segunda)* female.

Identity

So important are some instruments in a nation, region, or other entity that they take on symbolic value for that community and become part of its identity. We've already noted that the striking timbre of the bandoneón is much associated with Argentina, despite the instrument's German origins. As we'll see, the harp became closely identified with Paraguay, as the marimba did with Nicaragua and Guatemala.

Production

Instruments may be produced in consistent forms (standardized) or individually crafted. Many European or European-derived instruments, such as the vihuela, are mass produced nowadays although one can always find skilled craftspeople who prove the exception to the rule. Likewise, instruments in a symphony orchestra may be either handcrafted or mass produced, although the basic sizes and materials are generally consistent. A violin bigger than the standard size, however, is used in the music that accompanies *matachines,* dancers who enact medieval battles in brightly colored costumes, performing from Peru to New Mexico in a centuries-old dance ritual introduced by colonial missionaries but elaborated by indigenous peoples. Instruments such as the flutes once played by indigenous communities in Mexico and Guatemala are individually made.

Some instruments carry prestige. In Latin America, the piano, a European invention, has generally been confined to the homes of the wealthy. Instruments with elaborate carvings, paintings, or other artwork may also be highly valued. The latter instruments may also reinforce religious precepts, as in the carvings on ceremonial drums from pre-Conquest Mexico that depict a jaguar, which has godlike status. Critical here is *material culture,* or the physical artifacts of a community. What materials are available for instrument building? What tools are required? What are the methods of production? Clay, for example, which is both sturdy and versatile, proved ideal for pre-Conquest indigenous flutes and made it possible to construct flutes shaped like animals or human figures. Such designs, however, ensured that these instruments were not taken seriously in the Global North, where they were practically considered toys—or at least oddities—and displayed in museums, sometimes for imperialist motives. In the 1980s, a research team of archeologists, musicians, anthropologists, and ethnomusicologists studied their acoustic properties using tools such as X-rays and stroboscopes. They discovered that many are quite complex, with carefully calibrated tuning systems not replicated in other instruments.

VOLUME

The loudness or softness of a sound, called *dynamics* in Western European musical parlance, is also related to instrument technology. Certain instruments are designed to play more loudly than others. If you return to sound link 3.6 and turn up the volume as high as it can go on your recording device, you'll have at least some idea of the tremendous volume an ensemble of siku players can generate. A Brazilian *bateria* (drumming ensemble) in samba can be overwhelmingly loud; in fact, many drummers protect their hearing with earplugs. Other instruments, such as the acoustic guitar, play much more quietly. In European classical music, composers indicate dynamics in the score (sheet music), expecting performers to adhere to their instructions.

PITCH

As noted in chapter 2, a pitch is either high or low depending on frequency, the number of vibrations per second in the sound wave. Again, "highness" and "lowness" are relative terms, best considered along a continuum. The Andean *wayno*, normally sung by women, is often described as high-pitched by people in the Global North, a descriptor that represents only one perspective. Revisit sound link 3.3 and listen again to the indigenous charango. Its thin metal strings are often tuned so high that the instrument will "cry out like a cat," as indigenous players describe it (Turino 2008: 48). These players also find the deeper nylon strings of the mestizo charango less than satisfactory. In the end, perceptions of "high" and "low" are subjective: pitches have either a faster waveform or a slower one.

If pitch is on a continuum, can we nonetheless talk about specific pitches or notes? Again, different cultures take different approaches. In Western European music, pitches are identified with any of seven letter names (A, B, C, D, E, F, G) or, as is common in Spanish- and Portuguese-speaking regions, any of seven syllables (do, re, mi, fa, sol, la, ti/si). Music in the Global North is much influenced by a system called *equal temperament,* which divides a given range of pitches in equal parts. Musicians conditioned by equal temperament often refer to playing "in tune" or "out of tune," the technical term for which is *intonation.*

As you've probably anticipated, intonation is by no means universal. In many traditions, players have to set the pitch themselves, which may vary widely from one community to another or even from one musician to another. This is the case in northeast Brazil, where pitch is often outside the equal temperament system. An eminent ethnomusicologist named Mantle Hood (1918–2005) wrote of attending a professional conference in Latin America. (At such conferences, one speaker after another reads a talk or research "paper" summing up his or her research to an audience of scholars.) On this occasion, one of the speakers discussed an indigenous flute player. As is common in music conferences, he enhanced his presentation with recordings of this flutist's playing, which he described as "out of tune." What transpired reminded Hood of the familiar children's story "The Emperor's New Clothes" by Hans Christian Andersen (1805–75):

At the end of the paper I could scarcely believe my ears when the young man who had read it apologized for the out-of-tuneness of the performance. I waited for some kind of explosion of protest from the floor. None came. The emperor was riding naked through the streets! After some polite discussion about other matters, it appeared we were about to proceed with the next paper. I asked for the floor and as tactfully as possible pointed out that the emperor was nude. The observation generated a very heated discussion that clearly separated a few supporters of an older generation's point of view from the large majority of younger scholars who had no difficulty in accepting the Indian flute as being *in tune with its tradition*. (Hood 1982: 87, emphasis added)

To be "in tune with one's tradition" means, therefore, rejecting tuning systems that are foreign to one's culture. The indigenous flutist was being held, at least by some in the audience, to a system that he would have no particular reason to embrace. Being "in tune with one's tradition" can also involve the passage of time. An A in the eighteenth century was lower than the A to which classical symphony orchestras tune today, with a frequency of 440 cycles per second. In addition, weather can affect pitch. Mariachi players tune to the current standard of A, although they sometimes feel compelled to defend themselves against the idea that they are too unschooled or folksy to do so. As one mariachi violinist states, "contrary to popular belief, mariachi musicians . . . do tune to A440."

Figure 3.7 Mariachi violinist playing outdoors.
Javier García/Shutterstock.com.

This player adds, "unlike our classical counterparts, however, we don't always have the luxury of performing in a climate-controlled theater. Oftentimes our instruments get exposed to the extremities of Mother Nature [and] given that it's customary to make money on a per song basis—we often have to retune on the fly and succumb to tuning to each other" (Sandra Arias, email communication, January 10, 2017).

By the latter part of the twentieth century, being "in tune with one's tradition," as Hood so eloquently put it, became increasingly difficult to do. Thanks to radio, CDs, and the internet, the equal temperament system has encroached on local practices, as has Western-influenced music in general.

More on Pitch

Here is a fact that surprises many people: when we listen to a sound, we may think we are hearing a single pitch. In fact, the sound is actually a composite of many pitches. The main pitch (the one labeled with a letter name in the Western European system) is called the *fundamental.* It stands out from the many other pitches above it, which are called *partials;* the fundamental is the lowest partial. An alternative term for partial is "overtone," since partials lie over the fundamental.

In your outside reading, you may come across the terms "pitched" and "unpitched" sounds. These concepts are problematic. Does not a spoken utterance have a pitch? Listen to the song "Adentro" by the Puerto Rican rap-reggaeton artists Calle 13 and see if you don't hear changes of pitch in the spoken vocal line. As we'll discover when we study a shaman's chant from Tierra del Fuego, music and speech are not always that far apart. While some frequencies are whole-number multiples of the fundamental *(harmonics),* others are not, such that not all partials are part of the overtone series. These acoustical facts relate especially to percussive sounds and to various timbres common in traditional musics, which should not be devalued.

Range

If you hear a timbre and wish to identify the instrument, having an idea of its *range,* or the span of pitches the instrument is capable of producing, may help you make an educated guess. Most instruments are designed to play some pitches and not others. A violin tuned according to the norms of a mariachi ensemble will ordinarily not play lower than the pitch of its lowest string. If an inexperienced mariachi composer writes a pitch for the violin that is lower than that string, the violinist will rightly complain that the music is "out of range."

In Western European classical music, human voices are also categorized according to range. Many choruses include *sopranos,* who can sing the highest, and *altos,* whose range is not quite as high but who can sing several notes lower. Sopranos and altos, parts generally taken by women, are followed by the male ranges, the *tenors* and *basses,* each successively lower. ("In-between" ranges, such as *baritone,* exist as well; also, each range has its own quality.) Again, composers must be careful to write in an appropriate range for singers or they risk fatiguing their performing forces. Vocal ensembles using some combination of these ranges often perform without instruments, which is called *a cappella* singing and is a popular activity on many college campuses. Although many singers in the Global North identify themselves according to their vocal range, those from other cultures or performance traditions do not and instead simply sing music compatible with their comfort level. We do not generally refer to a cumbia soprano, for example.

MAKING A MELODY

Whether created spontaneously or written down, a melody consists of a series of pitches. It can be either high- or low-pitched, again, along a continuum. This placement of pitch is called *register* and it is not quite the same thing as range, which refers to an instrument's capabilities. Rather, register refers to the overall highness or lowness of a portion (passage) of music. As noted, in much Andean traditional music, melodies are in a high register, at least to the ear conditioned by Western classical and popular music.

Intervals

Besides register, another factor in melody is the distance between pitches, called *intervals.* A melody consisting primarily of close intervals is called a *conjunct* melody. "My Country 'Tis of Thee" is a conjunct melody, as is the opening of "Mi vida," an example of the Chilean *cueca,* a genre we'll study in chapter 6. A melody consisting primarily of intervals that are farther apart is called a *disjunct* melody and will generally be harder to sing.

Fun Fact.   Like so many musical terms, "register" is used in ordinary speech. In this sense, it was the focus of a well-known sketch by the British comedy troupe Monty Python from the 1970s. Using the search terms "monty python higher register" Google the video in which a man reporting a burglary to the police clerk is told to use different registers to make his report.

Figure 3.8 Piano keyboard with names of notes, C through B ("do" through "ti"). The note after B is C, which is followed by D, E, etc. On the piano, a half step is the very next key. A whole step consists of two half steps, encompassing two adjacent keys. David C. Rehner/Shutterstock.com.

In the Western European tradition, intervals are labeled with numbers. A *second,* for example, comprises two letter names or syllables (C-D; do-re), whereas a *sixth* comprises six letter names or syllables (C-A; do-la). An easy way to grasp these theoretical concepts is by looking at the piano keyboard, although a word of caution is in order. However familiar the piano keyboard may be in the Global North, it can limit our understanding of pitch and tuning systems because it is the quintessential vehicle of the equal temperament system, discussed above. Look in figure 3.8 at the interval of a second, C-D, just discussed. Then find the octave, a distance of eight white keys from C. The two pitches in an octave have the same name (C-C/do-do or A-A/la-la). If more than one instrument or voice sings the same pitch the resulting sound is a *unison,* mentioned in chapter 2.

When Andean end-blown flutes, panpipes, and side-blown flutes play a unison, however, the instruments often encompass a spectrum of intonation that can't be represented on the piano. Some players blow slightly higher or slightly lower, resulting in density of sound, the desired aesthetic for that community. If you have access to a keyboard, do use it. But understand that it is not a definitive point of reference.

PATTERNS OF PITCHES

Scale

A *scale* is a pattern of pitches. Scholars who have analyzed musical traditions around the world apply the concept of "scale" to the many hundreds of pitch patterns they have identified. In fact, a "scale" is just that, a concept. Although many musicians are aware of scales and think in terms of such abstractions, others do not. These two approaches to the concept of scale are just one example of the difference between musical theory and practice—thinking about music and what musicians actually do.

Scholars identify scales and draw conclusions about them in several ways, including deducing patterns from the music heard or studying instruments in detail. For example, by investigating the number of holes in Andean flutes, along with how the fingers would likely be placed, scholars have been able to advance hypotheses about how scales are configured. As we noted in chapter 2, the scale that is probably most familiar to you is the one on which the song "Do-Re-Mi" (Do, a Deer, a Female Deer) is based, widely used in Western classical and popular music. It comprises seven different pitches, with the eighth pitch repeating the first an octave higher (figure 3.8). Although the *heptatonic* (seven-pitch) scale may seem normative, scales around the world can have any number of pitches.

The scale in "Do-Re-Mi" consists solely of seconds and is called a *major* scale because of way the intervals are arranged. In the European system, we name intervals not only according to the number of pitches encompassed (second, third, octave, etc.) but by quality. Intervals "come in" more than one quality: the seconds that compose the major scale can be either *minor* (the very next key on the piano keyboard) or *major* (two minor seconds). Another name for the minor second is *half step* whereas another name for the major second is *whole step*, that is, two half steps. In the scale on which "Do, A Deer" is based, half steps occur between pitches 3 and 4 ("mi" and "fa") and pitches 7 and 8 ("ti" and "do"). This is the pattern that constitutes the major scale (sound link 3.17).

The *minor* scale consists of a different pattern of half and whole steps and has three variants, although for our purposes, the type heard in sound link 3.18 will suffice. At the very end of the minor scale, you'll hear an interval that encompasses three half steps: larger than a second but smaller than a third. This interval, the *augmented second*, is prominent in Spanish music deriving from the musical legacy of the Moors (ethnic Arabs and Berbers), who ruled Andalusia (Southern Spain) from 711 to 1492. Andalusia is also the region from which the greatest number of Spaniards came to Latin America during the colonial period. We'll study some Latin American genres influenced by Spanish-Arab music, along with genres that originated in Latin America and made their way back to Spain, an instance of cross-cultural exchange.

Composers of popular music from the Global North generally write music in either major or minor, as have many composers of classical music. This tendency is so common that the term "major-minor system" is sometimes used. Some Latin American genres are likely to be in either major or minor. The Chilean *cueca* is nearly always in major, whereas the Argentine *chacarera*, a dance from the center of the country, is generally in minor. Again, major and minor are on a continuum: in Northeast Brazil, some musicians play or sing in such a way that intervals fall somewhere in between the major and minor scales of Western European music.

In the Global North, we tend to associate minor keys with sadness, sometimes even tragedy. For example, "Ana's Theme" in *La historia oficial,* which introduces Ana early in the film and at key points punctuates Alicia's eventual confrontation with the truth, is in a minor key. Yet in other parts of the world major and minor keys are not necessarily perceived this way. For example, Andean peoples do not consider minor-oriented music sad.

A scale that uses seven pitches as just described is said to be *diatonic.* In other words, the pitches are not altered in any way but correspond to the established pattern of whole steps and half steps for that scale. An instrument tuned to play only notes in that scale is said to be a *diatonic instrument.* One such instrument is the Paraguayan harp, covered in chapter 5.

Beyond Major and Minor

If we incorporate notes from the *chromatic* scale, which consists solely of half steps, the situation changes, however. As shown in figure 3.8, on the piano keyboard, all the keys, black and white, are the same distance apart, an easy way to conceptualize temperament, which is based on the equalization of half steps. If we play all the pitches, the result is a chromatic scale (sound link 3.19). If we add chromatic notes to a diatonic melody, we say that the diatonic melody has been *chromatically altered.* The chromatic scale can be played and sung on many instruments besides the piano. When we study Guatemalan marimba music in chapter 5, you will hear a prominent chromatic scale played by several *marimberos* (marimba players).

However familiar the major-minor system may be to us today, it's only a few centuries old. Before 1600, European music was based on other patterns of pitches, called *modes,* which comprised whole and half steps but in different combinations than those just described. In music from other parts of the world, a mode can encompass both a pattern of pitches and a mood. Some Arab modes, called *maqam,* made their way into Andalusia, where they combined with European modes well before the major-minor system took hold. One version of such a combination is often called the "Phrygian" or "Andalusian-Phrygian" mode, in which the half steps fall between the first pitch and the second and between the fifth pitch and the sixth, although this pattern is subject to variation (sound links 3.20a and 3.20b). Such patterns, and sonorities based on them (sound link 3.20c), may appear in the *joropo,* a Spanish-influenced genre from Colombia and Venezuela discussed in chapter 5.

The *pentatonic* scale is also heard in many cultures around the world. It has five pitches, as its name suggests, and no half steps (sound link 3.21). Although most of the contexts in which the pentatonic scale occurs have nothing to do with piano music, the keyboard nonetheless provides an easy if imperfect point of reference since the black keys are grouped in twos and threes. If you play any group of 2 + 3 or 3 + 2 you can hear the basic quality of the pentatonic scale.

Pentatonic music figures in some indigenous communities, such as the Q'eros of Peru, and pentatonic songs are also part of European-influenced religious customs in the Ecuadoran highlands during Holy Week, the seven days before Easter Sunday in the Christian calendar. Celebrants in Yavi, Argentina (on the border with Bolivia), learned pentatonic songs through oral tradition, and sang them unaccompanied, also during Holy Week. Another source of pentatonic music is that of the Mapuche, indigenous inhabitants of southern Chile and southwestern Argentina, including areas of Patagonia. Their music draws on both the pentatonic and the *tritonic* scale, with three notes.

As noted above, the equal temperament system has encroached on music around the world, as has the major-minor system. To give just one example related to Latin America: In 1977, scholars recorded a series of flute melodies in the southern highlands of Bolivia, several of which were based on a six-note scale. Melodies played in the same village by the same instruments only ten years later, however, were far likelier to use a seven-note scale. An assault on local identity by hegemonic powers? An example of fluid intercultural exchange? These are some of the often controversial topics taken up throughout this book, especially in chapter 9.

Another way to grasp the limitations of the piano keyboard is to consider the phenomenon of *microtones*. A half step is the smallest interval possible on the piano but a microtone is smaller than that. Although many in the Global North consider microtones exceptional, most of the rest of the world uses them. Microtones can be produced on chordophones when the player slides his or her finger along the string, whereas players of aerophones use breath to the same end. Microtonal music in Latin America can be found in the Amazon basin, such as in the Kamayurá community, in which large flutes figure in various rituals.

European classical composers experimented with microtones before 1700, although the idea never particularly took hold. From the twentieth century on, however, when many classical composers began to find the major-minor system limiting and aesthetically unsatisfactory, several pioneering figures became interested in microtones. Among them was the Mexican classical composer Julián Carrillo (1875–1965), whose microtonal music was hailed as innovative by his admirers whereas his detractors found it weird.

Fun Fact. Children around the world have taunted one another with a three-note melody that you may have heard or sung yourself—at least when you were younger (sound link 3.22). If we wanted to theorize about these pitches, we would likely say that they form a *tritonic* scale. It is less likely that we would chide quarreling children by saying, "Will you kids cut it out with that tritonic scale?"

Figure 3.9 Marker in the Panteón Civil de Dolores cemetery in Mexico City for Julián Carrillo. "Sonido 13," Spanish for "thirteenth sound," refers to the composer's desire to go beyond the twelve half steps of traditional tonality.

Thelmadattar/Wikimedia.com.

TEXTURE

Previously, we introduced texture and identified two types: monophonic and homophonic. In deepening our understanding of this musical phenomenon, we'll see that although some textures can be clearly identified, others are not so easy to classify. Perhaps you have already guessed that such textures, like so many other aspects of music, exist along a continuum. One texture that can be classified is monophonic, discussed in chapter 2. Monophonic texture is common in much traditional music in Latin America and in religious chant of the Western European tradition that was brought to Latin America. As for homophonic texture, also mentioned in chapter 2, a main melody is accompanied by other pitches, often played by one or more instruments. This texture is common in certain Latin American genres, as we'll see in chapter 7, when we explore songs in which a singer accompanies him- or herself on the guitar.

Falling somewhere between monophonic and homophonic textures is a melody sung over a *drone,* a single pitch that is sustained throughout, as with a bagpipe. In Latin America, the music of the *matachines* generally includes drum, guitar, and the extralarge violin mentioned above, which can play a drone. Similar in concept to the drone is the *ostinato,* a pattern repeated many times. An ostinato might be played by a percussion instrument or clapped, and can involve pitches as well as rhythm. It occurs frequently in traditional Latin American music, both indigenous or African-influenced and, as we'll see in chapter 8, some Latin American classical music. (Another term for a repeated pattern, often applied to popular music, is *groove.*) Another texture is *heterophony,* in which many people sing or play the same melody but in which some individuals add a few additional pitches or adjust existing pitches. This is the case with the *haraví,* an indigenous Andean genre sung by women in various rituals who sing the three notes of a tritonic scale, each slightly varying the music as she sees fit.

Polyphonic texture is exactly what its name implies: "many voices." Two or more independent melodies sound at once, with each melody or series of pitches having its own profile. One form of polyphonic music likely familiar to you is the round ("Row, Row, Row Your Boat" or "Dona nobis pacem," for example), in which each singer or group of singers performs the same melody at staggered, predetermined entrances. Much polyphony, however, does not involve all parts singing the same music but rather different melodies. In popular music, for example, a singer or instrument may perform a *countermelody* against the main melody, such that both sound well together. In Western classical music, polyphony is governed by numerous rules that determine which pitches sound well together and which do not, all according to aesthetic judgment, convention, and cultural values. We'll study one example of this approach to polyphony in a mass written for the cathedral at Puebla, Mexico, during the colonial period. Other examples of polyphony are found in Afro-Cuban religious music, with multiple layers of instruments and voices punctuated by various idiophones, all yielding a wide variety of timbres.

We can also refer to musical texture more generally. A piece containing only a few instruments and relatively few accompanying parts may be described as light-textured. A piece with more instruments or more accompanying parts is said to be densely textured.

FINDING THE CENTER

As you recall from chapter 2, in much Western classical and popular music, we sense the presence of a tonal center confirmed by a cadence, a point of rest. We also noted that cadences often involve chords. (Some cadences are strictly melodic.) We'll now deepen our understanding of tonality—finding the center—which, moreover, informs several Latin American genres influenced by the Western European tradition. In that tradition, a hierarchy prevails, manifesting itself in scales, modes, and other patterns of pitches. For example, a certain pitch may occur more often than others, or the music may conclude on a particular pitch. Scales, which are labeled according to their starting pitch and their quality, for example, C major or G minor ("do mayor" or "sol menor" in Spanish), contain pitch hierarchies that govern the music. A piece using a given scale as its tonal center is said to be in that *key,* such that to be "in the key of C major" means to take the note "C" as its tonal center.

We have also touched briefly on chords, several pitches played simultaneously, and collectively known in European-influenced classical and popular music as *harmony.* One familiar chord from this tradition consists of notes 1, 3, and 5 (do, mi, sol) of the major scale (sound link 3.23). Because its foundation is the first note of the scale, we label this chord with a roman numeral I. (The corresponding notes in the minor scale are also a chord, which you can hear in sound link 3.24.) These three notes constitute a unit, as do similar combinations, such as those built on the fourth and fifth notes of the scale, labeled with roman numerals IV and V (sound links 3.25, 3.26). Composers arrange these and other chords so as to constitute a *chord progression,* a series of chords. One of the more common such progressions, I-IV-V-I, can be heard in sound links 3.27a, b, c, and d. Of course, chords can be built on scales from outside the Western European system, as we saw with the Andalusian-Phrygian sonority (another word for chord) in 3.20c. Any chord can be played with all the notes sounding together or separately, called a "broken" chord and common in guitar playing (shown in sound link 3.27c). Even in a broken chord it is the unit that counts—the fact that the notes belong together according to rules of Western European harmony.

One basic chord progression is the cadence, a point of rest discussed in chapter 2 apropos the scene in *La historia oficial* in which Alicia and Sara meet in the café at the end of montage, concluded by a cadence. This particular cadence consists of a chord built on the fifth note of the scale (the V chord), which contains "ti," the pitch that in the Western European system nearly always resolves to a chord built on "do" (the I chord). When we play these chords back to back (I-V-I-V-I-V-I, etc.) listeners used to that system perceive a need for resolution (sound link 3.28). Some scholars refer to *teleology,* progression toward a desired goal. Such goal-oriented thinking meshes well with the hierarchical nature of the Western European system but does not apply to other ways of hearing music around the world.

The cadence just described, which takes us from V back to the tonal center, I, is called an *authentic cadence* (sound link 3.29). We can liken an authentic cadence to a period, the finalization of a thought. A cadence that takes us from

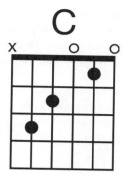

Figure 3.10 Diagram for a C chord on the guitar, with each vertical line representing a string and each dot indicating placement of the fingers so that the notes C, E, G (do, mi, sol) will sound.

StockAppeal/Shutterstock.com.

Figure 3.11 Realization of figure 3.10 on the instrument itself.

yellowsarah/istock.com.

I to V, on the other hand, called a *half cadence,* can be compared to a colon, the mark of punctuation that anticipates something to come (sound link 3.30). Sometimes a chord will surprise the listener by *not* affirming the tonal center but rather "going off" in some new direction. Such cadences are called *deceptive.* You can hear the potential for surprise in the deceptive cadence in sound link 3.31. As you work through this book, you'll notice that several Latin American musical genres follow the harmonic norms of Western European music. In the Mexican *corrido,* for example, we repeatedly hear the I, IV, and V chords, along with clearly defined cadences.

What happens when not the I chord but the V is the last sound we hear? Many people who listen to Latin American genres such as the *son jarocho* (Mexico) or the joropo are surprised to discover that they end exactly this way, a harmonic progression that stems from a long tradition rooted in Spanish-Arab music. Rather than imagine that something is missing, some scholars suggest that such music has two tonal centers, that is, two harmonic pillars of equal importance. Still, rather than end on a half cadence many players add a final I chord, perhaps because they think it belongs there or because they want to satisfy some teleological need they perceive on the part of their listeners. As we'll see in chapter 7, Latin Americans sometimes call this "the gringo way of ending" (Manuel 2002: 311).

Another device common in both Western classical and popular music is the *sequence* (sound link 3.32). Unlike a sequence in film, a musical sequence contains a progression of roughly four to ten chords, which are played first at one pitch and then at another. (Sometimes the term "chord progression" and "sequence" are used interchangeably.) The progression may be repeated at a third pitch level; indeed, it can be repeated as many times as the composer sees fit, although in Western classical music too much repetition is often considered tedious, despite the fact that plenty of other traditions involve a great deal of repetition. In most sequences, a melody will stand out, as in the Brazilian song we'll study in chapter 7.

MUSICAL TIME

Whenever we listen to music, our sense of time is fundamentally altered. Instead of linear or "clock time" (increasingly marked by the "ding" on our smartphone that tells us we have something to do), an alternative realm is created, one fundamentally different from that of nonmusical time. In chapter 2, we discussed several time-related aspects of music and noted that what we rather loosely call "rhythm" actually comprises several components.

ACTIVITY 3.2

Using the search terms "The World's Most-Used Musical Sequence" find on the internet the link to a program on this subject from National Public Radio. The program, which deals with a musical phenomenon introduced in this chapter, takes about an hour. Listen to it and then summarize its main points. What are the principal musical ingredients of this chord progression? In what Latin American music does it appear? In what other kinds of music? Write two pages or so and report to the class.

Beat, Rhythm, Meter

If you tap a tabletop and make steady, undifferentiated sounds, you are producing a beat or a pulse. Pulse is often compared to a heartbeat (at least a regular one). But what if you elongate some sounds or start to hear the sounds in patterns or groups, say, of four pulses, with pulses two and three joined together followed by several groups of five pulses? If you began speaking and gave each syllable a tap, it is unlikely that every syllable you utter would take up exactly the same amount of time. The syllables would have different *durations.*

> If only we didn't have an exam next week!
> ¡Ojalá que no tuvieramos un exámen la semana que viene!
> Se pelo menos a gente não tivesse um exame a semana que vem!

In the English-language version, you might give the first syllable of "only" extra time, perhaps following with quicker durations and giving extra time to the second syllable of "exam." Your emphasis would change depending on the meaning you want to convey. For example, if you're shocked that the exam is next week (instead of next month), you may well linger—painfully—on the word "week." The Spanish and Portuguese versions would contain their own emphases.

This simple exercise helps us appreciate some of the ways in which musical sounds can be organized in time. In one, generally described as free rhythm, pitches unfold without a steady pulse and in groupings so flexible as to seem incidental. Such pitches are often fitted to what is sometimes called "speech rhythm," the way the spoken language scans, as shown above. We'll consider this phenomenon in relation to opera, essentially a sung play, in which Latin America played an important role. In many other Latin American genres, musical time unfolds in units, that is, groups of beats. As noted, these regularly recurring groupings constitute what musicians trained in the Western European tradition call meter, which we discussed in chapter 2 apropos Gertrudis's polca. The polca is noteworthy for its consistent meter, as are other dances in duple meter, such as the Brazilian samba and Colombian cumbia, discussed in chapters 5 and 6. It's also worth noting that although the polca was brought to Mexico by Germans, Poles, and Czechs, it made its way into other Latin American countries as well, including Argentina, where it morphed into another genre, the *chamamé,* which is danced cheek to cheek.

As in nearly all duple-meter music influenced by Western European classical music, the first beat of these duple meter dances receives a slight stress (the downbeat):

1 2, 1 2, 1 2 . . . etc.

An *upbeat,* an incomplete metrical unit that precedes the downbeat of a phrase, section, or entire piece, is not emphasized. Several selections in this book contain upbeats.

In chapter 2, we also discussed triple-meter music, of which the song "Ojos de juventud" is an example. Again, the first beat in each three-beat unit generally receives a slight emphasis.

1 2 3, **1** 2 3, **1** 2 3 . . . etc.

Triple meter is the norm for another dance brought to Latin America, the waltz. Like the polca, it hails not from Spain or Portugal but from Central Europe. It too took on certain characteristics in its new locale, as we'll see with the *vals venezolano* (Venezuelan waltz), discussed in chapter 5. You can hear a familiar triple-meter song and a rendering of the same song in duple meter, in sound links 3.33 and 3.34.

Musical Time: More Possibilities

Another regularly recurring metric grouping contains four beats (**1** 2 3 4, **1** 2 3 4), called quadruple meter. At this point we might ask: Why are musicians influenced by European classical music so prone to emphasize the first beat? Why does the concept of the downbeat even exist? Again, the answer is cultural conditioning. As we'll see, it's not the only way to organize musical time.

Syncopation

Sometimes in lieu of emphasizing the regularly recurring downbeat, one or more of the weaker beats gets emphasized, *a situation often enhanced with rests*. In other words, a duple meter ordinarily felt as

1 2 3 4, **1** 2 3 4, etc.

could be felt as

1 **2** – 4, 1 **2** – 4, etc.

This practice, as well as variants thereof, is *the basis of syncopation* and appears in Latin American genres ranging from the *villancico* to bossa nova. Syncopation is common in jazz, including so-called Latin jazz. Likewise, in music performed by Latin rock artists, such as the Colombian singer Juanes (Juan Esteban Aristizábal Vásquez), the weak beats may be stressed. Indigenous music in Latin America may feature syncopation as well, although the basic structure is likely to consist of a single rhythmic pulse, steady and often highlighted with percussion, with only the vocal parts syncopated. We hear such an accompaniment (without syncopation in the vocal part) in the Yaqui Deer Dance, discussed in chapter 6. For a syncopated version of a familiar song, see sound link 3.35.

Simple and Compound Meters

In the European tradition, each beat can also be divided. This division relates to broad categories of *simple* and *compound* meters. In a simple meter, the beat is divided into two. With Gertrudis's polca, for example, we keep the same basic pulse and feel the division of the beat as follows, the "+" being the division:

1 + 2 +, 1 + 2 +, 1 + 2 +, etc.

With *compound* meter, we hear a division of the beat into *three*. The round "Row, Row, Row Your Boat" is in compound meter. Both simple and compound meter have a downbeat and a regularly recurring pattern. An easy way to grasp the difference between simple and compound meters is to multiply the duple, triple, and quadruple meters (simple) by three to arrive at groupings of six, nine, and twelve (compound).

Sesquiáltera

In much Latin American music, we hear the alternation of duple and triple metric groupings: either two groups of three beats or three groups of two beats in equal amounts of time. This metrical pattern, which also characterizes much Iberian music, is called *sesquiáltera*. Although not unique to Latin American music, sesquiáltera is widely associated with it. You'll hear quite a lot of it in our audio selections.

Compás

Sometimes both rhythm and harmony combine to mark musical time. When chord progressions such as I-IV-V are repeated in tandem with short rhythmic patterns, together they furnish an underlying structure called a *compás*, a phenomenon we'll encounter in the son jarocho.

Repetition

Repetition structures are a central factor in organizing rhythms in African music and are intimately linked to timbre. Return to sound link 3.14b of the African-influenced guaguancó and revisit the differences in timbres produced by the drums playing the guaguancó "groove." In much African music, rhythm and timbre are for all intents and purpose intertwined.

Interlocking Rhythm

Timbral patterns may emerge through a phenomenon known as *interlocking rhythm,* in which a steady pulse consisting of equidistant sounds furnishes the fundamental musical structure. Above this pattern, a contrasting rhythmic pattern may be played on a double bell similar to the agogô since the bell stands out and can be heard above a great many other instruments (revisit sound links 3.7 and 3.8). We often hear various bell patterns in salsa, discussed in chapter 6.

A host of other patterns is possible, played by different performers on contrasting percussion instruments, each with their own timbre yet all fitting together over the basic pulse. One scholar, who describes this interlocking format as "a three-dimensional jigsaw puzzle" (Stone 2005: 91), draws an analogy with conversational patterns among the Kpelle, a people of Liberia (West Africa). The Kpelle use short phrases that may or may not convey lexical meaning but nonetheless create connections between the speakers in a similar interlocking format. Another name for this phenomenon is *polyrhythm* (many rhythms). Still, in African-influenced Latin American music, such as Brazilian capoeira, performers will sometimes briefly play all the same rhythms at once. We call such situations *homorhythmic.*

These observations on African music take us back to the question of why the downbeat is so important in so much music influenced by Western Europe. In

---

ACTIVITY 3.4

Divide your class into four groups and have someone establish a pulse. Then experience timbral variety as follows:

- Line 1: students snap their fingers on each x. Repeat many times.
- Line 2: students clap their hands on each x and on each y clap their thigh. Repeat many times.
- Line 3: students stomp their right feet on each x and on each y stomp both feet. Repeat many times.
- Line 4: students bang on their desks on each x. Repeat many times.

	1	2	3	4	5	6	7	8
snap	.	x	.	x	.	x	x	.
clap	x	x	y	x	x	x	y	y
stomp	.	y	x	x	x	y	x	x
bang desk	.	.	x	.	x	.	.	.

Perform all these roles at once. Then switch roles. Also, try this exercise at a quicker tempo and then at a slower one.

a symphony orchestra, for example, a conductor establishes the first beat. She then guides all the beats that follow, as the players adhere to the metric foundation she establishes and respond to her interpretation of the music. In African ensembles, on the other hand, the relationships established between the interlocking patterns are collective. Players in these ensembles don't use sheet music but instead orient themselves by fitting their rhythmic patterns into those of the other players. Nor do they learn their own parts separately and come together only when they have mastered their individual roles, as is normally the case in Western classical music. Rather, the music is conceived in terms of the overall pattern, not as a series of discrete elements. Indeed, it is preferable to avoid thinking of these interlocking patterns in terms of meter since each consists of a group of beats with no overall meter-defining emphasis.

Africa, Musical Time, and Latin America

As noted, one important African-influenced metrical structure is *clave.* Listen again to sound link 3.16. Besides indicating the name of this idiophone, *clave,* which in English means "key," is a rhythmic pattern that is repeated constantly and serves as the basis for the rest of the music, one more way of marking musical time. A clave pattern will normally consist of two rhythmic patterns: one "straight" and one syncopated, either 3–2 or 2–3. In sound link 3.16, we hear the three pattern first, with which other instruments should interlock. If this does not happen, musicians will say that the song is "out of clave." Such a reaction gives an idea of its importance. Indeed, even when the distinctive sound of the claves themselves is inaudible the underlying structure provided is fundamental.

Additive Rhythm

Clave, with its 3–2 or 2–3 patterns, is a subset of *additive rhythm,* which can combine odd-numbered patterns of beats, such as seven (2 +2 + 3) and five (2 + 3), or even numbers, such as (2 + 2 + 4). Many rhythms in West African music, a major influence on Latin American music, are additive.

WORDS AND MUSIC

Recall our discussion of speech rhythm above. For many people, words go hand in hand with musical sound. Some people listen only to music that has words ("text") and many musical cultures worldwide sing in a way that hews closely to the spoken language. In others cultures, poetry may dictate the music. The *décima,* from Spain, derives from a centuries-old poetic form of ten octosyllabic (eight-syllable) lines and is common in Mexico, Cuba, Colombia, Peru, Nicaragua, Chile, and Puerto Rico, with variable instrumental accompaniments.

Other texted music relates closely to timbre. By using *onomatopoeic* language—words that actually sound like the thing they represent—African musicians add to the array of timbres fundamental to their music.

Composers often write music to enhance the meaning of the words or comment on them in some way. What if a bitter poem were set to gentle music? An analogy with film music may be helpful: if a calm melody, perhaps played by sweet-sounding violins, accompanies a violent battle scene the result will be very different than if loud brass instruments or vigorous drumming are used. Just as music may contradict the action on screen, a musical setting can "comment" similarly on the text, awareness of which will enrich the musical experience.

As we noted in chapter 2, putting words to music is called *text setting.* Two ways of setting individual words are *syllabic* and *melismatic.* In a syllabic setting, each syllable gets a note, whereas in a melismatic setting a single syllable gets many notes. In another expressive strategy, called *word painting,* the composer enhances the meaning of the words through music. For example, a composer of Catholic religious music might set the Latin word *Altissimus* ("highest" or "most exalted") to notes that are in a higher register than the rest of the piece, practices we'll discuss in light of colonial-period religious music from Mexico. Other syllables, called *vocables,* have no known lexical meaning but may be charged with spiritual significance, as we'll see when we study a curing song from Tierra del Fuego.

MUSICAL FORM AND LATIN AMERICAN MUSIC

If rhythm is the way individual sounds in a musical creation are organized in time, *form* or structure enables us to perceive how sections of music unfold. As we saw in chapter 2, musical structure can rest on principles of contrast: the music "goes" one way for a while and then does something different. Other forms rely on repetition, with some so generalized that listeners come to expect that the music will "behave" in certain ways, following a template, so to speak. Still other forms are unique in that they occur only once. Music that accompanies an activity such as a religious ritual, for example, will last just as long as that ritual requires. It too can be said to have a form, even if that form is unlike any other.

This question of unique forms brings us to *improvisation,* or composing extemporaneously (on the spot). Music that results from improvisation has a form but one that probably cannot be replicated. In the Global North, improvisation is much associated with jazz and rock, although it was an important part of classical training until around 1900. (Compare sound links 3.36 and 3.37, each of which takes a familiar song as a point of departure for improvising in different musical styles.) Some Latin American musical genres that involve improvisation do maintain certain formal requirements, such as the décima, which adheres to the ten-line octosyllabic format mentioned above. In our discussion of Paraguayan harp

Fun Fact. In 2012, a team of neurologists compared brain activity during improvisations by jazz musicians and freestyle rappers. The musicians lay flat on their backs and had their brains scanned while they improvised. The researchers found several points in common, including heightened activity in the prefrontal cortex, the part of the brain dedicated to, among other things, complex decision making.

music in chapter 5, we'll see how the harpist adds a few extra notes to the main melody, which are called *ornaments* in the Western European classical tradition and which the harpist probably improvises. In other music, such as *música guajira* (loosely translated as "Cuban peasant music"), improvisation is central.

Many people are surprised to learn that musicians learn to improvise, wrongly supposing that it "just happens." In fact, in many traditions musicians learn melodic patterns or chord progressions, mastering these so as to accumulate a copious reserve of materials for improvising. Many times in improvising, the player will enhance something already in the music—a melody, a rhythm, a relationship between players—which serves as a point of departure for creating new music.

What is the difference between composing and improvising? Many devotees of classical music believe that for music to qualify as a composition it must be written down. But the actual difference in sound between a piece that was written down and a piece that *could* have been written down but that was not is clearly negligible. As mentioned above, most of the world's music has not been notated. The reasons are manifold: some musicians from these traditions are simply uninterested in writing down their ideas, whereas others have prodigious memories and can reproduce much of what they have played without recourse to written transcriptions. This phenomenon brings us back to the continuum. Music may be more improvised or less so. The Chilean cueca we'll discuss in chapter 6 probably involves improvisation, since one of the performers sings in harmony above the main melody, common in many Latin American and Iberian traditional genres. Is this really improvisation or simply a long-established practice that people like to repeat? Certainly it does not substantively affect the form of the music, or its rich cultural context.

We now consider musical form in terms of several *general* formal procedures (templates) found in a variety of Latin American genres.

Call-and-Response Form

One such template is *call-and-response.* In it, a leader sings ("calls") a phrase or more of music, and a group responds. Call-and-response form is extremely flexible in that the response can repeat a fragment of the call, sing a melodically related phrase, sing a new melody, or answer back with heterophony, to give a few possibilities. Let's say the leader improvises, such that the call is of variable length and the response fixed. Of course, the reverse can take place, depending on the group interaction and the impulse of the moment. Additionally, the call may or may not overlap with the response. The call or the response can go on for quite a while or both can be relatively brief, such that the call follows the response in quick succession, almost like an echo. The same variables apply when call-and-response is used in instrumental music.

Common in African music, call-and-response form came to the Americas during the slave trade, where it emerged in the work songs and religious music of the slaves. Elsewhere in this book, we'll see how call-and-response singing is grounded in repeating patterns, short combinations of melody, harmony, or rhythm, especially in the music of Cuba and Brazil.

Strophic Form

In setting words to music, the composer often chooses a poem with a regular rhyme scheme. If the composer decides to use *strophic form,* each verse (strophe) of the poem is set to the same music. In chapter 2, we discussed the relative complexity of the Argentine national anthem. "The Star-Spangled Banner," the national anthem of the United States, on the other hand, is a strophic form with fewer internal melodies. Verses 2 through 4 are seldom sung.

In subsequent chapters, we'll study strophic form in relation to several Latin American genres and discuss modifications to strophic form.

Verse-and-Refrain Form

This form is also intimately related to sung music. In the verse, where the singer may tell a story or reflect on some emotion, one kind of music is used, which we can call "A." The refrain (*estribillo* in Spanish) is set to music that is different from "A," which we can call "B." "A" then repeats, but with different words and "B" follows, without variation in either music or words. This form works especially well when a soloist takes the verse and the chorus comes in on the refrain, as we'll see when we discuss political songs from Latin America.

Fun Fact. It's safe to say that nowadays few of even the most patriotic US citizens know all the verses of "The Star-Spangled Banner." During the Great Depression of the 1930s, however, when many were convinced that the capitalist system had failed, communism took hold in the United States. Communists were especially taken with verse 3 of the national anthem, which refers to the "foul footsteps" of the oppressor. A common joke in the United States was "How can you tell who's a member of the Young Communist League?" Answer: "Anyone who knows the third verse of 'The Star-Spangled Banner'" (Hochschild 2016: 102).

ABA Form and Beyond

As noted, letters make it easy to describe musical forms. If we say that a piece or song is in *ABA form*, we mean that the two outer sections are the same but that the middle section uses contrasting material. To be sure, when the A material comes back, sometimes it's slightly modified. But it's still recognizable as A.

When a form involves a greater number of contrasting sections, we simply add letters in our analysis. (Examples: ABCDCD, ABACADEA.) These loosely structured formal outlines figure in the Cuban *danzón,* a genre initially rooted in Western European music but that ultimately found favor with Afro-Cuban

---

ACTIVITY 3.5

Search on the internet for the following songs, which highlight some of the concepts we have just discussed. (Of course, each song manifests more than just one concept.) Timings given below may differ from one performance to another. Names of some of the artists are given.

- Major-key song: "Jarabe Tapatío"
- Minor-key song: "Veinte años" (Omara Portuondo); "Suavemente" (Elvis Crespo).
- Song that shifts from minor to major: "A felicidade" (Billy Eckstine, shift at 52 seconds)
- Duple meter: "La vida es un carnaval" (Celia Cruz)
- Triple meter: "Cielito lindo" (Mariachi de Tecalitlán)
- Compound meter: "Al Otro Lado del Rio" (Jorge Drexler, in the movie *Motorcycle Diaries*)
- Upbeat: "Las Mañanitas" (Pedro Infante, downbeat at 42 seconds)
- Call-and-response form: "Farão Divindade do Egito" (Olodum, call-and-response beginning at 1:23)
- Strophic song: "Gracias a la vida" (Violetta Parra, verse 2 begins at 44 seconds, verse 3 at 1:26, verse 4 at 2:05, verse 5 at 2:49, verse 6 at 3:30)
- Verse-and-refrain form: "Resistiré" (Dúo Dinámico, verse 1 starts at 20 seconds, refrain at 58 seconds, verse 2 starts at 1:59, refrain at 2:39). Incidentally, this song is an excellent opportunity to practice the present subjunctive in Spanish. Also, "Limon y Sal" (Julieta Venegas, verse starts at 24 seconds, refrain at 1:10; verse 2 starts at 1:53, etc. This song also has a coda, beginning around 3:18)
- Sequence: "Feliz Navidad" (José Feliciano, sequence starts at 45 seconds, "I wanna wish you . . . ")
- Vocables: "Bidi Bidi Bom Bom" (Selena)
- Melismatic setting: "Querida" (Juan Gabriel, often on the word "bien")
- Change of tonal center: "Amor Real" (Sin Bandera, tonal center changes at 3:04).

performers. Likewise, much Andean indigenous music consists of sectional groupings that some scholars label AABB, AABBCC, or AAB. Such procedures are examples of *multisectional* or free form. Also relatively free in the realm of musical form is the closing material known as a *coda,* common in the Western European classical tradition. Although generally the coda is relatively brief, it can sometimes take on unexpected weight and drama, as we'll see when we discuss a Latin American symphonic work.

CONCLUSIONS

In discussing these musical concepts that are especially relevant to Latin America, we have frequently referred to a continuum, proposing it as a guide for awareness of how these various concepts may or may not interact. The very idea of a continuum suggests something other than fixed norms; indeed, change and elaboration are facts of musical life. We may well wonder at what point musicians should refrain from introducing changes into a particular genre. A Venezuelan waltz may contain plenty of sesquiáltera but a preponderance of triple meter makes it recognizable as a waltz. A Mexican corrido in something other than strophic form may surprise listeners, however. Assessing how each performer and each listener responds to such changes, along with the meaning they and their community attach to them, is one more reason to experience music.

We now embark on our study of selected Latin American genres. We should never lose sight of the multiple cultural perspectives that inform this music, or consider them "other" or "different." The relationship between self and other vis-à-vis musical terminology is as complicated as in other manifestations of this dichotomy. Some people argue that music created by peoples who had no knowledge of the Western European system should not be subject to that system's terminology. Others make the same case for music by European composers prior to 1600, when the vocabulary of Western classical and popular music and the major-minor system that many take for granted today simply did not exist. This quandary will probably never be satisfactorily resolved. In the end, one has to balance the desire to learn about music with ongoing respect for the communities it represents, all the while constantly scrutinizing our own attitudes, points of reference, and ways of expressing ourselves.

STUDY GUIDE

Key Terms

organology

Sachs-Hornbostel system

performing forces

hocket

dynamics

fundamental

partials

range

a cappella

teleological

downbeat

compound meter

interlocking rhythm

ostinato

interval

ornamentation

improvisation

half step

whole step

tonal center

microtone

texture

polyphony

countermelody

syllabic, melismatic setting

call-and-response form

strophic form

verse-and-refrain form

coda

For Further Study

Bernstein, Leonard. *The Joy of Music*. New York: Simon and Schuster, 1954.

Broad, William J. "Complex Whistles Found to Play Key Role in Maya and Inca Life." *New York Times*, March 29, 1988.

Chernoff, John Miller. *African Rhythm and African Sensibility: Aesthetics and Social Action in African Music*. Chicago: University of Chicago Press, 1979.

Copland, Aaron. *What to Listen for in Music*. Rev. ed. New York: McGraw-Hill, 1999.

Hochschild, Adam. *Spain in Our Hearts: Americans in the Spanish Civil War, 1936–39*. New York: Houghton Mifflin Harcourt, 2016.

Hood, Mantle. *The Ethnomusicologist*. New ed. Kent: Kent State University Press, 1982.

Jones, LeRoi. "The Changing Same (R & B and New Black Music)." In *The Black Aesthetic*, edited by Addison Gayle Jr., 112–25. New York: Anchor, 1972.

Koetting, James, and Roderic Knight. "What Do We Know about African Rhythm?" *Ethnomusicology* 30, no. 1 (1986): 57–63.

Madrid, Alejandro L. *In Search of Julián Carrillo & Sonido 13*. New York: Oxford University Press, 2015.

Madrid, Alejandro L., and Robin Moore. *Danzón: Circum-Caribbean Dialogues in Music and Dance*. New York: Oxford University Press, 2013.

Manuel, Peter. "From Scarlatti to 'Guantanamera': Dual Tonicity in Spanish and Latin American Musics." *Journal of the American Musicological Society* 55, no. 2 (2002): 311–36.

Olsen, Dale A. *Music of Eldorado: The Ethnomusicology of Ancient South American Cultures*. Gainesville: University of Florida Press, 2002.

Olsen, Dale A., and Daniel E. Sheehy, eds. *The Garland Handbook of Latin American Music*. 2nd ed. New York and London: Routledge, 2008. See especially essays by Olsen.

Powell, John. *Why You Love Music: From Mozart to Metallica*. New York, Boston, and London: Little, Brown, 2016.

Shelemay, Kay Kaufman. *Soundscapes: Exploring Music in a Changing World*. 3rd ed. New York and London: Norton, 2015.

Stone, Ruth. *Music in West Africa*. Experiencing Music, Expressing Culture. New York: Oxford University Press, 2005.

Wade, Bonnie. *Thinking Musically*. Experiencing Music, Expressing Culture. New York: Oxford University Press, 2004.

Experiencing Latin American Religious Music

F ew religious traditions omit music. Whether through Catholic mass, Protestant hymns, indigenous chants, or African call-and-response song, worshipers have long enhanced the religious experience with singing, instruments, or both. To be sure, a few exceptions exist. For many Quakers, religious observance consists of sitting in silence and speaking only when moved by what congregants call the "inner light." Similarly, members of the Religión Cristiana Argentina (Argentine Christian Religion), established in Buenos Aires at the beginning of the twentieth century, sit quietly for long periods and no music figures in the service.

This chapter offers a small sample of the manifold ways in which religion and music have combined in Latin America by focusing on six genres, each with a different spiritual goal but all with significant points in common. First, we consider how music and religion have been studied, followed by an overview of the many religions practiced in Latin America and a few general points about religion and ritual.

RELIGION IN LATIN AMERICA: INDIGENOUS COSMOLOGIES

When musicology was established as an academic discipline, a central point of departure was religious music.

ACTIVITY 4.1

If you were raised in a religious environment or you currently attend religious services, write a paragraph on your musical experiences in worship. What stands out? Did the music enhance or detract from the religious observance? Try to isolate some aspects of the music you experienced (pitch, rhythm, melody, texture, and the like) and comment on these. Then, recall a time you attended a religious service in a faith other than your own. For example, if you are Jewish, discuss your musical impressions upon accompanying a Catholic friend to mass. If you are Christian or Muslim, consider a friend's Bar or Bat Mitzah. If you were not raised in a religious environment, think back to a time when you attended a service and reflect on the music you heard. If you have never attended a religious service, choose another activity.

Rather than concentrate on "pagan" or "primitive" music of the ancient world, scholars researched Catholic churches, cathedrals, monasteries, and convents during medieval times. They took the music performed there as their starting point, believing that it contained the fundamentals for the Western European classical music of later periods. Similarly, musicologists studying Latin America focused on the Catholic religious music the Spanish and Portuguese brought there during colonial times.

Yet long before the Europeans arrived, the first inhabitants of the region practiced a wide variety of religions in which music figured prominently. We know the most about the *cosmologies* of the Inca, the Mexica, and the Maya. Like a religion, a cosmology explains how the world and the universe came to be, often emphasizing some act of creation by a deity or deities. (We'll use the two terms interchangeably.) Each of these communities lived in a well-organized, urban society grounded in religious beliefs. The Inca, inhabitants of what is now Peru, worshiped six main gods, among them Viracocha, who created the Earth and all living things; another was Inti, the sun god and the progenitor of Incan rulers. Young women and girls were chosen to serve as priestesses, sometimes from the age of ten. Music was an important part of the splendid religious festivals that took place in Incan territories, some of which involved up to one hundred native musicians, and singing in Quechua, the language of the Inca.

The Nahuatl-speaking Mexica lived in what is now central Mexico. Although the term "Aztec" is common, scholars nowadays generally refer to the Mexica, a label that includes all the Nahuatl-speaking communities in this region, including the Aztecs, who lived around Tenochtitlán, the present-day location of Mexico City. Many Mexica believed that their own civilization was preceded by four worlds, each of which ended because of some catastrophe.

Figure 4.1 Ruins of Tiwanaku, Bolivia, an ancient city near the Lake Titicaca. The gateway has at its center an image of Viracocha's forerunner, a pan-Andean god.

Matyas Reyhak/Shutterstock.com.

These previous worlds were called the Four Suns (the actual world of the Mexica was the fifth). Like that of the Inca, the Mexica religion was polytheistic: they worshiped multiple gods who gave birth to other gods. For example, Coatlicue, the primary earth goddess, who bore the moon and the stars, was also the mother of the sun and of certain war gods. A good deal of cultural interchange and absorption affected indigenous religions. The deity Quetzalcoatl, the feathered serpent and patron of the powerful priesthood, is actually a god of the Toltec religion, a civilization older than that of the Mexica.

Among the Mexica, musicians enjoyed high social status. Most studied at music schools, where it was possible to specialize in a particular instrument. (Some of these instruments can be seen at Mexico City's celebrated Museum of Anthropology.) Among the membranophones was the *huehuetl*, a large drum that yields more than one pitch, depending on how and where the player strikes the tightly stretched animal-skin drumhead. The huehuetl enjoyed special status (the Nahuatl word "huehue" translates as "venerable man"). Idiophones included the *teponaztli*, a two-keyed xylophone made out of a log with an H-shaped slit in its front surface; other idiophones were the *grijutian*, a string of deer hooves, and *tenebari* (butterfly cocoon rattles). Among the aerophones were high-pitched flutes, made out of bone, and conch-shell trumpets. Besides this variety of instruments, singing and dancing were fundamental to the

Mexica, and a high standard of performance was expected. Music enhanced many a ritual, such as civic ceremonies, life passages such as birth and death, and preparation for war.

The Maya existed since before 2000 BCE, living in a region that comprised present-day southeast Mexico, the Yucatán peninsula, and parts of Guatemala, Belize, and Honduras. Two main languages have been spoken in this region: Quiche in the south and Yucatec in the north. Besides developing sophisticated systems of agriculture, mathematics, and astronomy, the Maya constructed impressive cities such as Chichen Itza and Uxmal (Yucatán peninsula) and Bonampák (Chiapas state). Equally spectacular are their temples, some of which sit atop imposing multilevel pyramids. Mayans worshiped a series of nature gods, with the supreme deity, Itzamná, both the creator and the god of fire, and Chac, the god of rain and lightning. Earthly rulers served as intermediaries between humans and the gods. After death, nearly everyone went to the underworld, which was inhabited by the jaguar, the god of the night. Heaven was reserved for those who had been sacrificed or women who had died in childbirth.

The Maya played a variety of musical instruments, including flutes, drums, rattles, and jingles. A trumpet made of cactus stalks was used in festivals and in war. Some Mayan instruments are pictured in a series of well-preserved images in the Temple of the Murals in Bonampák, mentioned in chapter 3, which dates from around the eighth century.

The Mystery of the Maya and Latin American Classical Music

From around 900 CE, the Mayan population began to decline in large portions of their territory. Ultimately, cities were taken over by the jungle, a phenomenon that has long puzzled historians since no one has been able to determine if the Maya succumbed to war, famine, civil unrest, or some other force. (Thanks to laser technology, archaeologists learned in early 2018 that population numbers were far greater and agricultural methods far more sophisticated than previously supposed.) Today nearly all of the approximately three million descendants of the Maya live in Guatemala and Chiapas. The allure of a civilization mysteriously lost has sparked the imagination of several classical composers, especially in the twentieth century. Two from Guatemala, Raúl Paniagua (1897–1953) and Jesús Castillo (1877–1946), composed *Mayan Legend* and *Mayan Suite* respectively, both for orchestra. Silvestre Revueltas (1899–1940) of Mexico wrote a powerful score for the film *La noche de los Mayas* (The Night of the Mayas), made by the Mexican director Chano Urueta, shot on location in the Yucatán, and released in 1939. Revueltas's score, eventually transformed into a concert work, is nowadays heard independently of the film.

Figure 4.2 Pyramid at Yaxchilan, an ancient Mayan city in what is now the state of Chiapas.
wayak/Shutterstock.com.

RELIGION IN LATIN AMERICA: CATHOLICISM

A central aim of the Spanish and Portuguese colonial project was to spread Catholicism, a campaign initially spearheaded by the so-called Catholic monarchs *(reyes católicos),* Fernando (1452–1516) and Isabel (1451–1504) of Spain. All Spanish monarchs are Catholic, but the moniker was attached to Fernando and Isabel because of their religious zeal and the political actions they took. These included the *Reconquista* (Reconquest) of 1492, in which they expelled from Spain all Jews and Muslims unwilling to convert to Catholicism despite the fact that these three communities had lived for centuries in relative harmony with Christians, a phenomenon known as the *convivencia* (coexistence). Besides promoting Catholicism, Fernando and Isabel sought political and commercial power. Many a *conquistador* (conqueror) went to the Americas to find El Dorado, the legendary city of gold, while others envisioned entire fields of the precious metal that would be theirs for the taking. Religion provided the moral justification for the Conquest and its consequences.

In the colonies, the Spanish established systems of local government, which were run by viceroys. These representatives of the king oversaw a foreign possession (viceroyalty), of which there were four in Spanish America, each with an administrative center. Under the viceroyalties, indigenous peoples were torn from the lives they had established in their own communities and pressed into the *encomienda* system (forced labor that, many argue, amounted to slavery). Many died from overwork, whereas others contracted illnesses brought from Europe to which they had no immunity. Sometimes the Indians were so desperate that they organized mass suicides. An assault on native religions was undertaken as well. Members of the clergy, convinced that the Catholic faith was the true one, were generally untroubled by the fact that they were disrupting centuries-old beliefs and practices of the indigenous.

Traditionally, Catholic clergy have lived in monasteries or convents, which in turn belong to a religious order, an association that embodies the principles of its founder. Members of the Franciscan order, for example, try to imitate Saint Francis of Assisi, the medieval monk who led a life of sacrifice and poverty. An administrative hierarchy oversees the orders, headed by the pope, traditionally seen as infallible. (Note that "church" is normally capitalized to refer to the Catholic Church whereas Protestant denominations are lowercased, as in "Methodist church.") During the Conquest, Spanish and Portuguese clergy in the Americas undertook the massive and often coercive goal of *evangelization,* or spreading the message of Catholicism. Because of evangelization, about 40 percent of the world's Catholics today live in Latin America and the Caribbean.

Of what did this message consist? Catholics believe that Jesus Christ, the son of God, was born as a human being to the Virgin Mary (celebrated at Christmas) to preach a message of redemption. Jesus, who gathered about him a group of disciples, was crucified under Roman authority but rose from the dead three days later (celebrated at Easter), symbolizing faith and renewal. The principal Catholic rite is the *mass,* which may be spoken or sung, and which has at its center the sacrament (an outward sign of inner grace) known as Communion, the ritual initiated by Jesus during the final meal he ate with his disciples. By telling them that the bread they were eating was his body and the wine his blood, Jesus invested the ordinary act of eating and drinking with sacred significance. At a predeter-

Viceroyalties in Latin America

- Viceroyalty of New Spain, established 1535. Included central and southern Mexico, nearly all the southwestern United States, Florida, Cuba, much of Central America, Puerto Rico, the Philippines, and other territories.
- Viceroyalty of Peru, established 1542. Initially included all of South America, but was later reconfigured after Viceroyalty of New Granada was established.
- Viceroyalty of New Granada, established 1717. Included Colombia, Ecuador, Venezuela, Panama.
- Viceroyalty of Río de la Plata, established 1776. Included Argentina, Uruguay, Paraguay, Bolivia.

mined point during the mass, worshipers process to the altar and receive bread, in the form of a wafer, and wine, a practice that has endured for centuries.

During the colonial period, the friars who officiated at mass and other rituals found music an especially effective tool for conversion. Since music was part of theological training in Spain, they were qualified to teach the Indians note-reading and instrument-building; many natives also learned to sing in Latin, then the language of Catholic worship. Admittedly, by promoting Catholic music, the clergy were often indifferent to existing native musical traditions. Yet some wrote music in indigenous languages for the Indians to sing, just as many clergy in Latin America established communities in which they could coexist with the natives. Unlike the English in North America, who pushed Indians further and further west, the Spanish founded *missions,* which focused on spirituality and sustainability. Natives learned Spanish, Latin, reading and writing, new agricultural methods, and, as noted, musical skills. These actions have been much debated. As one scholar has observed, in evaluating the missions and the evangelization project as a whole, historians are inclined to see "only misery or triumph" (Russell 2009: 12). One should try to take as balanced a view as possible.

Figure 4.3 Along with the Jesuits, the Franciscans were an especially strong presence in Latin America. This photo, from around 1903, shows Mission Santa Barbara (California), founded in 1786.

George Wharton James/Wikimedia.com.

In the sixteenth and seventeenth centuries, Catholicism faced a major challenge in Europe, the Protestant Reformation. Thanks to its leaders Martin Luther (1483–1546) and Jean (John) Calvin (1509–64), many people turned away from Catholicism. Protestants believed that religious services should be conducted in the *vernacular* (the local language) rather than Latin, and they rejected the Catholic veneration (worship) of saints, individuals elevated to special status. Also, whereas as Catholics believe that Christ's Real Presence is manifest during Communion, Protestants hold that the bread and the wine only symbolize Christ. The Church launched the Counter-Reformation, increasing evangelization around the globe, including in Latin America; in Europe, religious wars raged until the mid-seventeenth century. Reflecting from a distance of three centuries on this bloody strife, the Spanish philosopher Miguel de Unamuno (1864–1936) once quipped that wars were waged over whether "bread is bread and wine is wine."

RELIGION IN LATIN AMERICA: THE AFRICAN LEGACY

For over three centuries, the Spanish and Portuguese imported some twelve million Africans to Latin America, mainly to the plantation economies of Cuba and Brazil, both profoundly influenced by Africa. Slavery also existed in countries with a less visible African presence today, such as Mexico, Peru, Colombia, Venezuela, and Puerto Rico.

Most of the slaves were from West Africa and were twenty years old or younger. They traveled as human cargo under dangerous and demeaning conditions, and some did not survive the long sea voyage. Those who did were expected to relinquish any sense of personal liberty upon arriving in the Americas to work long hours at physically demanding tasks. Not surprisingly, many died in these unfamiliar and inhumane surroundings, victims of a value system that justified one human being owning another.

ACTIVITY 4.2

Click the link www.slaveryinnewyork.org/history.htm to find the exhibit "Slavery in New York" at the Museum of the New York Historical Society. When was slavery abolished in New York? Why was it abolished? Why do you suppose so many citizens of the United States are unaware that New Yorkers and New Englanders owned slaves? Also, search on the internet for recent reports on ways in which slavery influenced some of the most elite universities in the United States.

In Latin America, enslaved Africans could circulate in society somewhat more freely than their North American counterparts. For example, they could take advantage of social organizations called *cabildos,* the literal translation of which is "council" but which in practice resembled a support or community group for enslaved Africans of a particular ethnic or language background. In encouraging such associations, slave owners were often motivated by self-interest: if slaves were fragmented along ethnic lines, it was reasoned, revolts would be less likely. The cabildos also kept African music alive. Although the enslaved did not generally bring musical instruments from Africa, they certainly brought their musical sensibilities. In maintaining music and dance traditions, they ensured that interlocking rhythms, polyrhythms, call-and-response singing, and a penchant for timbral variety found their way to the Americas. Much of their music was tied to religion and much helped them both to endure and, at times, to resist slavery. Under the dire circumstances they encountered we can only marvel at the fact that enslaved peoples made any music at all.

Figure 4.4 This engraving from 1595 by Theodor de Bry (with modern watercolor) depicts African slaves processing sugar cane on the Caribbean island of Hispaniola.

Everett Historical/Shutterstock.com.

Although the Africans that were brought to Latin America as human chattel represented several ethnic groups, nations, languages, and dialects, the most numerous were the Yoruba, from southwestern Nigeria and southern Benin. Yoruba religious traditions involve deities called *orichas,* each known for certain qualities and abilities. Eshu, for example, is a messenger oricha, whereas Chango is the oricha of virility, fire, and magnetism. Orichas can take a variety of forms; for example, one manifests itself as the amniotic fluid in a pregnant woman's womb. Adherents of Yoruban religions believe that someday they will be one with the divine creator, Olodumare, who initiated all life with his own breath. Some Yoruba believe in reincarnation, at least within families, and several African religions attach great importance to ancestor worship, which is practiced through prayers or sacrifices. Orichas can also be ancestors, who in turn may become minor deities.

RELIGION IN LATIN AMERICA: OTHER GROUPS

In the late nineteenth century, Protestant missionaries began to travel to Latin America, often from the United States, and to attract converts, often by sponsoring sports, social activities, or English classes. Catholicism continued to hold sway until the 1960s, when Protestant Pentecostal churches began making major inroads in Latin America. Pentecostals have made music part of their message, strategically anticipating the tastes of their target population to ensure that the music heard in the service or in religious broadcasting is the same music people enjoy outside of church. The popularity of Latin American Christian artists such as Luis "Funky" Marrero (Puerto Rico) or the Christian rock band Rojo (Mexico) confirms that music is as persuasive a tool in religious conversion as it was five hundred years ago.

Jews began immigrating to Latin America in 1492, the year of the Reconquista, eventually settling in Brazil, Chile, Uruguay, Mexico, and Venezuela. Mainly, however, they went to Argentina, where Jewish holidays are legally protected today. Muslims, who initially came to Latin America with their fellow Africans as slaves, are a growing presence in Latin America. The Muslim population, concentrated mainly in El Salvador, Argentina, Colombia, Venezuela, and Brazil, now totals over four million. Although some Muslims reject music in worship, others do not.

To be sure, any number of Latin Americans are atheists or agnostics. Such individuals may feel little connection to religious music even if they recognize that many a secular musical practice is rooted in religion. For example, the *aguinaldo,* a Puerto Rican genre (the word means "gift" or "Christmas box"), was traditionally sung in serenades, much the way Christmas caroling is practiced in the United States, Great Britain, and Germany. In Latin America nowadays, aguinaldos are likelier to be piped through muzak systems at malls such as Buenos Aires's Galerías Pacífico or any of Bogotá's *centros comerciales* than heard in live serenades, leaving many to wonder whether Christmas is a secular or a sacred holiday. Sometimes the same music used in the United States to entice shoppers at holiday time is played in Spanish or Portuguese translation.

RELIGIOUS RITUAL

All the religious groups just described have in common the practice of *ritual.* Of course, not all rituals are religious—parades, political rallies, and sporting events all qualify as rituals. With regard to religious rituals, some general characteristics will likely prevail. For one thing, rituals often call upon our senses: sound, but also movement, smell, sight, touch, and, in the case of rituals that involve ingesting food, taste. Next, most rituals consist of a predetermined sequence of events. Participants who regularly practice the ritual know exactly what will happen next, such that this sequence means something to them. Thus, when expectations are disrupted—a change in language, in the order of worship, in music—a reaction can be expected. Another general characteristic of religious rituals is the fact that, in most instances, not all participants will have the same role. Rather, some people will assume positions of authority, granted either on account of an individual's special training or because a community has decided to confer it. Also, religious ritual can mark not only important life events (birth, marriage, death) but offer access to transcendence, a state of mind that transports participants to a realm beyond the everyday world and that obscures the markers normally imposed by linear or "clock time." Religious rituals also tend to be public, done in the company of others to cement the bonds of community.

ACTIVITY 4.3

Choose a ritual in which you've participated or which you've observed at close range. Although it need not be explicitly religious, it should include music. Possibilities include weddings, the quinceañeara (the coming of age celebration for fifteen-year-old Mexican women), graduation, religious ceremonies such as baptism and communion, Kwanzaa candle lighting, Passover, Hanukkah, or Muslim calls to prayer. Explain the purpose of the ritual and describe what is involved. Then, identify the music used and explore the ways in which it complements the ritual.

Finally, no religious belief can be expressed in its totality. For this reason, religious rituals rely on a special metaphorical language, confirming that we think or behave on the basis of truths that we can perceive only partially. In this way, ritual acknowledges the elusive nature of belief. The fact that such religious behavior is metaphorical does not make religion any less "true," nor does it diminish its meaning to participants. Music, with its immense power to affect us, is just as important a dimension of this metaphorical language as are words, movement, and objects invested with special significance.

We now consider six musical genres practiced in Latin America, along with the traditions they represent and their impact over time. We'll examine *Santería*, an Afro-Cuban practice that seeks transcendence, connecting participants with the orichas. We'll also study the musical-religious rituals of the Q'eros of Peru and how these reflect the cosmology of this indigenous community, specifically through the veneration of animals. Another indigenous community we'll explore is the Selk'nam of Tierra del Fuego, the southernmost extreme of Latin America, who used music in curing rituals practiced by a shaman-priest. As for Catholic Church music, we'll consider two instances of its use in evangelization, including a utopian project that purported to build unity between the Church hierarchy and the subjugated native populations. Finally, we'll study Jewish music in Argentina and ways in which it created community among congregants in an immigrant community. Throughout, we'll see how these musical-religious expressions confirm that no one religious tradition can be said to be "pure" or unaffected by the various cultural forces with which it comes into contact.

SANTERÍA, SLAVERY, AND SYNCRETISM IN CUBA

The Santería ceremony is a good example of this blending. Fusing movement and music, it transports participants to a state of transcendence. It also suffered skirmishes with the law and thus became a symbol of resistance.

The Conquest Begins

In 1492, the year Fernando and Isabel expelled from Spain those Jews and Muslims who refused to convert to Catholicism, Christopher Columbus (Cristóbal Colón, 1451–1506) made his first voyage. Sailing for the Catholic monarchs, he landed in what is now the Bahamas, where natives swam out from the shore to greet him. Columbus promptly took several of them prisoner on the premise that they would be able to tell him where he could find the fabled riches of the Americas. (He later brought Indians back to Spain.) He then sailed to what is now Cuba

ACTIVITY 4.4

Reflect on the following sentence: In 1492, sailing for Spain, Columbus discovered America.

- To what extent is the verb "discover" accurate? Why or why not? What or whose perspective does it express?
- Apply the same criteria to consider the familiar locution "New World." New to whom?
- Do you think these terminological distinctions are important? Why or why not?

and then to Hispaniola, which is now Haiti and the Dominican Republic. All the while, Columbus believed he was on the trail of entire fields of gold.

The most prominent group in Cuba was Arawak Indians known as the Taíno, who, in addition to hunting and fishing, planted a variety of crops. (Incidentally, the Taíno are credited with inventing the hammock: the word *hamaca* exists in both Taíno and Spanish.) At that time, the Taíno were the most numerous indigenous population in the Caribbean. Much of our information on them comes from Bartolomé de las Casas (1484–1556), a Spanish clergyman of the Dominican order. It is said that as a boy in Seville (Andalusia), Las Casas saw Taíno Indians and several brightly colored parrots from one of Columbus's expeditions paraded through the streets, an experience that evidently sparked his interest in things American. After studying at the University of Salamanca, Las Casas took minor orders and arrived in Hispaniola in 1502, when he was eighteen years old. From time to time, he returned to Spain. Initially, Las Casas favored slavery but he became increasingly troubled by his compatriots' abuse of the natives and eventually opposed it. He debated this point before the Council of Valladolid and then, in 1552, published his *Short Account of the Destruction of the Indies* (Brevísima relación de la destrucción de las Indias), which documents the natives' suffering at the hands of his compatriots.

In arguing before the Valladolid Council, Las Casas persuaded his compatriots of something not previously acknowledged—namely, Indians did indeed have souls and "peaceful Christianization" would benefit all. Clearly he did not consider a "live and let live" approach in which the Indians could simply continue practicing their own religions. Yet the fact that Las Casas was listened to at all in Spain and that Spanish jurists sought at least some remediation for the ills he described was hardly insignificant in an environment in which the divine right of kings was taken for granted and few stood up to authority.

The Black Legend in the Americas

Some scholars argue that Las Casas was at least partly responsible for the over-whelmingly negative image of Spanish-speaking peoples in the Americas, known as the Black Legend *(leyenda negra).* The Black Legend, which persists today if not by that name, originated with the English and the Dutch. As Spain's main colonial competitors, they sought to diminish the Spanish through propaganda. Historians, including those in the United States, followed suit. Many condemned the Spanish conquistadors as violent and gold-crazed but described the English and French as "colonizers" or "settlers." This bias must be questioned. Without doubt, the Spanish conquest was cruel and many a conquistador was greedy. But such behaviors characterize any imperialist endeavor, including that of the English and French, who in North America removed Native Americans to reservations, broke several treaties with the Indians, and undertook a succession of wars in which Indian populations met with indignity or death. Can we assert that Spaniards were *uniquely* greedy or violent in comparison with the other colonial powers?

African Slaves and Religious Syncretism in Cuba

In the absence of gold fields, the Spanish established sugar plantations in Cuba. As early as the 1550s, the Taíno population began to decline, however, due to forced labor and diseases introduced by the Europeans. The Spanish then saw fit to import African slaves. Because the Yoruba were the most numerous and because they arrived relatively late in the history of the slave trade, we know more about them and their musical traditions than we do about other groups.

As elsewhere in Spanish America, Roman Catholicism was compulsory in Cuba. But thanks to the cabildos, enslaved Africans maintained many of their traditions, such that some African religious practices ultimately blended with Catholicism. This tendency manifests itself in *Santería,* a ceremony in which the powers of the orichas find parallels with those of Catholic saints. (*Santo* means "saint" in Spanish; an alternative name for Santería is *Regla de ocha,* or "rule of the oricha.") The oricha Oggún, for example, who carries a machete, is the deity of iron and of the forge. His Catholic counterpart, Saint Peter, carries the metal keys to the kingdom of heaven. Anyone attending a Santería cere-mony who sees an image of Saint Peter would make this connection. Likewise, Ochosi, one of the warrior orichas, is associated with the Catholic archangel Santiago.

This melding of cultural practices, in which ostensibly conflicting belief sys-tems emerge in new and unexpected ways, is called *syncretism.* One scholar has written at length about syncretism's "ambivalent, not to say bizarre history" (Starkloff 2002: 188). Some Christian theologians have railed against syncretism, considering it an act of compromise or even weakness. (In doing so, they gloss over the fact that the Christmas tree was once a pagan symbol associated with the winter solstice.) In fact, syncretism affords those living in a state of oppression a way to reinterpret foreign symbols according to their own perspective, allowing them to reconcile themselves to their circumstances through a mixture of symbols and practices, as was the case among enslaved Africans in Cuba.

There are many reasons to attend a Santería ceremony. Let's say you, one of your friends, or a member of your family were ill. You might wish to summon the oricha Babalú Ayé, the deity of the Earth (sometimes known as "the father of the world") and protector against infectious diseases. Babalú Ayé has been syncretized with Lazarus, whom Jesus raised from the dead according to Christian tradition (New Testament, John 11:33–44). In turn, Lazarus is sometimes conflated with a New Testament beggar who is covered with sores but who was cured in the afterlife while a rich man who spurned him suffers (New Testament, Luke 16:19–31). Not surprisingly, the story of Lazarus has resonated with disadvantaged peoples for centuries.

The Santería ceremony would likely be held indoors, perhaps in a private home that has been granted special status. There, under the guidance of a religious leader, you would appeal directly to Babalú Ayé. Any images of saints you might see would be bathed in candlelight or the glow of Christmas-tree lights strung about the room, and you would likely inhale the aroma of flowers or herbs. Participants might be dressed in white, the color worn by initiates in some Santería traditions. Throughout, you would be surrounded by movement and energy: outstretched hands, men and women dancing (in free-form style rather than as couples), and heartfelt singing. Perhaps you too would dance, caught up in the ritual. Eventually, you might even find yourself in a trance-like state, necessary for the ultimate goal—possession. To be sure, spiritual guides in Santería recognize that possession is potentially dangerous and that a novice who is not yet ready to establish a relationship with the oricha may move jerkily or appear to be having a seizure. For their own benefit, such novices are led out of the room until such time as they can receive the spirit of the oricha.

The Music of Santería

However focused you were on dancing, you would constantly be aware of the music, especially the drums. These vary depending on the type of Santería being performed. For some ceremonies, sacred *batá* drums are used, which are double-headed, shaped like an hourglass, and played in sets of three. Batá drums are imbued with a spiritual force, one that aids communication with the orichas and, according to Cuban tradition, may be played only by men. Another kind of Santería ceremony, *bembe,* generally takes place in a home, and although participants propitiate the orichas, the drums do not undergo ritual

Figure 4.5 This woman, wearing the traditional white of Santería ceremonies, is holding flowers in front of a house where such a ceremony may take place.
Ellie Matsanova/Shutterstock.com.

consecration. Three such drums, heard in audio selection 4.1, are the *cachimbo*, the *mula*, and the *caja*. Of these, the caja is the lowest, and often improvises or plays along with the singer. The rhythms of the higher-pitched cachimbo interlock with those of the mula, the middle-range drum, although the caja and mula may do the same. In Santería rhythms, it's rare that players simply mark the downbeat; rather, polyrhythms repeat in cycles, with the caja taking the lead on improvising. You'll find this practice in your audio selection.

Other percussion instruments include the *chekere* (chéquere, in Spanish), an idiophone made from a hollowed-out gourd covered with loosely hung bead netting, which resonates against the shell of the instrument when the gourd is shaken. The chekere is associated with the oricha Ochún, the deity of love, fertility, and physicality. Another idiophone common in Santería is the cowbell. As you recall from chapter 3 (sound link 3.8), the player can produce both

Musical Example 4.1. Basic percussion pattern in musical notation.
Transcription by Brian Rice.

Bembe (güiro)
basic part and notation

closed and open sounds, depending on which part of the bell is struck and whether the tip or the middle part of the stick is used. As you see in online audio guide 4.1, your audio selection starts off with an open sound, after which the other instruments join in.

As for the singing, a leader performs phrases of a melody alone, sometimes taking turns with another soloist, and the chorus answers, in call-and-response style. As is common in this flexible musical form, the length of both the call and the response varies, and sometimes the leader overlaps with the chorus. The leader must have a voice that is strong enough to be heard over the drums, which, in addition to the details just described, offer yet another layer of meaning, which has to do with communication. At our hypothetical Santería session, you would note the difference in timbre and pitch among the drums. Some scholars believe these qualities replicate the sounds of African *tonal languages,* languages in which the pitch of the speaker's voice affects meaning or

Figure 4.6 In Cuba, the term "chekere" (the instrument in the photo) is sometimes used interchangeably with güiro, also a gourd. A güiro can also be the event itself, as in, for example, "We're having a güiro for Babalú Ayé."
Eric Krouse/Shutterstock.com.

grammar. Those who listen to Santería will often comment, "the drums are talking."

In fact, the mix of actual languages in Santería has yet to be satisfactorily unraveled. These complexities are due to (1) the numerous languages spoken in Africa and (2) the ways in which some of these languages changed when spoken outside their original setting. Lucumí, one language of the Yoruba people that often appears in Santería, is essentially a 150-year-old version of Yoruba and, because it is not used in conversation, has remained essentially frozen in time. (Lucumí is also the label for Yoruba beliefs as practiced in Cuba.) On the other hand, the names of two of the bembe drums, the cachimbo and the mula, are Bantú, an African language with over two hundred variants. There is also the influence of Arará, a language spoken by a people descended from two African ethnic groups, the Fon and Ewe, whose descendants lived around Havana and Matanzas. In Arará, the name for Babalú Ayé is Asohano. Both names appear in our audio selection, a tribute to the linguistic diversity of Afro-Cuban culture. As you study online audio guide 4.1, note the following: our previous guides were coordinated with films, and were designed to enable you to follow the music in relation to the action onscreen (the "What happens" column). In this and all the rest of the online audio guides, the "What happens" column will confirm that it is possible—and equally gratifying—to follow musical "events" the same way you would follow any other kind of narrative.

Santería ceremonies can last for hours. Even after participating in this Afro-Cuban ceremony you might still decide to make a pilgrimage to the Church of Saint Lazarus in El Rincón (Havana Province) on December 17, the feast of Saint Lazarus. Coincidentally, El Rincón was a primary destination for slave ships.

Santería over Time

In the late 1880s, cabildos were outlawed and people who continued to practice African traditions, including Santería, had to do so in secret. Santería itself was banned in the early 1920s, when journalists railed against it and white upper-class audiences disapproved of the ritual, with some believing that drumming with the hands was primitive. In the 1930s, the composer Margarita Lecuona (related to Leo Brouwer, discussed in chapter 2) published a popular song called "Babalú," which many Afro-Cubans might have found disrespectful. Further repression came in 1959, when the Cuban government turned to communism and advanced the official policy known as scientific atheism. Under its precepts, the government began harassing Santería practitioners. In the 1990s, however, during a period of economic hardship, the communist government relaxed its policies because it became clear that Santería-related tourist packages *(santurismo)* could generate income.

Many have debated whether Santería should be considered more African or more Cuban. Nowadays, it is practiced wherever Cubans are concentrated. In Los Angeles, the Santería Church of the Orichas maintains a schedule of services, including initiation. In New York City, one can find plenty of shops that sell the religious articles used in Santería in addition to a full roster of Santería ceremonies. The essay "Babalu in the Bronx" gives an idea not only of the power of Santería but of the irresistible pull of call-and-response singing in religious

ACTIVITY 4.5

Look up Beyoncé's album *Lemonade*. How do visual and musical elements interact? How does Santería figure? (Be sure to mention a specific oricha here.) How else has Africa influenced this musical-visual statement? Do these African-influenced gestures support or otherwise comment on the album's overall message and, if so, how?

observance. "As the cleansing started," its author writes, "Gina, formerly a professional folkloric dancer and dance teacher, started to sing, 'Bariba o ge de ma,' and those of us who knew the right response joined in, 'Mole yansa mole ya'" (Knauer 2010). These same words start off your audio selection.

PLAINCHANT AND RELIGIOUS CONVERSION IN MEXICO

Mexico was an important site for musical evangelizing. The genre studied here originated in Europe, was transplanted to the Americas, and continues to be performed in both regions, with some surprising twists and turns in its history.

The Conquest in Mexico

In 1519, twenty-seven years after Columbus first sighted land, Hernán Cortés (1485–1547) made his way from Cuba, passed through Mayan territory, and then went on to central Mexico. There, Cortés and his men confronted the Nahautl-speaking Mexica.

In the ensuing years, Cortés subjugated the Mexica, ensuring that the Spanish controlled large swaths of territory. One particularly critical moment in the Spaniards' campaign was Cortés's meeting with and subsequent capture of the emperor Moctezuma II (1466–1520). After several additional battles, Cortés and his men marched on Tenochtitlán and, in 1520, proceeded to undertake a brutal massacre in the Great Temple in that city during a religious celebration. Infighting among the Spaniards, the resistance of the Mexica, and doubt on the part of the Spanish crown complicated Cortés's grand design. By August 1521, however, he had prevailed.

Two Musician-Friars in Colonial Mexico

Given that the Mexica already took music so seriously, it was only logical to make it part of religious conversion. Cortés traveled not only with soldiers, but

---

Nahautl: Indigenous Languages Then and Now

Nahuatl has been spoken in central Mexico since the seventh century BCE. Unlike some indigenous languages, it was both spoken and written. For example, it was a vehicle for philosophy and poetry, as the works of the king Nezahualcoyotl (1402–72) attest; chronicles and documents such as administrative records also appear in Nahutal. This phenomenon raises several important questions. How do written cultures differ from oral ones? Does the presence of a written language necessarily confer greater legitimacy on a culture? What are the consequences of instituting an "official language," as has been attempted with English in the United States? Today, about 1.5 million Nahua people speak the language, often with the strong influence of Spanish. Throughout Mexico, over sixty languages are spoken, including Zapotec, Mixtec, Otomí, and Huastec in addition to Nahuatl and Spanish.

---

with clergy and musicians, each part of the colonial project. The first European music teacher in the Americas was the Franciscan friar Pedro de Gante (c. 1479–1572). He arrived in 1523, just as representatives of King Charles V of Spain began supervising Cortés's bold actions. In the schools that Gante established, natives learned to build European instruments and also sang, learning choral music that he hoped would convince them of Catholicism's virtues. Another tool Gante employed was language. Although Latin was then the language of the mass, Gante learned Nahuatl so that he could translate Bible verses for use in worship. Nahuatl was also one of the indigenous languages in which colonial-period European (and European-trained composers) wrote music for natives to sing. Gante's influence spread to what is now New Mexico, Texas, and California.

Another Franciscan friar arrived in New Spain in 1529. Bernardino de Sahagún (1499–1590) lived to be ninety years old, unusual in those days, and has been called the "first anthropologist" for his study of indigenous life. He too learned Nahuatl and is perhaps most remembered for the *General History of the Things of New Spain* (Historia general de las cosas de la Nueva España), in both Spanish and Nahuatl and over two thousand pages long. Sahagún did not actually write the *General History* himself but compiled it. It contains some twenty-five hundred drawings by native artists, documenting Aztec cosmology, culture, daily life, and history, including the conquest of Mexico from an indigenous perspective. The best-known manuscript of this famous book is called the *Florentine Codex* since it is held in a library in Florence, Italy. (A codex is a book, usually bound, with a handwritten text and often including drawings.)

"To Read, Write, and Sing."

In the *General History* we read: "Later we came to this region to implant the faith . . . and we began to teach how to read, write, and sing." Scholars are still trying to unravel this potent phrase. What, exactly, did the Indians learn? What was the role of musical literacy among the native populations, that is, the ability to read and write music? Many natives copied musical manuscripts but we cannot know for certain if they were aware of what they were writing or if they were simply copying a series of unfamiliar symbols by rote. Some natives learned the music the Europeans taught them so quickly that the friars despaired that they would never learn to read music. "They don't know how to sing except by memory and through continuous rehearsing," the friars lamented. This complaint is common among teachers of classical music today who teach students with prodigious memories for melodic patterns and an overall sense of musical form but no interest in reading music. Many with such gifts do read music, of course; it is not an either-or situation. As we noted in chapter 3, most of the world's music is not notated.

Plainchant

However much Gante and Sahagún strove to incorporate Nahuatl into their musical evangelization, most of the music the friars taught the natives was in Latin, some from the Vulgate (the Latin Bible). These texts were often set as *plainchant,* one of the oldest forms of music making in European music. In the early days of the Christian church, religious services were sung rather than spoken, a practice also common in Jewish observance of that period. By the fourth century, Christians were using chants from the book of Psalms (Old Testament) as well as nonbiblical texts. Plainchant, which involves a single melodic line sung without accompaniment, is an example of monophonic texture. It closely follows the free, unmetered patterns of speech and often contains melismas, which can obscure the meaning of the text but encourage a meditative state. It also contains points of rest (cadences), without harmony, as is normal in monophonic texture.

Audio selection 4.2 is one of several chants that honor the Virgin Mary. Its title, "Salve Regina," means "Hail, Holy Queen" and appeals to the Virgin Mary's mercy *(misericordiae).* For some time, musicologists believed that the author of this nonbiblical text was an eleventh-century monk but now this hypothesis seems doubtful. Nor is it clear who wrote the music. According to some historians, Columbus and his men sang the Salve Regina aboard ship to elevate their spirits while traversing the high seas. The words, found in online audio guide 4.2, give an idea of the Salve Regina's power to comfort, a power enhanced by music. As one Catholic Latina student has observed, "when you listen to religious music it's the equivalent of praying twice" (Mirelle Sandoval, email to author of February 21, 2017).

Not only do many Roman Catholics pray directly to Mary but some join societies devoted especially to her. Activities such as these are part of the so-called cult of Mary or Marian worship. Also significant are appearances or "apparitions" of the Virgin, including one that took place in Mexico in December 1531 at the hill of Tepeyac (now in Mexico City but then outside it). A peasant named Juan Diego encountered there a young woman who told him in Nahuatl that she was the Virgin Mary and "the mother of the true deity." Ever since, the Virgin of Guadalupe, known as *la Vírgen morena* (the dark-skinned Virgin), has been a strong symbol of Mexican Catholicism and, since the eighteenth century, the patron saint of Mexico. Her feast day, on December 12, celebrates both the Virgin and Mexico's mestizo heritage. The same can be said of the Basilica of Our Lady of Guadalupe, built near the hill at Tepeyac where "la Morena" first appeared.

Plainchant over Time

In the 1960s, the Church convened the Second Vatican Council, known informally as Vatican II, to consider how Catholicism could be made more relevant to modern life. One important change was to discard Latin in favor of the vernacular. Latin chant still continues to be performed in many European monasteries, however, along with their counterparts in the Americas. Some monastery choirs make recordings, which music scholars and chant aficionados welcome. Still, the audience for plainchant has generally been rather restricted.

All this changed in the late twentieth century when the monks of the Spanish monastery Santo Domingo de Silos (not far from Burgos) hit the pop charts. In the 1970s, the monastery choir had recorded chant on several LPs and, in 1994 and 1995, two of these albums were released on CD, titled *Chant* and *Chant II.* To the surprise of all, the singing monks were a sensation and people with no prior interest in classical music were suddenly listening to plainchant. What made it so popular? Mainly, plainchant was marketed as a way to overcome the complexity and stress of ordinary life. The monks' first CD sold six million copies worldwide, going both gold and platinum. Even more unusual is that *Chant* occupied the number one slot on the classical chart and number three on the pop chart, quite an accomplishment. Some of the monks even appeared on TV programs such as *Good Morning America.* Probably none of these men would ever have imagined that the simple, cloistered life to which they initially committed themselves would yield such surprises. Nor would they have been able to predict that the spiritual values of medieval chant would have such appeal in the late twentieth century.

MUSIC AND ANIMAL VENERATION IN PERU

The Q'eros, an indigenous community in Peru, may well predate the Inca. They speak a regional dialect of Quechua and live in a remote part of the Andes Mountains. Because animals are such an important part of daily life, the Q'eros honor them in musical-religious rituals, underscoring the community's common purpose while connecting with the natural world and its creatures.

The Conquest in Peru

In 1533, forty-one years after Columbus first laid eyes on the Taíno and fourteen years after Cortés confronted the Mexica, Francisco Pizarro (c. 1471–1541) and his men entered Cusco, the administrative and military center of the Incan Empire. Had you been a member of his party, you would have witnessed the execution of the Inca chieftain Atahualpa (c. 1500–33), part of a long line of Incan leaders who had sought to expand the Incan Empire (Tawantinsuyu), which extended to Peru, parts of Bolivia, much of Ecuador, central Chile, northwest Argentina, and some of southern Colombia. Pizarro imprisoned Atahualpa for his knowledge of the area, believing his understanding of military intrigue would prove useful to the conquerors. In the end, it was too risky to keep Atahualpa alive and Pizarro had him executed. Atahualpa's resistance to the Spaniards and his death have been the subject of paintings, dramatic works, and music, including opera.

After destroying Incan temples, the conquerors proceeded to build monasteries, convents, and churches on the sites where these temples and other structures had stood. One such edifice is the Cusco cathedral, constructed on the ruins of an Incan palace. (Note that a cathedral is not simply a big church but the site of ecclesiastical authority.) Begun in 1560, the Cusco cathedral took over one hundred years to be completed. Of course, if you were Incan and had seen all these events you would have been horrified. Indeed, if you had been alive at the time the Cusco cathedral opened its doors to Catholic worshipers, in the mid-seventeenth century, you might well have feared that Incan religions had been erased from history.

Yet native ways endured. From their community about one hundred miles southeast from Cusco, Q'eros communities have long preserved a traditional way of life, maintaining customs that have survived since Incan times and that are integrated with natural surroundings. For example, a typical Q'eros family might have three houses, each made of mud and grass and each at a different altitude. One would be situated on a treeless expanse at fourteen thousand feet, where the Q'eros pasture their animals. Another would be at thirteen thousand feet, an ideal altitude for growing potatoes. A third, at eight thousand feet, would be for growing corn. The Q'eros depend on domesticated animals, such as alpacas, llamas, and sheep, for their economic well-being, with Alpaca wool

Figure 4.7 An engraving based on an oil painting by the nineteenth-century Peruvian artist Luis Montero depicting Atahualpa's funeral. The Italian-born composer Carlos Enrico Pasta (1817–98) composed an opera on Atahualpa in 1875.

Marzolino/Shutterstock.com.

an important source of income. Because animals are also endowed with spiritual significance, the Q'eros *venerate* (honor) them, similar to the way a Jew will show reverence to a patriarch or a Catholic to the Virgin or a saint.

According to Q'eros cosmology, wild animals, including birds, are linked to mountain spirits (Apu), whereas domesticated animals represent humans. All sense the presence of the Pacha Mama (Mother Earth). A fundamental precept of Q'eros cosmology is *yanantin*, which refers to the union of two interdependent but different elements. These opposing elements are in constant motion, seeking balance in the face of their differences. Thanks to this perspective on duality, work is not especially distinguished from play, or childhood from adulthood.

The Q'eros venerate sheep and cows in a ritual called Sinalay, which takes place just before All Saints' Day (Todos los Santos), celebrated on November 1 to honor the saints of the Catholic Church. Thanks in part, to this coincidence, Sinalay is sometimes called Santos, another example of syncretism. Shortly after Sinalay a blessing of llamas takes place. On both holidays, female animals are recognized for their ability to give birth and to continue the loving relationships between all living creatures of the community.

Q'eros Musical Expression and Spiritual Values

The concept of yanantin manifests itself in Q'eros music in that some instruments are paired with men's voices whereas others are paired with the women's. As for instruments, some used by the Q'eros were common in Incan times, including several types of drums. A principal aerophone is the panpipe. It has sacred origins for the Q'eros, who believe that the mountain spirit who protects cows plays a set of panpipes to which human cowherders attend. Thus, the panpipe, which has two sets of tubes made out of reeds, connects humans and animals with the deity. In the music of the Q'eros, one set of tubes is never played. Nonetheless, the coexistence of the two sets embodies the concept of yanantin.

Another instrument is the end-blown flute, the *pinkuyllu,* in which the player blows into a mouthpiece. (This type of aerophone is sometimes called a duct flute.) The pinkuyllu is made in many sizes, with the five- or six-hole kind often accompanying women's voices. It figures prominently in some Q'eros animal veneration rituals, in which men play instruments and women sing. In following audio selection 4.3 with the corresponding guide, you'll hear a special quality in the women's voices when they bless the llamas, a ceremony that takes place shortly after Sinalay, voices that at times seem almost empathetically to evoke the animals' sounds. You'll also hear the words "mamallay" and "mama" repeated, which refer to the female llama walking alongside the singer, who is mindful of the sustenance animals provide. Throughout, the singer repeats phrases based on a pentatonic scale over all six verses of text accompanied by the pinkuyllu.

The Q'eros over Time

The Q'eros are known for maintaining traditional rituals far longer than other indigenous people in Latin America. As we've seen, some of these rituals are ultimately religious in that they connect the community with spirits, animals, Mother Earth, and one another. Music plays a fundamental role, resulting in nothing less than "social and cosmic renewal through song," as one scholar puts it (Wissler 2009: 208) Yet whether through radio, the internet, or other media, the Q'eros are well aware of music other than their own. As a result, some Q'eros keep the ancient ways alive while also experimenting with other musical practices of the Andean region, such as playing the harp, an instrument that the Europeans brought to the region but that is now widely associated with the Andes. Although some people find such forays outside the community inauthentic, others defend them, claiming that they help unite all Andean peoples, who are said to be "of the same heart" (Wissler 2009: 18).

MASS IN THE CITY OF ANGELS

Catholics say "I'm going to mass" the way Protestants say "I'm going to church" or Jews say "I'm going to temple." The word "mass" not only is shorthand for "central Catholic ritual" but refers to a series of sacred texts that have been handed down for centuries and set to music by many hundreds of composers. In colonial Mexico, mass could be a relatively simple affair or a splendid occasion, enhanced with incense, flowers, and sumptuous vestments, the ceremonial clothes worn by priests, altar boys, and the choir. The elaborate polyphonic mass discussed below is from the cathedral at Puebla, Mexico, a community that grew from a utopian impulse.

Puebla: A Social Experiment

The cathedral of Puebla de los Ángeles is on the road between Mexico City and the Atlantic port city of Veracruz. Puebla de los Ángeles, also known simply as Puebla, was founded in 1531, ten years after Cortés conquered the Mexica and the first city in New Spain built on a site not claimed by any native group. (Compare the history of the Cusco cathedral, discussed above.) Puebla was intended as a model community. Only Spanish colonists who had neither slaves nor indentured servants in the encomienda system were supposed to reside there, and once settled in Puebla, they would presumably set an example of Christian life, the social benefits of which would be widely admired. This utopian project promised relief after the havoc Cortés had wrought. To be sure, concepts of utopia change over time. Puebla, for example, was by no means free of discriminatory racial practices, which were often safeguarded by the Inquisition, based in Toledo, Spain, but whose "transatlantic system" reached into New Spain as well (Martínez 2008: 174).

ACTIVITY 4.6

Utopia, often considered to be an imaginary place (or state of mind) in which everything is perfect, has inspired many social experiments. Some utopian societies in Latin America were motivated by religion, as with Puebla. Other utopianists have included twentieth-century communists or socialists, who envisioned a society in which resources would be evenly distributed. Take a position on the following questions: Is there any difference between utopia and fantasy? Nowadays when we say that an idea is "utopian," do we simply mean that it is naïve? Or is the concept of utopia useful because it urges us to better ourselves?

Figure 4.8 Interior of Puebla Cathedral.
Editorial credit: gary yim/Shutterstock.com.

Puebla was known as the "City of Angels" thanks to a legend, according to which a troupe of angels told a Church official exactly where the city should be located. Its founding predated by 250 years another angelic city—El Pueblo de Nuestra Señora la Reina de los Ángeles, or the Town of Our Lady the Queen of the Angels, known today as Los Angeles, California, and second only to Mexico City as the largest concentration of Spanish speakers anywhere in the world.

Catholic Music in Puebla: The Mass

As a musical genre, the mass used certain words and followed certain procedures. One kind of mass is the *Ordinary*, which consists of five invariable sections, with all but one in Latin.

Text of the Mass Ordinary, summarized

Kyrie. The words mean "Lord have mercy, Christ have mercy, Lord have mercy." The Kyrie is the exception mentioned in the text: the words are in Greek, not Latin.

Gloria. Jubilant, and with a great deal of text that essentially proclaims "Glory to God in the highest."

Credo. Credo means "I Believe" in Latin. This section is a statement of faith and acknowledges God's forgiveness of sins. Of the five parts of the Ordinary, the Credo contains the most words (see online audio guide 4.4).

Sanctus. A simple, succinct text that emphasizes holiness (Holy, Holy, Holy), and anticipates the coming of the Lord.

Agnus Dei. Agnus Dei means "Lamb of God" (that is, Jesus Christ). This final portion of the Mass Ordinary petitions for peace.

In another kind of mass, the Proper, additional sections are added to the Ordinary depending on the feast day being observed. These variable sections are also interwoven with the spoken word and sometimes with instrumental music. Another kind of mass is the *requiem,* sung when someone dies. All these texts are *liturgical* in that they are part of an existing body of ritual words associated with a particular purpose that religious authorities have approved and that congregants recognize as such. Initially, all the words to the mass were sung in plainchant *(plainchant mass).* But eventually church musicians began harmonizing spontaneously and singing in more than one part, resulting in the *polyphonic mass.* Composers often used a fragment of plainchant as part of the polyphonic texture. In New Spain, composers of polyphonic music could do the same with a native melody. The rich texture of polyphony appealed to many worshipers. One disadvantage, however—and something to which church officials have objected at several points in history—is that sometimes the words are obscured, especially with melismatic, rather than syllabic, settings of the text.

An important composer in Puebla was Juan Gutiérrez de Padilla (c. 1590–1664), who was also a priest. Born in Spain, he received a solid education before emigrating in 1622, over a century after Cortés overthrew the Mexica. By this time, the Viceroyalty of New Spain was well established and its vast territories were the envy of Europe. A composer-priest of that era would generally seek a position in a house of worship. Such positions were competitive, and required passing a series of tests *(exámenes de oposición)* so that the best-qualified individual could be selected. Padilla managed to secure the top music position in

Puebla, becoming *maestro de capilla* (chapel master) at the cathedral. He was a prolific composer and many hundreds of his works survive. Padilla is especially known for his *villancicos,* a genre that flourished in both Europe and the Americas from the fifteenth to the eighteenth centuries.

Padilla also composed masses. Some are for double choir, in which two groups of singers are stationed in two different parts of the cathedral singing alternately, a choral analogy to call-and-response style (also called *antiphonal* singing). Audio selection 4.4, Padilla's *Missa Ave Regina caelorum* (Hail Queen of Heaven Mass), is an example of this format. Like the Salve Regina plainchant and the "Ave Maria," discussed in chapter 2, it honors the Virgin Mary.

In the Credo, the third section of the mass, Padilla faced the task of setting the avalanche of words that constitute this statement of Catholic belief. To express the meaning of the words, he employed various strategies. For example, to highlight the distance Christ traveled from heaven to Earth to sacrifice himself for humankind, Padilla elongated the word "descendit" (as in "[Christ] descended from heaven") through melisma and used word-painting in that the notes of the melisma go down (descend). Elsewhere, Padilla set the text syllabically, as with the faith-defining words "Et resurrexit tertia die" (and on the third day he was resurrected), a fundamental precept of Christian belief; choir one, moreover, sings this phrase in homorhythm, making its importance crystal clear. Throughout, Padilla carefully calculated the role of each choir, sometimes engaging them in dialogue and sometimes bringing them together for moments of greatest import. Such a moment of unification occurs at the end of the Credo, which expresses faith in forgiveness of sin and in "life in the world to come" by repeating the word "Amen" several times, enhanced with melismas. You can follow all these things in online audio guide 4.4.

Villancicos in New Spain

Latin American villancicos, often for choir with instrumental accompaniment, blur the boundary between religious and secular music. Since the texts were in the vernacular rather than Latin, they could be in Spanish, Nahuatl, Quechua, and African-inflected dialects. Although villancicos composed in Europe were generally secular, in Latin America they were religious but nonliturgical, which means that they could be performed either in or outside of church. With their light, often lively character, some villancicos could even pass for dance music and thus stood out in the sometimes austere environment of formal worship. The fact that the word "villancico" is often translated as "Christmas carol" reflects both the popularity of villancicos at Christmastime and the idea that at least on some level Mary and Joseph, the parents of Christ, were ordinary people.

The Mass over Time

The mass is both genre and ritual. Some people are surprised to learn that it is often performed in concerts of classical music, such that a mass can be appreciated as music rather than as a statement of faith. This practice raises several questions. Is *any* music intrinsically religious or does its religious content depend solely on context? Does listening to a mass in a secular setting such as a concert hall qualify as worship, perhaps in a highly personalized way for whoever is listening? Many non-Catholic classical music lovers, including atheists and agnostics, admire masses and have experienced them only in the concert hall.

After the Second Vatican Council, composers began writing masses in the vernacular. In Spanish, for example, the words "Kyrie eleison" (Lord, have mercy) were replaced with "Dios, ten piedad." One Latin American composer who took advantage of this opportunity was Ariel Ramírez (1921–2010) of Argentina, whose *Misa criolla* (Creole Mass) of 1964 uses Spanish texts and indigenous instruments. In 1974, the Nicaraguan composer Carlos Mejía Godoy (b. 1943) composed *La misa campesina nicaragüense* (The Nicaraguan Peasant Mass), which expresses solidarity between Christ, who advocated on behalf of the poor and disenfranchised, and Nicaraguan peasants (campesinos). In part, Mejía Godoy achieves this objective by incorporating the speech of everyday Nicaraguans, along with guitar accompaniment, into the music. In 1977, however, a performance of the mass was interrupted by the Nicaraguan dictator Anastasio Somoza (1925–80). In the twenty-first century, the mass remains alive and well both as a form of worship and as a musical experience. More recently, masses have come to include indigenous languages, such as Tzotzil and Tzeltal (McDonnell and Wilkinson 2016).

MUSIC AND HEALING RITUALS: THE SELK'NAM SHAMANS OF TIERRA DEL FUEGO

For centuries, peoples of different cultures have called upon the power of music to cure physical or mental ailments in religious rituals. In some societies, healer, religious authority, and musician were the same person. One such society was the Selk'nam of Tierra del Fuego, whose story is a tragic one.

The Extinction of a People

Tierra del Fuego is an archipelago located at the southernmost tip of South America. To get there, one has to cross the Straits of Magellan from the mainland. The straits are named after Ferdinand Magellan (c. 1480–1521), the Portuguese explorer who sailed for Spain in the early sixteenth century. The

Selk'nam may well have laid eyes on Tierra del Fuego centuries before Magellan arrived and they likely crossed over from the mainland by canoe.

Tierra del Fuego means "land of fire." Presumably the region got its name when Europeans saw smoke from Selk'nam bonfires on one of the islands. A hunter-gatherer community, the Selk'nam were among the last aboriginal groups in South America to make contact with Europeans. In the 1870s, Europeans began setting up sheep ranches and farms in the region. Whereas the Europeans considered sheep private property, the Selk'nam were completely unfamiliar with this concept, and hunted the sheep for subsistence. In reaction, the ranch owners colluded with the governments of Argentina and Chile, who sent armed groups to either kill or deport the Selk'nam. Other Selk'nam died of diseases brought by the Europeans for which they had no immunity, suffering the same fate as other indigenous populations centuries earlier at the time of the Conquest.

The fate of the Selk'nam became increasingly dire as cattle breeders, farmers, and adventurers from other countries converged on Tierra del Fuego. A handful of missionaries tried to save them, establishing missions for shelter in the early twentieth century. In the mid-nineteenth century, the Selk'nam population had numbered around three thousand. In 1919, there were 279, and ten years later, there were fewer than one hundred. In 1966, only ten remained, four of whose fathers were of European descent. Since so few Selk'nam survived, the missions were closed. In 1968, only eight Selk'nam remained and the last one died in 1974. It is no exaggeration to label the extermination of the Selk'nam *genocide,* the systematic killing of a particular people, such as Armenians by the Ottoman Empire in 1915 or Jews during the Nazi-engineered Holocaust in the 1940s.

Selk'nam Cosmology: Music and Illness

Selk'nam language, culture, and religion perished in the genocide as well. But thanks to several anthropologists, we know at least something about these matters. According to Selk'nam cosmology, there are four skies, each infinite and each representing a season. Selk'nam religion was polytheistic but one main god prevailed, the rest being mythological ancestors. Different points of the year were marked by ceremonies, including rites of passage, such as initiation. Healers or *shamans* would perform a variety of rituals involving music, with several shamans usually serving a kinship group.

These shamans, who trained for many years, were seen to possess special spiritual power called *waiuwin* and, because shamans could use this power either to cure or to inflict mortal illness, they were respected but also feared. For the Selk'nam, disease was caused by an imbalance or irregularity in a person's inner spirit. It could be counteracted only by the same kind of power, which shamans accessed through trance. Music, mostly in the form of chants, was the gateway to transcendence. Selk'nam chants could be passed down among family members or come to the shaman in a dream. When tapping into this spiritual power, the shaman would repeat vocables, which, as noted in chapter 3, are often employed for expressive or other reasons. Besides vocables, shamans often used a specialized, symbolic language.

Audio selection 4.5, recorded in 1976, features a shaman old enough to remember some of the horrific times just described. Ordinarily sacred chants would not have been recorded, but this shaman realized that she was among the last survivors of her community and decided to record several chants as a vestige of a vanquished people. As shown in online audio guide 4.5, the shaman, who did not speak fluent Spanish herself, mentions blood ("sangre") during a curing session. She is referring to the shaman's practice of inducing trance, locating the disease, and then "sucking out" (drawing) the bad blood through supernatural powers, avoiding any piercing of the skin. The shaman would then hold aloft the source of the bad blood—a rodent or a lizard, perhaps—although other members of the community could not see it. The chant consists of melodic fragments that sometimes lapse into speaking, suggesting that music and speech may not be so far apart as we often think.

Music and Healing over Time

The Selk'nam were just one of many indigenous communities in Latin America to rely on shamans for healing. The Warao shamans of Venezuela also immerse themselves in trance, aided by music. For the Warao, music's role in such religious rituals is central. As one scholar writes, music is "not simply an added feature to be used only on occasion and to make the shaman's performance pleasing, but is the very voice of the 'gods'" (Olsen 1975: 33). Whether or not we accept the notion that music is the voice of a higher power, the idea that music can help cure mental and physical illnesses has survived from ancient times into the present such that an entire profession, music therapy, has arisen to explore this intriguing possibility. Launched in the United States after World War I (1914–18), when musicians would visit hospitals to play and sing for the thousands of patients who were physically and psychologically maimed, music therapy was eventually codified into an academic discipline. In Latin America, music therapy programs exist in several countries, including Argentina, Brazil, Peru, Uruguay, and Venezuela, either in universities or in hospitals, giving rise to professional societies that function under the umbrella of the multinational organization CLAM (Congreso Latino Americano de Musicaterápia, or Latin American Congress of Music Therapy). With or without a spiritual component in mind, its members advocate for the idea that music can promote health.

To be sure, skeptics remain. Yet in 2004 a study showed that choral singing decreases the levels of the stress hormone cortisol, and researchers have discovered that listening to and playing music enables the body to produce more of the antibody immunoglobulin A, along with cells that attack invading viruses and boost the immune system. Additionally, patients who listened to music prior to surgery instead of taking prescription drugs experienced less stress. Although research on music and the neurological system may not explicitly address religion or spirituality, the well-being that music is capable of promoting is increasingly taken as a given.

HIGH HOLY DAYS IN BUENOS AIRES: JEWISH MUSIC IN LATIN AMERICA

The Jews who came to Latin America brought with them their language, their traditions, and of course their music. The piece we'll study here has offered solace and spiritual nourishment to Jews both worldwide and in Argentina, which, as noted, is home to 50 percent of Latin American Jews.

Jews in Argentina

The Viceroyalty of Río de la Plata, of which present-day Argentina was part, was established in 1776, over two hundred years later than the Viceroyalties of New Spain and of Peru and was initially much poorer than the other viceroyalties. In fact, after Brazil, Argentina is the second biggest Latin American country and rich in natural resources, thanks mainly to its fertile fields (*pampas*), which make up almost one-third of the country's total land mass and yield abundant wheat and other crops. By the early twentieth century, Argentina was second only to the United States in terms of wealth and opportunity and, like the United States, attracted many immigrants. Mostly they were workers and fortune-seekers from Italy and Spain, eager to take advantage of the country's historically flexible ("open-door") immigration policies.

Jews began coming to Latin America after 1492, when Fernando and Isabel expelled them from Spain. (A handful of *conversos*, or Jews who had converted to Catholicism, sailed with Columbus.) In Argentina, several waves of

---

ACTIVITY 4.7

Listen to "¡Ay vey! Being Jewish and Latino!" which is program 1549 in the NPR series *Latino USA* (http://latinousa.org/2015/12/04/1549-ay-vey-being-jewish-and-latino/). Report to the class on what you learned. Don't neglect to interpret the title words "¡Ay vey!"

immigration took place, including one in the mid-nineteenth century, such that, by the 1860s, Argentine Jews were worshiping in synagogues in Buenos Aires and enjoying centuries-old musical traditions. A few decades later, Russian and Eastern European Jews came to Argentina to flee the *pogroms*, a form of genocide generally initiated by anti-Semitic regimes. (The word "Semitic" refers both to a family of languages that includes Hebrew, Aramaic, Arabic, and several ancient languages and to the peoples who speak these languages.)

Anti-Semitism, of course, or hostility toward Jews, has been a part of life in Western Europe since medieval times, when descriptions of "perfidious Jews" figured in Latin polyphonic music. In the 1930s, when the Nazi party was beginning to assert its raging anti-Semitism, Jews were expected to wear a yellow star to identify themselves and suffered financial and psychological trauma due to vandalism of their property and loss of employment; consequently, another wave of immigration of Jews to Argentina and elsewhere in Latin America took place after Adolf Hitler came to power in 1933. But in 1938, the open door of the immigration policy was slammed shut because of anti-Semitic and pro-Nazi sentiment in the Argentine government. Although some sectors of the population supported their leaders, many other Argentines were appalled by Hitler and worked hard on behalf of imperiled Jews, with musicians among them giving benefit concerts for pro-Jewish charities. Although Jews often confronted anti-Semitism in their new homes, they at least avoided death in Nazi concentration camps. Refugees to Argentina from Nazi-controlled territories included about one hundred professional musicians.

Jewish Religious Music

Jewish religious music focuses on chants, mainly settings of the biblical Psalms, as noted above. Most of the music is entrusted to the *cantor,* who sings and leads the prayers in the synagogue. The cantor sings chants, also called *cantorials,* which often contain elaborate embellishments and melodic flourishes, sometimes melismatic. The congregation sings in response but usually with much simpler music. Often they chime in on words such as "Amen," which appears in the Hebrew Bible, the Christian New Testament, and the Muslim Qu'ran, in each instance with essentially the same meaning of "so be it." (The Hebrew word "āmēn" translates as "truth" or "certainty.") As we have seen, it appears, in extended form, at the end of the Credo of Padilla's *Missa Regina caelorum.* Orthodox Jewish communities adhere most strictly to the Torah (the word of God as passed down to Moses) and do not use instruments, whereas Conservative and Reform Jews do. Instruments may be featured if a recording is being made, as is the case with our audio selection.

Figure 4.9 Jewish prayer shawl (tallit) and prayer book (siddur).
MstudioG/Shutterstock.com.

One of the most important Jewish holidays is Yom Kippur, or the Day of Atonement, one of the High Holy Days. To *atone* is to recognize and pardon one's own shortcomings and those of others. Yom Kippur lasts from sunset to sunset of the next day, starting on a date established by the lunar calendar. On that day, Jews fast and do no work. They do, however, attend religious services. Some people wear white, as a symbol either of purity or of death, the ultimate detachment from earthly pleasures. Jews who wear white may feel that they can better focus on these ultimate questions during this most holy period of introspection.

A musical high point of the Yom Kippur service is the Kol Nidrei prayer, heard in audio selection 4.6. It is not Hebrew but Aramaic, and is recited as the opening prayer on Yom Kippur eve, the day before the actual holiday. Metrically free, filled with melismas and ornaments, and in a minor mode, the Kol Nidrei seeks forgiveness, with the cantor representing the sentiments of the entire community, often with a dramatic singing style. Online audio guide 4.6 identifies augmented seconds in the melodic line, the distinctive interval we discussed in chapter 3. We remarked that it was common in Andalusia—where Jews, Muslims, and Christians lived in relative harmony during the convivencia. It is easy to imagine that immigrant worshipers in Argentina, far from home and often fleeing injustice, would take comfort in these familiar sounds while finding strength in the ritual behaviors of Yom Kippur.

Jewish Music and Religion in Argentina over Time

Of the Jewish musicians who fled Hitler and made their home in Argentina, many were classically trained graduates of some of the best European conservatories. Others, equally well trained, were involved in jazz or wrote film scores. In whatever capacity, they enriched Argentine musical life. Dajos Belá (1897–1978) of Ukraine conducted jazz orchestras in Moscow and Berlin; in Buenos Aires, he wrote several successful popular songs. Victor Schlichter (1903–86) was a jazz musician who wrote musical theater works that were performed in Yiddish in Buenos Aires. Some of the immigrant musicians changed their names in Argentina, such as the classical composer Wilhelm Grätzer, who became Guillermo Graetzer (1914–93). In his new home, he wrote in a variety of genres and alluded to his religion in several compositions, as in his ballet *Jerusalén eterna* (Eternal Jerusalem) or his dramatic work about two Old Testament women, *Lea y Raquel* (Leah and Rachel). Other Jewish musicians arrived prior to the 1930s, such as Jacobo Ficher (1896–1978) of Russia, who wrote a piece for soloists, chorus, and orchestra called *Kadisch* (a hymn or prayer in the Jewish service) and the orchestral work *Three Symphonic Sketches Inspired by the Talmud.*

The Kol Nidrei continues to be performed on the Day of Atonement in synagogues worldwide and, like the mass, can also be heard in various guises in the concert hall. Surely the Kol Nidrei comforted Argentine Jews in the months after an ugly display of anti-Semitism in Buenos Aires in July 1994, when the AMIA, or Asociación Mutual Israelita Argentina (Argentine Israelite Mutual Association), was car-bombed, killing eighty-five people and wounding many hundreds. This episode, the most serious terrorist attack in Argentine history, has never been satisfactorily explained. Among those who called for justice was Cardinal Jorge Mario Bergoglio (b. 1936), now Pope Francis I and the first Latin American to preside over the entire Roman Catholic Church.

CONCLUSIONS

Consider the wide range of musical-religious expressions we have studied. In Santería, the timbral variety of "talking drums," call-and-response singing, the mixture of languages, and uninhibited movement define this Afro-Cuban expression. In the speech rhythms of Latin we encountered a significant element of Marian worship while experiencing chant's calming qualities. We saw how the female llama is equated to a mother in Q'eros song, just as the presence of Pacha Mama, the Earth Mother of the Andes, infuses these songs with spiritual significance. We discovered how composers can highlight the most salient points of the Catholic faith in the polyphonic mass and explored the power of trance through the half-sung, half-spoken Selk'nam shaman's chant, one of the last traces of a tragically exterminated people. Finally, we sensed echoes of the convivencia in the Jewish Kol Nidrei as performed in Argentina, cementing religious cohesion while awakening the memory of a homeland left behind. For their respective communities, all these musical rituals have deep meaning. Participants collaborate according to predetermined roles accepted by the community, thus strengthening the bonds that made them a community in the first place. These musical-religious rituals also offer the experience of transcendence, giving participants access to a realm not part of their ordinary world yet deeply connected to it.

As we've also heard, the music of these six religious expressions is tremendously varied. Catholic plainchant sounds nothing like Santería, nor would anyone mistake the pentatonic animal veneration song for the shaman's chant. If we have focused mainly on hearing those musical features that distinguish one genre from another, we ought not overlook points in common. Both the Kol Nidrei and the Credo seek forgiveness. Santería and Q'eros animal veneration involve syncretism. Latin plainchant reveres the Mother of Christ, just as Q'eros song praises a life-giving female animal. The Selk'nam chant pays homage to deep spiritual forces and, like the Credo, rests on faith. Surely these similarities are as noteworthy as any differences.

STUDY GUIDE

Key Terms

cosmology
Inca
Mexica
Aztec
Toltec
Maya
Communion
evangelization
encomienda
missions
Protestant Reformation
Counter-Reformation
vernacular

cabildo
tonal language
Yoruba
oricha
Pentecostal
Taíno
Arawak
Black Legend
Santería
syncretism
call-and-response style
batá drums
chekere
Florentine Codex

plainchant

yanantin

pinkuyullu

mass

plainchant mass, polyphonic mass

villancico

antiphonal singing

Selk'nam

shaman

genocide

vocable

converso

pogrom

cantor, cantorial

For Further Study

General

Cleary, Edward L., and Timothy Steinenga. *Resurgent Voices in Latin America: Indigenous Peoples, Mobilization, and Religious Change.* New Brunswick and London: Rutgers University Press, 2004.

Garrard-Burnett, Virginia, Paul Freston, and Stephen C. Dove, eds. *The Cambridge History of Religions in Latin America.* Cambridge: Cambridge University Press, 2016.

Kennedy, Merrit. "'Game Changer': Maya Cities Unearthed in Guatemala Forest Using Lasers." National Public Radio, 2018. www.npr.org/sections/thetwo-way/2018/02/02/582664327/game-changer-maya-cities-unearthed-in-guatemala-forest-using-lasers.

Penyak, Lee M., and Walter J. Petry, eds. *Religion in Latin America: A Documentary History.* Maryknoll: Orbis, 2006.

Shelemay, Kay Kaufman. *Soundscapes: Exploring Music in a Changing World.* 3rd ed. New York and London: Norton, 2015. See especially chapter 8.

Smith, Christian, and Joshua Prokopy, eds. *Latin American Religion in Motion.* New York and London: Routledge, 1999.

Santería, Slavery, and Syncretism in Cuba

Beliso-De Jesús, Aisha M. "Contentious Diasporas: Gender, Sexuality, and Heteronationalisms in the Cuban Iyanifa Debate." *Signs: Journal of Women in Culture and Society,* 40, no. 4 (2015): 817–40.

Brown, David H. *Santería Enthroned: Art, Ritual, and Innovation in an Afro-Cuban Religion.* Chicago and London: University of Chicago Press, 2003.

Cornelius, Steven. "Encapsulating Power: Meaning and Taxonomy of the Musical Instruments of Santería in New York City." *Selected Reports in Ethnomusicology* 8 (1990): 125–41.

Cornelius, Steven, and John Amira. *The Music of Santería: Traditional Rhythms of the Batá Drums.* Crown Point, IN: White Cliffs Media, 1992.

Gregory, Steven. *Santería in New York City: A Study in Cultural Resistance.* New York: Garland, 2000.

Hagedorn, Katherine. *Divine Utterances: The Performance of Afro-Cuban Santería.* Washington, DC: Smithsonian Institution Press, 2001.

———. "Resorting to Spiritual Tourism: Sacred Spectacle in Afro-Cuban Regla de Ocha." In *Sun, Sound, and Sand: Music Tourism in the Circum-Caribbean,* edited by Timothy Rommen and Daniel Neely. New York: Oxford University Press, 2014.

Knauer, Lisa Maya. "Babalu Ayé in the Bronx." http://etnocuba.ucr.edu/?p = 3974. December 19, 2010.

Hearn, Adrian H. *Cuba: Religion, Social Capital, and Development.* Durham and London: Duke University Press, 2008.

Mason, John. *Orin Òrìṣà: Songs for Selected Heads.* New York: Yoruba Theological Archministry, 1992.

Moore, Robin D. *Music and Revolution: Cultural Change in Socialist Cuba.* Berkeley: University of California Press, 2006.

Palmié, Stephan. *The Cooking of History: How Not to Study Afro-Cuban Religion.* Chicago and London: University of Chicago Press, 2013.

Reséndez, Andrés. *The Other Slavery: The Uncovered Story of Indian Enslavement in America.* New York: Houghton Mifflin Harcourt, 2016.

Starkloff, Carl F. *A Theology of the In-Between: The Value of Syncretic Process.* Milwaukee: Marquette University Press, 2002.

Wirtz, Kristina. *Performing Afro-Cuba: Image, Voice, Spectacle in the Making of Race and History.* Chicago and London: University of Chicago Press. 2014.

Plainchant and Religious Conversion in Mexico

Bergeron, Katherine. "The Virtual Sacred: Finding God at Tower Records." *New Republic* 212 (February 27, 1995): 29–34.

Llewellyn, Howell. "Meet the Monks: EMI's Next Hit?" *Billboard* 106 (January 29, 1994): 1.

Hilley, David. *Introduction to Gregorian Chant. Cambridge Introductions to Music.* Cambridge: Cambridge University Press, 2009.

Peña, Elaine A. *Performing Piety: Making Space Sacred with the Virgin of Guadalupe.* Berkeley, Los Angeles, and London: University of California Press, 2011.

Rodríguez, Jeanette. *Our Lady of Guadalupe: Faith and Empowerment among Mexican-American Women.* Austin: University of Texas Press, 1994.

Music and Animal Veneration in Peru

Baker, Geoffrey. *Imposing Harmony: Music and Society in Colonial Cuzco.* Durham and London: Duke University Press, 2008.

Dean, Carolyn. *Inka Bodies and the Body of Christ: Corpus Christi in Colonial Cuzco, Peru.* Durham and London: Duke University Press, 1999.

Schechter, John. *The Indispensable Harp: Historical Development, Modern Roles, Configurations and Performance Practices in Ecuador and Latin America.* Kent and London: Kent State University Press, 1992.

Wissler, Holly. "From Grief and Joy We Sing: Social and Cosmic Regenerative Processes in the Songs of Q'eros, Peru." PhD diss., Florida State University, 2009.

Mass in the City of Angels

Beauschene, Kim, and Alessandra Santos, eds. *The Utopian Impulse in Latin America.* New York: Palgrave Macmillan, 2011.

Brill, Mark. "The Oaxaca Cathedral 'Examen de oposición': The Quest for a Modern Style." *Latin American Music Review* 26, no. 1 (2005): 1–22.

Cashner, Andrew A. "Playing Cards at the Eucharistic Table: Music, Theology, and Society in a Corpus Christi Villancico From Colonial Mexico, 1628." *Journal of Early Modern History* 18 (2014): 383–419.

Koegel, John. "Music and Christianization on the Northern Frontier of New Spain." In *Conversion to Christianity from Late Antiquity to the Modern Age: Considering the Process in Europe, Asia, and the Americas,* edited by Calvin B. Kendall et al., 293–332. Minneapolis: Center for Early Modern History, University of Minnesota, 2008.

León-Portilla, Miguel. *Bernardino de Sahagún: The First Anthropologist.* Norman: University of Oklahoma Press, 2002.

Martínez, María Elena. *Genealogical Fictions: Limpieza de Sangre, Religion, and Gender in Colonial Mexico.* Stanford: Stanford University Press, 2008.

McDonnell, Patrick J., and Tracie Wilkinson. "In a Mass in Chiapas, Pope Francis Denounces the Exclusion of Mexico's Native Peoples." *Los Angeles Times,* February 15, 2016. www.latimes.com/world/mexico-americas/la-na-pope-mexico-20160215-story.html.

Pedelty, Mark. *Musical Ritual in Mexico City from the Aztec to NAFTA.* Austin: University of Texas Press, 2004.

Russell, Craig H. *From Serra to Sancho: Music and Pageantry in the California Missions.* Currents in Latin American & Iberian Music. New York: Oxford University Press, 2009.

Stevenson, Robert M. *Music in Mexico: A Historical Survey.* New York: Thomas Y. Crowell, 1952.

Tomlinson, Gary. *The Singing of the New World: Indigenous Voice in the Era of European Contact.* Cambridge: Cambridge University Press, 2007.

Wagstaff, Grayson. "Franciscan Mission Music in California, c. 1770–1830: Chant, Liturgical, and Polyphonic Traditions." *Journal of the Royal Musical Association* 126, no. 1 (2001): 54–82.

Music and Healing Rituals: The Selk'nam Shamans of Tierra del Fuego

Chanda, Mona Lisa, and Dan Levitin. "The Neurochemistry of Music." *Trends in Cognitive Sciences* 17, no. 4 (2013): 179–93.

Chapman, Anne. *Drama and Power in a Hunting Society: The Selk'nam of Tierra del Fuego.* Cambridge: Cambridge University Press, 1982.

———. "Selk'nam (Ona) Chants of Tierra del Fuego, Argentina." Liner notes. *Selk'nam Chants of Tierra del Fuego, Argentina.* Smithsonian Folkways, FE 4176, 1976. Reissued in 2007.

Eliade, Mircea. *Shamanism: Archaic Techniques of Ecstasy.* Princeton: Princeton University Press, 1964.

Olsen, Dale A. "Music-Induced Altered States of Consciousness among Warao Shamans." *Journal of Latin American Lore* 1, no. 1 (1975): 19–33.

High Holy Days in Buenos Aires: Jewish Music in Latin America

Glocer, Silvia. "Judaísmo y exilio: las palabras ausentes." *Latin American Music Review* 33, no. 1 (2012): 65–101. This text is in Spanish.

Rein, Raanan. *Argentine Jews or Jewish Argentines? Essays on Identity, Ethnicity, and Diaspora.* Leiden: Brill, 2010.

Weiss, Piero, and Richard Taruskin. "Music in Temple and Synagogue: The Judaic Heritage." In *Music in the Western World: A History in Documents,* 15–21. New York: Schirmer-Thomson, 1984.

Reading for Pleasure

Allen, Dexter. *Dawn at Tepeyac.* North Charleston, SC: CreateSpace Independent, 2012.

Cabrera, Lydia. *Afro-Cuban Tales.* Translated by J. Alberto Hernández-Chiroldes, Lauren Yoder, and Isabel Castellanos. Lincoln: University of Nebraska Press, 2005. Original: *Cuentos negros de Cuba* (2004).

Cather, Willla. *Death Comes for the Archbishop.* New York: Vintage, 1990. Originally published 1927.

Craig, Angela Charmaine. *Día de los Muertos: A Day of the Dead Anthology.* Richardson, TX: Elektrik Milk Bath, 2010.

Gardiol, Rita, trans. and ed. *The Silver Candelabra, and Other Stories: A Century of Jewish Argentine Literature.* Pittsburgh: Latin American Literary Review Press, 1997.

MacQuarrie, Kim. *The Last Days of the Incas.* New York: Simon and Schuster, 2007.

Nieto, Margarita, ed. *Pathways to the Heart: An Anthology of Mexican Literature in Translation.* Info@cognella.com.

Stavans, Ilan, editor. *¡Oy, caramba! An Anthology of Jewish Stories from Latin America.* Albuquerque: University of New Mexico Press, 2016.

5

Experiencing Latin American Music and Identity

I dentity" is a multifaceted term that encompasses a range of factors such as race, ethnicity, nationality, regional affiliation, language, gender, and class. To be sure, when no particular situation arouses our sense of any of these things we go about our normal routines largely unaware of them. "Identity taken for granted" is invariably easier for those belonging to majority groups or for those in power. Yet in times of strife or oppression a people may become deeply aware of identity and call attention to it. In either instance, we associate with one group or another because of the way we see ourselves, thus enacting anew the relationship between self and other. (Of course, the same criterion can make us distances ourselves from a given group.) Identity can be expressed musically, especially when a particular group feels a sense of ownership toward a certain type of music. We'll study this phenomenon in the eleven musical genres explored in this chapter.

IDENTITY AND SELF-AWARENESS

We experience identity in several ways. When we attend meetings with people interested in a hobby we practice ourselves, we feel connected to them, just as we do when our family assembles to mark a holiday, birthday, wedding,

> ### ACTIVITY 5.1
>
> With what group or groups do you identify? Was this process of identification instilled in you during childhood? If not, what factors contributed to it? At any point in your life have you changed your way of identifying? Write two paragraphs or so on these questions. If you like, exchange them with a classmate.

or funeral, during which we sense the bonds that make us a unit, however fraught these bonds may sometimes feel. Attending our high school reunion enables us to relive adolescent pranks and look back on a common history. To each of these situations we bring knowledge of our habits, our preferences, and, if we are willing to examine it, our cultural conditioning. As social beings, we are constantly striving to understand ourselves as individuals: how *I* react, why *I* behave as I do, how I realize *my* potential in light of my particular skill set. All combine to create self-awareness.

To these experiences, we also bring our sense of identity. Unlike self-awareness, however, identity is collectively negotiated and agreed upon by the group or community of which we are a part. Social identity is always multiple in that we may see ourselves as part of a family, a religion, a school, or some other community simultaneously. Social identities are also situational since, depending on the circumstances, we may identify more strongly with our gender identity, our sexual orientation, our race, our religion, or our family background. Our sense of identity cannot be separated from self-awareness. As one psychologist has written, "the central purpose of identity is to help you make meaning of your experience in the world" (Shapiro 2016: 91). Identity is also bound up with our physical presence or, as one student put it, is "the person you think you embody" (Daniela López, email communication of February 27, 2017).

We might well wonder how the process of *identity formation* works. What are the criteria that determine *how* we identity with a particular race, ethnic group, nation, region, socioeconomic class, or gender? Who gets to decide whether these criteria are valid? In Latin America, many negotiations that lead to identity formation relate to complex questions of race and ethnicity.

RACE AND ETHNICITY

Debates over race and ethnicity are often tied to questions of physical versus cultural attributes. One dictionary defines race as "each of the major divisions of humankind, having distinct physical characteristics," and ethnicity as "the fact or state of belonging to a social group that has a common national or cultural tradition" (https://en.oxforddictionaries.com/definition/race). Yet people continue to conflate ethnicity with race, wrongly assuming that both are bio-logical and unchanging. In fact, both are socially constructed and both have been subject to the contingencies of the moment. In the United States of the late nineteenth and early twentieth centuries, for example, Irish, Italians, and Jews were considered nonwhite. They were labeled as such because certain legisla-tors, fearful that the United States would become something other than a nation of white Protestants, passed anti-immigration laws against letting these "races" into the country. Attitudes on race evolve slowly. It was not until 1967 that the US Supreme Court ruled that whites and African Americans could legally marry. The offensive term "half-breed," denoting the offspring of a white and a Native American, was rejected in public discourse only relatively recently.

In Latin America, perceptions of race and ethnicity are generally more fluid than in the United States. Race is determined by color but also by context, which may include class, contributing to what one scholar calls "the processes of racial formation" (Rodríguez 2000: 106). (Note the similarity to the term "identity for-mation" above.) In other words, whereas a brown-skinned child born of parents classified as black might be considered white in some parts of the Spanish Carib-bean, that same child might not "pass" in other Latin American countries. Like-wise, a person born brown may accrue the privileges of whiteness—effectively "becoming white"—through upward mobility. Some scholars trace this phenom-enon to the colonial period, during which the Spaniards who came to the Ameri-cas, accustomed to contact with North Africans, brought with them a so-called Mediterranean perspective according to which racial mixing was common. In New Spain, a complex classificatory system arose for identifying the inhabitants of the empire, one that recognized three broad categories (Indian, black, white European) along with many more possibilities. These include *mestizo,* which, as noted, was half Indian and half European. A few other categories were *mulatto* (half African, half European), *morisco* (half mulatto, half European); and *coyote* (half indigenous, half mestizo); others denoted a quarter or even an eighth of one's racial background. One category, *color quebrado,* literally translated as "broken color," referred to a person who combined European, Indian, and black descent in random or hard-to-quantify proportions.

In colonial Brazil, racial mixing was common as well. Concubinage *(mance-bia)* was permitted in areas where there were no white women for the Portuguese to marry, meaning that indigenous or mulatta women had sexual relations with Europeans and bore children; the Church, moreover, did not oppose mixed-race marriages. Thanks to these practices, blacks and mixed-race individuals became a far more visible presence than their counterparts in the United States. Again, a classification system arose. As in Spanish America, a *mulatto* was half black and half white, whereas a *caboclo* was half white and half Indian, a *cafuzo* was half black and half Indian, and a *juçara* was black, Indian, and white. More general terms included *pardo* (dark-skinned, i.e., brown), *preto* (black), and *africano* (African-born). In the late nineteenth and early twentieth centuries, a program

Figure 5.1 Racial classifications in the Americas were depicted in a genre known as the *casta* painting, as in this work from the eighteenth century by an unidentified artist. Museo Nacional del Virreinato, Tepotzotlán (Mexico).

Wikimedia.com.

ACTIVITY 5.2

Read the essay "The Cosmic Race," written in the 1920s by José Vasconcelos (Burns 1993: 125–29). Be sure to look up Vasconcelos and his role in the post-revolutionary government in Mexico. Then, write a short reaction paper in which you address the validity of his objective: establishing a truly universal civilization. What role did Vasconcelos believe race should play in this enterprise? Evaluate his thinking on this point in light of the discussion above.

of racial engineering called *branqueamento* (whitening) took hold, one based on the notion of "white" versus "black" blood. Its proponents argued that if enough blacks and mixed-blood individuals married whites, "inferior" races would eventually be overwhelmed through the ongoing infusion of "superior" European (i.e., white) blood. In doing so, they conveniently overlooked both the racist precepts on which branqueamento rested and the simple fact that there is no such thing as white or black blood. Eventually branqueamento was discarded and Brazil's problems were increasingly attributed to poverty and unequal distribution of wealth, effectively confirming the effects of race on class.

Whatever the relative freedom with which races have mixed and interacted in Latin America, racial inequality nevertheless prevails. As in the United States, whiteness has traditionally promised the greatest opportunities for wealth, respectability, and access to political power. Of all the categories listed above, blackness imposes the greatest social and economic disadvantages.

What about Latin Americans or people of Latin American descent living in the United States? At the beginning of the twentieth century, immigrants from Puerto Rico, Cuba, Mexico, and other Spanish-speaking countries were simply lumped together as "Spanish." Racist landlords advertised apartments with the notice "No Dogs, No Negroes, and No Spanish" (Glasser 1995: 73) and a person from Spain introducing him- or herself might be asked the surprising question "So you're Spanish—from Spain?" The history of the US Census, an official count of the population taken every ten years to determine the number of seats for each state in the US House of Representatives, gives an idea of this confusion over race, ethnicity, and national origins. According to the census of 1930, you could be designated "Mexican" unless you self-identified as "white or Indian." Did that mean Mexicans were a race? If so, it wasn't for long: in 1940, the policy was reversed so that "persons of Mexican birth or ancestry who were not definitely Indian or of other nonwhite race" were classified as white. The term "Hispanic" appeared in the 1970 US census. In other words, it arose as an administrative category rather than from within the community, such that many people of Latin American descent living in the United States prefer the term "Latino." Those who object to the label "Mexican American" have self-identified as Chicanos or Chicanas, discussed in more detail in chapter 6.

Latinos and the US Census

In the 2010 census, question 8 asked "is person of Hispanic, Latino, or Spanish origin?" with possible answers to include "no," "yes, Mexican, Mexican Am., Chicano," "yes, Puerto Rican," "yes, Cuban," "yes, another Hispanic, Latino, or Spanish origin." One could also designate origin by printing in a box "Argentinean, Colombian, Dominican, Nicaraguan, Salvadoran, Spaniard, and so on." Question 9 states that, "for this census, Hispanic origins are not races." One wonders how the 2020 census will read.

ACTIVITY 5.3

In recent years some people of Latin American descent living in the United States have begun self-identifying as Latinx. (Chicanx is another category.) What do such labels mean and why would they be attractive? Why have some important members of the Latino community nonetheless spoken out against them? What is a neologism?

While societies worldwide wrangle over classification systems, some people will argue that race and ethnicity are completely arbitrary and should be eliminated in favor of a *human* race. Of course, people who are members of a privileged group will find it easier to maintain this position since they have greater latitude to play down one aspect of their identity over another. Others take genuine pride in identifying with a particular racial or ethnic group.

IDENTITY OF PLACE: NATIONALISM AND REGIONALISM

Identity is also linked to our sense of place. In what country did we grow up? What was the geography of that country and how did it influence our behavior? How is our country perceived on the world stage, that is, is it part of the center or the periphery? Have we a clear sense of our country's values and, if so, how have we acquired this sense?

Nationalism is often defined as awareness of a particular spirit of a nation and of aspirations common to its people. This concept especially gained currency in the nineteenth century, when the idea of "nation" or "nation-state"—a bounded, geographic entity—began to dominate geopolitics. It also became a way for individuals living in a given nation to make sense of the world and their role in it. Dictionaries treat nationalism in multiple ways, some frankly acknowledging chauvinism. For example, one defines it as "a sense of national consciousness" that may involve "exalting one nation above all others and placing primary emphasis on promotion of its culture and interests as opposed to those of other nations" (*Merriam-Webster,* www.merriam-webster.com/dictionary/nationalism). It is easy to confuse nationalism with *patriotism,* generally considered more benign. If we cheer on our team in the World Cup we are most likely expressing patriotism rather than nationalism. When we vote to close the borders of our country to "outsiders" who threaten "our way of life," we are using well-worn nationalist rhetoric and may be attempting, consciously or not, to mask racism and feelings of our own superiority. When we defend certain traditions deemed worthy of preservation because they mean something to us as a people—including musical traditions—we could be acting out of either nationalism or patriotism.

Both nationalism and patriotism normally involve an array of official and unofficial symbols. These may be mottos that appear on currency, physical objects such as the flag, or flowers (including the various species of orchids that represent Belize, Brazil, Colombia, Costa Rica, Guatemala, Honduras, and Venezuela). Animals can also fill this need. For instance, the condor, which symbolizes freedom and resilience, is associated with more than one Andean country. People attach great importance to these symbols, and often react to them viscerally or call upon them in times of national trauma to encourage unity or strength in solidarity. An example of this tendency is the emblematic white bandana worn by each of the Madres de la Plaza de Mayo in Buenos Aires. Sometimes people even devise their own symbols, convincing themselves and others of their supposedly deep cultural roots. This process is called "invented tradition," a term coined by two British historians in the twentieth century (Hobsbawm and Ranger 1983), who revealed that the Scottish kilt, long considered a "tribal" garment of ancient societies, in fact arose in nineteenth-century nationalist circles in the United Kingdom.

Symbols and mottos are invariably contested. The words "In God We Trust" on US currency may be heartening to some but offensive to those who argue that the founders of the United States intended to separate church and state. Other people don't much notice. Or they point out that as credit cards and other forms of electronic payment take over ordinary transactions, bickering about coins will soon be irrelevant. All sides, however, recognize on some level that symbols and

---

ACTIVITY 5.4

What is your family's nationality? Do you feel strongly attached to it? How does this attachment (or lack thereof) manifest itself? Are you acquainted with any music related to your family's national origins? Does the music you presently enjoy reflect these roots?

mottos intertwine with a nation's understanding of its history, even when versions of that history conflict, as expressed so compellingly in *La historia oficial.*

In their quest for the authentic, some people identify with an idealized vision of their nation, a "homeland" that bears little resemblance to day-to-day political life. One reason such ideas can take root so easily is because the very concept of "nation" is both amorphous and abstract: no one can know all the citizens of a particular nation and the precepts on which a nation is founded have often been subject to the whims of historical memory. Another potent factor in the identity of place is loyalty to a region *(regionalism),* also dependent on ethnic and cultural loyalties. Like nationalists, regionalists cultivate the idea of a shared historical memory. They may also search for authenticity, bringing to bear an array of symbols. Regionalists, however, may challenge the boundaries of the nation-state when the affective ties that bind the people of a region are stronger than any allegiance to the nation state.

As noted in chapter 1, citizens of poorer nations often argue that richer and more powerful countries dominate not only the world economy but global culture. The wealthy nations, at the center of international life, exercise *hegemony*

Folklore Study in Latin America and the Search for the Authentic

In the early decades of the twentieth century, scholars, performers, and music lovers began to fear that national and regional musical traditions were fading into oblivion because of urbanization, massive demographic shifts, and the overwhelming presence of "foreign" music in the music industry, including on the airwaves. (One particularly pervasive threat was popular music from the United States.) Since several Latin Americans wanted to preserve and protect their musical traditions, folk music study developed as an academic discipline. In Argentina, Carlos Vega (1898–1966) did field work and collected traditional music, becoming such an important figure that an institute bearing his name (Instituto de Investigación Musicológica Carlos Vega) was established at the Catholic University in Buenos Aires, which still thrives today. The Brazilians Mário de Andrade (1893–1945) and Luiz-Heitor Corrêa de Azevedo (1905–92) investigated the traditional musics of their country, the former establishing the Discoteca Pública Municipal in the 1930s, an impressive recording library in São Paulo that still serves a large public. Similar efforts were undertaken in Uruguay and Mexico, and even a poorer country such as El Salvador established a National Committee for Folklore Research. Many folklorists and folklore enthusiasts search for what they believe to be *authentic,* an infinitely debatable quality believed to encapsulate national or regional identity while eschewing any kind of interference from outside. People who use the term "cultural purity" are often disappointed to learn that many, if not most, cultural symbols are hybrids, involving borrowings or some other mixture of expressive strategies.

(influence or political control) over the smaller nations on the periphery. In chapter 3, we saw one way in which this hegemonic structure applies to music when we noted the influence of the major-minor system and equal temperament on Latin American traditional musics. In this chapter, we'll consider other manifestations of center and periphery, focusing on identity.

MUSIC AND IDENTITY

Music, with its immense power to awaken human emotion, can easily become a symbol of identity, ostensibly representing some essential quality that defines a particular group. Sometimes the text is the most significant element, as in the soaring rhetoric of national anthems. A song sung in a regional accent will celebrate the identity of a given language community. A text need not name the country or region: if it describes some agricultural task, for example, it may implicitly uphold the values of rural identity.

Music without words can also represent identity. Dances or rhythmic structures of traditional dances, from which composers may draw inspiration, can achieve this objective, as can music suggested by some historical event or traditional legend. When classical composers employ such strategies, they are said to be practicing *musical nationalism.* Writing nationalist music is not without its complications. First, there are the negative associations with the word "nationalism," discussed above. Also, composers who incorporate folk themes are sometimes considered provincial (i.e., on the periphery), especially since nationalist music may not be especially meaningful outside the region or country being represented. Unless a composer says so explicitly, it can be difficult to determine if the musical materials the composer uses really represent a nationalist ideology or if they are simply part of that composer's frame of reference and contain no ideological message.

Sometimes a political leader will promote a certain type of music, either by financially rewarding artists who perform or compose it or by offering those artists publicity and other opportunities. Such projects may be undertaken to unify a divided country. In other instances, a particular genre will become a marker of identity more spontaneously. To be sure, once a traditional or popular genre is assigned the exalted role of representing an entire country or region, it risks turning into a museum piece, one that becomes rigidified and perhaps even irrelevant to younger generations. Adherents of a traditional or popular genre enamored of nationalism or authenticity will argue that museums are essential to preserve the past; such people will likely resist modifying it in any way. Those who perform the genre may do so largely because they have put on a costume—a colorful embroidered "peasant" skirt or cowboy attire—to perform in a folklore festival, for example, or to display rural traditions for the benefit of tourists. This type of activity is a far cry from the spontaneous or participatory music making from the community that gave rise to the genre in the first place. If we experience this music, we will want to consider whether the musical genre sounds vital or whether it has become ossified, sterile, and irrelevant to the present. If the genre does undergo change—such as being played with instruments completely foreign to its origins—we will likely reflect on how much change a genre can sustain without losing *its* identity.

GENDER IDENTITY

Another lens through which many people experience identity is gender, the prism through which most societies have typically perceived human behavior as either male or female. This traditional binary, mapped onto two sexes, has assumed heterosexuality while excluding other identities, such as transgender. Sexual orientation, or feelings of attraction toward other people, is not the same thing as gender identity, which is one's deeply held view of oneself as a gendered human being—female, male, neither, or some blending of both.

We've already encountered some gendered musical practices, such as the well-defined roles in Q'eros animal veneration songs or the exclusive use of the Andean charango by young, single men. Both not only show that gender can be musically performed but point to the fact that much human activity, musical or not, is effectively a "performance." Scholars in the discipline of *performance studies* analyze the many manifestations of this phenomenon, taking into account not only theatrical and musical performance but less explicit examples of "performance," such as civic ceremonies, sporting events, and political rituals, borrowing from anthropology, psychology, sociology, and related disciplines to arrive at their conclusions. Gender-based musical behaviors are reinforced through repetition, the constant reenactment and ingraining of societal norms. Study of the performance of gender via music has been approached mainly according to the male-female binary, which is quickly giving way to a range of many other identities, such as LGBTQ (lesbian, gay, bisexual, transgender, and queer), and others loosely grouped under the rubric "gender nonconforming." All deserve further study from a musical perspective.

In this chapter, we'll explore ways in which gender identity overlaps with the identities just discussed. Mariachi music, long seen as a symbol of Mexican nationalism and traditionally played by men, has been performed by women far more than scholars have previously appreciated. Nowadays women are also performing música llanera, a traditional genre from the Orinoco basin that was also dominated by men. We'll also take up racial and ethnic musical expressions from Uruguay and Puerto Rico, along with invented musical traditions in Paraguay and Guatemala. As for regional musical identity, we discuss the Andes and the La Costa area of Colombia, addressing two genres that are also bound up in societal perceptions of class. We'll also examine the way musicians understand their respective nations, by studying first one Argentine composer's approach to a national symbol that underwent many changes of status and then a Brazilian genre believed to enshrine the country's multiracial population. In addition, we discuss the phenomenon of transplanted identity, that is, what happens when a musical genre with roots in one country flourishes in another, as with salsa.

MÚSICA VALLENATA AND LA COSTA (COLOMBIA)

Música vallenata, or simply *vallenato,* hails from the La Costa region of Colombia and arose from humble beginnings. Initially considered low-class by white Colombians, this local genre ultimately penetrated the mass media and the music industry, also attracting the notice of the journalist, screenwriter, novelist, and Nobel laureate Gabriel García Márquez. Here we discuss música vallenata in relation to Colombian identity.

Colombia: An Overview

The Spanish first entered the country we know today as Colombia in the early sixteenth century, led by Gonzalo Jiménez de Quesada (1509–79). During the colonial period the territory was part of the Viceroyalty of New Granada, which depended on the labor of African slaves and Indians. In 1819, New Granada became independent from Spain; then, in 1830, Venezuela and Ecuador split off, leaving Colombia and Panama. In 1903, Panama declared independence from Colombia, aided by the United States. Why would the United States, often dubbed "the Colossus of the North," help a small Central American nation gain independence? Much of the motivation was economic: at that time, the more than thirteen-thousand-mile journey from New York to San Francisco took many months, since ships had to inch their way around the tip of South America. The business community dreamed of building a canal connecting the Atlantic and Pacific Oceans. Imbued with the spirit of Manifest Destiny, or the notion that Anglo-Saxon US Americans were destined to impose their economic and social systems on other peoples, the administration of President Theodore Roosevelt (1858–1919) destabilized the Colombian government and sent the US military to support Panama in breaking away from Colombia. Roosevelt later justified this operation by claiming that Colombia was "utterly impotent" and that its government acted in ways that were "wicked and foolish" (Roosevelt 1920: 520). Many Latin Americans resented both his words and his actions.

Colombia is the fourth largest country in South America today (after Brazil, Argentina, and Peru). Besides the indigenous, African, and European populations, many immigrants from the Middle East live there, most of whom arrived in the twentieth century. Its geography is diverse, embracing three principal rivers (Amazon, Orinoco, Magdalena) and coastlines on the Pacific Ocean (west) and Caribbean Sea (north). In the east, we find the river-plains, or *llanos,* a complete contrast to the tropical coastal region and the rain forest in the south, which is part of the Amazon basin. The mighty Andes, the longest continental mountain range in the world, mark Colombia's "central spine," as one scholar puts it (Ochoa 2006: 3). In each region, different customs and traditions prevail.

Música Vallenata and Colombian Identity

Throughout its history, Colombia has strived to define its identity. Due to what one author describes as its "strong regionalization," different population groups are associated with these various geographical areas: Afro-Colombians in the Pacific littoral; indigenous and whites of European descent (many of whom were missionaries) in the Amazon and Orinoco jungles; whites in the highland interior and in large cities such as Bogotá and Medellín; and heavy concentrations of Afro-Colombians and indigenous peoples, along with some whites, in the Caribbean coastal region of Colombia known as La Costa (Wade 2000: 30–31). La Costa itself comprises eight of Colombia's thirty-two *departamentos,* or states. Given this variety of perspectives, the quest for a single Colombian identity has proved challenging, musically and otherwise, and since the nineteenth century, Colombian intellectuals and politicians have tried to instill a common national framework. It was only in 1886, for example, that the Colombian national anthem was composed.

Música vallenata is a good example of this "strong regionalization." "Vallenata" means "of the valley" and also refers to the triangular area that is bisected by the Magdalena River and that includes the city of Valledupar, in the inland La Costa departamento of César. Música vallenata confirms the cultural overlaps among the Africans, indigenous peoples, and Europeans who have interacted in this region for centuries. Among the traditional instruments of música vallenata is the gaita, one of numerous types of indigenous Latin American flutes. Many percussion instruments have African origins, such as the *guacharaca,* a scraper made from either a dried gourd or metal that presumably sounds like the raspy call of the guacharaca bird. Also African in origin is the *caja,* a single-headed drum. (The Spanish word "caja" means "box" although the drum is actually conical and thus shaped differently than the caja studied in chapter 4.) Eventually the Western European string bass came to be used in música vallenata, as did the accordion, brought to La Costa during the mid-nineteenth century. With its penetrating timbre, the accordion eventually replaced the gaita and became música vallenata's signature sound.

Several accordion players achieved legendary status, among them Francisco Moscote (1848–1953), about whose origins and accomplishments rumors have

Gabriel García Márquez, Magical Realism, and the Accordion

García Márquez was fascinated by the accordion and affirmed its emotive power in an essay for the Colombian newspaper *El Universal,* in which he confessed that the instrument "muddles our feelings" (Vega Seña 2005: 3). The author reportedly described *One Hundred Years of Solitude* as a "400-page vallenato." In this richly textured narrative, García Márquez tells of seven generations of the Buendía family, interweaving their dreams, illusions, and misfortunes with landmarks in Colombian history, including war, the introduction of the railroads, and the looming presence of US business. Events both real and fantastic unfold in Macondo, an isolated town that is more a state of mind than anything else. Francisco el Hombre, who is nearly two hundred years old, travels far and wide with his accordion, stopping in Macondo to perform the songs he has composed during his wanderings, all of which relate in minute detail the news from the villages he has visited.

swirled. It is claimed, for example, that Moscote had such command of the instrument that he won a duel with the devil by playing his accordion while singing the words to the Credo, that text-heavy portion of the Roman Catholic mass. (Not only that, but he sang the words backward.) In his celebrated novel *Cien años de soledad* (One Hundred Years of Solitude), published in 1967, García Márquez took Moscote as a model for the character Francisco el Hombre (Francisco the Man).

The *paseo* is a subgenre of música vallenata that dates from the mid-twentieth century and probably arose from the couple dance of the same name. (The traditional Latin American custom of taking an evening stroll in the open air is also called a paseo.) Unlike Francisco el Hombre's news updates, the paseo is filled with romantic and sentimental words. The genre can also be identity-conscious, emphasizing local customs and places, sometimes down to the neighborhood. One paseo, for example, "La cañaguatera," refers to a female resident of El Cañaguate, a neighborhood in Valledupar. Because performers make no attempt to standardize local speech patterns and expressions, listeners familiar with regional variations in Spanish can often guess the singer's origins. Usually a principal singer is joined by another who harmonizes on the refrain.

Audio selection 5.1, "Sin ti" (Without You), manifests the "strong regionalization" discussed above with its *costeño* pronunciation, with the aspirated "s" sounds suggesting that the singer is probably from Bolívar, one of the departamentos of La Costa. Like all paseos, it's in quadruple (common) time. In online audio guide 5.1, you'll notice the spoken part in the instrumental interlude, during which the singer dedicates the performance to a particular person. This gesture is common in música vallenata, as is the minor key. In fact, the accordion player and composer of this selection, Náfer Durán (b. 1932), is nicknamed "king of the minor key" because of compositions such as "Sin ti."

Música Vallenata over Time

Música vallenata was initially perceived as low-class by whites in cities such as Bogotá and Medellín. But in the 1940s, roughly the same time that the paseo evolved, música vallenata began to be recorded, ensuring that the genre expanded beyond La Costa. In the 1960s, some ensembles replaced the string bass with electric guitar, and by the 1970s, the group El Binomio de Oro (A Bundle of Gold) toured internationally, performing in 1981 at New York City's Madison Square Garden. As música vallenata changed, a new generation began asserting itself. In the 1990s, the La Costa native Carlos Vives Restrepo starred in a Colombian *telenovela* (soap opera) about música vallenata called *Escalona*. The title refers to the musician Rafael Escalona, who specialized in música vallenata and who was also a friend of García Márquez. Vives, a talented musician, was well cast and the program was a hit. In 1993, Vives released his album *Clásicos de la provincia* (Classics of the Province), in which he combined música vallenata with rock 'n' roll and pop music. As música vallenata gained wider recognition, Vives revived the gaitas. One scholar relates this decision to identity, observing, "city dwellers now [felt] far enough removed from their rural origins to not fear losing social status from association with such music" (Scruggs, in Moore and Clark 2012: 152). Clearly música vallenata had reached beyond La Costa. In 2009, the Colombian director and screenwriter Ciro Guerra (b. 1981) made the movie *Viajes del viento* (Wind Journeys), which highlights these modest beginnings. In it, música vallenata assumes a role as important as that of any character.

ACTIVITY 5.5

Look up Ciro Guerra and watch *Viajes del viento*. What do you think música vallenata symbolizes in the film? How do you evaluate the performance style of the protagonist, played by Marciano Martínez? How does the paseo "Sin ti" frame the movie? Comment on the dramatic role or symbolic meaning of another música vallenata selection also featured in the film, "Caballito." What connection, if any, can be drawn between the references in the film to the devil and Francisco el Hombre in García Márquez's *One Hundred Years of Solitude*? Discuss other features of the film as you see fit, such as the indigenous languages spoken, the landscape, and the role of music in the rural communities depicted.

THE WAYNO AND LIFE IN THE ANDEAN REGION

Like música vallenata, the *wayno* is associated with a region, namely, the *altiplano,* or highlands of the Andes. (The word is pronounced "wine-o" and is sometimes spelled *huayno* or *huayñu*.) Unlike La Costa, the altiplano spans several countries: Bolivia, parts of Ecuador and Peru, and sections of Chile, Argentina, Colombia, and Venezuela. The wayno discussed here describes a challenge, namely, how indigenous peoples from the altiplano negotiate identity when migrating to the city.

Andean Lifeways

The altiplano is the biggest stretch of high plateaus outside of Tibet, most of it in Bolivia and Peru. Its economy depends on mining (silver, tin, copper), agriculture (cotton, tobacco, coffee), and herding (llamas and alpacas). In the altiplano, the majority languages are Quechua, with nearly nine million speakers, and Aymara, with some three million. Dialects of both are also spoken, as is Spanish. The very concept of Andean identity denotes a regional sensibility and way of life.

   When people in the Global North think of Andean life, they may conjure up spectacular visions of Machu Picchu or tourist markets with colorful textiles

Figure 5.2 Llama crossing in Bolivia.
Pocholo Calapre/istock.com.

and ceramics sold by indigenous women in black bowler hats against a back-drop of arid mountains at ten thousand feet above sea level. These postcard images aside, life in the altiplano requires strength, ingenuity, and a connection to one's surroundings. Staples of the diet such as potatoes, maize, and wheat must be cooked for hours because of the lower levels of oxygen. Perhaps not surprisingly, poets and musicians of the altiplano often pay tribute to their environment, and traditional festivals confer spiritual significance on the region's immensity and quietude. In such challenging surroundings, communitarian values matter a great deal and, as noted in chapter 3, are reflected in the performance practice of Andean panpipe players, in which individual players overlap pitches to produce a shared melody.

The Wayno: Music and Social Reality

The wayno was performed by the Incas and then taken up by the Spanish, such that two basic types evolved: indigenous and mestizo. They share certain musical characteristics, including a long-short-short rhythmic pattern repeated throughout, sometimes varied; strophic form; pentatonic melodies accompanied by minor chords; and a quickening of the tempo toward the very end (called the *fuga*). The indigenous version, performed on panpipes, harp, and violin, usually has a quick tempo for dancing, and lyrics in Quechua that may describe the cycle of nature, animals, flowers, or important life events. The mestizo wayno, on the other hand, is usually at a slower tempo and is sung in Spanish or a mixture of Spanish and Quechua. Its lyrics dwell on life in the altiplano or on sentimental topics.

Another theme is migration. Many indigenous leave their communities in the altiplano to relocate in cities in the hope of finding a better life there. Thanks in part to these migrants, the population of Lima nearly tripled between 1940 and 1960; between 1960 and 1970, it almost doubled and it continues to grow today. Pursuing the urban dream far from one's roots can be a daunting experience and those from the altiplano found soon enough that in the city they were no longer the majority but outsiders. This shift of identity also has practical consequences, since the skills acquired in rural life do not necessarily transfer to the city. Consequently, many migrants from the altiplano have difficulty finding jobs and are reduced to living in shantytowns. In Andean countries, such people may be called *cholos*, which means "urbanized Indian." It is not a compliment.

It's hardly surprising that in yearning for their homes, for nature, or for loved ones left behind these migrants would turn to music. Although the words of some waynos are melancholy or nostalgic (others are playful), the wayno, rather than provoking actual sadness, is often *cathartic*. Catharsis (the Greek word is *katharsis*) means purification, perhaps through immersing ourselves in some artistic experience to cleanse out negative feelings such as resentment, fear, or sadness, a desire for purification that may be experienced by groups or by individuals. To take the latter instance, let's say you've just suffered a painful breakup. You may find yourself singing or listening to sad songs rather than cheerful ones. These songs, rather than make you feel even more miserable, actually provide strength because they require you to confront your grief while the music puts distance between you and your feelings. As you sing, you effectively *perform* the breakup—to an audience of one—and thus reap the benefits of catharsis.

It is too much to say that catharsis is the underlying purpose of the wayno. But the genre suggests an interesting angle on self and other: to listeners used to the harmonic system of Western European music, the preponderance of minor chords in many a wayno might suggest sadness. Yet Andean peoples do not necessarily consider wayno music sad. Besides, minor chords sometimes alternate with major ones, as is the case with audio selection 5.2, "Cholo orgulloso" (Proud Cholo). As you'll see in online audio guide 5.2, the singer describes the cholo's travails in a pentatonic melody against an accompaniment of predominantly minor chords, although the music also shifts from minor to major. Ultimately, the singer tells a tale of triumph: although people poked fun at the cholo when he first arrived in the city, he quickly attracted the interest of the ladies and soon his boss decided that he was more capable than any of the other employees. All these events unfold via the wayno rhythm and at a brisk tempo, with spoken interjections punctuating the music, a common feature of wayno performance.

The Wayno over Time

Over decades, new arrivals to the cities of the Andean region began organizing social events through which they could enjoy aspects of rural life in the city, such as drinking *chicha* (corn beer) and listening to Andean music. (Chicha is also a musical genre, discussed in chapter 6.) Once the recording industry

ACTIVITY 5.6

Find three songs or pieces in minor keys. (You can consult activity 3.5 in chapter 3 for some minor-key selections from Latin American popular music.) They need not be sad or nostalgic. Comment on their emotional content and, for each song, identify two additional aspects of the music (pitch, rhythm, melody, texture, and the like), writing at least two sentences on each. Then choose one or two major-key works that strike you as cathartic and analyze your reaction in the way described above. You might wish to investigate the Mexican ranchera, described in chapter 2.

began promoting Andean music, the commercial wayno was born. In it, a solo singer performs on stage with an ensemble, maintaining the basic ingredients of the traditional wayno but sometimes adding nontraditional instruments such as nylon-stringed guitars, violins, saxophones, electric guitars, and synthesized electronic sounds. A lonely or despondent migrant from the altiplano could still experience catharsis through such music but now through the filter of a professional performance. Whether the modifications just described intensify or reduce feelings of identity is up to each individual listener.

Like música vallenata, the wayno became popular with mainstream audiences who initially considered it low-class. We can compare both genres to so-called hillbilly music in the United States, which many people with no particular connection to Appalachia enjoy on an emotional level. Regional identity thus transcends the borders of nations while making inroads into unexpected environments—such as the music industry—and finding new listeners and new identities.

IDENTITY FORMATION AND RACE: AFRO-URUGUAYAN CANDOMBE

Sometimes musical expressions of identity will lie unrecognized by the mainstream for years, coming to light only when reflecting on a given country's past becomes an urgent matter. One country that has seen this phenomenon is Uruguay, bordered by Argentina and Brazil, and, after Suriname, the second smallest country in Latin America. The musical vehicle for awakening that identity is Afro-Uruguayan *candombe.*

The "Switzerland of Latin America"

Some of the early inhabitants of what is now Uruguay were an indigenous people called the Charrúa, who lived there for hundreds of years before 1680, when the Portuguese established the first stable settlement in the territory. By the early eighteenth century, the Spanish had settled in Montevideo. Conflicts between Spain and Portugal ensued and in the long struggle for Uruguayan independence, from 1811 to 1824, the two European powers vied for the region. Nowadays approximately 3.3 million people live in Uruguay, with roughly one-third residing in Montevideo and its environs.

Uruguay has been nicknamed "the Switzerland of Latin America" for its economic and social stability. (Of course, the label is hardly congenial to those Uruguayans who feel that such comparisons are not only idle but uphold a standard of the Global North largely irrelevant to Latin Americans.) By 1913, the country boasted the highest per capita GNP, the lowest birth and death rates, and the highest literacy rate in Latin America. One hundred years later, the respected

British publication *The Economist* ranked Uruguay "country of the year [2013]." To be sure, Uruguay's history has sometimes been marred by dictatorships, most recently between 1973 and 1985. Nor is Uruguay particularly diverse, and it is informally known as one of Latin America's "white republics."

Yet Montevideo was once a port of call for slave ships. By 1800, 25 percent of the national population was African or Afro-Uruguayan. As in other parts of the world, Africans in Uruguay established social organizations based on models from their respective countries, at least to the extent possible. Halls *(salas)* in which Africans gathered in Uruguay were called African Nations (Naciones Africanas) and were named according to their members' origins, such as the Sala Congo. A king, queen, or prince presided over each. Mainly, the salas opened on Sundays or on those rare occasions when enslaved Africans got a day off. One especially meaningful celebration was Epiphany (January 6), the Christian celebration of the visit of the Three Kings to the infant Jesus, during which the Uruguayan salas honored the black king, Balthasar.

In 1842, slavery was abolished in Uruguay, twenty-one years before President Abraham Lincoln signed the Emancipation Proclamation in the United States. Over the next 150 years, blacks faced discrimination, which they countered with a black-run press and various civic and cultural organizations. Ultimately, however, the African population decreased such that by 2011 it totaled only 4.6 percent. Despite these reduced numbers, civic and cultural groups have revitalized Afro-Uruguayan culture in recent decades, part of a broader effort to acknowledge more completely the role of blacks in Uruguay's past.

Candombe in Context

"Candombe" refers to a complex of activities, including the music and dances performed in the Naciones Africanas and in street parades. Once such activity was ambulatory theater, in which actors would perform on quickly assembled stages *(tablados)* dressed as *stock characters,* dramatic types *(tipos)* with predictable behaviors. These stock characters might include authorities in traditional African societies, such as the king or queen; the *gramillero,* a medicine man gifted at prescribing herbs; the *escobero* (broom maker); or the *mama vieja* (old woman). Participants would identify themselves as belonging to one sala or another by displaying motifs such as stars or half moons, which could also be associated with a particular neighborhood. Nowadays people still dress up as these characters although they are likelier to take part in parades than appear on stage.

Participants dance to music performed by the *comparsa,* or candombe ensemble. At the heart of candombe are the drums, each with its own role. The solo drum is the medium-pitched *repique,* whose player reinforces a basic rhythm and improvises, in addition to controlling tempo and dynamics. The *chico* is high-pitched and often plays a repeated rhythm or ostinato, whereas

Figure 5.3 Gramillero (medicine man) in street festival in Montevideo.
Rudimencial/istock.com.

the largest drum, called the *piano,* has the lowest range. Another drum, the *tamboril,* is tubular and single-headed and players support it with a strap, carrying it over their shoulders so that they can play while walking through the streets. As with Cuban Santería, the different registers of the drums suggest a conversation. One Uruguayan music scholar notes that candombe music is "fundamentally collective" in that it arises from exchanges between one drum and another (Goldman 1999); also, certain norms govern the familiar call-and-response format. For example, a drummer can give the "call" that directs the others to switch patterns but the drummers aren't supposed to call all at once, just as in a respectful yet stimulating conversation. A variety of rhythmic patterns *(toques)* subject to variation in dynamics and tempo also moves the conversation along. ("Cordon," in the title of audio selection 5.3, refers to a toque.) In the same way that stars and half moons identify candombe participants by neighborhood, styles of drumming can disclose the performers' neighborhood, at least to experts. The interlocking patterns in our audio selection, all of which are improvised, give an idea of how challenging this can be. When you listen with the help of online audio guide 5.3, try to isolate the timbres of the different drums, focusing first on the repique, then repeating to focus on the chico, and then repeating again to concentrate on the piano. There is no tamboril in audio selection 5.3.

Nonmusicians have been drawn to candombe. The late Uruguayan author Eduardo Galeano (1940–2015) admired the genre and waxed poetic over the power of drumming. Candombe was also a favorite subject of the Uruguayan painter Pedro Figari (1861–1938). With their flat surfaces and unmixed colors, his paintings challenged artistic norms but captured the raw energy of the comparsa.

Candombe over Time

Over the twentieth century, candombe came to appeal to white Uruguayans. Captivated by its rhythms and variety of timbres, they too began parading through the streets at holiday time, imitating Africans by going about in blackface and wearing clothing that more or less passed for African costumes. Unfortunately, they sometimes indulged in imitations that were less than flattering to black people, such as highly sexualized dance steps. As white performers imitated blacks, however, black performers began imitating whites imitating blacks, a situation one historian calls a "troubling hall of mirrors" (Chasteen 2004: 63). In short, candombe's identity was becoming distorted.

All the while, Afro-Uruguayans were agitating for equal rights and rising to prominence in public life. Among them were two important women, the poet Virginia Brindis de Salas (1908–58) and the politician Alba Roballo (1910–96). In 2006, the Afro-Uruguayan congressman Edgardo Ortuño (b. 1970) proposed establishing a national holiday to honor Afro-Uruguayan culture. The Day of Candombe now takes place in early December and encourages

ACTIVITY 5.7

Research Pedro Figari. After finding out basic biographical information on him, get a sense of his style. What are its main ingredients? Even if you have little background in art, you can comment on those things that most catch your attention, such as Figari's sense of color, his depiction of the human figure, and his composition (i.e., how he arranges his subjects). Last, comment on Figari's interest in candombe. Do the style traits you've just described suit this musical genre? Why or why not?

Uruguayans to enjoy this musical genre but also to reflect beyond it by asking what steps must still be taken to ensure full racial equality in Uruguay. In 2009, candombe was recognized by the worldwide body UNESCO (United Nations Educational, Scientific, and Cultural Organization) as an example of "Intangible [nonphysical] Cultural Heritage of Humanity." This honor not only affirms Afro-Uruguayan identity but recognizes the power of music more generally.

THE INVENTION OF TRADITION IN PARAGUAY: THE HARP

Paraguay, along with Bolivia, is one of Latin America's two landlocked countries. Today a full 95 percent of Paraguay's population is mestizo and the country has two official languages, Spanish and Guaraní, an indigenous language also spoken in parts of Argentina, Bolivia, and Brazil. The harp has been hailed as an instrument capable of consolidating all these constituencies and is the national instrument. In fact, it came from outside of Paraguay.

Colonial Paraguay and the Jesuits

This preponderance of mestizos was no coincidence. Almost immediately after the Spanish explorer Juan Díaz de Solís (1470–1516) entered the territory we know today as Paraguay, in 1515, the goal of uniting the Spanish and indigenous populations drove many decisions in the new colony. At least on paper, the indigenous were to be treated well. In a document from 1537, Pope Paul III (1468–1549) condemned enslaving them and the Spanish king Felipe IV (1605–65) approved of mestizaje in a formal declaration of 1662. Certainly many Indians suffered under the encomienda system. But those who worked on various civic projects, which were more closely supervised, likely received somewhat better treatment. A relatively small number of African slaves were also brought to the territory.

Missionaries from the Jesuit order, known as the Society of Jesus, began arriving in the seventeenth century. Known for their intellectual rigor and independent thinking, Jesuits have often challenged Church and political authority

---

ACTIVITY 5.8

Research the former US ambassador to Paraguay James Cason. Of what do a diplomat's duties consist? What sort of farewell gift did he give to Paraguay when he left his post in 2008? How did his tribute reflect the demographics and language policies of Paraguay? How did Paraguayans react? Is Cason's gesture one that other diplomats should emulate?

since their founding in 1534 by Saint Ignatius Loyola, a Spaniard who underwent a religious conversion after being wounded in battle. In the wake of the Counter-Reformation, they were especially committed to missionary work, in part to stave off the rise of Protestantism. Like Spain, Portugal once headed a vast empire, settling not only in Latin America, but Africa (Angola, Mozambique, São Tomé) and Asia (Goa, Macau, East Timor). Initially the Jesuits were stationed in the Portuguese dominions, including what is now the state of São Paulo. In 1607, when the Jesuit Province of Paraguay was established, it set about evangelizing the Guaraní. The Jesuits built *reducciones* (reductions), essentially the same thing as missions. Some were near the spectacular Yguazú Falls on the present-day border of Brazil, Argentina, and Paraguay. Even critics of the Church, such as the French Enlightenment philosopher Jean-Jacques Rousseau (1712–78), praised the reductions for the self-sustaining and harmonious life they inculcated. An important element of life on the reductions was education, for the Indians learned reading and writing, catechism, practical skills, and music, including singing, instrument making, and playing different instruments. One instrument that the Jesuits brought to Paraguay was the harp, long used in Europe but not part of music making in pre-Conquest Latin America.

The Jesuits also safeguarded the Guaraní from slave hunters. This was not so difficult when the reductions were protected by the Spanish crown, but in 1750 the Treaty of Madrid transferred Jesuit Paraguay to Portugal, which did permit slavery. The transfer posed a major dilemma: if the Jesuits ceded to Portugal, the Guaraní would be enslaved, but if the Jesuits protected the Guaraní, Portugal would condemn the order and risk dividing the Church, already under threat from Protestantism. The Jesuits decided in favor of the Guaraní and in 1767 were expelled from Paraguay, such that the reductions disappeared. Some Guaraní continued to practice the skills the Jesuits had helped them cultivate, including instrument making and harp playing.

The Paraguayan Harp and the New Nation

In 1811, Paraguay proclaimed independence from Spain. But the fledgling nation was nearly annihilated during the War of the Triple Alliance (1865–70), when Paraguay faced off against Argentina, Uruguay, and Brazil in a bloody conflict over boundaries and tariff disputes. Paraguay's armed forces were severely outnumbered and civilians suffered disease, malnutrition, and torture. The war ended with the death of Paraguay's president and total devastation for the country. A lengthy period of reconstruction then began, as Paraguayans tried to bring their afflicted nation back to health.

Over this decades-long process, music helped persuade Paraguayans that they were a strong people. It also suggested that they were undivided by racial prejudice, a salient theme in the discourse of Paraguayan reconstruction. The harp, used for worship during the Jesuit period, now became increasingly

Figure 5.4 Harp in a shop in Asunción, Paraguay.
Mlifshitsz & Aij/Wikimedia.com.

attractive to secular musicians. Most *arperos* (harpists) were from lower social classes, which complemented another salient theme in Paraguayan reconstruction, that *la gente sencilla* (the simple people) would be the foundation on which the new Paraguay would be built. For decades, the harp grew in popularity and by the early twentieth century, when radio became common, harpists were broadcasting their talents throughout the country. Harp instruction became available to children through the Paraguayan school system and harpists participated in festivals of traditional music.

The most successful invented traditions respond to existing longings, in this case a desire to rejuvenate the country through mestizaje, the dual nature of

Fairs, Festivals, and Public Celebrations of Identity

Anyone who has visited a state fair, a rodeo, or any other kind of large gathering in which a variety of talents are on display can observe rituals and symbols related to identity. When a panel of judges at a state fair awards prizes for agricultural products or for baked goods made from those products, participants are effectively celebrating a community's stewardship of the Earth's bounty. A rodeo, such as the Mexican *charreada,* showcases equestrian skill and grace, much valued by the Mexican *charro* (cowboy). World's Fairs peaked in the last century, mostly in the Global North, although one was held in Buenos Aires in 1910 and another in Porto Alegre (Brazil) in 1935. Each showcased the national image of the host country through food, architecture, scientific advancement, art, and music. Likewise, folk music festivals promote a community's cherished principles expressed in music and dance, strengthening the bonds of place and identity.

Paraguayan nationhood. One critic, writing of a performance, claimed that a certain harpist had captured both Guaraní culture and "the soul of [Paraguay's] musical tradition" (Colman 2015: 5), adding for good measure that the performance evoked "the singing of birds and the sounds of the Yguazú Falls" (5). Given such enthusiasms, it's not surprising that the harp came to be known as the *arpa paraguaya* (Paraguayan harp).

Traditionally the Paraguayan harp was diatonic, able to play in only one key unless the harpist retunes. The key, with its sense of a tonal center, can be reinforced through what is sometimes called a "walking bass." It works something like this: the harpist, who generally uses his or her left hand to accompany, can also use the left hand to punch out a bass line by "walking" up and down the lower strings, called *bordonas.* Paraguayan harpists may improvise on the bass line itself and also add *glissandi,* in which many consecutive notes are played so quickly that they have no metrical value (singular: *glissando*), creating a rush of sound.

A favorite genre is the *polca paraguaya* (Paraguayan polka), which is completely different from its duple-meter counterpart, discussed apropos *Como agua para chocolate.* The Paraguayan polka often uses sesquiáltera, the alteration of duple and triple metrical groupings studied in chapter 3. It may also contain syncopation, which, when combined with its typically short melodic phrases, almost gives the impression that the melody is falling slightly behind the beat. Because the genre doesn't correspond to standard definitions of the polca, Paraguayans themselves have been less than satisfied with the name of their national genre and have proposed alternatives, including some in Guaraní. The term "polca" is so entrenched, however, that no other name has ever taken hold. Nowadays *arperos* often play with other instruments, such as guitar or string bass. The latter may reinforce the walking bass by playing *pizzicato* (i.e., plucking the strings rather than using the bow), as is the case with audio selection 5.4, "Piririta." (A *piririta* is a type of songbird.) As shown in online audio guide 5.4, a main theme is heard three times, each slightly varied and separated by interludes, with plenty of sesquiáltera throughout. The melody is enhanced with broken chords and also several *glissandi*, which may well be improvised; frequent *ornaments* ("extra" notes that embellish a melody) are probably improvised as well. Over the course of the piece, excitement accumulates, resulting in a real tour de force.

The Paraguayan Harp over Time

In 1985, 115 years after national reconstruction began in war-ravaged Paraguay, the Festival del Arpa Paraguaya (Festival of the Paraguayan Harp) was held in the capital city of Asunción, the first festival dedicated to harp playing. For three days, harp aficionados gathered for classes, workshops, concerts, and informal music making. Professional performers gave concerts centered on themes such as "The Harp and Patriotic Sentiments," "The Harp and the Home," and "The Harp and Our Landscape." The eighth such festival took place in 2014, confirming that the harp and its music continue to symbolize national identity for Paraguayans, as does the fact that it continues to be taught in many primary schools. For their part, the Jesuits, who played such a fundamental role in the invented tradition of the Paraguayan harp, eventually returned to various parts of Latin America, where they continue to be active, establishing schools, supervising health care, and running social service centers under their motto, "Siempre más alto" (Strive ever higher).

THE INVENTION OF TRADITION IN CENTRAL AMERICA: THE MARIMBA

Marimba playing, much associated with Central America, is an invented tradition in that the instrument was originally played by Africans. Yet as this population eventually disappeared as an identifiable group in some Central American countries, the origins of the marimba were suppressed. Below, we explore the nature of the instrument and the circuitous route by which this invented tradition took hold.

Central America and Race

The seven countries of Central America encompass the Pacific and Caribbean coasts. Although most of the region consists of tropical lowlands and rain forests, mountains run north-south through the middle of Central America. At the time of the Conquest, the region was inhabited by indigenous peoples, some of whom were later purchased by slave owners in Peru, the wealthy colony to the south. The Spanish presence was generally stronger in the western part of Central America whereas the eastern region has been more exposed to Caribbean culture. Central America has seen plenty of racial and cultural mixing between Europeans and indigenous peoples. In this region, the term for mestizo is *ladino*.

Since the terrain allowed for little sugar cultivation, relatively few enslaved Africans were brought to Central America, although some were deported from British territories in the Caribbean (mainly Jamaica) as a result of slave rebellions there. Even after slavery gradually ended throughout Central America during the first decades of the nineteenth century, Africans faced discrimination, with some countries enforcing a system of what amounted to *apartheid*, or strict racial segregation. Eventually, the African community began to shrink, and its remaining members mixed with the indigenous and ladino populations. Afro-Guatemalans, for example, some of whom are from the West Indies and speak English, comprise just 3 percent of the population nowadays, whereas the population of Afro-Nicaraguans is about 8 percent.

The Marimba of Central America

The word "marimba" means "many sounds" and, since the instrument is made of wood, it is sometimes called a "singing tree." Imagine a xylophone with large wooden keys and you have the essential idea of how the marimba is configured. The keys, which rest on a frame, are arranged from left to right (large to small) and range from low to high. The *marimbero* strikes the keys with mallets, which are also made of wood, and underneath each key is a resonating chamber, made from either a gourd or a wood cylinder. When pig intestines are inserted into the resonator, a buzzing sound *(charleo)* results, a feature of most Latin American marimbas. Because marimbas can play quite loudly they are often used at dance parties.

Among the several types of marimbas are the simple marimba *(marimba sencilla)*, diatonic and with one row of keys, sometimes as many as forty, although marimbas with twenty-two keys are common. More than one musician is generally required, with one player taking the bass line, another the melody, and another the inner parts, including chords. Another type of marimba, bigger and with two rows of keys, is the *marimba doble* or *grande* (double or big marimba), which can play chromatic notes. Central American marimba ensembles often use two such marimbas with a total of seven players, four on a large marimba and three on a smaller one. Some ensembles add string bass and a *drum kit*, a group of several kinds of drums, including a cymbal, and often used in dance bands.

Despite the capabilities of the marimba grande, it was the simple, twenty-two-key marimba to which Nicaraguans gravitated as a national symbol. Traditionally the simple marimba accompanied the *baile* (dance) *de la marimba*, a Nicaraguan tradition during which couples do a series of traditional dances,

Figure 5.5 Group of marimberos playing in Antigua, Guatemala.
lulblub/istock.com.

sometimes on a saint's day or sometimes just for enjoyment. Evidently the chromatic marimba grande was less authentic to Nicaraguans than its simpler counterpart. Other Central American nations have embraced the marimba with equal enthusiasm: besides Nicaragua, it is common in Guatemala, Honduras, Costa Rica, and parts of El Salvador. As one scholar has written, "it is safe to say that at any given time there is probably a marimba being played somewhere in Central America" (Scruggs, in Schechter 1999: 82).

To Whom Does the Marimba Belong?

Yet it was Africans who brought the marimba to Central America, as they did elsewhere in Latin America. We know, for example, from drawings made by enslaved Africans that the marimba was once played in Brazil, although for reasons that remain unclear, the instrument largely disappeared from that country. Marimbas are also found in African communities along the Pacific in Colombia and Ecuador and in the southern Mexican states of Chiapas and Oaxaca. The question of ownership became more fraught in Guatemala when some Guatemalans became convinced that the marimba had originated not with Africans but with their Mayan forbears. A few individuals went to great lengths to argue this point, with one writer actually forging a drawing in the style of ancient Mayan art depicting a marimba being played and going so far as to claim that he had received the drawing from Mayan priests. In short, this person was simply unwilling to admit that blacks had contributed to the national culture. His ruse—which some people undoubtedly accepted as fact—shows the extent to which a musical instrument can figure in the national imagination and, as in this case, spark a "ferocious debate" (Scruggs, in Schechter 1999: 83).

Many Guatemalans are undoubtedly unaware of this racist baggage and simply enjoy the marimba's timbre and versatility. One who has written for the instrument is Wotzbelí Aguilar (1897–1940), who made his name as a composer of dance music. Aguilar evidently led a rather colorful life, often selling his music for a mere bottle of rum. He wrote "Los trece" (The Thirteen), audio selection 5.5, in honor of thirteen eminent citizens of Quetzaltenango, the second largest city in Guatemala and Aguilar's hometown. As you follow online audio guide 5.5, you'll hear two marimbas (played by seven people), enhanced by the buzz of the charleo. Pay special attention to the frequent sesquiáltera, which is one characteristic of the *guarimba*, the genre heard here. The entire composition is in free form (A B B1 C). Listen also for the prominent chromatic scale, punctuated by a "choked cymbal," a percussion technique in which the drummer strikes the cymbal with a drumstick and then grabs the cymbal with the other hand to muffle the sound. See if you notice the various changes of tonal center.

The Marimba over Time

In 1978, the Congress of the Guatemalan Republic issued a government decree declaring the marimba the national instrument, thereby making its identity official. Latin American classical composers have also taken advantage of the instrument's special qualities. In his ballet *H. P.* (Horsepower), written for symphony orchestra, Carlos Chávez of Mexico (1899–1978) calls for marimba in a scene that depicts the tropics, suggesting that at least some in the classical audience were aware of the instrument's associations. Chávez even scored the marimba part for three players, just as in traditional Central American ensembles. In the *Misa campesina nicaragüense* (chapter 4), the Nicaraguan composer marimba Carlos Mejía Godoy used the marimba, drawing on the instrument's unmistakable timbre to arouse feelings of solidarity and common purpose during a period of strife.

PLENA AND PUERTO RICO

The musical genre *plena* encompasses both Africa and Europe, profound influences in Puerto Rican culture. As such, it affirms Puerto Rican identity. The plena also shows that as a people's identity changes, music does too, even while certain characteristics endure. In the case of the plena, the main agents of change were musical practices from the United States, the country that stepped into the power vacuum left when Spain relinquished the last of its colonial possessions, one of which was Puerto Rico.

Puerto Rico, Spain, and the United States

Columbus arrived on this small Caribbean island in 1493 (on his second voyage to the Americas). As in his first voyage, he was greeted by the Taíno, the once-populous group that reportedly fascinated Bartolomé de las Casas when he saw them paraded on the streets of Seville. For over five centuries the Spanish ruled Puerto Rico, with the island serving for a time as a military post. Because it was such a convenient stepping-stone between Europe and various points in Central and South America, Puerto Rico was coveted by the English, the Dutch, and the French, all Spain's competitors. During the American Revolution, Puerto Ricans fought against the British, led by a Spanish field marshal eager to challenge Spain's great enemy. As in the other colonies, enslaved Africans were imported to work the plantations, although they never numbered more than 15 percent of the total population. The few rebellions they undertook were unsuccessful.

In the nineteenth century, Puerto Rico began selling agricultural products to countries other than Spain, mainly coffee, sugar, and tobacco. Coffee was grown in the mountainous area in the center of the island, while sugar and tobacco were cultivated in the coastal regions. Urban centers such as San Juan attracted immigrants from Spain and elsewhere in the Caribbean, but infrastructure was poor and many people lacked education. Eventually Puerto Rico began agitating for independence, one rebellion coming to a head in 1868. Although it did not achieve the desired goal, some social reforms did result and, in 1897, Spain granted Puerto Rico autonomous rule.

In 1898, the Spanish-American War broke out, thanks in part to what would nowadays be called fake news. Many US journalists encouraged war fever by printing sensational Black Legend stereotypes about Spanish administration in the Caribbean, whipping the public into war frenzy. The war, which the United States won handily, cost Spain the last vestiges of its once mighty colonial empire: Puerto Rico, Cuba, and the Philippines. (Two autonomous cities in North Africa, Ceuta and Melilla, are still Spanish enclaves.) In Spain, the war was known as *el desastre* ("the disaster"), confirming for many Spaniards that their country had largely slid off the world stage just as the upstart United States was begin to flex its military muscle.

After gaining independence from Spain, Puerto Rico was immediately ceded to the United States, however, which imposed military rule. In 1917, when the United States entered World War I, US citizenship was granted to Puerto Ricans, which meant that they could be drafted into the US military. Along with US African Americans, Puerto Ricans of African descent suffered the inequities of the segregated armed forces. After the war ended, in 1918, many Puerto Ricans immigrated to the United States, with New York attracting the greatest numbers.

Figure 5.6 Antiracist, anti-imperialist caricature originally published in January 1899: Uncle Sam, the United States, is lecturing four brown children labeled Philippines, Hawaii, [Puerto] Rico, and Cuba, while a Native American boy, isolated from the others, is too ignorant to hold his book right side up; also, a black boy does the menial work of window washing and a Chinese boy waits tentatively outside.

Louis Dalyrymple/Library of Congress, Prints and Photographs Online Catalogue.

Music in Puerto Rico

Puerto Rican music has been shaped by this variegated history. One genre from Spain is the décima, the musical-poetic form consisting of ten octosyllabic lines (chapter 3) and common in several Latin American countries. In its Puerto Rican version, poets would improvise verses to the accompaniment of the *cuatro*, a small guitar with steel strings, usually arranged in *courses*, two closely placed strings tuned at the unison or the octave and played simultaneously to amplify the sound. Other musicians would play the güiro (sound link 3.11) while others strummed the standard guitar. The people who performed this music were generally *jíbaros*, the descendants of the Spanish ranchers and farmers of the coffee plantations, often from Andalusia and Extremadura, the poorest regions in Spain. Sometimes they played the Arab-influenced music of Spain, including a genre called the *seis*, whose musical vocabulary drew on the Andalusian-Phrygian scale (sound links 3.20a, b, and c). Eventually *música jíbara* (jíbaro music) came to be considered the music of poor country people.

African influence emerges in *bomba*, a genre initially associated with Puerto Rican slaves that dates from the seventeenth century. It consists of call-and-response singing accompanied by a wealth of traditional percussion instruments, including maracas and pairs of sticks, all playing different rhythms. A *baile de bomba*, a big gathering at which bomba was performed, was a chance to release the psychological abuses of slave life. (Sometimes the bailes de bomba were called *descargas*. "Descargar" means "to release.") Slave owners often feared that such events portended rebellion. Yet this cathartic experience surely animated these enslaved Africans and gave them the chance to express through music desires otherwise denied them.

Not all Puerto Rican genres are so easily categorized. Many would consider the *danza*, a salon dance that combined steps from England, Spain, and France, an upper-class, European-influenced genre and, indeed, it was performed at parties for Puerto Ricans of European descent. Yet the musicians who played it were generally mulattos or lower-class whites, since playing music was not considered an acceptable activity for the upper classes. Ultimately, the danza was a "new synthesis that reflected African and jíbaro as well as European elements" (Glasser 1995: 25), another example of class affecting musical identity.

Plena

Like bomba, plena speaks to the experience of African-descended Puerto Ricans, although its reach was ultimately multiracial. Many *pleneros* began as *bomberos* and, as in bomba, early plena involved percussion and call-and-response singing. It evolved in the early twentieth century, when the United States was assuming control over Puerto Rico. Initially, plena flourished in the Afro–Puerto Rican neighborhoods of Ponce, a city on the southern coast of the island that attracted immigrants from elsewhere in the Caribbean, including the British territories of Barbados, St. Kitts, and the Virgin Islands. Many plenas are narrative, telling of some local news or perhaps neighborhood gossip. They could also advocate for social justice. One scholar has called plena "an integral part of the labor movement," as it has served as a vehicle to demand higher wages or better working conditions, sometimes describing labor conflicts, such as a dockworkers' strike in the early twentieth century (Duany 1990: 290). The urban working class with which plena was identified could be black, mixed race, or white.

The instruments of plena also distinguish it from bomba. The mainstay is the *pandereta,* a round, handheld frame drum borrowed from Spanish and Arab cultures that comes in different sizes. The size known as the *seguidor* (sometimes called the *tumbador*) is the lowest pitched; *segundo* (sometimes called the *punteador*) lies in a middle range; and the *requinto* is the highest pitched. The drums are capable of a variety of sounds. A resonant, open tone results when the skin is struck with a flat hand or the edge of the thumb whereas a muffled sound, in which the player leaves the hand on the skin, closes off the resonance. With a "slap" tone, the player strikes the center of the drumhead with the palm or strikes the drum with a "loosely cupped hand with most of the energy going into the fingertips," as one percussion expert notes (Brian Rice, email communication September 18, 2017). Although the slap tone is most common in the requinto, each drum can produce several kinds of sounds.

Another common instrument, also used in música jíbara, is the güiro. Along with the requinto, it figures prominently in our audio selection. Over the years, other instruments were added, such as the button accordion or the cuatro, also from the jíbaro tradition. An African instrument called the *marímbula,* a thumb piano consisting of a wooden box with "keys" made from the metal of rum barrels, is sometimes used in plena.

Plena is usually in duple meter and often begins with a chorus (response), which is subsequently repeated between the verses (call) of the leader and which may or may not be improvised. Each drum will play a different rhythm and throughout the drummers show off their abilities. In audio selection 5.6, we hear this format, which also features a splendid performance on the requinto, indicated in online audio guide 5.6. This plena is also a *plena corrida,* or "running plena," which distinguishes it from the *plena lamento,* a slower variety.

ACTIVITY 5.10

Watch the video *Plena Is Work, Plena Is Song* by Susan Zeig and Pedro Rivera, first shown on PBS in 1991 and now available on YouTube. How does it enhance your understanding of plena? What is the video's main thesis? How is the United States represented and how does the South Bronx effectively become an extension of San Juan?

Plena over Time

Since the plena mixes African, Arab, European, and jíbaro traditions, it represents Puerto Rico's heterogeneous culture. Yet because of its working-class, mixed-race origins, it was considered inferior by wealthier people. This status began to change, however, after World War I, when so many Puerto Ricans immigrated to the United States, including several pleneros (plena musicians). These musicians, already accustomed to African-influenced music, became fascinated with genres such as jazz, then becoming popular in the United States, and in the 1920s, plena began to be recorded in the studios of New York City. Once a chronicle of hardscrabble working-class life, the plena was now commercial, and a *plena de salón* evolved for ballroom dancing, using dance band arrangements influenced by jazz. Still, although figures such as the bandleader César Concepción (1909–74) played the plena to great acclaim, many people continued to associate it with the urban poor. This narrative was especially compelling in the coming decades, as Puerto Ricans continued to arrive in New York, often working at menial jobs. Some commercially successful pleneros alluded to the poverty out of which the plena arose. In 1983, a group called Los Pleneros de la 21 was founded in the Bronx, taking its name from a bus route that once ran through a poor, predominantly black neighborhood outside of San Juan, where two of its members lived before coming to New York. The group uses some jazz instrumentation and timbales (sound link 3.15). Another group, Víctor Montañez y Sus Pleneros de la 110, marks out a neighborhood and an identity with *its* name: 110th Street, on the West Side of Manhattan, is the boundary with Harlem, where many impoverished African Americans and Puerto Ricans have lived during the twentieth century.

SHIFTING IDENTITIES IN ARGENTINA: THE MALAMBO AND THE WORLD OF THE GAUCHO

Since no population is static, symbols of identity can change in surprising ways. In Argentina, a longtime struggle between sophisticated Buenos Aires and the rural interior was ameliorated, at least symbolically, by the *gaucho,* a figure roughly equivalent to the US cowboy and championed by Argentine intellectuals since the 1870s. Here we study the *malambo,* the gaucho's signature dance in which he displays manhood and endurance. We'll see not only how the genre came to represent national identity but how it was reconceptualized for consumption by classical music aficionados.

"Civilization and Barbarism"

For much of its history, Argentina has been conflicted over the proper relationship between Buenos Aires, with its immigrant population and penchant for

European culture, and the interior, dominated by the pampas, the inhabitants of which, along with other regions of the country, have often felt overlooked by the capital. Tensions arose in the mid-nineteenth century, for example, when Argentina was ruled by a strongman, General Juan Manuel Rosas (1793–1877), who imposed censorship and other forms of violent repression on the citizenry. Although born in Buenos Aires, Rosas had amassed a considerable amount of land in Buenos Aires province and came to identify with the gaucho, the free-spirited horseman of the pampas. The gaucho could be identified by his attire: *bombachas* (billowy trousers), a poncho (cape), and a *chiripá* (loincloth worn over the pants). He also had at his disposal an assortment of spurs and weapons, the most fearsome of which was the *boleadora,* two or three leather-covered stones tied together that the gaucho would whirl around over his head and hurl at an enemy. (Rosas, it was said, could shoot the *boleadora* with the best of them.)

One outspoken opponent of Rosas was the Argentine statesman and writer Domingo Faustino Sarmiento (1811–88). In 1845, Sarmiento published *Civilization and Barbarism, or The Life of Juan Facundo Quiroga*, a book that is part novel, part sociological study, and part historical treatise. The protagonist of the title is a fictitious local strongman, a gaucho obsessed with raw power and deaf to such niceties as education or manners, clearly an attack on Rosas.

Figure 5.7 Gaucho attire on display in a festival in Cafayate, Argentina, in 2014.
sunsinger/Shutterstock.com.

Sarmiento thus set forth a dichotomy of which Argentines remain mindful today: "civilization," in which enlightened ideals hold sway, and "barbarism," a might-makes-right attitude that can encourage dictatorial regimes. In Sarmiento's book, the latter is represented by the gaucho, who lives amid the "uncertain, vaporous, and ill-defined horizon" of the pampas, as the author puts it. Not surprisingly, Sarmiento was frequently in exile during the Rosas years, mainly in Chile.

In 1852, Rosas was overthrown and a constitutional government established. During these times of change, Argentines began reevaluating the gaucho and, over the next few decades, came to embrace the horseman of the plains as a symbol of identity. An epic poem by José Hernández (1834–86) was partly responsible. In 1872, he published *El gaucho Martín Fierro* (The Gaucho Martín Fierro), in which the protagonist embodied not "barbarism" but independence and resourcefulness, freedom from society's sterile conventions. *Martín Fierro* was such a popular success that Hernández did what many authors and filmmakers do in such circumstances: in 1879, he came out with a sequel, publishing *La vuelta de Martín Fierro* (The Return of Martín Fierro).

Reality was considerably less romantic. Although gauchos lived in natural beauty under the endless sky of the pampas, they were usually exploited by landowning elites, who employed them on *estancias* (large, estate-like ranches) in daily toil. Besides exhaustion and deprivation, in times of war the gaucho was expected to take up arms to defend the interests of his oppressors, and over the nineteenth century, the gaucho population declined. But the image of the gaucho was well entrenched, a positive symbol of identity that appealed to those nostalgic for a simple rural life, one, moreover, that seemed threatened by increasing immigration and urbanization. Ultimately, the gaucho came to represent "what is collectively Argentine and genuinely 'ours,'" as the author Ricardo Rojas stated (Rojas 1948: 630–31).

The Gaucho and Classical Music

From around 1900, several Argentine classical composers began evoking the gaucho and his world, composing piano music, music for the stage, and music for orchestra. They recognized that the traditional gaucho was musical, skilled not only at athletic dancing but at playing a guitar-like instrument called the *vigüela* and at improvising verses. Among the many composers who drew on the musical practices of the gaucho was Alberto Ginastera (1916–83). Born in Buenos Aires, he studied at the conservatory there, an unusual career move in that era, when most aspiring Latin American classical composers dreamed of studying in Europe, often Paris. Besides declaring himself an Argentine composer right from the start of his career, Ginastera took the rhythms and melodic structures of Argentine songs and dances, including those of the gaucho, as a point of reference.

One of Ginastera's early works is a score for a ballet called *Estancia*. Framed by words from the poem *Martín Fierro*, the ballet glorifies life on the pampas. The action, danced on stage, unfolds via the daily cycle of life on the ranch. For example, Ginastera musically suggests flocks of birds and the movement of cattle and dancers; he also depicts the *peones* (workers) beginning their chores. A young man from a nearby village arrives and is attracted to a young woman of the estancia, but she rejects him because he is inept at ranch work. When a group of gauchos tames wild horses, the village lad proves that he can rise to such challenges as capably as they, and of course the young woman capitulates.

Among the traditional idioms that attracted Ginastera was the *malambo*. Its steps, which gauchos traditionally improvised, involve vigorous stomping and kicking, symbolizing the qualities of the gaucho himself: endurance, agility, ingenuity, virility. Not surprisingly, it was often danced competitively. In reinterpreting this traditional genre for symphony orchestra, Ginastera emphasizes these characteristics through driving rhythms and relentlessly repeated motives, often laced with sesquiáltera. Perhaps most remarkable is the coda. In many classical compositions, this section is little more than a postscript. But as heard in audio selection 5.7 (guide 5.7), the coda of Ginastera's "Malambo" is unusually imposing, with driving chords and new thematic material, also relatively unusual in a coda. One might even suggest that the coda threatens to take over the piece.

The Malambo over Time

A ballet such as *Estancia* can be quite expensive to produce since it involves not only the orchestra but dancers, a choreographer, scenery, and costumes. Like many classical composers of ballet, Ginastera extracted some of the work's peak moments—making sure to include the malambo—and worked them into a *suite*, several sections of music to be played by a symphony orchestra without dancers or scenery, ensuring that at least the music survives. *Estancia* remains one of Ginastera's most frequently performed compositions.

Whether in Argentina or worldwide, malambo enthusiasts flock to see the dance in festivals and competitions. The first such festival took place in 1966, in Laborde (Córdoba province) and continues today. According to its website, of the many festivals that have sprung up since, the one at Laborde is "the most Argentine of all," attesting to the power of musical symbols of national identity. Sometimes performers flirt with danger. In the publicity materials for malambo performances in 2015–16, we read that the choreography is enhanced with boleadoras. Ginastera's malambo can also be heard in environments having little to do with Argentine identity: the work has been arranged for marching band and has enlivened many a football game as half-time entertainment in the United States.

ACTIVITY 5.11

Search on the internet for folkloric versions of the malambo. Watch at least two performances and consider them in relation to Ginastera's score. Then, listen to the ballet-suite version of *Estancia* in its entirety. How do the four sections compare? What does the title of each convey? Which section appears in the film *The Artist,* directed by Michel Hazavanicius and released in 2011? Is it dramatically effective? Why or why not?

SAMBA: BRAZILIAN IDENTITY AND MUSIC OF THE FAVELAS

Samba, for many the quintessential Brazilian genre, also emblematizes the African presence in Brazilian history. The term harkens back to circle dances from the Congo and from the Portuguese colony Angola, in which participants would invite one another to dance through a mutual touching of belly buttons, a move called *semba* in Kimbundu, one of Angola's main languages. With its interlocking rhythms and the timbral variety of its percussion instruments, samba is much identified with the northeastern state of Bahia, sometimes nicknamed "the Africa of the Americas" for its large black and mixed-race population. The samba also took hold in Rio de Janeiro, the phenomenon we'll study here.

Samba in Rio de Janeiro and the African Presence in Brazil

How did an African dance find its way to a large cosmopolitan city such as Rio? The answer is tied to Brazil's history. In 1500, the Portuguese seaman Pedro Álvares Cabral (1467–1520) sailed past the African coast and continued westward into the Atlantic, eventually making landfall on what he believed was a large island. In fact, Cabral was on the eastern coast of what is now Brazil. There he encountered the Tupi Indians, some of whom were cannibals and some of whom owned slaves. African slaves, mainly from Angola and the Congo, began to be imported, and would eventually total some 4.5 million. They toiled on sugar plantations, in gold and diamond mines, and on tobacco farms, often under dire circumstances exacerbated by the economy. For example, during a sugar boom starting around 1570, the slaves had to work even harder than normal to meet demanding quotas.

In Brazil, some enslaved people could secure their freedom. Three avenues were available: a master could (1) release a slave with no further obligations, (2) release a slave with some obligations, or (3) allow an enslaved person to purchase his or her freedom. The third option was advantageous mainly to those with marketable skills who could pay their master in installments over a period of years. To be sure, masters were often motivated by profit rather than altruism: since the market rate would invariably be higher than the slave's initial price, they would make money. In that fundamentally racist society, even freed slaves did not enjoy total liberty. They were not permitted to hold government office, nor were many careers open to them, although freedmen often went into the military. These restrictions were one more means of maintaining a social order "that was more separate than equal" (Klein and Luna 2010: 254).

In 1850, the slave trade ended, and in 1888, slavery was officially abolished. Many people of African and mixed-race backgrounds relocated to cities, having worked on sugar and coffee plantations until production of these crops fizzled in the mid-nineteenth century. By the early part of the twentieth century, a substantial Afro-Brazilian community had relocated to Rio de Janeiro. Signs of social stratification there emerged in Carnaval, the celebration that ushers in the penitential season of Lent (before Easter), which is still celebrated with great abandon in Rio. At the turn of the twentieth century, the city would hold three separate Carnaval celebrations. Which one you would attend depended on whether your neighborhood was wealthy, middle-class, or poor, with poor neighborhoods home to greater numbers of blacks and mixed-race people. This population was even further isolated when, thanks to a series of construction projects in the center of Rio de Janeiro, dilapidated homes were swallowed up by newer and more expensive buildings. Pushed farther and farther away from downtown, the poor erected shantytowns, or *favelas,* on the hills surrounding the city, which exist today. Arising from an unmet need for housing, favelas, the individual dwellings of which are often distinguished by their corrugated tin roofs, seldom follow building codes and lack public services. By 1940, 95 percent of the favela population was black or mulatto.

It was in such environments that samba took hold. One, "Pelo telefone" (By Telephone), was conceived in 1916 in a poor neighborhood, and when it was recorded the following year it became the first commercial samba. The words themselves describe samba, referring to the new genre as "pulsating" and "thrilling." Samba, a duple meter song and dance, would become even more "thrilling" than this modest composition suggests. It's characterized by lively percussion parts, which often call for a great variety of instruments. One subgenre of samba that makes these African roots even more explicit is the *batucada,* performed solely by percussion instruments, the bateria mentioned in chapter 3. *Samba schools* (escolas de samba) were established not as educational institutions but as neighborhood clubs that prepare all year long for Carnaval. Members rehearse their dances, make costumes and floats, and devise logistics for the elaborate parades that go on for weeks during Carnaval. The first school was founded in 1928 and had the provocative name "Deixa falar" (Let 'em talk). As such, samba acted as "an identity marker" for poor blacks increasingly bereft of their territory; in fact, many sambas were written and performed by ex-slaves and their descendants (Shaw 1999: 5).

ACTIVITY 5.12

Watch the film, *Orfeu negro* (Black Orpheus), released in 1959, by the French director Marcel Camus. It retells the Orpheus myth against the backdrop of twentieth-century Rio de Janeiro at Carnaval time. First, review the myth. Then consider how it was adapted for the film. (Example: Instead of playing a lyre, Orpheus plays the guitar.) Then reflect on the music of *Orfeu negro*. How do all-percussion passages figure throughout? Note that one of the main songs in the film, "A felicidade" (Happiness), is abruptly juxtaposed with a batucada at the conclusion of the opening credits. What might the director be trying to communicate? Describe in musical terms Orfeu's songs and people's reaction to them. Finally, address the fact that some critics complained that the film romanticizes poverty. Do you agree or not? Why?

Samba and the National Image

The lyrics of early sambas often treated stock characters such as the *malandro,* a shiftless man who lived off women or gambled. Generally black or mulatto, the malandro can ultimately be traced to the African tradition of the "trickster" or the so-called bad man who nonetheless stands up to society's injustices and can thus be seen in a positive light. Samba lyrics often took into account the poverty in which the malandro lived, along with his cleverness in overcoming social obstacles. Many middle- and upper-class Brazilians found these topics distasteful, however, while racists objected to African musical influences, one referring to "vulgar Negroid sambas" (Clark 2002: 265).

This situation changed during the regime of the dictator-president Getúlio Vargas (1882–1954). He came to power in 1930 through a disputed election and eventually presided over an authoritarian state, the Estado Novo (New State). Styling himself the "father of the poor" (*o pai dos pobres*), Vargas employed several strategies for uniting the country. Among these was the idea that Brazil's racial diversity could be made into a strength rather than a social weakness. To promote the rosy vision of Brazil as a land of racial harmony through samba, the composer, pianist, and lyricist Ary Barroso (1903–64) was enlisted. Born in the state of Minas Gerais, Barroso claimed to be fed up with sambas that glorified immoral habits and set about to improve upon the genre that would help make Brazil strong.

Audio selection 5.8, "Aquarela do Brasil" (Watercolor of Brazil), proves his intention. Barroso wrote both the music and the lyrics for this sung samba (*samba canção*), which describes Brazil's beauties just as a skillful painter would do. He praises greenery and "murmuring springs" but also emphasizes the racial mixing in Brazilian society. As you'll see online audio guide 5.8, the

Figure 5.8 The Rio Carnaval today is the biggest in the world. This photo, of dancers at the Sambódromo in Rio, is from February 10, 2013.

Migel/Shutterstock.com.

first image to emerge in the watercolor is a mulatto, which Barroso equates with Brazil itself. He also relies on several stereotypes that would offend many today, such as the black wet nurse (i.e., the enslaved woman who nurses the master's children) and the "headstrong mulatto girl with the indiscreet look," who might astutely exact tribute from the master for her sexual favors. In their time, such images suggested that Brazil was a happy, uncomplicated country in which everyone knew their place—in the authoritarian scheme. So aptly did "Aquarela do Brasil" correspond to Vargas's nationalist goals that some have called it the *segundo hino nacional* (second national anthem).

The Good Neighbor Policy and Cultural Diplomacy

Patriotism and the desire to unify Brazil intensified during World War II. As noted in chapter 1, the US president Franklin D. Roosevelt launched the Good Neighbor Policy to improve relations with Latin America in the event of an invasion by the Axis. A significant aspect of the Good Neighbor policy was *cultural diplomacy,* the idea that people of different countries can better understand one another through a deeply shared experience of the arts. Under

President Roosevelt, the State Department sponsored goodwill tours to the region by US classical composers, jazz musicians, artists, playwrights, dancers, architects, filmmakers, movie stars, and authors. They performed, lectured, gave press interviews and radio broadcasts, met Latin American artists and musicians, and interacted with average citizens throughout Latin America.

Brazil was a prime target for Good Neighbor cultural diplomacy because once the war broke out in September 1939, it was unclear which side Vargas would take. Sometimes he expressed admiration for Hitler (it was rumored that he once sent Hitler a birthday card) but other times seemed to lean toward the United States. A massive cultural diplomacy project was launched: a ballet company, two symphony orchestras, architects, artists, and musicians were dispatched to woo the Brazilian public. Among them was Walt Disney (1901–66), who traveled through several Latin American countries with a team of artists, composers, and writers to make cartoon features about Latin America to be shown in the United States and in Latin America. While in Brazil, he heard "Aquarela do Brasil" and gave it pride of place in *Saludos amigos!*, the first of these cartoons. Audio selection 5.8, a reissue of a historic recording from the 1930s, captures this context in that it features the *big band* sound then popular

---

The Good Neighbor Policy and the Path to World War II

1933 (January). Hitler comes to power in Germany.

1933 (March). US president Franklin D. Roosevelt gives his first inaugural address, alluding to the Good Neighbor policy.

1933 (April). On Pan American Day (April 14), Roosevelt describes the Good Neighbor policy in greater detail.

1933 (December). At an inter-American conference in Montevideo, the United States promises to give up intervening in Latin American governments.

1936 (December). At another inter-American conference, this time in Buenos Aires, Roosevelt is enthusiastically cheered by Latin Americans.

1938 (March). Germany annexes Austria.

1938 (August). The Division of Cultural Relations is established under the State Department, launching official cultural diplomacy in the United States.

1938 (September). Hitler annexes the Sudentenland, an area of the former Czechoslovakia inhabited by German speakers.

1939 (September). Hitler invades Poland and World War II begins.

1941 (December). After the Japanese attack Pearl Harbor, the United States declares war on Japan, Germany, and Italy. Several Latin American countries lend support to the United States while others remain neutral or uncommitted.

in the United States, which consists of twelve to fifteen players, usually saxophones, trumpets, trombones, and drum kit. (Note that the recording, which lacks some of the polish of more recent technology, captures this historical moment.) Did Disney's cultural diplomacy project influence Vargas? We can't say for sure, but in August 1942, Vargas decided to throw in his lot with the Allies and declared war on Germany and Italy. To mark this important announcement, *Saludos amigos!*—under its Portuguese title *Alô amigos!*—was shown at a special ceremony in Rio de Janeiro.

However much the Disney cartoon sought to cement North-South amity, the race relations hinted at in "Aquarela do Brasil" don't correspond to reality. Under Vargas, immigration officials established quotas to control the number of blacks coming into the country, and in 1942, when the US film director Orson Welles tried to make a documentary on samba, this Good Neighbor cultural diplomacy effort stalled because Welles wanted to emphasize the genre's African roots and it was feared that the film would give the impression to the world that Brazil was something other than a sophisticated and predominantly white nation ready to do its part in the global conflict.

Samba over Time

As one scholar explains, "Since the 1930s, Carnaval has been a metaphor for Brazil," adding that the elaborate floats, parades, and costumes disclose "where the country is at the moment" (Aidi 2014: 18). The fact that Muslims are increasingly participating in Carnaval confirms that this is indeed the case. Over the history of slavery in the Americas, Brazil received more Muslims than any other country, and in 2010, the country's Muslim population was 35,167, with the greatest concentration around São Paulo and Paraná. Muslims tend to be well integrated into Brazilian society. The second largest TV network in the country is owned by Arab-Brazilians, for example. How does a Brazilian Muslim celebrate Carnaval? In 2011, the members of a top-rated samba school called the Gaviões da Fiel (Hawks of Faith) performed the "Dubai samba," named after the Arab emirate and city. Singers wore Arabian headdresses and dark glasses, while the parade floats featured dancing nomads on stuffed camels. Spectators wore turbans, some dressing as sheiks or veiled women. All provide a measure of Brazil's shifting identity.

PAN-LATINO MUSICAL IDENTITY: SALSA

Salsa (the word means "sauce" in Spanish) takes as its main ingredients an African-influenced Cuban genre called the *son*, elements of the Puerto Rican bomba and plena, jazz, and melodies rooted in the Western European system of classical and popular music. As such, salsa is a *hybrid* genre, one that began to flourish in Latino immigrant communities in New York City in the 1970s and ultimately became popular worldwide.

Salsa and Musical Hybridity

Many musical genres are hybrids and there is nothing pejorative about describing them as such. As we've seen in the "Over Time" sections throughout this book, musical change often means absorbing influences of other cultures, be they instruments, language, or musical form. Salsa confirms yet again that no musical genre can be "timeless" and that authenticity is a highly debatable concept. Many people have argued over the extent to which one group or another has contributed to salsa. One might instead choose simply to admire the richness of this musical hybrid.

Certainly the Cuban influence is significant. It takes as its starting point the *son,* initially a nineteenth-century rural dance music played on African percussion instruments and stringed instruments of European origin. In the son's urban incarnation, which dates from the 1920s, bongos, maracas, string bass, and trumpets were added, as was the *tres,* a small instrument in the guitar family with three courses of double strings, with each course tuned to a note of a major or minor chord. (Keyboard instruments in salsa often play in parallel triads, a practice likely derived from the *tres.*) Another identifying timbre was that of the claves, which played the familiar combinations of 3–2 or 2–3 patterns (revisit sound link 3.16). The Cuban son was also influenced by immigrants from Haiti, Jamaica, and Puerto Rico besides Spaniards and Africans, long a presence in Cuba.

In the 1950s, timbales and congas were added to the ensemble. By then, Cuban musicians had begun traveling between Havana and New York, where they listened to jazz, like their Puerto Rican counterparts a few decades earlier. In fact, the 1950s saw a fresh wave of Puerto Rican immigration in part because the island was changing due to massive capital investment by the United States. For the first time in its history, Puerto Rico was becoming more urban than rural and many country people were out of work. After trying their luck in San Juan or Ponce, they came to New York in such vast numbers that the city eventually boasted the highest concentration of Puerto Ricans anywhere (more than one million by 1980). These Puerto Ricans were the first audience for salsa, although it quickly became popular among other Latino immigrants.

Salsa's hybridity rests on a few essential musical elements that are now familiar to you. These include the interlocking rhythms and the variety of percussion instruments typical of Afro-Caribbean music, the call-and-response form of plena and bomba, and melodies rooted in the norms of the Western European system. Unlike the smoother Cuban son, which generally uses two trumpets at most, salsa can involve many more brass instruments, including the trombone, as you'll hear in your audio selection. Like some plena, early salsa lyrics often dwelt on poverty and marginality. Although the *barrios* of New York were not unlike the poor neighborhoods of San Juan, Havana, and Santo Domingo, unskilled Latino workers confronted both the challenges of adjustment and anti-Latino prejudice. Salsa thus became a strong identity marker and was often associated with resistance. An important component was language. Over the decades, many important salsa artists were Nuyoricans (born in New York of Puerto Rican parents) who found it easier to carry on a conversation in English than in Spanish, including Willie Colón, the artist in your audio selection. Yet the language of salsa is almost always Spanish, an assertion of identity.

The Music of Salsa

Audio selection 5.9 features a two-part form common in salsa, the *canto* (verse) and the *montuno* (refrain). In the canto, we pay attention to the narrative, whether an actual story being told or a series of reflections on some generalized sentiment. The montuno can be in call-and-response style between solo and chorus, and the words may not be the same each time, as is the case here. When the players insert jazz-derived solos or improvised passages, the percussionists respond. Here the *bongocero* (bongo player), the *conguero* (conga player), and the *timbalero* (timbales player) also play cowbells, and vary the number of drums they play. Some players refer informally to the percussion as either "down" (quiet, without cowbells) or "up" (loud, with cowbells).

The audio selection represents *salsa dura*, one of two principal types of salsa. Literally translated as "hard salsa," it arose in the 1970s in New York. Faster than the Cuban son, it often strikes listeners as driving and the words frequently express some political sentiment. Surprising to many Anglos is the fact that Latinos dance to music with tragic or politically sensitive words. As one Latina student puts it, "We dance to show affirmation" (Trinidad Alcalá-Arcos, email communication March 5, 2017). In "¡No!," Willie Colón decries social injustice and vows to resist corrupt powers. Among the many typical salsa instruments featured are the shaker, maracas, bongos (especially prominent), güiro, timbales, and cowbell, along with trumpets, saxophone, trombones, and keyboard. As shown in online audio guide 5.9, these instruments are all capable of special effects, such as the *abanico* produced by the timbales, a roll that suggests the sound of an old-fashioned fan being snapped open. ("Abanico" means "fan" in Spanish.) More than mere backup, the instruments are a fundamental part of the music, propelling the song's defiant message.

Salsa dura was first recorded on small, New York–based labels, such as Fania Records, which were bought out by big corporations in the 1980s, as salsa became commercially successful. *Salsa romántica* (romantic salsa) dates from this period. It is generally at a more relaxed tempo than salsa dura and may also have a slow introduction. The words often focus on some sad or sentimental topic, which can range from the personal (unrequited love) to the societal (drive-by shootings). Whereas salsa dura involved little studio manipulation,

Musical Example 5.1a. Salsa percussion in musical notation, 2–3 clave.

Transcription by Brian Rice.

Musical Example 5.1b. Salsa percussion in musical notation, 3–2 clave and notation key.

Transcription by Brian Rice.

3-2 Clave

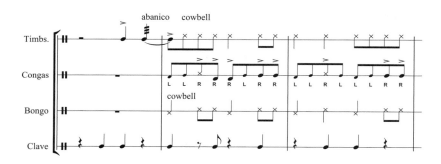

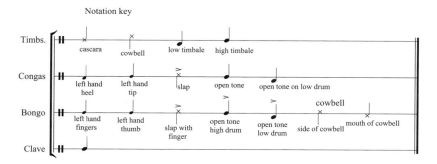

ACTIVITY 5.13

Look up salsa artist Celia Cruz. What was her background and relationship to the United States? In what ways did she project her gender onstage? On gender norms in salsa performance, see Abreu 2007 and Aparicio 1998, listed in the bibliography.

salsa romántica may add reverb for greater expressivity, or combine synthesizers with percussion instruments typical of salsa. Listeners who miss the incisive words and propulsive tempo of salsa dura often disparage salsa romántica, calling it *salsa monga* (limp salsa).

Salsa over Time

As noted, salsa was a vehicle for Pan-Latino solidarity. As the decades passed, Latino immigrants to the United States and their descendants observed that Latin American history and culture were marginalized in the public school system. They longed—and still long for—adequate representation in movies, television, and other media. In the sprawling metropolis of New York City, Latinos united through salsa to celebrate the countries they'd left behind, the country they now called home, and some less-defined state of mind in between.

Pan-Latino identity expressed itself musically well beyond Manhattan and the Bronx. Thanks to artists such as Rubén Blades of Panama (b. 1948), Celia Cruz of Cuba (1925–2003), and Oscar D'León of Venezuela (b. 1943), salsa also took on a greater presence throughout Latin America, acquiring new traits depending on locale, as in Colombian and Venezuelan salsa, for example. Europe, Africa, and Asia also embraced salsa. In 1984, a salsa band of Japanese musicians called the Orquesta de la Luz formed, which sang in Spanish and gained an enthusiastic following in Latin America. Who owns salsa? If it "belongs" to everyone who enjoys it, what does that say about Pan-Latino identity? In chapter 9, we'll explore these issues in terms of globalization and the extent to which it threatens or enhances identity.

MARIACHI: FOR MEN ONLY?

Some musical genres are so regularly associated with either men or women that the possibility of changing listeners' expectations seems remote. One such genre is mariachi, which is also known internationally as a musical symbol of Mexican identity. In recent years, our understanding of mariachi and gender has changed dramatically.

Mariachi, the Charro, and Mexican Identity

Traditionally, mariachi was associated with the Mexican cowboy, or *charro*, who, like the Argentine gaucho, is independent and rugged. A superb horseman, the charro often displays his skills in roping and bronco riding at rodeos or other exhibitions. In his wide-brimmed sombrero, spurs, snug-fitting pants, and bandolera, he cuts a striking figure. Even his horse is elegant, performing rope tricks and dancing after a fashion. The charro must also be a gentleman and behave in a refined manner so as to charm the ladies and show them due respect. This code of behavior is called *charrería*. Charros may be gallant but in their male-dominated culture they are very much in charge, with women playing rather restricted roles. The *china*, for example, is the demure young lady who is honored with serenades, perhaps under her balcony. A *charra*, on the other hand, rides, smokes cigars, shoots, and kicks back shots of tequila even as she is aware of her exceptional status and knows that she risks being seen as unattractive to men.

The Pacific-coast state of Jalisco is the center of both charro culture and mariachi music. The two worlds overlapped to the point that, at least in the public imagination, mariachi musicians were for all intents and purposes equated with charros. For example, they wear the charro dress outfit, enlivened with silver buttons running down the leg *(botonadura)* and other ornaments. (To be sure, few charros would actually dress in such a fancy style. Nor do mariachi musicians necessarily spend much time with horses.) In 1907, a mariachi ensemble performed at the residence of the Mexican president Porfirio Díaz, and in the 1930s, the beginning of the "golden age" of Mexican cinema, films began featuring mariachi music. Over the following decades, mariachi ensembles sprang up all over the world such that the international community also came to understand mariachi as a representation of Mexican identity.

The Music of Mariachi

Initially mariachi ensembles consisted solely of stringed instruments. Around 1900, a typical group might contain one or two violins, harp, and members of the guitar family, including the standard guitar, the guitarrón (Sound Link 3.1), and the five-string *vihuela* (sound link 3.2). All these instruments are rooted in the Spanish colonial heritage. Because these ensembles often played at weddings, the erroneous idea arose that the term "mariachi" is related to the word French word *mariage* (marriage).

In the 1940s, an instrument that we nowadays take for granted in mariachi entered the ensemble—the trumpet, with its penetrating timbre. The ensemble became *standardized,* that is, listeners came to expect a certain instrumentation. A standard mariachi ensemble includes two trumpets, three to six violins,

Figure 5.9 Mariachis perform in Oaxaca, Mexico, in 2015 on the Day of the Dead, one of the most popular holidays in Mexico.

Kobby Dagan/Shutterstock.com.

guitarrón, vihuela, and six-stringed guitar. Still, standardization allows for flexibility and no one would be surprised to hear more than six violins playing in a mariachi ensemble, for example. The harp disappeared largely because mariachi musicians (simply called mariachis) began performing *al talón*, wandering from place to place in search of an engagement or "gig" ("hueso" in Mexican Spanish). Clearly it would be difficult to drag a harp around in Mexico City's Plaza Garibaldi, the prime location for seeking mariachi gigs.

Besides wedding receptions, mariachis play at baptisms, *quinceañeras*, civic events, and even funerals. They may ocassionally be hired to preserve the custom of the serenade, recalling the days of charros singing their hearts out under the balcony of a blushing *china*. Passionate about music, mariachis often learn their craft from their fathers or other male relatives, sometimes by ear rather than by learning to read music. Nowadays, many mariachis are professionals in that they are paid but, as in the past, many are devoted amateurs, reminding their listeners of how much music enriches our lives whether we are professionally trained in it or not.

Among the many genres mariachis perform is the *canción ranchera* (or simply *ranchera*), part of the general category of música ranchera. As in "Paso del norte," heard in *Como agua para chocolate*, a ranchera may express nostalgia.

It can also dwell on masculine themes, with narratives about honorable men who get jilted (dumped) by their girlfriends, whereas other struggles, also related by men, lament the cost of excessive drinking and high living. A title such as "Cuando lloran los hombres" (When Men Cry) gives us a taste of the emotional scope of the canción ranchera. Another important mariachi genre is the Mexican son (not to be confused with the Cuban son discussed above). In Mexico, the word "son" is usually clarified through an accompanying adjective that denotes a region. For example, the *son jarocho,* discussed in chapter 6, is from Veracruz. The *son huasteco,* from the Huastec region in northeast Mexico, is in syncopated triple meter and was traditionally intended for dancing. The *son jalisciense* (Jalisco son), which applies to much mariachi music, contains strumming that emphasizes beats 1, 3, and 5 of a six-beat unit, followed by a pattern that emphasizes beats 2 and 5, along with other performance practices. One frequent feature of the son jalisciense is the abrupt ending: a sudden cessation of musical energies, such as that heard in audio selection 5.10, "Las Abajeñas." The title refers to the high-spirited women from Bajío, a region in the lowlands of Jalisco state. (Male inhabitants are *abajeños.)* You can hear the standard mariachi ensemble of guitarrón, guitar, vihuela, violins, and trumpets, which accompany the male singers, who sing in harmony and whose utterances are enhanced with shouts *(gritos)* and whistles, a common feature of mariachi performance. Online audio guide 5.10 shows the alternation of vocal and instrumental passages and the bright timbre of the trumpets.

Mariachi over Time

What happens when women want to perform mariachi? Recently, several have been doing just that, with some contemporary groups even claiming to be the first of their kind. In fact, women have been performing mariachi for over a century, as an exhibit in 2014 at the San Gabriel Mission Playhouse in San Gabriel, California, revealed. The exhibit was organized by the researcher Leonor Xochitl Perez, who was once discouraged from playing mariachi

---

ACTIVITY 5.14

Research mariachi in your community (or near where you live). If there are no mariachi musicians in your area, research some other manifestation of mariachi music outside of Mexico, such as the Mariachi Academy of New York. When was it founded and by whom? What is its mission? An alternative research topic is the mariachi music performed at Disney World (Epcot). Do you think mariachi corresponds to the Disney brand? Why or why not?

because it would mean frequenting bars. She is committed to educating the public about the role of women in this vibrant tradition, talented women who were restricted by gender norms. Perez tells, for example, of Doña Rosa Quirino, who as a thirteen-year-old girl in the early twentieth century would play the violin with a shawl crisscrossed over her chest, like a bandolera. Sometimes men would tease her but, whenever this happened, she would simply explain, "Gentlemen, I am working"—and then flash her gun at them.

Perez tracked down several other elderly women, many of whom had been forced to give up playing the trumpet or the violin because of domestic responsibilities. She learned of an all-female mariachi group established in 1948, Las Adelitas, and found out about a team of four sisters from Texas that called themselves Las Rancheritas who entertained troops in 1968, during the Vietnam War. Sometimes women performers were hassled by male mariachis in the Plaza Garibaldi, where competition for gigs could be stiff. Marginalized for decades, these women are finally telling their stories. One of Perez's informants, an eighty-three-year-old woman named Frances Angulo, put it this way: "I hear a mariachi play and it's like you set me on fire. I have to dance, I have to sing, I have to do something."

MÚSICA LLANERA: FOR MEN ONLY?

Another Latin American genre traditionally associated with men is *música llanera.* It gets its name from the *llanos,* or inland prairies of the Orinoco river basin in Venezuela and eastern Colombia. Música llanera shows that lived culture in a given environment challenges the political borders drawn on a map. The dramatic performance style in our audio selection owes something to Spanish influence while also asserting masculinity, one aspect of música llanera that women have challenged in recent years.

Musical Features

A música llanera ensemble consists of three instruments. One, the Venezuelan *cuatro* (not to be confused with its steel-stringed Puerto Rican counterpart), is one of the smaller members of the guitar family, with four nylon strings. In música llanera it is strummed, often quite vigorously. Another instrument is the maracas. Maraca players in música llanera are among the most skilled in the world, and move their arms vigorously. The third instrument is the harp, which plays the lowest notes in a rhythmic pattern, marking the beat although sometimes adding syncopation. Some harpists even damp the strings of the instrument to imitate the dry picking of the *bandola,* a pear-shaped chordophone resembling the mandolin and associated with Venezuela and Colombia. In recent years, some música llanera ensembles have added string bass.

A subgenre of música llanera is the *joropo.* (In fact, joropo is so common a term that it is often used interchangeably with música llanera.) Like many Spanish words, "joropo" is of Arab derivation and, as a dance, is influenced by Spanish colonial-period practices, in which couples would do independent steps with a good bit of energetic footwork instead of a coordinated group choreography, all at a lively tempo. Spanish influence can also emerge in Phrygian melodic patterns and sonorities (sound links 3.20a, b, and c). As noted in chapter 3, this tradition often calls for ending on a half cadence, as is the case with audio selection 5.11.

Traditionally, women joropo dancers in Venezuela have worn colorful embroidered skirts, and men sport white cotton pants, long-sleeved shirts buttoned to the neck, and felt sombreros. But not all joropos are danced. Among the basic types of joropo is the *pasaje,* relatively melodious and with a *golpe* many people find both driven and exhilarating. (The verb *golpear* means "to hit" or "to beat." It refers here to the percussive strummed patterns of the cuatro.) Like música llanera in general, *golpes* can be either instrumental or vocal. For example, a singer may introduce the joropo with a *golpe con leco,* a sustained cry. Rhythmic interactions enhance the often propulsive quality of música llanera: the cuatro might strum in triple meter, following the upper notes of the harp, while the lower notes of the harp punch out other pitches in compound meter. This is also the case with the *pajarillo,* another subgenre of música llanera, which is heard in your audio selection. It is further intensified with short melodic fragments repeated insistently in the bass. The pitch of the vocal line is generally high, cutting through the instrumental ensemble, and is a frequent characteristic of música llanera. Some música llanera singers improvise, inventing verses on established rhyme schemes and inserting many percussive consonants. These singers, called *copleros,* add to the dense texture of the joropo and its overall energy.

For two centuries, the lyrics of música llanera have extolled rural life in all its beauties and challenges—as faced by men. How have men dominated nature? What heroic deeds have men undertaken in combat? How deeply do they love their region and the loyal women who have supported them in their

ACTIVITY 5.15

Antonio Estévez (1916–88) was a Venezuelan classical composer. Listen to his piece for orchestra and chorus *Cantata criolla.* What does the word "criolla" mean in this context? What is the subject matter of this composition? Who wrote the words? What is the role of the coplero and how does the coplero's presence enhance the music and relate to Latin American tradition? Comment more generally on the piece, making sure to elaborate on at least three aspects of the music (pitch, rhythm, melody, texture, and the like).

Figure 5.10 The caimán (crocodile) of the Orinoco, which the plainsman of "Llanero, sí, soy llanero" claims to outwit, is now an endangered species.
wayak/Shutterstock.com.

endeavors? This style of singing such music is called *canto recio,* translated more or less as "rough or robust singing." You can hear these qualities in our audio example, in which the singer describes in rapid-fire delivery acts of daring such as breaking a colt, grabbing a bull by the tail, and outsmarting alligators in the river, as shown in online audio guide 5.11. All the while, he proudly proclaims his identity, repeating, "I am a plainsman."

Música llanera over Time

Despite this emphasis on masculinity, one of the best joropo singers today is a woman. Ana Veydó was born in the plains of eastern Colombia, where her parents herded cattle. Even as a little girl, she loved música llanera and eventually moved to Bogotá to study and pursue a career in music. By age fifteen, Veydó was performing in festivals and now has a successful career singing this music, markedly different from the sentimental or romantic songs more typically associated with women singers. She and other women who sing música llanera are called *cantantes recias.* Veydó knows that female joropo singers still have to struggle to assert themselves in this male-dominated genre. Like their counterparts in mariachi, they are determined to pursue their goal.

CONCLUSIONS

We have seen a striking variety of ways in which music can express identity. Whether in the regional accent of música vallenata, in the poignant tale of the cholo negotiating a new life in the city, or in Afro-Uruguayans asserting themselves politically, music inscribes in pitches, timbres, and rhythms these human stories of region, class, and race. We have seen how invented tradition manifested itself musically in Paraguay and Central America, just as the rich mixture of cultural influences inherent in Puerto Rican plena is practically synonymous with that island's history. The Argentine malambo enshrines a symbolic figure and is versatile enough to figure in folkloric festivals or in symphonic format. Samba, traditionally a barometer of Brazilian mixed-race society, has proved ample enough to include Muslim performers who affirm *their* identity. The hybrid genre of salsa not only was claimed by Latinos but became popular worldwide, including in Japan. Finally, we've seen that mariachi and música llanera, although initially "for men only," are quickly changing in terms of gender identity.

Each musical creation combines aspects of music in different ways while reflecting the prevailing culture and helping to create new norms. It would be difficult to argue that musical characteristics—melody, form, instrumentation, and the like—can express one kind of identity or another in and of themselves. Yet the cultural contexts in which these different musical features are configured and the meanings that a given culture attaches to them confer identity on what would otherwise be abstract sounds.

STUDY GUIDE

Key Terms

identity, identity formation
ethnicity
race, racial formation
mestizo
mulatto
branqueamento (whitening)
nationalism
patriotism
regionalism
center and periphery
gender
música vallenata
La Costa (Colombia)
magical realism
paseo
wayno
altiplano
catharsis

commercial wayno
African Nations
candombe
stock character
comparsa
Guaraní
Jesuit order
reduction
polca paraguaya
ladino
apartheid
marimba
marimba sencilla
marimba grande
baile de la marimba
danza
bomba
plena
course (guitar strings)

pandareta

güiro

requinto

malambo

pampas

gaucho

Tupiniquim (Tupi)

samba

favela

samba school

batucada

big-band jazz

salsa

Cuban son

canto

montuo

salsa dura

salsa romántica

gender identity

mariachi

charro

música llanera

canto recio

For Further Study

General

Bendix, Regina. *In Search of Authenticity: The Formation of Folklore Studies.* Madison: University of Wisconsin Press, 1997.

Born, Georgina, and David Hesmondhalgh, ed. *Western Music and Its Others: Difference, Representation, and Appropriation in Music.* Berkeley: University of California Press, 2000.

Brill, Mark. *Music of Latin America and the Caribbean.* Boston, Columbus: Pearson/Prentice Hall, 2011.

Carlson, Marvin. *Performance: A Critical Introduction.* 1996; New York and London: Routledge, 2013.

Finkel, Jori. "What's in a Name? Some Say Inclusion." www.nytimes.com/2017/09/11/arts/design/pacific-standard-time-getty-latino.html?mcubz = 3.

Forbes, Jack D. *Black Africans and Native Americans: Color, Race and Caste in the Evolution of Red-Black Peoples.* Oxford: Basil Blackwell, 1988.

García Canclini, Néstor. *Hybrid Cultures: Strategies for Entering and Leaving Modernity.* Translated by Christopher L. Chiappari and Silvia L. López. Minneapolis: University of Minnesota Press, 1995. Originally published in Mexico City in 1989.

Glasser, Ruth. *My Music Is My Flag: Puerto Rican Musicians and Their New York Communities, 1917–1940.* Berkeley: University of California Press, 1995.

Gleason, Philip. "Identifying Identity: A Semantic History." In *Theories of Ethnicity: A Classical Reader.* Edited by Werner Sollors. New York: New York University Press, 1996.

Gómez, Laura. *Manifest Destinies: The Making of the Mexican American Race.* 2nd ed. New York and London: New York University Press, 2018.

Herndon, Marcia, and Susanne Ziegler, eds. *Music, Gender, and Culture.* Wilhelmshaven: Florian Noetzel, 1990.

Hobsbawm, Eric, and Terence Ranger. *The Invention of Tradition.* Cambridge: Cambridge University Press, 1983.

Huxley, Michael, and Noel Witts, eds. *The Twentieth-Century Performance Reader.* 2nd ed. New York and London: Routledge, 2002.

Koskoff, Ellen. *A Feminist Ethnomusicology: Writings on Music and Gender.* Urbana, Chicago, and Springfield: University of Illinois Press, 2014.

———, ed. *Women and Music in Cross-Cultural Perspective.* Urbana and Chicago: University of Illinois Press, 1989.

Magrini, Tullia, ed. *Music and Gender: Perspectives from the Mediterranean.* Chicago and London: University of Chicago Press, 2003.

Moore, Robin D., and Walter A. Clark, eds. *Musics of Latin America.* New York: Norton, 2012.

Morales, Ed. *Latinx: A New Force in American Politics and Culture.* New York: Verso, 2018.

Nash, Manning. *The Cauldron of Ethnicity in the Modern World.* Chicago: University of Chicago Press, 1989.

Pérez-Torres, Rafael. "Mestizaje in the Mix: Chicano Identity, Cultural Politics, and Postmodern Music." In *Music and the Racial Imagination,* edited by Ronald Radano and Philip V. Bohlman, 206–30. Chicago and London: University of Chicago Press, 2000.

Pernet, Corinne A. "'For the Genuine Culture of the Americas!'" In *Decentering America,* edited by Jessica C. E. Gienow-Hecht, 132–68. New York and Oxford: Berghahn, 2007.

Rodríguez, Clara E., ed. *Changing Race: Latinos, the Census, and the History of Ethnicity in the United States.* New York and London: New York University Press, 2000.

Shapiro, Daniel. *Negotiating the Nonnegotiable: How to Resolve Your Most Emotionally Charged Conflicts.* New York: Viking, 2016.

Skinner, Thomas E. *Black into White: Race and Nationality in Brazilian Thought.* New York: Oxford University Press, 1974.

Sollors, Werner. "Foreword: Theories of Ethnicity." In *Theories of Ethnicity: A Classical Reader.* New York: New York University Press, 1996.

Música Vallenata

Brill, Mark. *Music of Latin America and the Caribbean.* Boston, Columbus: Pearson/Prentice Hall, 2011.

Moore, Robin D., and Walter A. Clark, eds. *Musics of Latin America.* New York: Norton, 2012. See especially the essay by Scruggs.

Ochoa Gautier, Ana María. "García Márquez, *Macondismo,* and the Soundscapes of Vallenato." *Popular Music* 24, no. 2 (2005): 207–22.

———. "Introduction." Liner Notes. *Un fuego de sangre pura,* Smithsonian Folkways Recordings, SFW CD 40531, 2006.

Roosevelt, Theodore. *Theodor Roosevelt: An Autobiography with Illustrations.* 1913; New York: Scribner's, 1920.

Sheehy, Daniel. *¡Ayombe! The Heart of Colombia's Música Vallenata.* Liner notes. Smithsonian Folkways CD 40546, 2008.

Vega Seña, Marcos Fidel. *Vallenato: Cultura y sentimiento.* Bogotá: Universidad Cooperativa de Colombia, 2005. This text is in Spanish.

Wade, Peter. "Music, Blackness, and National Identity: Three Moments in Colombian History." *Popular Music* 17, no. 1 (1998): 1–20.

———. *Music, Race, and Nation: Música Tropical in Colombia.* Chicago and London: University of Chicago Press, 2000.

Wayno

Brill, Mark. *Music of Latin America and the Caribbean.* Boston, Columbus: Pearson/Prentice Hall, 2011.

Moore, Robin D., and Walter A. Clark, eds. *Musics of Latin America.* New York: Norton, 2012. See especially the essay by Ritter.

Romero, Raúl R. *Debating the Past: Music, Memory, and Identity in the Andes.* New York and Oxford: Oxford University Press, 2001.

Wade, Peter. *Music, Race, and Nation: Música Tropical in Colombia.* Chicago and London: University of Chicago Press, 2000.

Candombe

Chasteen, John Charles. *National Rhythms, African Roots: The Deep History of Latin American Popular Dances.* Albuquerque: University of New Mexico Press, 2004.

Goldman, Gustavo. Liner notes. *Uruguay: Tambores del Camdombe.* Musique du monde. Buda Records, 1999 (92745–2).

Moore, Robin D., and Walter A. Clark, eds. *Musics of Latin America.* New York: Norton, 2012. See especially the essay by Schwartz-Kates.

Paraguayan Polca

Colman, Alfredo C. *The Paraguayan Harp: From Colonial Transplant to National Emblem.* Lanham, MD: Lexington, 2015.

———. "The Paraguayan Harp and Its Music." Liner notes. Maiteí América: Harps of Paraguay. Smithsonian Folkways, SFW CD 40548, 2009.

Hobsbawm, Eric, and Terence Ranger. *The Invention of Tradition.* Cambridge: Cambridge University Press, 1983.

McNapsy, Clement J., S. J. "Conquest or Inculturation: Ways of Ministry in Early Jesuit Missions." In *Critical Moments in Religious History,* edited by Kenneth Keulman, 77–94. Macon: Mercer University Press, 1993.

Marimba

Amado, Andrés. "The Foxtrot in Guatemala: Cosmopolitan Nationalism among Ladinos." *Ethnomusicology Review* 16 (2011): 1–19.

Brill, Mark. *Music of Latin America and the Caribbean.* Boston, Columbus: Pearson/Prentice Hall, 2011.

Garfias, Robert. "The Marimba of Mexico and Central America." *Latin American Music Review* 4, no. 2 (1983): 203–28.

Lehnhoff, Dieter. "Introduction." Argentina." Liner notes. *Chapinlandia: Marimba Music of Guatemala.* Smithsonian Folkways, CD 40542, 2007.

Moore, Robin D., and Walter A. Clark, eds. *Musics of Latin America.* New York: Norton, 2012. See especially the essay by Scruggs.

Schechter, John, ed. *Music in Latin American Culture: Regional Traditions.* New York: Schirmer-Thomson, 1999. See especially the essay by Scruggs.

Plena

Brill, Mark. *Music of Latin America and the Caribbean.* Boston, Columbus: Pearson/Prentice Hall, 2011.

Duany, Jorge. "Popular Music in Puerto Rico: Toward an Anthropology of 'Salsa.'" *Latin American Music Review* 5, no. 2 (1984): 186–216.

———. "Review: 'Salsa,' 'Danza,' and 'Plena': Recent Materials on Puerto Rican Popular Music." *Latin American Music Review* 11, no. 2 (1990): 286–96.

Flores, Juan. *From Bomba to Hip-Hop: Puerto Rican Culture and Latino Identity.* New York: Columbia University Press, 2000.

———. *Viento de Agua: Materia Prima Unplugged.* Liner Notes. Smithsonian Folkways, CD 40513, 2004.

Glasser, Ruth. *My Music Is My Flag: Puerto Rican Musicians and Their New York Communities, 1917–1940.* Berkeley: University of California Press, 1995.

Menkart, Deborah, ed. *Caribbean Connections: Puerto Rico.* Washington, DC: Network of Educators of the Americas, 1992.

Mintz, Sidney W., and Richard Price. *An Anthropological Approach to the Afro-American Past: A Caribbean Perspective.* Philadelphia: Institute for the Study of Human Issues, 1976.

Moore, Robin D. *Music in the Hispanic Caribbean.* Experiencing Music, Expressing Culture. New York: Oxford University Press, 2010.

Malambo

Holden, Robert H., and Eric Zolov, eds. *Latin America and the United States: A Documentary History.* New York: Oxford University Press, 2000. See especially the essay by Sarmiento.

Moore, Robin D., and Walter A. Clark, eds. *Musics of Latin America.* New York: Norton, 2012. See especially the essay by Schwartz-Kates.

Rojas, Ricardo. *Los Gauchescos.* Buenos Aires: Losada, 1948. This text is in Spanish.

Slatta, Richard. *Gauchos and the Vanishing Frontier.* Lincoln: University of Nebraska Press, 1983.

Samba

Aidi, Hishaam. *Rebel Music: Race, Empire, and the New Muslim Youth Culture.* New York: Pantheon, 2014.

Clark, Walter A. "Doing the Samba on Sunset Boulevard: Carmen Miranda and the Hollywoodization of Latin American

Music." In *From Tejano to Tango: Latin American Popular Music,* edited by Walter Aaron Clark, 252–76. New York and London: Routledge, 2002.

Hess, Carol A. "Walt Disney's *Saludos Amigos:* Hollywood and the Propaganda of Authenticity." In *The Tide Was Always High: The Music of Latin America in Los Angeles,* edited by Josh Kun, 105–23. Oakland: University of California Press, 2017.

Iyanaga, Michael. "Why Saints Love Samba: A Historical Perspective on Black Agency and the Rearticulation of Catholicism in Bahia, Brazil." *Black Music Research Journal* 35, no. 1 (2015): 119–47.

Klein, Herbert S., and Francisco Vidal Luna. *Slavery in Brazil.* Cambridge: Cambridge University Press, 2010.

Murphy, John P. *Music in Brazil. Experiencing Music, Expressing Culture.* New York: Oxford University Press, 2006.

Shaw, Lisa. *The Social History of Brazilian Samba.* Aldershot, UK: Ashgate, 1999.

Williams, Daryle. *Culture Wars in Brazil: The First Vargas Regime, 1930–1945.* Durham and London: Duke University Press, 2001.

Salsa

Abreu, Christina D. "Celebrity, 'Crossover,' and Cubanidad: Celia Cruz as 'La Reina de Salsa,' 1971–2003." *Latin American Music Review* 28, no. 1 (2007): 94–124.

Aparicio, Frances R. *Listening to Salsa: Gender, Latin Popular Music, and Puerto Rican Cultures.* Hanover, NH: Wesleyan University Press, 1998.

Crook, Larry. "The Form and Formation of the Rumba in Cuba." In *Salsiology: Afro-Cuban Music and the Evolution of Salsa in New York City,* edited by Vernon Boggs. Westport, CT: Greenwood, 1992.

Duany, Jorge. "Popular Music in Puerto Rico: Toward an Anthropology of 'Salsa.'" *Latin American Music Review* 5, no. 2 (1984): 186–216.

Flores, Juan. *Salsa Rising: New York Latin Music of the Sixties Generation.* New York: Oxford University Press, 2014.

Manuel, Peter. "The Anticipated Bass in Cuban Popular Music." *Latin American Music Review* 6, no. 2 (1985): 249–61.

Moore, Robin D. *Music in the Hispanic Caribbean.* Experiencing Music, Expressing Culture. New York: Oxford University Press, 2010.

———. *Nationalizing Blackness: Afrocubanismo and Artistic Revolution in Havana.* Pittsburgh: University of Pittsburgh, 1995.

Quintero-Rivera, Ángel G., and Roberto Márquez. "Migration and Worldview in Salsa Music." *Latin American Music Review* 24, no. 2 (2003): 210–32.

Rondón, César Miguel. *The Book of Salsa: A Chronicle of Urban Music from the Caribbean to New York City.* Chapel Hill: University of North Carolina Press, 2008.

Washburne, Christopher. "Play It 'Con Filin!': The Swing and Expression of Salsa." *Latin American Music Review* 19, no. 2 (1998): 160–85.

Waxer, Lise. "'En Conga, Bonga, y Campana': The Rise of Colombian Salsa." *Latin American Music Review* 21, no. 2 (2000): 118–68.

Mariachi

Bermúdez, Esmeralda. "Exhibit Highlights Women Who Made Mariachi History." *Los Angeles Times.* March 5, 2014 http://articles.latimes.com/2014/mar/05/local/la-me-mariachi-women-20140306.

Brill, Mark. *Music of Latin America and the Caribbean.* Boston, Columbus: Pearson/Prentice Hall, 2011.

Moore, Robin D., and Walter A. Clark, eds. *Musics of Latin America.* New York: Norton, 2012. See especially the essay by Koegel.

Sheehy, Daniel. *La Bamba: Sones Jarochos from Veracruz.* Liner notes. Smithsonian Folkways CD 40505, 2003.

———. *Mariachi Music in America.* Experiencing Music, Expressing Culture. New York: Oxford University Press, 2006.

Terry, Don. "Mariachi Musicians Sustaining Their Traditions." *New York Times,* October 31, 1997.

Música Llanera

Brill, Mark. *Music of Latin America and the Caribbean.* Boston, Columbus: Pearson/Prentice Hall, 2011.

Moore, Robin D., and Walter A. Clark, eds. *Musics of Latin America.* New York: Norton, 2012. See especially the essay by Scruggs.

Reading for Pleasure

Asturias, Miguel Ángel. *Legends of Guatemala.* Translated by Kelly Washbourne. Bilingual ed. Latin American Literary Review Press: Pittsburgh, 2012. Original: *Leyendas de Guatemala* (1930).

Berrigan, Daniel. *The Mission: A Film Journal.* New York: HarperCollins, 1986.

Brazaitis, Mark. *The River of Lost Voices: Stories From Guatemala.* Iowa City: University of Iowa Press, 1998.

Burr, William. *Fall from Grace: A Novel of the Utopian Jesuit Villages in Colonial Paraguay.* Amazon Digital Services, 2015.

Diniz, Andre. *Picture a Favela.* Amazon Digital Services, 2012.

García Márquez, Gabriel. *100 Years of Solitude.* Translated by Gregory Rabassa. New York: Harper, 2006.

———. *Love in the Time of Cholera.* Translated by Edith Grossman. New York: Knopf, 1988.

Güiraldes, Ricardo. *Don Segundo Sombra: Shadows on the Pampas.* Translated by Harriet de Onís. New York: New American Library, 1966. Original: *Don Segundo Sombra* (1926).

Hernández, José. *The Gaucho Martín Fierro.* Translated by Walter Owen. Bilingual ed. McMinnville, TN: Saint Claire, 2000.

Hijuelos, Oscar. *The Mambo Kings Play Songs of Love.* New York: Farrar, Straus, Giroux, 1989.

Kingston, William Henry Giles. *The Young Llanero: A Story of War and Wild Life in Venezuela.* Los Angeles: Library of Alexandria, 1884.

Machado de Assis, Joachim Maria. *The Alienist, and Other Stories of Nineteenth-Century Brazil.* Indianapolis: Hackett, 2013. Original: *O Alienista* (novella, 1882).

Recacoechea, Juan. *Andean Express.* Brooklyn: Akashic, 2009.

Sarmiento, Domingo Faustino. *Facundo, Or Civilization and Barbarism.* Translated by Kathleen Ross. Berkeley and Los Angeles: University of California Press, 2004. Original: *Facundo, o civilización y barbarie* (1854).

Experiencing Latin American Music through the Body

S urely one of the most fundamental ways to experience music is through the body. Our bodies respond, often instinctively, to beat, rhythm, and meter. We spontaneously tap our toes, move our heads, or wiggle our shoulders when we hear music. These are natural, human reactions to music. Do they constitute dance?

As noted in chapter 1, music and dance are so intertwined in some Andean communities that people playing music refer to this activity as "dancing." We've already discussed several Latin American genres that involve bodily movement: Santería, malambo, samba, salsa, and joropo. In this chapter, we explore eight new genres explicitly from the standpoint of the body. We'll consider ways in which the body's mode of expressing meaning can reinforce the music's basic structure and how dance can also represent identity, the phenomenon discussed in chapter 5.

SOCIAL DANCE AND SOCIAL MEANING

For centuries, dance has involved organized bodily movement. Yet nowadays most people who dance in the industrialized world engage their bodies freely. Whether dancing at a wedding reception, a prom, a sporting event, or in a club, they eschew prescribed steps and are generally

ACTIVITY 6.1

Think of a dance associated with your country of origin. If you can, watch a demonstration of it on YouTube. Listen to the music and write two sentences describing its basic characteristics, such as pitch, melody, rhythm and meter, timbre, and
the like. Observe the dancers and write a few lines on their movements. Then discuss in at least five sentences why you think this dance has acquired national connotations. (It is fine to speculate here, a point of view you can convey to your
reader with expressions such as "It may be that . . . " or "Possibly . . . ") Finally,
research the dance and compare your speculations with what you have learned.

unaware if they are performing any dance in particular. If you ask them what
they are doing they will simply reply, "dancing." Other people who dance
may offer a list of their favorite named dances—salsa, bachata, lambada,
merengue—which can be done in couples or in groups.

Any of these movements has the potential to facilitate flirtation, and
throughout history, social dancing has tested one's attractiveness to a potential
mate. As a dance manual that circulated in Europe during the late sixteenth
century explained to its male readers: "if you desire to marry, you must realize
that a mistress is won by the good temper and grace displayed while dancing"
(Arbeau, in Cornelius and Natvig 2012: 198). Dance thus serves as one of many
societal patterns that reinforce gender norms, with certain poses and movements suggesting pursuit, retreat, or acceptance. It has also been seen to promote health, both individual and collective, with well-coordinated dancing
presumably reflecting a calm, organized society and excessively wild or uninhibited dances considered a threat to the social order. The phrase "social dancing" takes into account these connotations while tacitly acknowledging the
power of the body.

DANCE AND MUSIC

Dance is the embodiment of music. The body can react to many aspects of
music, but in dancing, it's that most fundamental unit of musical time, the beat
or pulse, that attracts our attention. Some body movements are coordinated
with individual beats and others outline extended metrical groupings. Besides
pulse, timbre can also be integral to a dance. The reason is that some dance traditions are so associated with certain instruments that the dance seems
unthinkable without their distinctive timbres.

Until recently, relatively few scholars took seriously the relationship between
music and dance. In part, this lack of interest was due to the mind-body split

upheld by Western philosophy for centuries, discussed in chapter 1. Those who subscribed to this philosophy were convinced that dance (even more so than music) was unworthy of intellectual pursuit. A further obstacle to rigorous study of dance was the fact that dance movements were often not written down. Scholars had to speculate on what dancers actually did, relying on written descriptions and dance treatises. Eventually various systems of dance notation were devised, and a discipline known as *choreology* developed, the purpose of which is to study dance steps and their relationship to music. Nowadays, thanks to video recordings, scholars can observe bodily movement in minute detail, often through frame-to-frame analysis; likewise, YouTube has made dance accessible to anyone with a computer. Dance scholars relate individual steps to the music while also taking into account the configuration of the group, how space is organized, and the extent to which leadership may be delegated. Where relevant, scholars may consider the behavior of onlookers, as well as differences between presentational dances (i.e., dances by professionals) and participatory ones. They also weigh any political significance a dance may have. All of these scholarly perspectives involve analyzing movement in terms of some broader context.

Often these factors interconnect. In Catalonia, a region in northeast Spain, people have danced the *sardana* for hundreds of years. Dancers join hands, form a circle, and perform a series of steps that look simple but that actually require a good bit of counting: any tourist who believes it's possible to casually join in is in for a rude awakening. Unlike dances that highlight spontaneity or the virtuosity of an individual, the sardana depends on group coordination and collective effort, communitarian values that also inform Catalonian society. As such, the sardana is a symbol of regional identity. For this very reason, it has been banned at various points in Spanish history, most recently between 1939 and 1975 under the dictatorship of Francisco Franco, who repressed regionalism. Thus, dancing it can be a political act.

A similar multiplicity of perspectives applies to the dances of the mixed-race Garífuna, mentioned in chapter 3 in relation to gendered instruments. Descended from African slaves and Arawak or Carib Indians, many Garífuna settled in Belize after facing near extermination by the British in the late

---

ACTIVITY 6.2

In the town of San Jerónimo, Peru, a dance ritual takes place during the fiesta held there annually for the patron saint. Wearing masks, dancing participants relate contemporary events. Read about this phenomenon and explain (1) what sort of music is used and (2) how the dancers both enact and shape social reality. Report to the class.

Figure 6.1 Singers, dancers, and drummers make their way along the main road in the village of Hopkins, Belize, during the annual Garífuna Settlement Day celebrations.
Roijoy/istock.com.

eighteenth century. Art-historical evidence reveals that their drums are not only gendered but are symbols of the historical trauma the Garífuna endured; drums also figure prominently in religious ritual, which involves dance. Although men initiate the singing, a woman presides over the religious ceremony. Known as the *buyei,* or spiritual authority, she leads a sacred circle dance in which she gestures with shakers to the various places where the spirits can be accessed, either low (close to the Earth) or high (closer to the heavens). The drummers respond to the dancers' movements, a three-beat step with halting at certain positions. Anyone studying the sacred dance of the Garífuna must consider religion, gender, and the rhythmic patterns of the drums in relation to the body.

SOME ASPECTS OF DANCE IN LATIN AMERICA

Dance scholars also examine transmission. For each Latin American genre discussed in this book, we've seen in the "Over Time" sections how music is transformed depending on place, historical period, and social change. The same is true of dance. For centuries before the Conquest, indigenous peoples of Latin America danced to unite members of their communities, to propitiate their gods, make contact with their ancestors, or celebrate the interconnectedness of the universe and its various components. After the Conquest, some European and indigenous dances blended, perhaps to reenact a historical event in a dance drama. Among these were the dancers of the matachines, whose dance initially re-created medieval battles between *moros y cristianos* (Moors and Christians) but has accrued a range of meanings depending on where it is danced. As one scholar notes, if Latinos "in New Mexico have maintained the *matachines* as an icon of Spanish tradition, in Mexico *matachines* allow for the expression of indigenous ideals and formats" (Romero 2009: 186).

Transmission can also be multidirectional. Some dances that originated in the Americas found their way to Europe, each with its own type of music. Among these dance-music genres from New Spain was the *chacona*, which the Spanish authors Miguel de Cervantes (1547–1616) and Lope de Vega (1562–1635) described as a dance of enslaved Africans and Native Americans. Another was the *zarabanda*, the first reference to which is found in a manuscript in Panama, but which was mainly performed in Mexico. The Church condemned these and other dances. It considered the chacona, with its exuberant character, to be the work of the devil and banned the *zarabanda* for its purported obscenity in 1583. Naturally such qualities made these dances all the more interesting to Europeans; indeed, Spanish literature contains references to the zarabanda well past 1583. The dances, which were performed in a variety of settings, often turned up in the compositions of European classical composers attracted to their rhythmic and metrical structures.

A term related to transmission is *criollo*, someone of European descent born in Latin America. *Música criolla* therefore refers to a music or dance genre that originated in Europe but was reimagined in Latin America. An analogy with migration is apt: just as immigrant parents are often surprised by the way their children behave in their adopted country, music and dance genres may take some unexpected turns. These new characteristics distinguish the "immigrant" version from the original and can vary according to region or country.

So far, we've mentioned dances enjoyed by ordinary people, that is, nonprofessionals who either do unstructured dances or who follow a certain

ACTIVITY 6.3

Research an indigenous dance drama not discussed in the text. Possibilities include the *danza de los voladores* and the *mitotes* (pre-Conquest and colonial-period Mexico respectively), the *marujada* (Brazil), the *satiri* (Comina, Peru), *diablada* (Bolivia), the *güegüense* (Nicaragua), and the *morenada* (Bolivia). Consider the history of the drama, the event it commemorates, and the type of music used. Try also to get an idea of the dance itself, from YouTube if necessary.

choreography, a predetermined order of steps and movements that has arisen over time. In professional dance, with its far more elaborate choreography, movements are devised by a *choreographer*, who also rehearses the dancers to ensure that these steps are realized according to his or her artistic vision. Choreographers often make extreme demands on the bodies of professional dancers, many of whom have been studying dance since childhood; professionals must also watch their diets carefully and spend hours a day practicing in the studio. (To be sure, choreographed dances don't necessarily have a monopoly on testing dancers' physical endurance. In the *quebradita*, popular on the US-Mexican border in the 1990s, the female partner is expected to do a backbend.) Choreographers also decide how many dancers should be onstage, how they should be dispersed, and often what they should wear. Since the same music can be choreographed in more than one way, choreographers invariably leave a personal stamp on a musical composition, each "translating" music into movement in his or her own way.

Some main areas of choreographed dance are jazz, modern, and ballet. Latin America boasts many fine dance companies, such as the Cuban National Ballet, founded in 1948 by Alicia Alonso. Also noteworthy are the ballet of the Teatro Colón (the principal concert hall in Buenos Aires) and the National Ballet in Montevideo. Besides the ballets by Ginastera and Chávez discussed above, the Brazilian composer Heitor Villa-Lobos (1887–1959) wrote several ballets. One of them, *Uirapurú*, depicts an enchanted bird that flies among an indigenous community of the Amazon.

In this chapter, we first study Afro-Brazilian *capoeira*, a dance closely linked to martial arts. Next we explore the *tango*, a dance associated with Argentina that far exceeded the boundaries of ordinary flirting in its enactment of gender roles, effectively testing societal views toward sexuality. We then discuss dance in religious rituals of the Yaqui, an indigenous people inhabiting the borderland region of northwest Mexico and the southwest United States, followed by the *cueca* of Chile, which was originally a rural courtship dance but was profoundly affected by politics. The next national genre, the *vals venezolano* (Venezuelan waltz), is a variant of the European triple-meter waltz, an example of

---

ACTIVITY 6.4

Research the Cuban National Ballet (Ballet Nacional de Cuba) and its founder, Alicia Alonso. What is her background in dance? Why did she initially start the company and how were her dancers trained? How was Alonso's company affected when Fidel Castro came to power in 1959 and what has been its relationship to the communist government?

Figure 6.2 Young ballerinas taking class at the Pro Danza Ballet dance school, affiliated with the Ballet Nacional de Cuba.

Joseph Sohm/Shutterstock.com.

música criolla that also helped legitimize an instrument long stigmatized in classical music circles, the guitar. We'll also see how the traditional *cumbia,* a couple dance that originated in Colombia, defies racial stereotypes. Then we'll study the links between the movements and musical structure of the Mexican *son jarocho,* a genre associated with Mexican identity that also serves as a springboard for new meanings in the United States. Finally, we'll study a controversial example of choreographed dance that purports to represent the experience of Latinos in the United States. Please note that merely reading descriptions of these dances and listening to the music that accompanies them will give you only a rough idea of the dances themselves. Luckily, all can be viewed on YouTube.

BRAZILIAN CAPOEIRA: FIGHTING DANCE OF SLAVES

In its earliest stages, Afro-Brazilian capoeira enacted a fight in which slaves performed physically demanding movements that were coordinated with music that unfolds in certain predetermined forms. Eventually, capoeira came to include particular instruments. The text of our audio example imparts a lesson on the history of slavery in Brazil. We'll also consider the meaning of capoeira outside of this context.

Slavery and Resistance in Brazil

We've seen that some enslaved Africans in Brazil were able to secure their freedom. Others, however, rebelled. Perhaps the most significant revolt was that of 1835, over five decades before abolition. It took place in Salvador de Bahia and was led by African-born enslaved Muslims, along with freedmen influenced by Muslim teachings. These rebels were either put to death, flogged, or deported; also, stringent measures were taken to convert these Muslims to Catholicism.

Slaves who managed to escape their masters often established refuges in the forests or other remote areas called *quilombos*. Modeled on African societies, the quilombos were governed by kings. They were also under constant attack by the Portuguese and the Dutch and often had to support an army. The biggest quilombo was Palmares in Alagoas state, and one of its most noteworthy kings was Rei (King) Zumbi dos Palmares, born in Palmares in 1655 and the nephew of a previous king. In 1694, the Portuguese launched an artillery assault on Palmares. Zumbi, who challenged their vastly superior forces, was roundly defeated and on November 20 of the following year, he was beheaded, becoming a martyr to Afro-Brazilians.

Whether in the quilombos or under their masters' control, Afro-Brazilian slaves practiced their religion. A Brazilian version of *Santería* called *Candomblé* endures today (the variant from Rio de Janeiro is called *Macumba*). As in Cuba, African deities (*orixás* in Portuguese) and Catholic saints are blended. One of these is Santa Bárbara, who protects navigators against hurricanes, storms, and lightning. Through syncretism, she is linked in some traditions with Iansã, the Afro-Brazilian deity who presides over storms, wind, and lightning. As we'll see in our audio selection, Santa Bárbara-Iansã is a source of considerable strength.

Movements of Resistance

Most scholars believe that capoeira grew out of resistance to oppression. Thanks to its demanding movements, enslaved Africans in Brazil were able to improve their agility, coordination, and concentration—their fighting skills.

Many who practice capoeira today nonetheless call themselves "players" *(joga-dores)* rather than fighers *(lutadores)* or dancers *(dançarinos),* suggesting that the element of interactive play is paramount. Participants must have a good strong kick and be able to spin on a dime while also controlling the whole body, with rolls and even cartwheels, making for an impressive display. The fundamental movement is the *ginga,* in which the player drags one leg behind the other and then reverses legs. Because the whole leg is used (along with arm movements) the range of motion can be quite wide. More significant, the swaying motion of ginga, which is coordinated to the music, can confuse the opponent, since it can be difficult to tell if the other player is going forward or backward. In other words, a major element of capoeira is deception. By leading your opponent astray, you make that individual vulnerable without actually attacking.

Traditionally, two players would stand in the middle of a circle made by the other participants, the *roda de capoeira* ("roda" meaning "circle" or "wheel"). As the pair in the center repeat the motions just described, they incorporate additional steps into the ginga. Some wear white, adding another challenge: Can they walk away from a capoeira session without a speck of dirt on their clothing? Throughout, the movements of the players both cohere and compete, through either repetition or variation, each a moving target at all times.

During the colonial period, capoeira was sometimes repressed by the authorities, and in 1890, two years after abolition, it was formally prohibited. (In some circles, the word "capoeira" came to mean "scoundrel" or "thief.") Naturally, it continued to be secretly practiced. During this so-called underground period, two figures in the history of capoeira stand out, both called "mestre" (master), a title bestowed on teachers of capoeira, who are respected for their capoeira skills and for their general wisdom. One, Manuel dos Reis Machado (1900–74), or Mestre Bimba, advocated for capoeira's place in Brazilian society, arguing that an important dimension of the nation's history was enshrined in the dance. Thanks in part to Mestre Bimba, capoeira became legal again in 1930. He also established a school of capoeira, devising a formal system of various rhythmic patterns, some of which he created himself, although because his innovations proved attractive to people outside of the usual capoeira circles (including the white middle class), Mestre Bimba was criticized for failing to adhere to capoeira's African roots. The second leader in capoeira, Vicente Ferreira Pastinha (1889–1981), or Mestre Pastinha, was more intent on cultivating the genre's African characteristics, specifically through the Angolan style. Nowadays, capoeiristas engage in this activity not so much to develop combat skills but for the sheer pleasure of experiencing physical coordination, group dynamics, and the self-knowledge martial arts can afford. Many also do so to honor their African heritage and recapture something of their own past.

Figure 6.3 Brazilian capoeira group performs in Salvador, Bahia, in 2016.
Cassiohabib/Shutterstock.com.

The Music of Capoeira

Besides these physical exertions, practitioners of capoeira must be sensitive to the music, which is performed by a small ensemble called a *bateria*. Listen again to the berimbau (sound link 3.4) and recall its appearance. As noted in chapter 3, the timbre varies depending on whether the player strikes the string with a stick or presses it with a coin or a small stone. In capoeira Angola, a bateria will usually contain three berimbaus, each in a different register. Some scholars contend that the instrument derived from Angola or the Congo and was brought to Brazil in this form. More scholars, however, believe that although the berimbau did come from Africa, it was modified in Brazil.

Also revisit sound link 3.10 and review the different timbres produced by the caxixi, the small, closed basket with seeds inside. Figure 3.2 shows how the berimbau player holds on to the instrument and the stone with one hand and manipulates the caxixi and the sound-producing stick with the other. Additional capoeira instruments are the agogô bell and the pandeiro (sound links 3.7 and 3.9). The bateria also includes the *atabaque*, a tall, wooden hand drum with calfskin heads played with the hands, and the *reco-reco* (scraper). Together the players establish a variety of *toques* (rhythmic patterns), some of which are linked to melodic patterns and are repeated but which are also subject to variation. A leader will often sing solos, sometimes improvising, or collaborate in call-and-response singing with participants; indeed, group response is fundamental to capoeira's communicative power. Besides singing, participants in some capoeira traditions may clap as they wait their turn to test their physical and mental stamina in the middle of the roda.

Rather than simply accompany movement, the music of capoeira is deeply integrated into the ongoing action, feeding into the dancers' exertions while energizing the roda. Each section of music is part of an overall form—again, defined as the laying out of the sections of a musical creation in time—which, in capoeira, depends on repetition and variation. Each musical section demands certain responses both from the dancer-fighters and from the audience. For example, some sections always elicit call-and-response singing, whereas some toques, when repeated, quickened, or elongated, usher the participants into another section. The different sections of the form are signaled by instruments, with the lowest berimbau, the *gunga*, as the leader. The gunga establishes a toque and signals to the dancers when it is time to begin and end each capoeira game. The *medio*, or middle-register berimbau, is the least varied, for it plays the same rhythm as its lower-pitched counterpart, although it may play the high and low pitches in reverse. The *viola* (or *violinha* in the diminutive form) is the highest, and either plays an additional pattern or matches that of the gunga. More so than the other berimbaus, the viola improvises. Normally the bateria keeps a steady tempo, but when the "feel" for the prevailing toque starts to shift, the musicians yield to whatever new series of groupings is being established, while participants react with their bodies. The result is a natural tension that pushes and pulls in combination with the internal impulses of the players and the receptivity of the musicians. In sum, capoeira requires consummate balance within a flexible framework. Total concentration is required to sense these variations and ultimately return to the basic structure.

Audio selection 6.1 represents the Angolan style of capoeira. As online audio guide 6.1 shows, it relates the historical account of Rei Zumbi's martyrdom, outlined above. In the first part, the *ladainha* (litany), the leader sets forth the facts, mentioning November 20, the day of Rei Zumbi's beheading, and May 13, when abolition became law in 1888. The tale told is one of frustration, for not only has Rei Zumbi's sacrifice been inadequately acknowledged, but history itself has deceived Afro-Brazilians, since so little changed with abolition. (The ladainha can sometimes be improvised although that is probably not the case here.) You'll hear the Angolan-style toque, along with the entrances of the three berimbaus and the other instruments, as the narrative unfolds. During this part, the players sit on their heels, heads bowed, waiting for the music to tell them when it is time to start moving. The next part, the *chula*, is in call-and-response form. This particular chula resembles another type of capoeira song, the *louvação,* or salutation, in which capoeiristas salute their master and proclaim, "the time has come." Accordingly, the members of the chorus bow their heads and raise both hands toward God, toward their ancestors, or whatever else they may wish to honor. The final section, the *corrido,* signals that the actual movements are about to begin. (The corrido should not be confused with the Mexican genre of the same name, discussed in chapter 7.) In this section, the singers honor Santa Bárbara, syncretized with the orixá Iansã, by calling attention to flashes of lightning. With shorter toques and an accelerating tempo, the corrido urges the fighter-dancers to exert themselves as they move into the roda.

Capoeira over Time

Since the era of Mestre Bimba, Afro-Brazilians have made some progress toward equality, although much ground remains to be traveled. More than half the people in the favelas of Rio de Janeiro are black, for example, and the 2010 census revealed that "the income of whites is slightly more than double that of black or brown Brazilians" (*The Economist,* 2012: www.economist.com/node/21543494). Nowadays, November 20 is celebrated as the *Dia da Consciência Negra* (Black Consciousness Day) and it can involve educational events, demonstrations, and music. (Sometimes it is called "Zumbi Day" in tribute to Rei Zumbi's sacrifice.) As for capoeira, it is practiced for its physical, spiritual, and psychological benefits, and has spread to many countries beyond Brazil. In the United States, capoeira communities have sprung up in virtually every state. Thanks to this phenomenon, Brazilians and non-Brazilians assemble to compete but also to enjoy the affective bonds capoeira has offered for centuries, celebrating the links between the body, music, and mental well-being. Some practitioners see the movements as a path to discipline and enlightenment. As one informant in Sacramento, California, explains, "I was a street kid, into drugs and all sorts of things. Capoeira turned all that around" (private communication, March 12, 2016). Clearly capoeira's promise of liberation can be experienced in many ways.

ACTIVITY 6.5

Assuming that you are unable to travel to Brazil while enrolled in this class, visit a live capoeira performance in your area. (To prepare, watch a few YouTube videos of capoeira beforehand.) After reading the section "Interviewing Strategies" on page 339, arrange in advance to interview at least one non-Brazilian performer. How did he or she become involved in capoeira? Then write a short essay about why people outside of Brazil might want to practice capoeira.

ARGENTINE TANGO: THE BODY AND THE VOICE

We have discussed Argentina's generous immigration policy of the late nineteenth and early twentieth centuries and the extent to which Jewish immigrants enriched musical life in their adopted country. The tango arose in another immigrant community, that of poor and working-class people from Spain and Italy. Intimately linked to the body, the dance was initially considered scandalous. Over the years, however, whether sung or danced, it became both an international success and a national symbol.

Immigrant Culture in Argentina and the Evolution of Tango

During the 1870s and 1880s, Spanish and Italian immigrants made their homes in the slums *(arrabales)* on the outskirts of Buenos Aires. Some were single men looking for adventure while others simply wanted to better their economic circumstances. If they were married men, they generally came alone, found work, and sent for their wives, children, and other family members later. Displaced gauchos also relocated to the arrabales when their opportunities in the pampas declined.

This immigrant population distinguished itself from the mainstream in several ways. Many spoke *lunfardo,* which combines Spanish with words from Italian, including Italian dialects. At least some lunfardo vocabulary related to criminal activity, the aura of which was further enhanced through an array of stock characters whose images circulated in sketches, paintings, literature, and the media. One, the *compadrito,* slouched on street corners in a snug black suit, knife at the ready and with a kerchief loosely tied around his neck. Accompanying this urban gaucho was the *mina,* the lunfardo word for an unmarried woman, who might be abandoned or reduced to prostitution. Another was the *malevo,* or ruffian. Just as Mafiosos such as Tony Soprano and Don Vito Corleone have fascinated the US public, the mystique of these hard-bitten characters took hold in Argentina. Of course, plenty of noncriminals lived in the arrabales and anyone posing as compadrito might be doing just that—posing.

In this environment, tango arose. Because there were not always enough women to go around, two men might dance the tango together, with the result that the steps could be aggressive; also, the tango was sometimes danced in houses of prostitution. When women and men danced together, they would lock in a tight embrace, their faces often inches apart or actually touching. The basic step is a confident stride in a timed progression around the dance floor. Following the steady beat of a duple or quadruple meter, the man places a firm hand on his partner's back and steers her around the floor. It is important for the man to have "floor sense" and avoid colliding with others. In tracing various patterns, the dancers may or may not be conscious of how closely their movements actually correspond to the musical phrases.

Tango dancers have at their disposal a whole series of steps or "figures," several of which can be provocative, as in the *gancho,* in which one partner hooks his or her leg around the other person's. In the *sacada,* the upper body is turned while the free foot of one dancer crosses the imaginary line between the partner's feet. With the *boleo,* the knees are kept together while one calf whips upward. Throughout, the man leans forward over the woman, a confrontational position that has occasioned comparisons between the tango and a violent act, such as a knife fight. More often, however, it's compared with sexual intercourse and is seen as a performance of male domination. While it is true that some women claim they barely need to concentrate when the man leads with authority, others confide that, while dancing, they conduct themselves in such a way as to make the man *think* he is leading, subtly interjecting cues of their own.

Figure 6.4 Skilled dancers performing the tango in front of the entrance to a restaurant in Buenos Aires.

Kobby Dagan/Shutterstock.com.

Gradually immigrants integrated with mainstream Argentine society. Lunfardo words and expressions shed their criminal origins or worked themselves into ordinary speech. (Some survive today. For example, the word "laburo," derived from the Italian "lavoro," which means "work," is often used in Buenos Aires instead of "trabajo," Spanish for work.) Tango cafés began to flourish in downtown Buenos Aires, and by the 1940s, the classic tango orchestra, known as the *orquesta típica* (typical orchestra), was established. Such orchestras generally consisted of six players, with piano and string bass providing the harmonic foundation and two violins playing the melody. At the heart of the tango orchestra was the bandoneón, introduced in chapter 2, two of which play in the six-piece orquesta típica. The bandoneón itself is an "immigrant," one whose history shows how dramatically musical function can change: in Germany, the bandoneón was sometimes used in smaller churches that lacked an organ, a context quite different from that of the scandal-tinged tango.

Also in the 1940s, the Argentine strongman Juan Domingo Perón (1895–1974) decided to make the tango a symbol of national unity, much the way Vargas did with samba. Perón, who came to power in 1946, was known for championing poor and working-class Argentines and his wife, María Eva Duarte (Evita), was even more beloved than he in some sectors. To be sure, Perón was a divisive figure who curtailed civil liberties and weakened the economy. But when he and Evita decided that the tango was an ideal symbol for the nation, his populist base paid attention. All the while, authors and social critics assigned the tango an important place in the national psyche.

Borges and the Tango

Jorge Luis Borges (1899–1986) was one of Argentina's most celebrated authors, turning out short stories, poetry, essays, and literary criticism. His works are known for their complex embrace of philosophical concepts, engagement with memory, and allusive power. Many a literary tour de force, such as the ambiguous narrator, can be found in his writings. At age fifty-five, Borges became blind, a condition some critics believe further stimulated his already vivid imagination. He responded deeply to the tango, addressing it in more than one literary work. In his essay "History of the Tango," Borges is not so much concerned with the dance's actual history but rather with its power to unify a sometimes fractious society. In doing so, he refers to memory. "The tango gives all of us an imaginary past," he once remarked in a lecture, the recording of which was recently discovered and reported on in the press. "To study the tango is . . . the same as studying the different vicissitudes of the Argentine soul" (Borges "Oyendo un tango viejo," www.clarin.com/sociedad/borges-vision-particular-tango_0_BJRx5ufswml.html).

It should be noted that despite the overwhelming tendency to associate the tango with Argentina, many Uruguayans claim credit for it, since it was an Uruguayan who composed not the first tango but probably the most famous one, "La Cumparsita," in 1916. The composer was Gerardo Matos Rodriguéz (1897–1948) and the title refers to a carnival march.

Audio selection 6.2a, detailed in online audio guide 6.2a, is the classic tango "El choclo," by Ángel Villoldo (1861–1919), a native of Buenos Aires. The title, which translates as "the ear of corn," has been the cause of some speculation. According to one account, "El choclo" was first performed at an elegant restaurant in Buenos Aires in 1905 (i.e., before tango had reached the height of its popularity). The orchestra leader wasn't sure that the exclusive clientele would appreciate it. Yet, because he admired Villoldo, a pioneer of tango, he wanted very much to perform Villoldo's latest creation. So the orchestra leader decided to announce it without a title, simply calling it a *danza criolla*, that is, a dance with European credentials, a characterization he believed would appeal to cosmopolitan Buenos Aires. Eventually Villoldo arrived at "El choclo," claiming that the ear of corn was the tastiest part of the stew, or *puchero*. Since "ganar el puchero" means "earn a living," perhaps he was also alluding to his hope of becoming wealthy with his new tango. As a classic, this tango has been arranged many times and performed by numerous artists, including for dance and freer interpretations.

The Tango Abroad

Another factor in the acceptance of tango was international interest. A French dancer and choreographer toned down some of the steps so as to be suggestive yet suitable for the ballroom, and as one scholar explains, "upper-class Argentines had no choice but to accept it, since they upheld Paris as the model of cultural refinement" (Schwartz-Kates, in Moore and Clark 2012: 296). Indeed, on the eve of World War I, tango was all the rage in Paris, as a novel about this period demonstrates, *The Four Horsemen of the Apocalypse,* (Los cuatro jinetes del apocalípsis) by the Spanish author Vicent Blasco Ibañez (1867–1928). In it, a young Argentine man makes his living teaching tango in Paris. The silent-film version of the novel, from 1921, featured the movie idol Rudolph Valentino in this dancing role, which provoked sighs and heartthrobs among female moviegoers the world over.

During World War I, tango also came to the United States, where it was an immediate hit. Some precautions were in order, however: clergymen railed against what they believed to be its inherent lewdness and Yale University banned the tango from its 1914 prom. Harvard responded by saying that it *would* permit the tango at its prom, and when the mayor of New York and the secretary of the treasury began dancing it, it was clear that the tango had arrived. Naturally, the whiff of scandal made it all the more fashionable.

Helping in the campaign for respectability was the famous husband-and-wife dance team, Vernon and Irene Castle, known for "cleaning up" risqué dances. Their sanitized version of the tango emphasized erect posture and eliminated "the swaying that made the Argentine tango so objectionable," as they stated (Castle, in Cook 1998: 141).

Tango Canción

The tango also has a long history of being sung, often with guitar accompaniment. For example, "El choclo" acquired words and thus became a *tango canción* (sung tango), with two sets of lyrics. In one set, from the 1930s and by Juan Carlos Marambio Catán (1895–1973), the singer tells of pain and longing. The other set, from 1946 and by Enrique Santos Discépolo (1901–51), came at the request of an Argentine movie star who wanted to sing it in a film. The words are just as mournful but are laced with plenty of lunfardo. In both, the singer comments on the tango itself and its emotive force.

The most celebrated tango singer in history was the movie star Carlos Gardel (1890–1935), who began recording tangos in the 1920s. Of his several films that feature tangos *(Tango on Broadway, Tango Bar),* some were shot in New York at the Paramount studios in Queens. Gardel took the sung tango to new heights, delivering its lyrics in a markedly dramatic style. The words often tell of inestimable loss, whether through death, rejection, or separation, all attributable to an inscrutable fate that no human being can understand, much less control. As if to confirm the dark power of tango lyrics, sometimes Argentines describe a tragic or melodramatic event by saying, "es todo un tango" (it's one big tango).

Audio selection 6.2b is "Adios muchachos" (So Long, Boys), by Julio Sanders (1897–1942) and with lyrics by César Vedani (1906–79), tells of a man beset by ill fortune: not only has he lost his sweetheart and his beloved mother but for reasons that remain obscure, he must leave his friends and resign himself to the "law of God." At a brisk tempo, "Adios muchachos" is in a major key, further debunking the idea that minor is sad and major is happy. As shown in online audio guide 6.2b, two guitars accompany Gardel's inimitable voice.

ACTIVITY 6.6

Research Carlos Gardel and find out the basic facts of his biography. Why do you suppose he became such an important figure in Argentine culture? How do the circumstances of his death contribute to his mystique? Return to *La historia oficial* and the sequence beginning at 22:55. Why might Ana have had a poster of Gardel in her apartment? Why might his image be used as an advertising icon?

Figure 6.5 In this photo from 2013, a woman jogs past a mural of Gardel in the Palermo neighborhood of Buenos Aires. Evidently the owner of the building gave permission to paint on the side of the building, which is otherwise illegal.

Natacha Pisarenko/APimages.com.

The Tango over Time

By the 1960s, when Perón had been out of power for several years, young Argentines rejected the tango in favor of rock 'n' roll. It never lost its hold on musicians, however, and the classically trained Argentine composer Astor Piazzolla (1921–92), saw the tango as an invitation to experiment. He composed tangos in a wide variety of styles and also wrote challenging works for the bandoneón, at that time not considered a legitimate instrument in classical music circles. Purists criticized Piazzolla for combing tango with jazz.

In the 1990s, the dance became popular again. Touring companies based in Argentina began performing it, albeit in a highly choreographed, almost athletic version. Still, people who saw these performances found themselves entranced by the tango, even if they could not themselves dance it in such a dazzling style. As a result, classes in "Argentine tango" have become available to dance amateurs worldwide, with many people finding in tango an emotional and physical outlet, along with the physical gratification that comes with mastering the bodily demands of the dance.

BELIEFS, BORDERS, AND THE BODY: THE YAQUI DEER DANCE

The Yaqui are a Native American people from northwest Mexico (the present-day state of Sonora) near the Yaqui River. Many eventually settled in the border region of the Southwest United States, primarily in Arizona. Yaqui cosmology and its rituals include dance. The Deer Dance, studied here, speaks to both Yaqui and Catholic belief systems and is thus an example of syncretization. It also mirrors the borderland itself, which one Chicana scholar describes as a zone in which "two or more cultures edge each other . . . where the space between [different peoples] shrinks" (Anzaldúa 1999:19).

Catholic Faith, Yaqui Cosmology, and Dance

Before the Conquest, the Yaqui practiced agriculture and hunting. Their social system rested on a kinship network, a system of coparenthood according to which a child could have many pairs of godparents, who are responsible to the child's biological parents, to all the other godparents, and of course to the child. The Yaqui believe that all beings are connected, whether through blood or spirit, and, seeing themselves as one with nature, revere all living creatures. For the Yaqui, five different worlds exist: (1) the desert or wilderness world, (2) the mystical or enchanted world, (3) the world of flowers, (4) the world of dreams, and (5) the world of the night.

When the Spanish came, the Yaqui defended their land fiercely. They were not unreceptive to Jesuit missionaries, however, whom they first encountered in the seventeenth century. The Yaqui embraced many aspects of Catholicism, including the message of Christ's sacrifice for humankind, and some Yaqui even came to believe that Jesus had once lived in their own villages during ancient times; some also saw Mary as the equivalent of an Earth mother. The five worlds of the Yaqui also found a parallel in Catholic theology, which embraces (1) earthly life, (2) heaven (for the virtuous), (3) hell (for the damned), (4) purgatory (a state of purification after earthly death), and (5) limbo (for those not sinful enough to go to hell).

Another shared characteristic was dance. Sensing native interest in spectacle, the missionaries drew on a long tradition of religious dramatization in Catholic Europe, which often combined music and dance and which was especially strong in Spain. Throughout the country, religious dramas such as the *auto sacramental* were enacted in the town square with costumes and pageantry. During Semana Santa (Holy Week), which commemorates Christ's final days before he was crucified, Sevilla (Andalusia) celebrates in an especially grand style, with processions and music drawing tourists from all over the world to this day. Sevilla is also noted for religious dance: on various holidays, ten boys, called *seises,* perform sacred dances in the cathedral for the benefit of the faithful. In sum, people *perform* their faith. Compare this outlook to that of certain Protestant denominations, such as those of the Puritan communities in colonial New England, who were convinced that dancing encouraged sinful behavior. Some Protestant denominations prohibit dancing today.

Dance and music combine in the Deer Dance, which is related to Holy Week. The deer merits special respect and gratitude for the Yaqui: willing to pray to Jesus, they also recognize certain animal "saints," such as a water serpent that brings a flood. The deer, once an important element of their subsistence, is honored despite the fact that the Yaqui no longer rely on hunting. Selected individuals perform a special dance in the deer's honor. As they do so, they embody questions of community, good and evil, or life and death, questions that also inform the beliefs and practices bound up in the Christian holiday of Lent, or Waehma in Yaqui.

The Deer Dance as Ritual

Some key participants in the Deer Dance are introduced on Palm Sunday, the first day of Holy Week. These include the *pascolas,* individuals who will dance and tell jokes throughout the week. The word probably derives from "Pascua" (Spanish for Easter) although the pascolas largely overlook any sacred messages, instead dedicating themselves to entertaining. The pascolas are accompanied by drummers and *cantoras,* women who sing in either Spanish, Latin, or Yoreme, an indigenous language. In enacting parts of the Holy Week story, group roles are also possible: one crowd of participants will agitate to have Jesus killed while another defends Jesus.

The dance portion of Holy Week reaches its climax the night before Easter Sunday, when the dancers perform at an all-night ceremony called a *pahko.* Its central feature is the Deer Dance, which is accompanied by a deer song called *maso bwikam,* celebrating the community's reverence for the deer and for the interconnectedness of all things. According to Yaqui cosmology, a community leader initially learned this practice from a father deer teaching his children. The Yaqui use the ceremony to ask forgiveness of the deer, who had to be sacrificed for the survival of the community, a parallel with Christ's sacrifice for humankind. The dancer may hold out two gourd rattles *(aiyam)* in his hands to represent the front legs of the deer and wear butterfly cocoon rattles *(tenebari)* on his legs. Fastened to his head is a small, stuffed deer head or antlers. Taking small steps, he keeps his feet close to the ground. His arms wave back and forth slightly as he shakes the rattles, and most of the time his head moves only slightly but for a few deeper bowing gestures, a dance vocabulary that is both modest and repetitive. In audio selection 6.3, the music mirrors these features, consisting of a melody that is built on conjunct intervals and that repeats itself many times. Accompanying this melody are two idiophones, both with symbolic significance. One, the rasping sticks, are notched sticks that are scraped together and represent the deer's breathing. The other, a water drum *(ba kubahe),* is half a gourd placed in a wooden bowl of water (or half of a larger gourd) with the open side downward, and symbolizes the deer's heartbeat. As shown in online audio guide 6.3, the words tell of the antler crown as well as flowers and the flower world.

The all-night event has a festive mood. The Yaqui believe that religious observance must take place in a group so that individuals bond with the community through ritual and thus hundreds of people attend. They stay up until dawn not just because they are having a good time but because dawn is important in Yaqui cosmology, another parallel with the Easter message of resurrection. As we saw above, flowers are important to the Yaqui belief system as well. In Holy Week celebrations, flowers represent the drops of Christ's blood shed during the crucifixion. They are also flung at the Hurasim, the group that represents those who wanted to kill Jesus. In all, participating in the pahko is to participate in being Yaqui.

The Yaqui and Borders

How did the Yaqui come to perform these rituals in the southwestern United States? They have long been a beleaguered people. After Mexico gained independence from Spain in 1821, the Yaqui were persecuted so that elites could seize their land, agriculturally the richest in Sonora. It was when Yaquis began to be extradited to other parts of Mexico (Oaxaca or the Yucatán) or sold as slaves that they began relocating to Arizona. In doing so, they became part of a vast swath of territory that was once Mexico—New Mexico, Colorado, Utah, California, Nevada, Wyoming, Texas, Kansas—but that has been contested territory at various points in history. One such point was the US-Mexican War in the mid-nineteenth century.

Whenever the Yaqui encountered danger in the borderland, they gave up their ceremonies, fearful of being deported back to Sonora, whether from Tucson, Phoenix, Scottsdale, or Yuma. When they eventually felt safe enough to revive ceremonies such as the Deer Dance, they were forced to rely on memories of older people to guide them in re-creating this genre, one that acknowledges the borders between two belief systems and between two nations and that despite all obstacles has allowed the Yaqui to assert themselves bodily, musically, and spiritually.

The Deer Dance over Time

In preserving the Deer Dance and its creative fusion of indigenous cosmology and Roman Catholicism, the Yaqui ultimately did attract the notice of the authorities although not as an object of attack. Just as the Spanish tourist industry entices visitors to Sevilla during Holy Week, the Tucson Chamber of Commerce decided in the 1920s that the "Indian Easter Dances" could attract visitors to the area, and offered a small yearly subsidy to ensure

Borders and the US-Mexican War

After independence, Mexico struggled to maintain control over its territories. But national unity had not yet solidified in the young country, and some areas, including Yucatán, Oaxaca, Zacatecas, and California, were more loyal to regional than to central authority. In the early nineteenth century, the United States, a nation only slightly older than Mexico, was bent on expanding its territories westward, a spirit of acquisition justified through the ideology of Manifest Destiny. In 1836, Texas declared independence from the Republic of Mexico, supported by Tejanos, Spanish-speaking settlers in Texas. It was during this time that the now-legendary Battle of the Alamo took place. For nine years, the Lone Star Republic lasted as an independent entity. When California followed suit in the Bear Flag Revolt in June 1846, the US-Mexican War had already broken out, with its first significant battle in spring 1846 near Brownsville, Texas. Subsequent battles incurred heavy casualties for Mexicans, as in the storming by the United States of Chapultepec, a castle in a defense position for Mexico City. Many historians today consider the invasion of Mexico by the United States unjustified. Ultimately Texas and California were annexed by the United States, which could now boast a much expanded southern border and a gateway to the Pacific.

this. Given the symbolic power of the deer dance, it's natural that the practice caught the attention of the Mexican artist Diego Rivera (1886–1957), probably the best-known Mexican artist of the twentieth century. Born in Guanajuato, Rivera studied in Paris, where he absorbed all the recent trends in modern art, such as cubism, which rejects realistic representation. Upon returning to Mexico in 1921, he changed his style to paint fanciful but realistic scenes of his native land. In 1929, he married the artist Frida Kahlo (1907–54), an equally talented Mexican artist. Rivera is especially famous for his murals. In the 1920s, he painted a series of murals for the Secretariat of Public Education in Mexico City, portraying in one the Yaqui deer dancer in the traditional butterfly-cocoon leggings and antler headgear as the community meditates on kinship and the life cycle before a bonfire, shown in figure 6.6. In another of Rivera's realizations of the Deer Dance, the bodies of the two dancers interlock in complementary movements, which unfold beneath the motif of a snake biting its own tail. This "infinity sign" represents the timelessness of indigenous culture while also subtly hinting of the repetitive cycles of the music.

Figure 6.6 Diego Rivera, *The Dance of the Deer*, 1928. Secretariat of Public Education, Mexico City.

Photo credit: Schalkwijk/Art Resource, NY.

THE CUECA: THE BODY AND CHILEAN HISTORY

Like the tango, the Chilean *cueca* is a couple dance. True to its rural origins, it imitates farm animals: a rooster and a hen sizing each other up and showing "attitude," which in classical ballet terminology means a particular position of the body. Here, "attitude" also refers to the personalities these birds suggest. The analogy with animals is only a point of departure, however, for while the couple is engaged in high stepping or circling around each other, they make steady eye contact. As we'll see, the body movements of the cueca also help explicate one of the darker chapters of Chilean history.

Chile: An Introduction

Bordering Argentina to the east, the Pacific to the west, and Peru and Bolivia to the north, Chile is a long, slender strip of a territory divided into several geographical and cultural zones. The landscape is marked by mountains but also valleys and central plains, which yield wheat, several kinds of fruit, and Chile's world-famous wine. Prior to the Spanish Conquest, native inhabitants included the Incas in the north and the Mapuches in the south-central part of the country, whose descendants struggle over land rights and social justice today. Another group was the Araucanos, a people known for valor and the subject of works of literature, art, and music. Chilean classical composers who wrote pieces based on Araucanian lore include Carlos Isamitt Alarcón (1887–1974), who composed *Friso Araucano Americano* (Araucanian American Frieze) for solo voices and orchestra, *Mito araucano* (Araucanian Myth) for orchestra, and *Símbolos araucanos* (Araucanian Symbols) for piano. The African presence in Chile has been slight. Once slavery was abolished in the 1820s, Africans went to warmer climates in nearby Pacific countries, leaving relatively little influence on traditional Chilean music.

Population is distributed unevenly. Nearly 40 percent of Chileans live in Santiago, founded in 1541, or in its environs. Classical music has flourished there, especially during the twentieth century, when the influence of Europe was extremely strong. Chileans have shown particular devotion to the German composer Johann Sebastian Bach (1685–1750), dedicating entire concerts to his music and founding Bach societies in Santiago. Another large city is Valparaíso. Patagonia, a region shared with Argentina, is far more sparsely populated. This relative shortage of urban environments has ensured that apart from classical music, most genres associated with Chile have been traditional, that is, rural. As one scholar notes, "the development of a modern, urban, and mass-mediated popular music in Chile has been difficult" (Gonzalez 2005: 254).

In 1810, Chile became the first of the Spanish colonies to agitate for independence. It took many years to achieve this objective, but the last Spanish troops were defeated in 1817. After independence, the founding father and military hero Bernardo O'Higgins (1778–1842) ruled Chile with an iron hand until he went into exile in 1823. In 1833, a constitution was promulgated but it gave only the appearance of a republican government. Over the course of the twentieth century, however, Chileans have sought democracy, and several effective presidents served the country until 1973, when the military dictator Augusto Pinochet (1915–2006) took control in a coup. As in Argentina, opponents of Pinochet's regime were disappeared, exiled, or executed.

The Cueca in Chile

The cueca has absorbed these broad societal changes. In the traditional rural format the male partner is a *huaso*, a Chilean cowboy, rancher, or cattle driver well accustomed to physical endurance. The huaso and his female partner each wield a large handkerchief or scarf, an important part of the dance, with which they signal to each other. Tracing a circle on the ground, their steps depict pursuit or retreat: in the *escobillado* (brushing) the partners come together, but then separate with a sliding step and a *vuelta* (turn). To repel or attract the *huaso*, the woman swirls her skirt, and in some versions, the dance ends when the *huaso* drops to his knees and wraps his handkerchief around the woman, as if to seal the mating ritual. While the dancing is going on, other participants may sing, sometimes in improvised harmony. The music of the cueca generally unfolds in a three-part (tripartite) form, all in a rather relaxed tempo. Audio selection 6.4 contains three verses separated by instrumental interludes. The verses are further divided into three internal phrases, which are repeated in a pattern, as online audio guide 6.4 shows. These cyclic repetitions mirror the circularity of the dance step.

Cueca texts can address any number of subjects, such as love (either fulfilled or frustrated), historical events, or community. Often the onlookers shout gleefully. The traditional instruments for the cueca are guitar and accordion, or harp, as in our audio example. Diatonic and triangular, the traditional harp has

Figure 6.7 Chilean dancers in traditional costume.

billyfoto/istock.com.

approximately thirty-five strings. But for a few glissandi, the style of playing is far from flamboyant, a restraint that is said to characterize many traditional Chilean harpists. Percussion instruments in the cueca can include tambourine, various drums, or simply hand clapping; sometimes guitarists and harpists drum on the body of their instruments. The cueca is almost always in a major key.

At various points in its history, the cueca came to be considered both old-fashioned and unsophisticated. During the 1950s, the Chilean folk singer Margot Loyola (1918–2015) was concerned that the tradition was dying and began teaching the cueca at the University of Chile in Santiago. Thanks in part to her efforts, "hundreds of students spread all over the country" were now "helping to keep our . . . dance alive . . . Finally!" as she once enthused (Moreno Chá, in Schecter 1999: 257). Popular variants of the cueca arose throughout Chile. The *cueca nortina* (from the north) uses some Andean instruments, such as the *bombo* (a large Andean drum) and panpipes. The southern version is perhaps the most energetic choreographically whereas the populous central region of Chile has given rise to the greatest number of variants, one of which is the urban *cueca brava.* That version can be accompanied by accordion or piano, and is danced in ordinary street clothes rather than the whirling rustic skirts and cowboy attire of the rural cueca. From the 1960s, the cueca brava was a favorite among working-class Chileans.

In 1979, six years after Pinochet came to power, the cueca was officially made the national dance of Chile. No longer a picturesque glimpse of bygone rural culture or a winning snapshot of urban life, it now symbolized the dictatorship, sometimes to the point of being featured in military parades. A somber variant of the dance arose, the *cueca sola.* If a woman's son or husband or boyfriend was disappeared, she would dance the cueca by herself ("sola" meaning "alone") such that the traditional couple dance, with its playful, fixed gaze between two partners, was now reduced by half. Observing a woman dancing alone under these circumstances was painful enough but even more wrenching was seeing her dance in the absence of music. With neither guitar, harp, bombo, nor accordion to support her, she would move in silence in memory of her absent loved one and of the country she once knew, an eloquent subversion of the customary interrelationship between music and the dancing body.

ACTIVITY 6.7

Research the artist Sting. Then listen to his music video "They Dance Alone," released in 1988. What is the subject matter? Construct a formal diagram of this piece, using letters (A, B, etc.). Comment also on the words and on the instrumentation. Do you hear any timbres associated with Latin America? How did Sting, an Englishman, become interested in Chile?

The Cueca over Time

Given that a ruthless dictator gave the cueca a seal of approval, it's hardly surprising that the dance was unpopular after Pinochet stepped down in 1990. But the cueca has been rehabilitated and is making a comeback. In Santiago, Carmen Gloria Araya owns a dance hall called El Huaso Enrique (Enrique the Cowboy) that features a weekly Cueca Night. People of all ages pack the place. Some younger dancers may be unaware of the cueca's history, seeking little more than a release of the week's tensions, whereas other young people want to recuperate a past their parents knew. Many wear jeans and Converse sneakers, a far cry from traditional rural attire. Clearly the cueca will prove vital enough to sustain whatever transformations it may undergo in the future.

VALS VENEZOLANO: DANCE AND THE GUITAR

Sometimes a classically trained composer is attracted to a particular dance. In his or her hands, the dance becomes a point of departure for a new piece, one that won't accompany actual dancing but that conjures up bodily movement in the listener's imagination, adding to the enjoyment of the music. One such composer was Antonio Lauro of Venezuela (1917–86), who not only admired a Latin American version of the waltz *(vals)* but composed for an instrument few people in classical music circles of his day took seriously—the guitar.

Classical Music in Venezuela: The Waltz as Música Criolla

Besides música llanera and various other traditional musics, Venezuela boasts a long tradition of classical music. During the colonial period, Venezuela was part of the Viceroyalty of New Granada and one of the poorer regions of the Spanish empire. As elsewhere, friars taught music to the indigenous peoples. Among them was the Spanish-born Diego de los Ríos (?–c. 1670), who worked in missions established throughout the territory, sometimes using Carib, an indigenous language. (Today Venezuela's indigenous population makes up only about 2 percent of the population and lives mainly in the rain forest state of Amazonas or the northwestern state of Zulia.) In the late eighteenth century, the Caracas cathedral distinguished itself musically with composers such as Juan Manuel Olivares (1760–97), a mulatto, and José Ángel Lamas (1775–1814) writing Latin-texted religious works. Over the next two centuries, Venezuelan classical composers wrote pieces for orchestra, piano, and voices. An especially important figure was Juan Bautista Plaza (1898–1965), who not only composed but lectured, taught, wrote, and gave radio broadcasts to promote classical music in his native land. In general, Venezuelan composers have sought inspiration from both European models and the traditional music of their own country.

One genre in which these two orientations combined was the waltz. This dance, in brisk triple meter, was initially popular in nineteenth-century Vienna but promptly achieved worldwide fame. This celebrity was due not only to the lilting music but to the scandalous position the dancers assumed, in which the gentleman would hold the lady around the waist and clasp her close to him. Priggish onlookers wondered what thoughts might enter the heads of young couples spinning around the dance floor at such a dizzying pace. As with the Argentine tango, the Viennese waltz catapulted to international fame in part because it pushed the boundaries of social convention.

Like the polca and other nineteenth-century European dances, the waltz came to Latin America, taking on new characteristics depending on the region that adapted it. The Brazilian waltz is rather relaxed whereas the Peruvian version *(vals peruano)* typically uses both European and African instruments. The Venezuelan waltz *(vals venezolano)* tends to have a quick tempo and is often rhythmically intricate. All are examples of música criolla. Two additional categories of the Latin American waltz apply more generally, the *vals de salón* (parlor waltz) and *vals popular* (popular waltz). Parlor waltzes sounded in the elegant homes of the moneyed classes during the mid-nineteenth century and were usually played on the piano, a high-status instrument that only this stratum of society could afford. Space permitting, some people might have danced spontaneously, although most probably contented themselves with tapping their feet to the unmistakable meter. Waltzes performed on the piano maintained certain basic attributes of the genre (triple-meter accompaniment, multisectional form, homophonic texture) but often the harmonies and melodic figurations were more complicated than those found in waltzes for dancing. Parlor waltzes were all the rage in Latin America in part because they were fashionable in Europe, the cultural standard to which Latin American elites aspired. The vals popular, on the other hand, is rooted in traditional music. The Venezuelan variant is especially associated with the region on the border with Colombia, with instruments including the violin and the bandola.

Antonio Lauro and the Guitar

During the 1930s, Lauro studied piano, violin, horn, and string bass in Caracas, along with academic subjects. He also enjoyed singing traditional music and frequently accompanied himself on the guitar, mainly as a hobby. One day, Lauro had the then-rare experience of hearing a classical guitar recital by no less than the celebrated Paraguayan guitarist Agustín Barrios (1885–1944). It galvanized Lauro, who had never imagined the guitar was capable of such expressivity. He resolved to devote himself to the instrument, perfecting his own technique and exploring the guitar's potential.

Figure 6.8 Classical guitarist in concert dress.
ABB Photo/istock.com.

Why was the guitar once disparaged in classical music circles? Many listeners associated it with street musicians, who often asked for money in exchange for playing a few ditties. Anyone playing the guitar would automatically be considered part of the marginal social class of street beggars and derelicts, as the story of one musician, Johnny Rodríguez (1912–97) of Puerto Rico, attests. Johnny's father forbade him from playing the guitar but the boy bought one anyway and hid it under his bed. When Rodríguez Sr. found it, he confiscated the instrument and scolded his son, saying, "I don't want to have a drunkard *[borrachón]* here" (Glasser 1995: 33). Rodríguez solved this problem by waiting until his parents were asleep and sneaking out of the house to play a different guitar at the home of a friend. He also proved his father wrong, eventually forming a quartet (Cuarteto de Estrellas Boricuas) that led to a contract with RCA and fame throughout the Americas, especially during the Good Neighbor period.

Another factor that worked against the classical guitar was its volume. In the era before amplification, people who regularly attended symphony concerts or operas believed that the guitar was too quiet to command the public's attention. In fact the opposite is true: a fine performance on the guitar will easily engage the public, since listeners instinctively focus carefully on the most minute shading of dynamics, just as we concentrate on a speaker who is soft-spoken but riveting. As often happens in cases of musical snobbery, a handful of gifted pioneers succeeded in turning the tide. Thanks to forward-looking guitarists of the twentieth century such as Barrios and Andrés Segovia (1893–1987) of Spain, prejudice against the guitar has largely evaporated. Still, it was only in the 1960s that it became possible to major in guitar in US universities and conservatories.

Given this lack of serious attention, it's no wonder that in Lauro's day the guitar lacked first-rate classical pieces. The few guitarists of that period generally had no choice but to play pieces originally composed for other instruments arranged for guitar. Lauro set about to remedy this problem. After hearing several valses de salón performed on the piano, he decided to transfer this piano genre to the guitar, resulting in a series of valses venezolanos, one of which is audio selection 6.5. As you follow online audio guide 6.5, you'll notice that the tempo is quite quick, such that we feel the obligatory triple meter (**1** 2 3, **1** 2 3) compressed into one main pulse or "in one," as musicians often say. Thanks to this pronounced metric structure, we can easily imagine bodily movement. Other factors, such as sesquiáltera, symmetrical phrases, and shifting from major to minor, enhance the listening experience.

Latin American Guitar Music over Time

Besides evoking bodily movement in this series of waltzes, Lauro wrote many other guitar pieces, including a work for guitar and symphony orchestra. Other classical composers from Latin America responded to the growing interest in the guitar, such as Ginastera, who wrote a widely played composition, and Chávez, who wrote for the guitar both early and late in his career. A far more prolific guitar composer was Guido Santórsola (1904–94) of Uruguay, who wrote fifty pieces for either one or more guitars, including half a dozen works for one, two, or four guitars with orchestra. The Brazilian composer Heitor Villa-Lobos was particularly taken with the instrument and even met Segovia, at whose request he wrote several pieces. Like Lauro, Villa-Lobos was inspired by the body, as in his "Brazilian Dance" for solo guitar confirms.

ACTIVITY 6.8

Choose a Latin American guitarist, either classical or popular, acoustic or electric. Research the basic facts of that artist's biography. Then consider his or her main contributions to guitar playing. If your chosen artist is also a composer, select one of that individual's works and discuss it.

CUMBIA: TRICULTURAL FUSION AND DIGNIFIED DANCING

We return to La Costa, Colombia, to study the traditional cumbia, a courtship dance. Although mainly associated with Afro-Colombians, the cumbia offers an interesting angle on the interpenetration of indigenous, European, and African influences in La Costa and their manifestations in the body. It also challenges an unfortunate stereotype.

Racial Stereotyping and Eroticism

We've seen that lurking behind certain dances was the fear that bodily movement could give rise to unbridled passion. Dances as different from one another as the tango and the waltz threatened the worldview of those who believed the body had to be kept in control at all times. When it came to dances that were markedly non-European, moreover, these fearful individuals could target a clearly defined other. For example, in the early days of jazz, which hailed from African American communities, middle- and upper-class whites in the United States looked askance at the newest jazz dances, the bold movements of which seemed wild and unchecked. Jazz's pronounced rhythms portended wanton behavior both on and off the dance floor, as one writer fretted in the opinion piece "Does Jazz Put the Sin in Syncopation?," written in 1921 (Faulkner 1999).

Such reactions stem from racism. Throughout history and in many different parts of the world, blacks have been the victims of sexualized imagery. This stereotype stems from a completely unsubstantiated notion that blacks are uninhibited, instinctual, and physically potent. "White civilization," on the other hand, was to be admired for its purity and self-control, such that the capacity to resist sexual impulses could be seen as one more component of the larger project of advancing Western values. With the aid of religious and civic institutions, whites could at least imagine that such impulses did not exist. Quite likely some secretly envied what they wrongly held to be black characteristics, such as naturalness, spontaneity, and sexual energy.

The Movements of Traditional Cumbia

In Colombia, several musical genres from La Costa are traditionally performed by Afro-Colombians and thus draw on a "generalized notion of Caribbean 'relaxation'" (Wade 2000: 206). One such genre is cumbia. Given the stereotypes just described, however, it is supremely ironic that the traditional cumbia, a couple dance, is extremely modest and respectful. Throughout, the dancers refrain from touching each other, instead circling around musicians seated on the ground. The woman wears a full skirt, which she may manipulate to send signals to the man (alternatively, she can remain aloof) while the man, who generally wears a white suit with a red neckerchief, might use his hat to catch her attention. As if to confirm that no touching is going on, the dancers raise their arms frequently and also make circular movements with their wrists. All unfolds against the backdrop of the night sky.

Cutting through the darkness, however, is candlelight, an important enhancement of the traditional cumbia. In one version, the woman holds a bundle of lit candles wrapped in a cloth, and in another, the man holds a candle and tries to get the woman to accept it, something he might have to attempt several times. Often the candle is a thick block of wax made from several candles melted together. (Both parties have to be careful of the dripping wax as they dance.) Once the woman finally takes the candle from the man—at this point their hands may touch—she blows it out and the music ends. Even while celebrating union and procreation the dance remains dignified.

Who were these stereotype-defying dancers? The cumbia was born during the colonial period, when Colombian cities such as Cartagena were ports of entry for slaves. (Some historians claim, rather fancifully, that the dance represents slaves trying to extricate themselves from their shackles.) Occasionally a source describes a dance between an Afro-Colombian man and an indigenous woman, claiming that the woman is more reserved than her companion and less prone to sexual inhibition, resulting in mutual acceptance between black and indigenous people that is "both represented by and encouraged by music and dance" (Wade 2000: 61).

The Music of Cumbia and Tricultural Fusion

The African, indigenous, and European influences on cumbia emerge in the music. The three drums used are all of African origin. The *tambora*, the lowest-pitched, often laid on its side, is struck with wooden sticks either on the head or on the side. Whoever plays the narrower and higher-pitched *tambor llamador* (caller drum) uses the hands and generally plays on the weak beat. The third drum, the *tambor alegre* (happy drum), is also pitched high, and players improvise rhythmic patterns, sometimes replicating the singer, but are more active when no singing is taking place. Other percussion instruments contribute to the timbral variety: maracas and *guaches* (tubes of either metal or cane filled with seeds) and sometimes claves or güiros.

The indigenous feature of the cumbia is the *gaita* ensemble, the backbone of the traditional cumbia, one type of which was used in música vallenata before the accordion took it over in the late nineteenth century. Made from cane or bamboo, gaitas can be close to two feet long and are played in pairs called male and female *(macho and hembra)*. Scholars have not determined exactly how these terms arose, although it is tempting to associate them with the dance. When the mood strikes them, gaita players improvise, adding extra notes. The tambor alegre, the drum that often improvises, sometimes interacts with the female gaita. Tricultural fusion is completed through the words of the cumbia, which are in Spanish. Audio selection 6.6, "Así lo grita Totó" (That's How Totó Shouts It), was composed by Nicolás Hernández Pacheco (1932–2013) for a cumbia festival in El Banco in the *departamento* of Magdalena, which featured the much admired Totó la Momposina (b. 1940). This Afro-Colombian singer, also the subject of this cumbia, sees Colombian music as a mirror of her country's history. "Colombia is a mixture of the Indian, the black, and the Spaniard," she states, "so the force of history imposes itself . . . and creates an identity which is that of the Indian, the black, and the Spaniard" (Wade 2000: 201). Elaborating on the idea that cumbia has been shaped by "the force of history," Totó la Momposina suggests that music from La Costa "can be described as the result of a musical project that perhaps began its process over five hundred years ago" (Wade 2000: 59). Clearly cumbia has assumed mythic status.

In the audio selection, you'll hear the two gaitas, the three drums, the guaches, and a large maraca played with one hand by the gaita macho player, who fingers the gaita with the other hand. As shown in online audio guide 6.6, the words describe the traditional cumbia, with the singer registering the various instruments, the candles ("paquetes de vela"), and the dance itself, which he looks forward to performing with his partner. You'll also hear shouts of "¡Cumbia, cumbia!" and "¡Uepa!," roughly the equivalent of an enthusiastic "Yeah!" in Colombian Spanish.

Figure 6.9 People of all ages dancing their own versions of the cumbia.
Magaiza/istock.com.

Cumbia over Time

The "force of history" to which Totó la Momposina refers could just as easily describe cumbia's international ascent. In the early twentieth century, white Colombians from the interior rejected the genre as low class. By the 1940s, cumbia artists began experimenting with guitars, accordions, piano, and organ, sometimes adding instruments common in jazz, such as trumpets, trombones, and saxophones. The result was what one scholar calls the "dance-band cumbia" (Moore, in Moore and Clark 2012: 21). It abandons candles and sweeping skirts and has steps that are easy to master, consisting mainly of backward stepping, pauses, and coordination of the arms that can nonetheless be stylishly executed by people of any age or musical sensibility. Cumbia became especially popular in Mexico and fell under the label "música tropical," along with other Caribbean styles. A Peruvian version of cumbia is less tropically oriented: known as *chicha* or *cumbia andina,* it combined some of the melodic features of the wayno and retained the strong percussive element while incorporating instruments ranging from panpipes to electric guitars. An Argentine version is called *cumbia villera* and an El Salvador version is the *chanchona. Tecnocumbia* uses electronic drums and electric guitars.

Cumbia also came to the border region of the United States. *Cumbia norteña,* brought by Mexican immigrants, blended "hip hop, rock, and electronica elements" (Ramos-Kittrell 2011: 203). In south Texas, it's known *cumbia tejana,* and in yet another borderland context, the Tohono O'odham people of southern Arizona may have influenced cumbia by dancing it in a "non-coupled, counterclockwise form similar to waila," a Native American dance (Hutchinson 2011: 46).

Because fewer Colombians migrated to the United States than Puerto Ricans, Cubans, or Dominicans, cumbia never achieved the international presence of salsa or merengue, both of which were snapped up by the music industry. Still, this genre of fusion has continued absorbing all manner of influences and the body has responded accordingly.

ACTIVITY 6.9

Choose any type of cumbia from the "Over Time" section. Watch as many live performances or YouTube videos as you can and report to the class on (1) dance steps, (2) lyrics, (3) instrumentation, and (4) other musical features, such as form, melody, rhythm, and the like. Draw general conclusions from your observations.

MEXICAN SON JAROCHO AND THE BODY

European dances circulated widely in Mexico, as elsewhere in Latin America. Like the waltz, the polca was once restricted to large cities but was eventually taken up in rural settings not unlike the ranch in *Como agua para chocolate*. In contrast to the polca, the *son jarocho* is readily perceived as Mexican, its body movements relating to the musical structure. In recent years, the son jarocho has been taken up by Chicana/os.

Some Mexican Dances

One element of dance in Mexico was the complex known as the *jarabe*, dating from colonial times. It consisted of a set of related pieces played consecutively but with different steps for each section. Because the movements of the jarabe could be quite suggestive, the Church condemned it, although people continued to dance it in various forms. In the twentieth century, the *jarabe tapatío* from Jalisco became famous. ("Tapatío" means "inhabitant of Guadalajara," the capital of Jalisco.) Known in the United States as the "Mexican Hat Dance," it is performed worldwide and in arrangements for a variety of instruments.

The Mexican *son*, discussed in relation to mariachi, can also be a dance, as is the case with the *son jarocho* of Veracruz state, which boasts over two thousand different ethnic groups. Besides indigenous and mestizo populations, Afro-Mexicans have a strong presence and history in Veracruz. The Gulf Coast town once known as San Lorenzo de los Negros was originally founded by fugitives, some of the half million enslaved Africans brought to Mexico starting in the sixteenth century and who managed to escape their masters. In 1932, San Lorenzo de los Negros was renamed after its founder, Yanga, a Muslim man from Nigeria. The meaning of "jarocho" remains a puzzle, however. One possible derivation is the word for spear, "jolocho" in the language spoken by the Totonac, one of Veracruz's many indigenous communities.

Traditionally, the son jarocho was danced at a *fandango*. (A fandango is also an Iberian dance but in this context it refers to an event.) The root of the word is Angolan and in its original sense means "making order out of chaos" (Hernández 2014: 12). People of all ages participate, with adults dancing together or perhaps teaching the steps to children. A fandango often lasts from evening to dawn, with a son jarocho called "El siquisirí" kicking things off. In it, participants ask permission to sing and to enter the world of the fandango, sometimes introducing themselves in song, with improvised lyrics. Over the course of the fandango, different *sones* reflect the mood of the participants, with livelier *sones* to start the evening but slower *sones de madrugada* (dawn sones) played in the wee hours, as if replicating the general fatigue.

Son Jarocho: Movement and Music

Dances can be performed either in couples or by women only. Footwork, called *zapateado,* is lively, rapid, and intricate. ("Zapato" means "shoe" in Spanish.) Dancers perform on a raised wooden platform called a *tarima* and link their movements to the music. For example, on the downbeat they let loose a vehement stomp of the heel. They also use the ball and the flat of the foot, sometimes incorporating an upward kick from the ankle and frequently dividing the beat with the sound of their tapping feet. These energetic sounds are especially prominent during the instrumental interludes, whereas during the singing the footwork is less active. Because the tapping is part of the music, the tarima effectively serves as a percussion instrument.

Dancers keep an erect posture, arms at their sides, although a woman may hike up her skirt slightly so that she can move more freely. The reason for the erect posture is that, during colonial times, son jarocho dances were among those the Catholic Church considered scandalous. One of these was "El cuchumbé," which presumably involved dancing "belly to belly" (Hérnandez 2014: 46). (The word "chuchumbé" is slang for male genitalia.) At one point, ordinary people played African drums in such dances, but these were confiscated with the result that feet, rather than hands, became the focus of movement. With the upper body thus contained, no mutual touching takes place. (Sometimes even two individual tarimas are used instead of one large enough to accommodate two people.) There is often little difference between the movements of the men and the women.

Within these restrictions, dancers nonetheless executed spectacular movements. A firsthand account comes from 1844, roughly two decades after independence, in which a chronicler described the graceful dancing of the jarochas. According to this observer, these high-spirited women would begin dancing the moment a son was played, on the *tarima.* The same writer exults over

> the agility with which they tap their heels, make a thousand movements, carrying a glass filled with water on their heads without spilling a single drop, or forming a noose with a sash laid on the ground that they adjust with their feet and then untie without using their hands at all. (Sheehy, in Olsen and Sheehy 1998: 605–6)

Clearly dancing the son jarocho was no mean feat. But what were the sounds that made these dancers so eager to tap their heels on the tarima? Over history, several instruments have been used in son jarocho. These include an idiophone called the *quijada,* the jawbone of a horse or cow struck with a stick, and an African instrument called the *marimból,* consisting of a large wooden box that serves as a resonator with lamella (metal tongues). Sometimes drums, confiscated during the colonial period, were used. A common ensemble for son jarocho nowadays consists of three instruments: the harp and two instruments in the guitar family. The harp *(arpa jarocha)* is about five feet tall with thirty-odd strings. One of the guitars, the *jarana,* is small, shallow, and carved from a

Figure 6.10 Dancers with the son jarocho group Zarahuato performing at the Museo de Arte Popular in Mexico City in 2012.
Thelmadatter. Wikimedia.com.

single piece of wood. Its eight to twelve strings usually include three double courses and two single strings. The other guitar is the *requinto* (not to be confused with the instrument in Puerto Rican plena), also carved from a single piece of wood but with four single strings. Whereas the jarana is strummed, the requinto player uses a pick, called a *púa*.

The musical form rests on repetition, specifically the *compás*, the underlying structure discussed in chapter 3. Three harmonies (I-IV-V-V) repeat over and over in tandem with short rhythmic patterns. Superimposed over the compás is a melody, also consisting of short phrases. According to one scholar, these features are "strikingly similar to the cyclical rhythmic patterns of West and Central African music, the point of origin of most of the African peoples who populated this hemisphere, including Veracruz" (Sheehy, in Schechter 1999: 68). The dancers change their footwork pattern in accordance with the compás, marking the musical form with their bodies

Audio selection 6.7, "La bamba," is easily one of the most celebrated son jarochos. As shown in online audio guide 6.7, it has all the characteristics just outlined and is also one of the sones that is played at a fandango to liven things up if energies are flagging. Notice also that the last of the repeated *compases* sounds as thought it might end on V rather than I, that holdover of Iberian practices (revisit sound links 3.29 and 3.30). Such an ending may sound like something is missing, but rather than imagining that "La bamba" goes unresolved, we can instead conclude that I and V have equal weight. Listen to how this performance of "La bamba" actually ends.

You may find the words to "La bamba" puzzling. Over 150 versions of the lyrics exist, but since sometimes a verse or two from one version may be "pasted together" from the verses of another, stray lines of text often don't make a great deal of sense, a situation similar to that encountered in the cueca. Extra syllables, repeated words, and vocables fill out the impetus of the musical line, just as frequent and spontaneous shouting enlivens the texture. In verse 2 of this version, the singer refers to "la Vírgen morena" (the dark-skinned Virgin) or the Virgin of Guadalupe.

"La bamba" became especially well known in the United States when Richard Steven Valenzuela (1941–59), the singer known as Ritchie Valens, recorded it in 1958 in rock 'n' roll style. Valens's tragic death in a plane crash in February 1959, along with singer-songwriter Buddy Holly (1936–59) and musician, songwriter, and disk jockey J. P. Richardson (1930–59), was a tremendous loss for music.

ACTIVITY 6.10

Watch the movie *La Bamba,* directed by Luis Valdez, released in 1987, and set in the late 1950s. Research basic historical facts about the main character. How does the rock 'n' roll version compare to the traditional rendering in our audio selection? Explain how the traditional son jarocho "La bamba" is transformed over the course of the film, making sure to discuss each scene in which it appears and to account for as many musical characteristics as you can (pitch, rhythm, melody, texture, and the like) throughout. What does this transformation say about the protagonist's cultural heritage? What did rock 'n' roll represent in terms of youth culture and social change in the United States during this period?

The Son Jarocho over Time

In the United States, son jarocho can be performed in its traditional format but it has also become a symbol of social justice, figuring in events organized by the United Farm Workers, the labor union cofounded by César Chávez (1927–93) and Dolores Huerta (b. 1930), and accompanying demonstrations on behalf of immigrants' rights or events organized by the Occupy Movement. In addition, the son jarocho has enlivened gatherings of the activist organization MEChA (Movimiento Estudiantil Chicanx de Aztlán), an organization that promotes *chicanismo,* or the rejection of the label "Mexican American," which Chicanas and Chicanos believe encourages assimilation and accommodation. (Aztlán, referred to in the organization's name, is the homeland of the Mexica but now part of the southwestern United States.) MEChA established itself in colleges, universities, and high schools in 1969 and remains active today. Groups such as the Los Angeles–based *Las Cafeteras* have taken the son jarocho as a point of departure for innovation. Initially comprising students enrolled in a son jarocho class in East Los Angeles, this band combines the genre with Afro-Mexican idioms and the spoken word, rap style. Many of their songs revolve around Chicana/o pride and social justice. One topic they address in their songs is the DREAM Act (Development, Education, and Relief for Alien Minors), which would conditionally grant residency to children of undocumented immigrants who entered the United States prior to age sixteen. Introduced to the US Senate in 2001, the DREAM act never became federal law and has been the subject of much debate, especially since the 2016 election. As the son jarocho changes, so does the body movement that complements it: some dancers perform the zapateado in tennis shoes or do break dancing during the instrumental interludes.

PERFORMING LATIN AMERICA: PUERTO RICO ON BROADWAY

Unless we are dancing in solitude, perhaps in the privacy of our homes, dance is a performance. Even at social dances, people are generally aware that others may be watching them. Naturally it is the thrill of performance that animates professional dancers, who execute steps conceived by a choreographer before a nondancing audience that carefully follows their every move, much the way they would an athletic event. We in the audience invariably see them in the glare of the spotlight—through the lens of performance—not as "people just like us" whom we might encounter in social dancing. What considerations might come into play when professional dancers and choreographers seek to represent Latinos?

Choreography and Folklore

As noted, the choreographer puts his or her personal stamp on any created dance. This personal vision can become controversial if a choreographer brings traditional dances to the stage. For example, a choreographer may be attracted to the cueca and have a reasonable idea of how it looks in traditional practice but may incorporate into the choreography high kicks, leaps, and exuberant arm motions that would surprise many a campesino. Still, even if the steps of the "real" dance are so obscured as to be unrecognizable, the choreographer may believe that he or she has captured its essence. When choreographers proceed in this way we say that the resulting dance is *stylized.* Choreographers who stylize traditional dances insist that the basic movements are vital enough to accommodate change; further, they argue that any tradition worth its salt requires change to keep it alive. Others will preserve existing norms in the interest of that much debated phenomenon "authenticity."

Representing Latinos on Broadway

Stylization and representation came to the fore in the musical *West Side Story,* first produced in 1957 and made into a film in 1961. It's a collaboration of the

Traditional Latin American Dance on the Worldwide Stage

In 1952, the classically trained dancer and choreographer Amalia Hernández (1917–2000) founded the Ballet Folklórico de México. As she often stated, her aim was nothing less than to "rescue" traditional dance in Mexico. One reason for her success was that she "effectively integrated official discourses" of Mexican identity, specifically by representing the indigenous and mestizo populations (Hutchinson 2009). With her award-winning, government-sponsored company, Hernández has told numerous stories from Mexican history through dance. In a ballet about the Mexican Revolution, a group of young aristocrats do European-style dances until revolutionaries break up the party, at which point we hear a famous song of the Revolution, "La Adelita," named after a *soldadera.* In the Feather Dance, the Ballet Folklórico honors the indigenous past by reenacting Zapotec customs, which require the dancers to manipulate elaborate feather headdresses. One of the company's best-known pieces was based on the Yaqui Deer Dance. Hernández's stylized dances often combined the techniques of classical ballet with folk tradition. Whether she achieved authenticity, either of the letter or of the spirit, is left to the public to decide.

US composer and conductor Leonard Bernstein (1918–1990), the lyricist Stephen Sondheim (b. 1930 and also a composer), and the choreographer Jerome Robbins (1918–98). Arthur Laurents (1917–2011) wrote the script, or "book," as it's called in the world of the *musical*. In a musical, lines are spoken but every now and then the characters sing, either a solo, a duet, or a chorus. Fans of musicals appreciate this feature whereas people who don't like the genre find the practice of "bursting into song" contrived. Because dance is often featured, musicals may involve "bursting into dance."

Perhaps because of this admittedly artificial, entertainment-oriented format, initially musicals treated lighthearted themes, such as day-to-day family conflicts or boy-meets-girl encounters, in which all problems are happily resolved. Along with several other musicals in the post–World War II period, *West Side Story* departs from this orientation. Certainly boy meets girl, but each is from a different "tribe": Maria, a young Puerto Rican woman, falls in love with Tony, a Polish American, both of whom live in tenements on New York's West Side. Tony is a member of the Jets, an all-white gang, whereas Bernardo, María's brother, is the leader of the Sharks, an all–Puerto Rican gang. Anglo and Puerto Rican cultures frequently clash, sometimes in subtle ways and sometimes through unabashed violence. An *adaptation* of Shakespeare's *Romeo and Juliet*, *West Side Story* takes the play as a point of departure but reshapes it according to the tastes of contemporary audiences and the social reality its creators wanted to represent. *West Side Story* became one of the most famous musicals in history. Yet some people think it should never have been written.

Why should this be the case? When *West Side Story* premiered on Broadway, tension between Puerto Ricans and white US Americans was very real. The 1950s saw the peak of Puerto Rican immigration, with approximately one-quarter of the island's population coming to the United States as conditions in Puerto Rico deteriorated, especially in rural areas. In 1952, Puerto Rico became a *commonwealth*, a self-governing territory with its own constitution although it remains part of the United States, a status that does not, however, afford the rights enjoyed by the fifty states. (Puerto Rico's congressional representative is nonvoting, for example.) When Puerto Ricans came to the United States in the 1950s, they entered not only a country that spoke another language but one that was conflicted over its racist policies and that, frankly, had been wondering what to do with Puerto Rico ever since the Spanish-American War.

These Puerto Ricans often found low-skilled jobs in construction, manufacturing, and service, working as dishwashers, waiters, or janitors. Their experience, especially if they were black or mixed-race, was quite different from that of Anglo US Americans, then enjoying unprecedented prosperity. On May 30, 1955, *Time* magazine exulted that "the people of the U.S. have never been so prosperous" (Quintero-Rivera and Márquez 2003: 214). The rise in personal income between 1940 and 1955 totaled a whopping 293 percent and the average Anglo consumer spent freely, finding a spate of appliances, automobiles, labor-saving devices, and various luxuries increasingly within his or her reach. In addition, those avidly pursuing the so-called American Way of Life left the cities for the burgeoning suburbs, a phenomenon some demographers have dubbed White Flight.

Alongside this social and economic backdrop was the cultural dimension of Puerto Rico's relationship with the United States. For many Puerto Ricans, the media—radio, print, television, film, advertising—were synonymous with US hegemony. We can see this trend in music. Back home on the island, popular music was ubiquitous thanks to radio and film, but most of it was from the United States, resulting in a "one-way flow of mass media products" (Glasser 1995: 40). If you were a Puerto Rican musician living on the island, you might play in a band with a decidedly Anglo name, such as Augusto Rodríguez's Midnight Serenaders, or write commercial jingles to sell US products. If you were a Puerto Rican primary school teacher you would likely be informed by a US official that your school would observe US holidays, with the result that Puerto Rican schoolchildren sang "America" ("O Beautiful for Spacious Skies"), also played by municipal bands all over the island.

Add to this economic and psychological background a broader problem: stereotyping in the United States of Latinos, especially in film. Since the silent era, with movies such as *The Greaser's Revenge* (1911) and *Licking the Greasers* (1914), Hollywood had shown little respect for Latinos. In the 1930s and 1940s, major studios spewed forth an array of stereotypes, such as the bandido, the temperamental Latin lover, the spitfire señorita, or the mañana-is-good-enough-for-me buffoon. (Nowadays the drug lord is a commonplace.) In movies about Latin America, Hollywood often did little fact-checking, such that Brazilian characters might speak Spanish or a sign would be misspelled; moreover, *gringo* actors tended to get the leading roles, often playing Latin Americans while actual Latin American actors were relegated to crowd scenes. Latin American music was also stereotyped. Largely because of its lively rhythms and variegated timbres, Latin American music was widely considered "'fun,' lightweight, and essentially trivial," resulting in "a crushing stereotype," as one commentator described it (Roberts 1999: 84).

ACTIVITY 6.11

Watch the documentary *The Bronze Screen,* directed by Alberto Domínguez and Nancy de los Santos and released in 2002. In two paragraphs, explain its basic premises. (Note: if you decide to write a longer paper on Latinos in the US film industry, this documentary could serve as one of your sources.)

Music and Dance in *West Side Story*

The creators of *West Side Story* were likely unaware of all but the broadest outlines of this situation. Yet with these realities in mind, we can "read" the music
and dance in *West Side Story* more perceptively. Bernstein wanted to differenti-
ate musically the Puerto Ricans from the US Americans while also conveying
the love, elation, and despair the script called for. If you watch the entire film,
you'll see that in the number "Cool," which describes the US Americans as represented by the Jets, Bernstein uses elements of cool jazz, which was popular in
the United States in the 1950s and 1960s and to which people did not dance,
unlike earlier jazz. The music makes it clear that the Jets are so "cool" that one
of their big dance numbers starts out with nothing but finger snapping. By contrast, the song "America," which focuses on the Puerto Ricans, is anything but
"cool." Here, Bernstein may be hinting at the fact that performers of Latin jazz
in the United States during the 1950s, unlike those who played cool jazz or
bebop, *did* want people to dance to their music.

Dance is also part of *West Side Story*'s plot. When you watch the film, you'll
see that Bernardo becomes angry at María for dancing with Tony at a social
event. Bernardo's girlfriend, Anita, defends her, arguing that María was "only
dancing" with Tony. "She is in America now!" says Anita, whereupon Bernardo
snaps, "Puerto Rico is in America now," perhaps an allusion to tensions over
Puerto Rico's often misunderstood status in the United States. Dance is also a
temporary release from the stress of poverty and discrimination the characters
in *West Side Story* face daily. Maria, realizing that the two gangs will fight each
other that evening, asks Anita why "the boys" always have the urge to fight.
"Well, you saw how they dance," Anita shrugs. "Like they gotta get rid of something, quick. That's how they fight." "Get rid of *what?*" Maria asks. "Too much
feeling," Anita replies. This excess of feeling, which Anita seems to understand
as a toxic mix of anger, desperation, and fatalism, factored into the production.
So central a theme is anger in *West Side Story* that the choreographer even
decided to foment genuine rage among the actors, hoping that their pent-up
feelings would explode in the dance sequences and make them more effective.
To ensure mutual hatred, Robbins separated the actors playing the Jets from
those playing the Sharks and spread rumors about each group.

Anger infuses "America," audio selection 6.8. At least half the words are a cry
of protest: whenever the Puerto Rican women praise life in the United States
("here you are free and you have pride"), the men retort sarcastically, citing discrimination in employment ("free to wait tables and shine shoes"), in housing
("better get rid of your accent"), and in US society in general ("life is all right in
America if you're a white in America"). As discussed in our study of film, music
often comments wordlessly on the way a story is unfolding. If we were to listen
to the music of "America" in the absence of any context, we might well find it
exuberant, a counterweight to the "cool" outlook of the Jets. We might also

Figure 6.11 Billboards in Times Square in New York City in September 2010 advertising one of the many revivals of *West Side Story*.

Sean Pavone/Shutterstock.com.

conclude that Bernstein was simply reviving the "crushing stereotype" attached to Latin music. Certainly he draws on familiar musical gestures, marshaling a vast array of percussion instruments, including bongos, cowbells, conga, timbales, snare drum, güiro, cymbals, maracas, woodblock, and marimba. He also showcases sesquiáltera, which underscores the fundamental words, "I Want to be in A-me-ri-ca." (Say these words and clap along. You will forever after be able to identify sesquiáltera.)

Yet these are the very words that are so difficult to interpret if we dig below the surface of the lively music. What are the boundaries of America? Is Puerto Rico in America in any but the most technical sense? We cannot be sure that the women are simply gullible; indeed, they may be better than their men at resigning themselves to difficult circumstances or are mocking their men. It would also be too easy to propose that the men are simply immature or too lazy to work their way up in US society, for perhaps they are resisting assimilation or are fearful of losing their identity. At one point (4:00) both groups forgo English, Spanish, and Spanglish, and bark like dogs while clapping their hands. Since the last forty seconds of the song are strictly instrumental, neither side can claim victory.

We might also expect to hear a clave rhythm, which one scholar describes as "immediately identified as Latino" by listeners in the United States (Reyes 2004: 52–53). As shown in online audio guide 6.8, Bernstein launches "America" with a 3–2 clave (revisit sound link 3.16). But when maracas enter a few seconds later, they are "out of clave" with the 3–2 pattern, accenting the first beat in an eight-beat pattern. Whether he did so deliberately or not, Bernstein thus hints that "America" as most of his audience knew it was conflicted about Latinos. As for the dance steps in "America," they consist mainly of zapateado, high kicks, swirling skirts, and exuberant hand gestures. Yet the choreography for the Puerto Ricans in "America" is no more or less angry or flashy than the Jets' dances, even if the actual dance vocabulary differs from group to group. In short, both music and dance leave open the question: What does it really mean to be "in America"?

When you watch the entire movie, you find an answer. Toward the end, "America" is heard again, as a thematic recall (chapter 2). The scene is Doc's candy store, where Anita has shown up unexpectedly and the Jets rough her up, choreographically enacting a rape. By inserting "America" at this painful moment, Bernstein reminds the viewer of Anita's plucky spirit, so much on display in the initial number but now completely crushed. This, not good-humored sassiness, is the effect of "America" on these Puerto Rican immigrants.

West Side Story over Time

One critic writing about *West Side Story* has maintained that "no one in Puerto Rico ever refers to the United States as 'America' and no Puerto Rican ever did" (Delano 1990: 4). Certainly we have seen plenty of justification for this point of view, even as we have pointed to certain gestures in *West Side Story* that suggest empathy for Puerto Ricans; further, poor whites, represented by the Jets, are also degraded and consumed by anger. *West Side Story* was richly rewarded, for it was nominated for six Tony awards, the prize recognizing excellence in live theater. (Robbins received a Tony for his choreography.) But when the film version was made in 1961, Hollywood did not exactly rise to the occasion. Just as Carol Lawrence, a US American, had played the leading role of Maria on Broadway, along with a Latina actor, Chita Rivera, in the supporting role of Anita, in the film version Natalie Wood, born in Californian of Russian parentage, played Maria and Rita Moreno, a Puerto Rican, played Anita. (Nor did Wood sing, for she was dubbed by the late Marni Nixon.) Likewise, the actors playing the Puerto Ricans were directed to use accents and were made up to have brown skin, despite the fact that many Puerto Ricans speak unaccented

> ### ACTIVITY 6.12
>
> Research basic facts on Lin-Manuel Miranda. What are his main accomplishments? Next, investigate the way he used music from *West Side Story* to respond to Hurricane María, which devastated Puerto Rico in fall 2017.

English and are light-skinned. Concerns over diversity in Hollywood continue to plague the industry, as the fierce debate over the 2016 Academy Awards ceremony has shown. Happily, Latin Americans triumphed in 2018, garnering Oscars in several categories.

CONCLUSIONS

We've seen several ways in which music and bodily movement interact, each embedded in a particular social or cultural context. In capoeira, the body masks a fight with music and dance, just as it celebrates a religious ritual with the Yaqui Deer Dance. Politics and political change are part of the history of the cueca, whereas the music of cumbia and the son jarocho celebrates Latin America's multiethnic heritage in ways that sometimes take a stand against stereotypes. Throughout history, dances such as the tango can shock, whereas others, such as the vals venezolano, suggest music for listening. As we've also seen, choreographed dances, including "Latin" dancing on Broadway, are easy to unthinkingly applaud but become much richer when we look more deeply into movement, music, and context.

STUDY GUIDE

Key Terms

social dance	waltz
choreology	tango
choreography, choreographer	lunfardo
quilombo	bandoneón
capoeira	tango canción
ginga	Yaqui
roda de capoeira	US-Mexican War
berimbau	Manifest Destiny
toque	religious drama
Black Consciousness Day	*seis* (dancer)
	deer dance

rasping stick

water drum

cueca, cueca sola

attitude (in dance)

huaso

cumbia

gaita (macho, hembra)

chicha

tecnocumbia

jarabe

son jarocho

tarima

fandango

jarana

requinto

course (guitar)

compás

Carib

música criolla

parlor waltz, popular waltz

bandola

musical

adaptation

commonwealth

cool jazz

For Further Study

General

Brandes, Stanley. "The Sardana: Catalan Dance and Catalan National Identity." *Journal of American Folklore* 103, no. 407 (1990): 24–41.

Cornelius, Steven, and Mary Natvig. *Music: A Social Experience.* Boston: Pearson, 2012.

Hanna, Judith Lynn. "Dance." In *Ethnomusicology: An Introduction,* edited by Helen Meyers, 315–26. London and New York: Macmillan and Norton, 1992.

———. *Dance, Sex, and Gender.* Chicago: University of Chicago Press, 1988.

Madrid, Alejandro L. "Dancing with Desire: Cultural Embodiment in Tijuana's Nor-Tec Music and Dance." *Popular Music* 25, no. 3 (1996): 383–99.

Manuel, Peter. "From Scarlatti to 'Guantanamera': Dual Tonicity in Spanish and Latin American Musics." *Journal of the American Musicological Society* 55, no. 2 (2002): 311–36.

Querol, Miguel. "La Chacona en la época de Cervantes." *Anuario Musical* 25 (1970): 49–65. This text is in Spanish.

Romero, Brenda M. "*Matachines Danza* as Intercultural Discourse." In *Dancing across Borders: Danzas y Bailes Mexicanos,* edited by Olga Nájera-Ramírez, Norma E. Cantú, and Brenda M. Romero, 185–205. Urbana and Chicago: University of Illinois Press, 2009.

Russell, Melinda. "'Give Your Body Joy, Macarena.'" In *From Tejano to Tango: Latin American Popular Music,* edited by Walter Aaron Clark, 172–92. New York and London: Routledge, 2002.

Sachs, Curt. *World History of the Dance.* New York: Norton, 1963.

Thomas, Helen, ed. *Dance, Gender, and Culture.* Basingstoke, UK: Macmillan, 1993.

Capoeira

Capoeira, Nestor. *Capoeira: Roots of the Dance-Fight-Game.* Berkeley: North Atlantic, 2002.

Díaz, Juan Diego. "Between Repetition and Variation: A Musical Performance of *Malícia* in Capoeira." *Ethnomusicology Forum* 26, no. 1 (2017): 46–68.

Downey, Greg. *Learning Capoeira: Lessons in Cunning from an Afro-Brazilian Art.* Oxford and New York: Oxford University Press, 2005.

———. "Listening to Capoeira: Phenomenology, Embodiment, and the Materiality of Music." *Ethnomusicology* 46, no. 3 (2002): 487–509.

Graham, Richard. "Technology and Culture Change: the Development of the 'Berimbau' in Colonial Brazil." *Latin American Music Review* 12, no. 1 (1991): 1–20.

Graham, Richard, and N. Scott Robinson, eds. "Berimbau." In *Continuum Encyclopedia of Popular Music of the World,* edited by John Shepherd et al., vol. 2, 344–45. New York and London: Continuum, 2003.

Green, Thomas A., and Joseph R. Svinth, eds. *Martial Arts in the Modern World.* London: Praeger, 2003.

Klein, Herbert S., and Francisco Vidal Luna. *Slavery in Brazil.* Cambridge: Cambridge University Press, 2010.

Lewis, J. Lowell. *Ring of Liberation: Deceptive Discourse in Brazilian Capoeira.* Chicago: University of Chicago Press, 1992.

Moore, Robin D., and Walter A. Clark, eds. *Musics of Latin America.* New York: Norton, 2012. See especially the essay by Magaldi.

Pressing, Jeff. "Black Atlantic Rhythm: its Computational and Transcultural Foundations." *Music Perception: An Interdisciplinary Journal* 19, no. 3 (2002): 285–310.

Röhrig Assunção, Matthias. *Capoeira: The History of an Afro-Brazilian Martial Art.* London and New York: Routlegde, 2005.

Shelemay, Kay Kaufman. *Soundscapes: Exploring Music in a Changing World.* 3rd ed. New York and London: Norton, 2015.

Tango

Baim, Jo. *Tango: Creation of a Cultural Icon.* Bloomington: Indiana University Press, 2007.

Borges, Jorge Luis. "Oyendo un tango viejo." www.clarin.com
/sociedad/borges-vision-particular-tango_0_BJRx5ufswml
.html.

Cara, Ana C. "Entangled Tangos: Passionate Displays, Intimate
Dialogues." *Journal of American Folklore* 122 (2009): 438–65.

Collier, Simon. *Tango! The Dance, the Song, the Story.* New York:
Thames and Hudson, 1995.

Collier, Simon, and María Susana Azzi. *Le Grand Tango: The Life
and Music of Astor Piazzolla.* New York: Oxford University
Press, 2000.

Cook, Susan. "Passionless Dancing and Passionate Reform:
Respectability, Modernism, and the Social Dancing of Irene
and Vernon Castle." In *The Passion of Music and Dance:
Body, Gender, and Sexuality,* edited by William Washabaugh,
133–50. Oxford: Oxford University Press, 1998.

De Buenosaires, Oscar. *Tango: A Bibliography.* Albuquerque:
FOG, 1991.

Goertzen, Chris, and María Susana Azzi. "Globalization and the
Tango." *Yearbook for Traditional Music* 31 (1999): 67–76.

Moore, Robin D., and Walter A. Clark, eds. *Musics of Latin
America.* New York: Norton, 2012. See especially the essay
by Schwartz-Kates.

Roberts, John Storm. *The Latin Tinge: The Impact of Latin
American Music on the United States.* 2nd ed. New York and
Oxford: Oxford University Press, 1999.

Savigliano, Marta E. *Tango and the Political Economy of Passion.*
Boulder: Westview, 1995.

Taylor, Julie. "Tango: Theme of Class and Nation." *Ethnomusicology* 20, no. 2 (1976): 273–91.

Tobin, Jeffrey. "Tango and the Scandal of Homosocial Desire." In
*The Passion of Music and Dance: Body, Gender, and Sexual-
ity,* edited by William Washabaugh, 79–102. Oxford: Oxford
University Press, 1998.

Wendland, Kristin F. *Tracing Tangueros: Argentine Tango Instrumental Music.* Oxford University Press, 2016.

Yaqui Deer Dance

Anzaldúa, Gloria. *Borderlands La Frontera: The New Mestiza.*
2nd ed. San Francisco: Aunt Lute, 1999.

Avila Hernández, Juan A. "Yoeme (Yaqui) Deer Dance." In *Amer-
ican Indian Religious Traditions: An Encyclopedia,* edited by
Suzanne J. Crawford and Dennis F. Kelley, vol. 3, 1165–68.
Santa Barbara: ABC-CLIO: 2005.

Crumrine, N. Ross. *The Mayo Indians of Sonora: A People Who
Refuse to Die.* Tucson: University of Arizona Press, 1977.

———. "A New Mayo Indian Religious Movement in Northwest
Mexico." *Journal of Latin American Lore* 1, no. 2 (1975):
127–45.

Downing, Mary Katherine. "Yaqui Cultural Continuity: A
Question of Balance." *Wicazo Sa Review* 8, no. 1 (1992):
91–98.

Evers, Larry, and Felipe S. Molina. *Yaqui Deer Songs Maso Bwikam: A Native American Poetry.* Tucson: Sun Tracks and the
University of Arizona Press, 1987.

Gómez, Laura. *Manifest Destinies: The Making of the Mexican
American Race.* 2nd ed. New York and London: New York
University Press, 2018.

Greenberg, Amy S. *A Wicked War: Polk, Clay, Lincoln, and the
1846 Invasion of Mexico.* New York: Vintage, 2013.

Hutchinson, Sydney. "The Ballet Folklórico de México and the
Construction of the Mexican Nation through Dance." In
Dancing Across Borders: Danzas y Bailes Mexicanos, edited
by Olga Nájera-Ramírez, Norma E. Cantú, and Brenda M.
Romero, 206–25. Urbana and Chicago: University of Illinois
Press, 2009.

McGuire, Thomas R. "Ritual, Theater, and the Persistence of the
Ethnic Groups: Interpreting Yaqui Semana Santa." *Journal of
the Southwest* 31, no. 2 (1989): 159–78.

Romero, Brenda M. "*Matachines Danza* as Intercultural
Discourse." In *Dancing across Borders: Danzas y Bailes
Mexicanos,* edited by Olga Nájera-Ramírez, Norma E.
Cantú, and Brenda M. Romero, 185–205. Urbana and Chi-
cago: University of Illinois Press, 2009.

Sheridan, Thomas E. "How to Tell the Story of 'A People without History': Narrative versus Ethnohistorical Approaches to
the Study of the Yaqui Indians through Time." *Journal of the
Southwest* 30, no. 2 (1988): 168–89.

Spicer, Edward H. "Contrasting Forms of Nativism among
the Mayos and Yaquis of Sonora, Mexico." In *The Social
Anthropology of Latin America: Essays in Honor of
Ralph Leon Beals,* edited by Water Goldschmidt and Harry
Hoijer, 104–25. Los Angeles: University of California Press,
1970.

———. *The Yaquis: A Cultural History.* Tucson: University of
Arizona Press, 1980.

Spicer, Rosamond B., and N. Ross Crumrine. *Performing the
Renewal of Community: Indigenous Easter Rituals in North
Mexico and Southwest United States.* Lanham, MD: Univer-
sity Press of America, 1997.

Cueca

Espinosa, Christian Spencer. "Imagining Traditions: Perfor-
mance and Social Imagination in the Urban Cueca Scene in
Santiago de Chile (2000–2010)." In *Made in Latin America:
Studies in Popular Music,* 64–75. Routledge Global Popular
Music Series. New York: Routledge, 2016.

Gonzalez, Juan Pablo. "The Making of a Social History of Popular Music in Chile: Problems, Methods, and Results." *Latin
American Music Review* 26, no. 2 (2005): 248–72.

Murphy, Annie. "The History of Modern Chile, Mirrored
in Dance." National Public Radio, 2009. www.npr.org
/templates/story/story.php?storyId = 120619384.

Robertson, Carol E. "Power and Gender in the Musical Experiences of Women." In *Women and Music in Cross-Cultural
Perspectives,* edited by Ellen Koskoff. Westport, CT: Greenwood, 1987.

Schecter, John, ed. *Music in Latin American Culture: Regional
Traditions.* New York: Schirmer-Thomson, 1999. See especially the essay by Moreno Cha.

Vals Venezolano and the Guitar

Burton, Cyndy. "Reflections on Segovia's Guitars at the Metropolitan Museum of Art, New York." *American Lutherie:*

The Quarterly Journal of the Guild of American Luthiers 21 (1990): 32–34.

Josel, Seth F., and Ming Tsao. *The Techniques of Guitar Playing.* Kassel: Barenreiter-Verlag Karl Kotterle, 2014.

Labonville, Marie Elizabeth. *Juan Bautista Plaza and Musical Nationalism in Venezuela.* Bloomington and Indianapolis: Indiana University Press, 2007.

Zea, Luis. "'I Thought of It in Terms of Pure Music': An Interview with Antonio Lauro." *Classical Guitar* 21, no. 1 (2002): 11–16.

———. "The Works for Solo Guitar by Antonio Lauro: Analysis and Interpretation." *Classical Guitar* 21, no. 11 (2003): 51–53.

Cumbia

Brill, Mark. *Music of Latin America and the Caribbean.* Boston, Columbus: Pearson/Prentice Hall, 2011.

Faulkner, Anne Shaw (aka Mrs. Marx E. Oberndorfer). "Does Jazz Put the Sin in Syncopation?" In *Keeping Time: Readings in Jazz History,* edited by Robert Walser, 32–36. New York and Oxford: Oxford University Press, 1999.

Hutchinson, Sydney. "Breaking Borders/*Quebrando fronteras:* Dancing in the Borderscape." In *Transnational Encounters: Music and Performance at the U.S.–Mexico Border,* edited by Alejandro L. Madrid, 41–66. New York: Oxford University Press, 2011.

List, George. *Music and Poetry in a Colombian Village: A Tri-Cultural Heritage.* Bloomington: Indiana University Press, 1983.

Moore, Robin D., and Walter A. Clark, eds. *Musics of Latin America.* New York: Norton, 2012. See especially the essay by Scruggs.

Ramos-Kitrell, Jesús. "Transnational Cultural Constructions: Cumbia Music and the Making of Locality in Monterrey." In *Transnational Encounters: Music and Performance at the U.S.–Mexico Border,* edited by Alejandro L. Madrid, 191–206. New York: Oxford University Press, 2011.

Simon, Alissa. "The Costeño Hip Movement: A Conceptual Framework for Understanding Sexuality in Afro-Colombian Folklore Music and Dance." PhD diss. University of California, Los Angeles, 1994.

Wade, Peter. *Music, Race, and Nation: Música Tropical in Colombia.* Chicago and London: University of Chicago Press, 2000.

Son Jarocho

Hernández, Alexandro. "The Son Jarocho and Fandango Amidst Struggle and Social Movements: Migratory Transformation and Reinterpretation of the Son Jarocho in La Nueva España, México, and the United States." PhD diss., University of California, Los Angeles, 2014.

Hernández, Alexandro, and Micaela Díaz-Sánchez. "The Son Jarocho as Afro-Mexican Resistance Music." *Journal of Pan African Studies: Africans in México: History, Race and Place,* edited by Itibari M. Zulu, 6, no. 1 (2013): 187–209.

Loza, Steven. *Barrio Rhythm: Mexican American Music in Los Angeles.* Urbana: University of Illinois Press, 1993.

———. *Essay on Chicano/Latino Music.* Los Angeles: UCLA Chicano Studies Research Center Press, 2017.

Olsen, Dale A., and Daniel E. Sheehy, eds. *The Garland Encyclopedia of World Music: South America, Mexico, Central America, and the Caribbean.* New York and London: Garland, 1998.

Peña, Manuel. *The Texas-Mexican Conjunto: History of a Working-Class Music.* Austin: University of Texas Press, 1985.

Reyes, David. *Land of a Thousand Dances: Chicano Rock 'n' Roll from Southern California.* Albuquerque: University of New Mexico Press, 1998.

Sheehy, Daniel. "Popular Mexican Musical Traditions: The Mariachi of West Mexico and the *Conjunto Jarocho* of Veracruz." In *Music in Latin American Culture: Regional Traditions,* edited by John M. Schechter, 34–79. New York: Schirmer-Thomson, 1999.

Vargas, Deborah L. *Dissonant Divas in Chicana Music: The Limits of La Onda.* Minneapolis: University of Minnesota Press, 2012.

Broadway, Representations of Latinos

Acevedo-Muñoz, Ernesto. *West Side Story as Cinema: The Making and Impact of an American Masterpiece.* Lawrence: University Press of Kansas, 2013.

Delano, Jack. *Puerto Rico Mío: Four Decades of Change.* Washington: Smithsonian Institution Press, 1990.

Domínguez, Alberto, and Nancy de los Santos, directors. *The Bronze Screen: One Hundred Years of the Latino Image in Hollywood.* Questar, 2002.

Hutchinson, Sydney. "The Ballet Folklórico de México and the Construction of the Mexican Nation through Dance." In *Dancing across Borders: Danzas y Bailes Mexicanos,* edited by Olga Nájera-Ramírez, Norma E. Cantú, and Brenda M. Romero, 206–25. Urbana and Chicago: University of Illinois Press, 2009.

Laird, Paul. *Leonard Bernstein: A Guide to Research.* New York: Routledge, 2001.

Quintero-Rivera, Ángel G., and Roberto Márquez. "Migration and Worldview in Salsa Music." *Latin American Music Review* 24, no. 2 (2003): 210–32.

Ramirez Berg, Charles. "Stereotyping and Resistance: A Crash Course on Hollywood's Latino Imagery." In *The Future of Latino Independent Media: A NALIP Sourcebook,* edited by Chon A. Noriega, 3–14. Los Angeles: UCLA Chicano Studies Research Center, 2000.

Reyes, Adelaida. *Music in America.* Experiencing Music, Expressing Culture. New York: Oxford University Press, 2004.

Rodríguez, Clara E. *Latin Looks: Images of Latinos and Latinas in the U.S. Media.* Boulder: Westview, 1997.

Wells, Elizabeth. *West Side Story: Cultural Perspectives on an American Musical.* Lanham, MD: Scarecrow, 2011.

Woll, Allen L. *The Latin Image in American Film.* Rev. ed. Los Angeles: UCLA Latin American Center Publications, University of California, 1997.

Reading for Pleasure

Antush, John. *Nuestro New York: An Anthology of Puerto Rican Plays.* New York: Signet, 1994.

Blasco Ibañez, Vicente. *The Four Horsemen of the Apocalypse.* Rockville, MD: Borgo Press, 2002 Original: *Los cuatro jinetes del apocalípsis* (1916).

Borges, Jorge Luis. *Evaristo Carriego: A Book About Old-Time Buenos Aires.* Hialeah, FL: Dutton, 1984. Contains the essay "History of the Tango." Original: *Evaristo Carriego* (1930).

García Márquez, Gabriel. *The General in His Labyrinth.* 1st ed. Translated by Edith Grossman. New York: Vintage, 2003. Original: *El general en su laberinto* (1989).

Giddings, Ruth Warner, compiler. *Yaqui Myths and Legends.* Tucson: University of Arizona Press, 1974.

Huston, Nancy. *Black Dance.* New York: Grove Press, 2014.

Martínez, Tomás Eloy. *The Perón Novel.* Translated by Helen Lane. New York: Knopf, 1998. Original: *Novela de Perón* (1997).

———. *The Tango Singer.* Translated by Anne McLean. London: Bloomsbury, 2014. Original: *El cantor de tango* (2004).

Pratter, Frederica. *Carlos Gardel: Volver (To Return).* North Charleston, SC: CreateSpace Independent, 2015.

Robertis, Carolina de. *The Gods of Tango.* New York: Knopf, 2015.

Savala, Refugio. *Autobiography of a Yaqui Poet.* Tucson: University of Arizona Press, 1980.

Thom, James Alexander. *St. Patrick's Battalion: A Novel of the Mexican-American War.* Indianapolis: Blue River, 2008.

Experiencing Latin American Music and Politics

I n summer 1967 in Havana, Cuban singers Pablo Milanés (b. 1943) and Silvio Rodríguez (b. 1946) helped organize the First Protest Song Conference, which yielded the declaration, "song must be a weapon at the service of the peoples, not a consumer product used by capitalism to alienate us" (Holden and Zolov 2000: 261). During the Argentine dictatorship, the singer and champion of the poor Mercedes Sosa (1935–2009) received death threats from the regime and in 1979 was arrested onstage at a concert in La Plata (Argentina). In 1998 in London, the dictator Augusto Pinochet was arrested for crimes against the Chilean people and a crowd of Spanish-speaking protesters chanted, "¡El pueblo unido jamás será vencido!" In 2008, at the beginning of the so-called Great Recession in the United States, the same chant resounded in English translation ("The people united will never be defeated!") during a workers' strike in Chicago; the Chilean composer Sergio Ortega (1938–2003) set this street chant to music and a classical composer, Frederic Rzewski (b. 1938) of the United States, wrote a set of variations on Ortega's theme in a virtuosic work for solo piano as a tribute to the Chilean people.

In each instance, music cements solidarity and advances a political point of view. How is it that some songs are so powerful that they endure both as gratifying music and as symbols of resistance? How and why do they

> **ACTIVITY 7.1**
>
> Think back to the last time you became aware of a political protest through the news media (or perhaps witnessed or participated in one). Where did it take place and what point of view was being advanced? How would you describe the participants? Was there any music and, if so, what was its effect?

reappear in new guises, cutting across boundaries of time and place? In this chapter, we examine five examples of politically motivated music from Latin America in light of these questions.

MUSIC OF THE PEOPLE: AN OVERVIEW

A high point in the history of politically motivated music was the worldwide labor struggle during the late nineteenth and early twentieth centuries, a time when workers exploited by business or by the political power structure began to organize. Many of their leaders looked up to intellectuals such as Karl Marx (1818–83) and Friedrich Engels (1820–95), whose *Communist Manifesto* of 1848 attacked the very foundations of capitalism. Seeking to abolish private property and the profit motive, these leaders argued for collective ownership and advocated a system in which an individual's income would correspond to his or her contribution to society. Communists and their supporters believed that art and music should affirm this vision. Bent on eliminating any trace of class structure or elitism, many rejected classical music, with its emphasis on specialized training. They were equally mistrustful of the burgeoning popular music industry, fearing that the authentic "voice of the people" was being silenced by conformity and commercialism. For these social activists, the solution lay in promoting traditional music and in encouraging composers to write new songs in a folk style that would be accessible to the average person. (As noted in chapter 1, the labels "traditional" and "folk" are sometimes used interchangeably.)

Such songs were often participatory, drawing on the immensely satisfying feeling collective singing generates. Few experiences can compare with joining one's own voice with those of hundreds of others on behalf of some deeply felt cause. To ensure that as many people as possible can sing, a political song will likely have a melody consisting of smaller rather than larger intervals; likewise, the form is generally uncomplicated, with strophic or verse-and-refrain form both reliable options. (In the latter, a leader often sings the verse and everyone else joins in on the refrain.) Words are usually set syllabically, without melismas or other artifices that bear no resemblance to ordinary speech. A political song may be aspirational, treating a generalized sentiment such as solidarity with the poor or the hope that humankind's better nature will some-day prevail. A political song can also be about a specific event, such as a labor strike, a war, or a presidential campaign, in which case the event is often explained in detail, with places, dates, and individuals identified by name. Alternatively, some political songs are metaphorical rather than literal. In the plena "El león" (The Lion), for example, the singer tells of a lion escaping from the zoo and all the people fleeing, with the lion symbolizing unchecked political authority. To be sure, not all politically driven songs are musically simple, as some involve more elaborate forms or wider intervals, calling for solo singing. Soloists in this repertory have filled coffee houses, stadiums, and even august venues such as Carnegie Hall in New York City, where Sosa performed in 1988.

Figure 7.1 The Argentine singer Mercedes Sosa in an undated photo taken in her hometown of San Miguel de Tucumán (northern Argentina).
La Gaceta/APimages.com.

> **ACTIVITY 7.2**
>
> Choose a political matter that means a great deal to you. After deciding on a musical form, write lyrics in the language of your choice. Decide also if your song will be literal (i.e., about a specific event) or metaphorical. If the former, you must be well informed about the event you are depicting. If you can, compose a melody. If you know how to write it down, do so; if not, simply sing it enough times so that it stays in your memory. Alternatively, you can use an existing melody that matches your lyrics, a common strategy in political songs. If you know how, add guitar chords or get a classmate to do so.

Latin America enjoys a rich tradition of politically motivated music. One period in which such music flourished was the Cold War, which affected Latin America in ways not seen elsewhere in the world.

THE COLD WAR: FOCUS ON LATIN AMERICA

When World War II ended in 1945, the United States was one of two undisputed world leaders. The other was the Soviet Union, communist since the Russian Revolution of 1917. The Western capitalist democracies, led by the United States, and the Soviet satellites in Eastern Europe, led by the Soviet Union, eyed one another warily until 1991, when the Soviet Union fell. This period, from roughly 1945 to the fall of the Soviet Union, is known as the Cold War. (The term "cold" is used because no direct fighting between the two superpowers took place, despite smaller proxy wars.) Thanks to the atom bomb, first used in 1945 to hasten the end of World War II, each superpower knew it had the capacity to eliminate the other. Each also saw fit to demonize the other, with the Soviets railing against capitalist consumerism and the United States against "godless communism."

Cold War frictions came to Latin America under Roosevelt's successor, President Harry S. Truman (1884–1972). Intent on containing communism in the aftermath of World War II, his administration initiated economic aid programs to persuade the poorer Latin American countries to adopt free-market capitalism. Whenever an anticommunist dictator established himself in a Latin American country, the United States would generally support that regime, often granting diplomatic recognition within days of its seizing power, as was the case with Fulgencio Batista (1901–73), who assumed control in Cuba through a military coup in 1952. (Batista had served as an elected president during the 1940s.) The United States also resumed intervening in Latin American governments, a practice it had largely given up under the Good Neighbor policy. The Central Intelligence Agency (CIA), established in 1948, identified those Latin American countries believed to be leaning toward communism, seen to threaten both the world order and US business interests, which included copper mining in Chile and fruit cultivation in Central America. These businesses earned huge profits for US shareholders and Latin American business elites but often exploited Latin American workers through low wages and sometimes dangerous conditions, especially in mining. One example of US interventionism took place in 1953, when the administration of President Dwight D. Eisenhower (1890–1969) toppled the legally elected president of Guatemala, Jacobo Arbenz (1913–71), who was tagged a communist in part because he expropriated land claimed by the United Fruit company. The CIA organized a force of exiled Guatemalans to overthrow Arbenz and replaced him with a military man.

Many Latin Americans resented these actions. The Guatemalan poet, essayist, and diplomat Luis Cardoza y Aragón (1901–92) wrote that the United States had destroyed "a stammer of freedom in a very small, very backward country, which in no way could endanger anyone" (Holden and Zolov 2000: 205). A more fervent expression of anti-US sentiment came in spring 1958, when Eisenhower's vice president, Richard M. Nixon (1913–94), took a good will tour through Latin America, presumably to revive the spirit of the Good Neighbor era. Instead, he engaged in a shouting match with student groups in Peru and Uruguay, and riots broke out in Venezuela when an angry mob overturned his car such that Nixon had to be whisked away to safety. The fact that the United States had given a Legion of Honor award to the Venezuelan dictator General Marcos Pérez Jiménez (1914–2001) undoubtedly motivated many of those who shouted anti-US slogans on the streets of Caracas that day in 1958.

Cuba was another story. On New Year's Day 1959, Fidel Castro (1926–2016) and his followers seized power in Cuba, eventually creating a communist state. One of Castro's corevolutionaries, Ernesto (Che) Guevara (1928–67), served as finance minister. The United States promptly broke diplomatic relations with Cuba and, in 1960, imposed an embargo *(bloqueo)* to prevent trade between the two nations. In April 1961, a CIA-trained Cuban paramilitary force tried but failed to overthrow Castro in an operation known as the Bay of Pigs. Castro responded by asking the Soviet Union for nuclear missiles, resulting in a stand-off between the United States and the Soviet Union in October 1962, thirteen days of sheer panic for US citizens aware that deadly nuclear weapons were stationed ninety miles off the Florida coast. The Cuban Missile Crisis ended when President John F. Kennedy (1917–63) promised not to repeat maneuvers such as the Bay of Pigs, whereupon the missiles were withdrawn.

As far as the United States was concerned, Cuba was a litmus test for the rest of Latin America. Countries that rejected Cuba earned US respect, whereas those that supported Castro or sought rapprochement with his government earned its suspicion. Certainly not everyone in the US government

US Presidents During the Cold War

Harry S. Truman (Democrat) 1945–53
Dwight D. Eisenhower (Republican) 1953–61
John F. Kennedy (Democrat) 1961–63
Lyndon B. Johnson (Democrat) 1963–69
Richard M. Nixon (Republican) 1969–74
Gerald Ford (Republican) 1974–77
Jimmy Carter (Democrat) 1977–81
Ronald Reagan (Republican) 1981–89
George H. W. Bush (Republican) 1989–93

approved of these measures. In 1965, when Washington officials believed the Dominican Republic was on the verge of a communist takeover, President Lyndon B. Johnson (1908–73) excluded his vice president, Hubert H. Humphrey (1911–78), from the decision to send twenty-three thousand troops there because he knew Humphrey would oppose interventionism. In his book *The Arrogance of Power,* published in 1966, Arkansas senator J. William Fulbright (1905–1995) lamented that "nowhere has the ambivalence in the American attitude toward revolution been more apparent and more troublesome than in the relations of the United States with Latin America" (Fulbright 1966: 82).

MUSIC AND PROTEST: THE SOUNDTRACK

At mid-century, the entire world seemed to be in ferment. In the United States, African Americans and their supporters took to the streets to demonstrate for fair voting procedures, desegregation, equal access to education, and antidiscriminatory hiring practices; others protested the Vietnam War, undertaken to contain communism in Southeast Asia. In Paris, in May 1968, workers and students rioted not only against involvement in Vietnam but also against capitalism and consumerism, effectively bringing France to a halt through a wave of massive strikes. In countries such as Poland and the former states of Czechoslovakia and Yugoslavia, people agitated against communism and its restrictions on civil liberties, often at considerable personal risk. Latin Americans demonstrated as well: against the Vietnam War, labor conditions, what they saw as US imperialism, and repressive governments in their respective countries.

In addition, many Latin Americans were tired of hearing the Beach Boys or Diana Ross and the Supremes over the airwaves in Chile or Bolivia. Resentful of the ubiquitousness of music from the United States, they, like the attendees of the Havana Protest Song Conference, considered its pervasiveness one more form of imperialism designed to lure Latin Americans away from their roots ("a consumer product used by capitalism to alienate us"). They also disparaged the "American Way of Life," which privileged middle-class comfort and material abundance while glorifying inauthentic values, such as consumerism for its own sake.

Another significant force in Cold War Latin America was liberation theology, which rocked the Roman Catholic Church. A social justice movement that started in the 1950s among Catholic priests, it ultimately took its name from the book *Teología de la liberación: Perspectivas* (Theology of Liberation: Perspectives) by the Peruvian priest Gustavo Gutiérrez (b. 1928), published in 1971. Advocates of liberation theology defended the poor on the premise that Jesus himself associated with the lower rungs of society and protected the downtrodden. They challenged the Church hierarchy, accusing it of collaborating in a system that marginalized oppressed peoples while keeping corrupt or violent ruling classes in power. Some Church officials did, in fact, link liberation theology to communism and largely maintained the status quo. (Recall the conversation in *La historia oficial* between Alicia and her priest.) Any number of musicians were drawn to liberation theology. As noted in chapter 4, the Nicaraguan composer Mejía Godoy composed an entire mass that defends the poor and the exploited.

We've already seen how genres such as plena, salsa, and capoeira can express resistance. Here we study five additional selections, focusing explicitly on their political context and the historical events that surrounded them, mainly in relation to the Cold War in Latin America. In "Guantanamera," our Cuban selection, poetry, politics, and intellectual property come to the fore. Then, the Mexican *corrido* offers an account of student activism along with a sober message about historical memory. In "Zelão," we see a very different picture of Brazil than that depicted in the celebratory "Aquarela do Brasil." Our discussion of Chilean *nueva canción* shows how one musician who resisted Pinochet ultimately lost his life. The final example, from the 1930s, is a work for

ACTIVITY 7.3

Interview an older friend or family member who remembers any protest movement of the 1960s. What political activities, if any, did that person undertake during this time? What was the soundtrack of the era and what music did this person favor? Why was it attractive to him or her? Was there any point at which this music was especially important to this individual? After reading the section "Interviewing Strategies" on page 339, formulate at least six questions for your interview.

symphony orchestra by the Mexican classical composer Silvestre Reveultas, whose short but intense career challenged the assumption that classical music is incapable of expressing the voice of the people.

GUANTANAMERA: MUSIC FOR THE CUBAN PEOPLE

"Guantanamera," in verse-and-refrain form, is one of the best known of all Latin American songs in part because its simple refrain encourages participatory singing. It has the curious distinction of being an unofficial national anthem for communist Cuba but also an international hit, the latter thanks largely to the US folk singer and activist Pete Seeger (1919–2014). Its complicated history reflects some of the difficulties between Cuba and the United States.

José Martí and the Struggle for Cuban Independence

Like Puerto Rico, Cuba won independence from Spain in the Spanish-American War of 1898. Given that so many other colonies in Spanish America gained their independence in the 1820s, it may seem surprising that Spain managed to hang on to Cuba and Puerto Rico for such a long time. The reason was economic: especially in Cuba, sugar was so lucrative that local elites preferred not to disrupt their profits by revolting against the colonial power. Some landowners opposed taxation, however, and in 1868, they and other Cuban patriots declared independence from Spain. In the Ten Years' War that followed, several races and social classes united in the struggle but failed to gain independence. The peace that was achieved was uneasy at best.

One of the most eloquent agitators for Cuban independence was the poet José Martí (1853–1895), author of the verses of "Guantanamera." A prolific writer, Martí saw art as one with life and wrote copiously even while relentlessly pursuing political activities. Because he spent long periods in the United States to garner support for Cuban independence, he understood the concept of "America" from many perspectives. His most celebrated essay is undoubtedly "Nuestra América" (Our America) of 1891, which is still widely read. In it, Martí criticized Latin Americans who blindly accepted the dictates of powerful foreigners. He had little patience for formal education, advocating instead the innate wisdom of what he called "natural people," those untainted by ideas alien to their circumstances. He also alluded to Sarmiento, writing,

> No struggle exists between civilization and barbarism but rather between false erudition and natural knowledge. Natural people are good; they respect and reward wisdom as long as it is not used to degrade, humiliate, or belittle them. . . . Natural people resent the imposition of foreign solutions, the insidious result of sterile book learning, because they have little or nothing to do with local conditions and

realities. . . . The history of the Americas, from the Incas to the present, must be taught in detail even if we forego the course on ancient Greece . . . European and Yankee books hold no answers for our problems and our future. (Burns 1993: 111–12)

In "Nuestra América," Martí also called attention to the vast populations outside US borders who call themselves Americans, rejecting both European and US imperialism.

Also in 1891, Martí wrote "Versos sencillos" (Simple Verses), the words that would eventually be set to music in "Guantanamera." In that long series of four-line strophes, Martí upholds yet again the values of "natural people," declaring that a sense of fundamental truth is more important than diplomas or degrees. Martí casts his lot with "the poor of the earth," since it is they who can claim moral authority, not those in positions of power. He also offers an array of nature images—a mountain stream, a palm tree, a wounded bird seeking shelter—to underscore the perspective of "natural persons."

In 1895, a second war for independence began and Martí, now back in Cuba, was killed in one of its first battles. Days before he died, in May of that year, he addressed the United States in even more dire terms, writing a friend, "I have lived in the monster and I know its entrails" (Holden and Zolov 2000: 63). Three years later, the United States handily eliminated Spain from the hemisphere in

Figure 7.2 Statue of Jose Martí in Cienfuegos, Cuba, with Cuban flag.
Zoran Kaparencev/Shutterstock.com.

the Spanish-American War and Cubans imagined they could look forward to freedom. Yet like Puerto Rico, Cuba did not enjoy independence. Rather, it became a protectorate, a state that is protected but also controlled by another, in this case the United States. Although this status was revoked during the Good Neighbor period, the United States retained a naval base at Guantánamo Bay in Guantánamo province (southeast Cuba), which it maintains to this day, along with the detention camp established there in the aftermath of 9/11.

"Guantanamera": A Special Verse-and-Refrain Form

Unlike Martí's verses, filled with imagery and exhortation, the refrain of "Guantanamera" consists of just two words: "guantanamera, guajira, guantanamera." A *guantanamera* is a woman from Guantánamo province and *guajira* translates as "Cuban peasant woman" or "Cuban country girl." In *música guajira*, rural singers often improvised verses, rounding off each with a refrain, sometimes playing the tres, the small guitar with double strings discussed in chapter 5, and other instruments in the guitar family. In the 1920s, as conditions in farming changed, Cuban peasants flocked to cities in search of work, bringing música guajira with them. In time, it was taken up by the music industry to be written down as sheet music or recorded, effectively becoming a commodity in that it could be bought and sold.

Thanks to the Cuban radio host and composer Joseíto Fernández (1908–79), the spontaneity of improvised performance in música guajira was not entirely lost, however. In the 1930s, Fernández started concluding his radio program by improvising verses on current events or some juicy bit of local gossip, complementing these verses with music that closely resembled the refrain of "Guantanamera" we know today. Radio disseminated these performances far and wide, and the simple, repetitive refrain became ingrained in the minds and ears of Fernández's listeners. The improvised verses, which changed daily, did not, however, become ingrained. One listener to Fernández's radio program was the Cuban classical composer Julián Orbón (1921–91). Attracted to the refrain, Orbón decided to couple it with his own music, setting Martí's "Versos sencillos" for the verses. As a prominent classical composer, Orbón also taught music composition. One of his students, Héctor Angulo (b. 1932), played a significant part in the next installment of the complicated history of "Guantanamera."

We now fast-forward to the Cold War. In 1960, Angulo traveled to the United States to study at the Manhattan School of Music in New York City. Like many a student, Angulo needed money, and in summer 1962, he began working as a counselor and teacher at the politically progressive Camp Woodland in New York state. Camp Woodland attracted a diverse group of young people, with many races, religions, and socioeconomic classes represented. Besides outdoor activities, group singing was part of camp life. For that reason, the folksinger Pete Seeger would frequently visit.

During one visit, Angulo sang "Guantanamera," which consisted of Martí's
poetry set to music by Orbón and Fernández's refrain. Seeger was entranced
and asked Angulo about the song. Because the young composer–camp counselor told Seeger only that "Guantanamera" was anonymous and a "very old
melody," Seeger felt justified in performing it at his concerts, including an
appearance at Carnegie Hall. It also figured in his album *We Shall Overcome*,
released in 1963. We'll listen to two versions of this famous song, audio selections 7.1a and 7.1b, which give a good idea of Seeger's enthusiasm. (As you
follow online audio guide 7.1, notice how the public joins in and harmonizes on
the refrain.) One version ends on the V chord and the other uses "the gringo
way of ending" (Manuel 2002: 311).

"Guantanamera" over Time

Thanks to Seeger, "Guantanamera" became famous worldwide. But Fernández,
who remained in Cuba after the Revolution, learned of the song's success and
believed he had been cheated out of his intellectual property. To complicate the
matter, several other composers began writing their own versions of "Guantanamera." When some of these versions were published, a spate of lawsuits
ensued, such that three ethnomusicologists were called in as consultants to
resolve this legal battle. The main point of contention was the catchy refrain,
which Fernández claimed to have created for his radio program of the 1930s.
When these ethnomusicologists compared the intervals and rhythms of Fernández's refrain with other traditional music, however, they discovered that at
the time of Fernández's broadcasts, similar versions of the refrain were already
in circulation and that Fernández could not claim it as his own.

Seeger, on the other hand, recognized that while he had been collecting royalties for his performances of "Guantanamera" its real creator, Orbón, had
received nothing. He set up a special fund to compensate the Cuban composer
but, because of the embargo, these monies could not be distributed. In short,
this emblematic song, which exalts solidarity with "the poor of the earth" (los
pobres de la tierra), was ultimately fraught with conflicts over money and with
US-Cuban politics.

STUDENTS MAKING A DIFFERENCE: MEMORY AND THE MEXICAN CORRIDO

As noted, the cohesiveness of a community depends on shared memory, a historical account that, at least in principle, all can agree on. The following section shows that when state authorities try to repress the memory of a particular event, it can still live on in music, here, in a Mexican *corrido,* a genre sometimes known the "musical newspaper." In this case, the "newspaper" reports on student activism.

Student Protest in the Americas

Students have long participated in protest movements, either on their college campuses or in society at large. In February 1960, four African American college students seated themselves at a whites-only lunch counter in Greensboro, North Carolina. When no one served them, they sat quietly, and when they were pelted with food or squirted with ketchup, they remained seated. Although the students were arrested, restaurants in the South eventually abandoned their policy of segregated lunch counters. The following year, racially mixed groups of university students rode buses through the Deep South to help enforce voting rights denied to African Americans. Local law enforcement did not protect the Freedom Riders, as they were known, and three young idealists were killed by white supremacists. Today, many Black Lives Matter activists are students.

Student activism has a strong tradition in Latin America. In Colombia, June 8 is the Día del Estudiante Caído (Day of the Fallen Student), which commemorates the death in 1929 of a student at the hands of the police. In 1954, on the anniversary of this event, the forces of the dictator Gustavo Rojas Pinilla (1900–75) killed eleven students and wounded fifty who were taking part in a commemorative demonstration. Three years later, students helped bring down Rojas Pinilla. Today, at the National University of Colombia, closures and rescheduling due to student demonstrations are not infrequent and professors, many of whom are sympathetic in principle to the students' demands, despair that they won't get through their syllabi.

ACTIVITY 7.5

Research the history of student protest movements on your campus. What protest activities can be found there now and how do they make their presence felt? Are they related to any national or international movements? How does your university's administration handle these protests? How do the local media? What role does music play in these protests?

In Mexico City, student protest erupted into violence immediately before the opening of the 1968 Olympics. Since these were the first Olympics held in Latin America, many foreign journalists had traveled to Mexico City, presenting a golden opportunity to the demonstrators. Thanks to these reporters, it would be possible to call to worldwide attention the oppressive government of President Gustavo Díaz Ordaz (1911–79). On October 2, students and their working-class supporters converged on the Plaza de Tres Culturas (Square of Three Cultures) in the Tlatelolco neighborhood of Mexico City. The protesters had formulated several demands, including releasing political prisoners and dismantling a government-sponsored riot squad. Soldiers began to fire, shooting for nearly two hours, and the exact number of civilian casualties, among whom were hundreds of students, may never be known.

The Corrido and Memory

Just as the Freedom Riders lifted their spirits by singing on those long bus trips, Mexican activists found both release and purpose in song. The ideal genre to describe an event such as the massacre at the Plaza de Tres Culturas is the *corrido,* the Mexican version of the ballad. (It should not be confused with the corrido in Brazilian capoeira, discussed in chapter 6.) In strophic form, the corrido can accommodate a great deal of detail because it contains many verses. A typical corrido accompaniment consists of one or more guitars (accordion and harmonica are sometimes added), which generally play the familiar I, IV, and V chords (revisit sound links 3.23 and 3.25–3.27a, b, c, and d). If more than one person sings, close harmony is the norm; also, corridos can be in either duple or triple meter.

The corrido has thrived in times of uncertainty or turmoil, such as the Mexican Revolution. Often factually oriented, the genre frequently addresses the five questions journalists habitually consider—who, what, when, where, and why—and thus differs from an aspirational song such as "Guantanamera." Over multiple verses, corrido singers tell of heroes, villains, or ordinary people, ranging from the revolutionary general Pancho Villa to Gregorio Córtez, a simple man who avenged his brother's death at the hands of the law. Singers specify place names, the year of the event being described, and even the time ("on the seventh day of August" in "El contrabando de El Paso," for example, or "about ten PM" in "El deportado"). So that such details can be readily grasped, the setting is syllabic. Through its direct musical language, the "musical newspaper" shapes collective memory, like a good journalistic account.

Corridos recount the traumatic events of 1968 in Mexico City. One, "Canción del Politécnico" (Song of the Polytechnic Institute), details the point at which the military took over the National Polytechnic Institute, one of Mexico's largest public universities. In audio selection 7.2, "Tragedia de la Plaza de las Tres Culturas" (Tragedy of the Square of the Three Cultures), you'll hear the guitar accompaniment, the basic I-IV-V chords, and the regular verse structure, all in the service of the narrative, as shown in online audio guide 7.2. As that narrative progresses, we learn who, what, when, and where, although *why* the tragedy occurred, a question over which the singer anguishes, goes unanswered. In verse 9, the singer mentions Oriana Fallaci (1929–2006), an Italian journalist and author famous for her coverage of conflict in the twentieth century. In verse 12, we hear of Demetrio Vallejo Martínez (1912–85), a union activist who organized a railway workers' strike and was in prison at the time of the protest.

The Corrido over Time

More recent examples of the genre include "Corrido de las Torres Gemelas" (Corrido of the Twin Towers) in memory of the 9/11 terrorist attacks, along with several from the 2016 US presidential campaign, such as "El corrido de Donald Trump," "Arriba con Hillary Clinton" (Up with Hillary Clinton), and "El Quemazón" (a play on Bernie Sanders's campaign slogan, "Feel the Bern"). A subgenre, the *narcocorrido*, relates the exploits of drug lords and their power. Singers of narcocorridos do not necessarily admire such individuals but rather report on such activity as part of daily reality, especially in the border region between Mexico and the United States. Feminist corridos by the late Jenni Rivera (1969–2012) are exceptional given that traditional corridos often emphasize the activities of men.

Reviving collective memory through music or other means is seldom straightforward. For decades after the events in the Plaza de Tres Culturas, the tragedy was barely spoken of, appearing neither in history textbooks nor in public discourse. Today a museum of memory stands in the Plaza de Tres Culturas dedicated to the protesters, living and dead, who took a stand in the plaza that day. On October 2, 1993, the twenty-fifth anniversary of the massacre, a stone slab was erected as a memorial. Like the corrido, with its aural power, these physical monuments remind us that repressive governments will invariably seek to dismantle any history that challenges their authority and that it is the duty of any people to remember both the noble and the ignoble aspects of its political history.

A SONG FROM THE FAVELAS

Our next selection, from Brazil, is more complicated musically than "Guantanamera" or "Tragedia de la Plaza de Tres Culturas." It tells a sobering tale of life in the favelas, the hillside shantytowns surrounding large cities such as Rio de Janeiro. Surprisingly, this solo song uses a bouncy samba-like rhythm to convey this political message.

Brazilian Music and the Cold War

By any standard, Brazilian music during the Cold War was a major success story. In the late 1950s, *bossa nova* burst onto the world stage, its very name proclaiming originality ("bossa" means "tendency" or "direction" in Portuguese and "nova" means "new"). Bossa nova eschews the exuberant African percussion of so many sambas, sometimes relying solely on guitar and voice. Over gentle, syncopated rhythms and with harmonies often inflected by jazz, singers reflect in breathy and intimate tones on the complexities of love or the beauties of nature. One creator of bossa nova was the classically trained composer, arranger, singer, pianist, and guitarist Antônio Carlos Jobim (1927–94), also known as Tom Jobim. He holds the distinction of composing "Garota de Ipanema" (Girl from Ipanema), released in 1964, which is the most celebrated and widely recorded bossa nova in history. In it, a young man gazes across the sands of Ipanema, one of Rio's splendid beaches, at an attractive but indifferent woman. The melody corresponds to the rhythms of natural speech, even to the point of suggesting the young man's sighs. Another important figure was the guitarist, composer, and singer João Gilberto (b. 1931), who recorded "A garota de Ipanema" in addition to many other accomplishments. Bossa nova, to which Brazilians generally do not dance, has been called "a blend of chilled-out Brazilian samba and jazz" (May 2008). It also endures into the present: nowadays a combination of bossa nova and electronica known as *bossatrônica* is popular worldwide.

In the early 1960s, Jobim and Gilberto were optimistic about their country. Brazil had elected a left-leaning president, João Goulart (1918–76), who advocated social security and wanted to increase the minimum wage. He was also willing to recognize communist countries diplomatically and forge closer relations with them, including Cuba. As a result, relations between Brazil and the United States began to suffer and the Kennedy administration became convinced that Goulart was taking Brazil down the path of "a second Cuba," as declassified documents later revealed (Hershberg 2004: part 2, 12). The US Ambassador to Brazil requested covert resources from the CIA in case the

ACTIVITY 7.6

Research basic facts on "Garota de Ipanema" (Girl from Ipanema). Then, listen to at least three recordings of this famous song. Some important ones are those by Amy Winehouse, Frank Sinatra, and the saxophonist Stan Getz. Research each artist and compare his or her approach to that of the others, taking into account as many aspects of the music (pitch, rhythm, melody, texture, and the like) as you can.

Figure 7.3 Ipanema beach in Rio de Janeiro with the mosaic sidewalks characteristic of Brazil.
Caterina Belova/Shutterstock.com.

Goulart government had to be destabilized. These funds, and other secret activities, enabled a military regime to take power in April 1964. The dictatorship, to which the United States promptly granted diplomatic recognition, lasted twenty-one years and sustained five military presidents who not only suspended civil liberties but tortured, exiled, or "disappeared" their opponents.

From Bossa Nova to the Favelas

What was it that the military wanted to suppress? Besides advocating for social security and a decent minimum wage, Goulart had tried to improve education. He was sympathetic to the work of the anthropologist and educational pioneer Paulo Freire (1921–97), then testing his theories on how best to raise literacy. Freire was convinced that humankind was at a crossroads and that the species could either "humanize" or "dehumanize" itself, depending on whether the great masses of the world's poor could be genuinely lifted up beyond sporadic charity or politically motivated aid programs. One of Freire's best-known books is *Pedagogy of the Oppressed* (1968), in which he noted not only the prevalence of worldwide exploitation of the poor but the corrosive effect of this system on the oppressors themselves. Those "who oppress, exploit, and rape by virtue of their power," Freire argued, "cannot find in this power the strength to liberate either the oppressed or themselves" (Freire 1968: 27–28).

The Afro-Brazilian singer Zelia Barbosa (1926–2006) focused on similar issues. In an album released in 1968, she sang of the favelas and the poverty and despair their inhabitants confront on a daily basis. Audio selection 7.3, "Zelão," describes one such inhabitant. As shown in online audio guide 7.3, Zelão can only weep despite the fact that it is Carnaval time, usually a joyous occasion. The samba-like rhythms confirm that it is indeed Carnaval but also serve as a foil to the sadness expressed in the lyrics. The melody, rich in sequences, expresses this sadness as well, taking some unexpected chromatic turns. Listeners also learn of Zelão's sad fate through figures of speech ("in the woodstove of a shack you can only cook illusions"). All of these are apt expressive gestures in a solo song. Songs such as "Zelão" can also be considered a reaction against bossa nova, which some Brazilians saw as socially irrelevant during these years: Barbosa herself once stated that in the face of overwhelming poverty, "to sing of the sea, the sky, the flowers is not enough" (Smithsonian liner notes: 1968 [no author]). Clearly "Zelão" is a far cry from Ari Barroso's upbeat "Aquarela do Brasil."

Other musicians who reacted to the dictatorship included performers of Música Popular Brasileira (Brazilian Popular Music, or MPB), known for lyrics that explicitly attacked racism, social inequity, and the military regime. A leading figure in MPB was Chico Buarque (b. 1944), a composer, singer, guitarist, playwright, and poet. A great admirer of Jobim and Gil, Buarque wrote a protest song that was censored and a play that landed him in prison. He left Brazil for eighteen months but returned to continue his political-artistic mission. Another movement of the 1960s, *Tropicália,* was more international, embrac-

Figure 7.4 Favela in Rio de Janeiro.
Tetiana Tuchyk/Shutterstock.com.

ing not only Brazilian music but psychedelic rock and the British invasion; theater, dance, poetry, and pop art were also part of the Tropicália movement. In fact, this consuming and "spitting out" of multiple influences had long been a practice in Brazilian artistic circles.

Tropicália musicians experienced few such doubts, however, and went decisively forward with their mission. Some of the words in Tropicália songs are disjointed, as in much modern poetry. Other songs explicitly criticize the dictatorship and the state of the world in general. The name of one celebrated group influenced by the Tropicália movement, Os Mutantes (The Mutants), gives an idea of this freewheeling eclecticism. Two key Tropicália figures who collaborated with Os Mutantes were Caetano Veloso and Gilberto Gil, both born in 1942 and both singers, guitarists, and songwriters. (They also teamed up with MPB artists.) They were not always greeted warmly, precisely because they drew on pop and other kinds of commercially successful music, which Marxist audiences found objectionable. In 1968, Veloso, backed by Os Mutantes, sang at the Catholic University in Rio de Janeiro and was practically booed off the stage by Marxist students. Yet because both Veloso and Gil continued to criticize the dictatorship, in 1969 they were arrested, imprisoned, and exiled. They went to London but eventually returned home, enjoying immensely successful international careers. In 2003, Gil became minister of culture, only the second black person to serve in a cabinet post in Brazil, and Veloso, who performs frequently in English, has received numerous Grammy and Latin Grammy awards.

Cultural Cannibalism

For decades, Brazilians had sought to define themselves artistically. Although many wanted to be independent from Europe, they were unwilling to forgo all the latest artistic trends that had evolved there. Back in 1928, the Brazilian poet and essayist Oswald de Andrade (1890–1954) completed his *Manifesto Antropófago* (Cannibalist Manifesto), advocating cannibalism—metaphorically speaking—of Europe. Just as the Tupi Indians had devoured Portuguese missionaries, Andrade argued, Brazilian artists should ingest European techniques and theories and combine them according to Brazilian reality, including aspects of indigenous art. Such a process, which creates a transformative dynamic between self and other, promised to engender new forms of artistic expression. Yet the twentieth-century Brazilian "cannibals" were plagued by ambivalence, as Andrade's quip—"Tupi or not Tupi?"—suggests. Were indigenous art forms really compatible with European cultural expressions? Was cannibalizing Europe truly a new path? These questions were debated for decades.

Music of the Favelas over Time

The favelas continue to show the sharp divisions in Brazilian society. One, the Complexo de Alemão, is a short distance from Rio de Janeiro's elegant beaches and faces the gigantic statue of Christ the Redeemer, who watches over the city. Residents of Complexo de Alemão wryly joke that Christ doesn't see them. In the late twentieth century, new types of music have sprung up in the favelas. *Funk carioca* first became popular in the 1970s, usually involving sampled songs, recordings of melodies chopped up into small fragments (or no melodies at all), and repeated patterns (grooves), some of which came from the United States. With lyrics often focusing on social justice, *funk carioca* makes a political statement, as do *bailes funk,* the big dance parties held in the favelas that involve very energetic dancing and attract big crowds. Funk carioca was not immediately accepted, however. Some compared it unfavorably with samba, considering funk carioca "an inauthentic expression" of favela culture for its use of electronics and North American grooves (Moehn 2012: 136–37). Rap is also a strong presence in the favelas, with Brazilian rappers speaking on behalf of the poor and the marginalized, just as their counterparts worldwide do. MV Bill (b. 1974), a popular hip hop artist from the favela Cidade de Deus (City of God) in Rio de Janeiro, has made it his mission to persuade the youth of the favela to reject drugs.

PROTEST AND NUEVA CANCIÓN IN CHILE

One Latin American genre that aptly expresses a political point of view is *nueva canción* (new song). The dictatorship of Augusto Pinochet, studied in chapter 6, considered the genre subversive to the point of banning it, along with some of the instruments that accompanied it.

Nueva Canción throughout Latin America

In the 1950s and 1960s, many Latin Americans believed that local values were dying in a world increasingly dominated by homogenized mass culture and consumerism. One musician who was convinced of this trend was Atahualpa Yupanqui (1908–92). (His real name was Héctor Roberto Chavero but he took the name of two Incan rulers.) He rode on horseback through his native Argentina, not only absorbing local customs and songs but also gaining an appreciation of the circumstances of poor people. Another musician, Violeta Parra (1917–67), collected songs from rural areas of her native Chile. Most nueva canción artists did not sing the music they gathered, however, but songs they composed themselves that were strongly influenced by traditional music. For example, Parra wrote "Cueca de los poetas" (Cueca of the Poets) after the traditional Chilean dance.

Nueva canción, popular throughout Latin America, was called *nueva canción chilena* (Chilean nueva canción) in Chile and *nueva trova* in Cuba, where it effectively set to music the ideals of the revolution of 1959. Some nueva canción artists aspired to a Pan-Latin American reach. Although Chilean, Parra played the *cuatro*, the small, four-stringed guitar of música llanera. (She called it her *guitarrilla*, or "little guitar.") Others played Andean instruments, such as the *kena*, one of several types of vertical flutes, and the *charango*, studied in chapter 3. It's worth pointing out that earlier in the twentieth century, middle- and upper-class urban youths were discouraged from playing these Andean instruments because the social establishment associated them with indigenous peoples, whom they believed were indolent, passive, and prone to alcoholism. Merely playing these instruments was therefore an act of rebellion.

The Cold War in Chile: Politics and Music

When Pinochet took power in 1973, he ousted a legally elected socialist president, Salvador Allende (1908–73). (The author mentioned in chapter 2, Isabel Allende, is Salvador Allende's first cousin once removed.) Allende, who was trained as a medical doctor, well knew the effects of poverty on public health.

ACTIVITY 7.8

Find on the internet Victoria Parra's performance of "Gracias a la vida" (Thanks to Life or Here's to Life), an emblematic work from the nueva canción repertory. If you don't know Spanish, look up an English translation. How would you describe the timbre of Parra's *cuatro?* Comment also on the form and texture of "Gracias a la vida." Then, listen to performances of the same song by Mercedes Sosa and Joan Baez of the United States, who recorded it in 1974 on her album of the same title. Compare each performance, taking into account the vocal quality, accompaniment, and mood created. Can "Gracias a la vida" be considered a political song? Why or why not?

Among other things, he wanted to improve education and health care for the poor and nationalize industry and banking, which meant defying local elites who collaborated with foreign-owned, profit-driven businesses, such as the big US mining companies. Allende's electoral victory was nothing short of remarkable given that the CIA massively funded his opponent and fomented labor strikes to frustrate the electorate.

Allende was also an enthusiastic supporter of nueva canción. In 1969, while still a presidential candidate, he attended the First Festival of Nueva Canción Chilena, held at the National Stadium in Santiago. Before a large crowd, he stood under a banner that proclaimed, "there can be no revolution without songs." A second nueva canción festival took place there in 1970, and after Allende was elected, LPs of nueva canción were released on the government-subsidized label DICAP (Discoteca del Cantar Popular). One of the most celebrated nueva canción artists at this time was the Chilean singer Víctor Jara (1932–73). Sometimes Jara performed with other musicians but more often than not he relied solely on his guitar and his distinctive voice. In one song, "Manifiesto" (Manifesto), he declares that his guitar is "not for the rich," endorsing Allende's socialist values. In "¿Quién mató a Carmencita?" (Who Killed Carmencita?), Jara sings of a young woman from a working-class Santiago neighborhood who, deceived by "lies and bottled happiness," commits suicide, a victim of mindless consumerism. In the bitter and dramatic "Preguntas por Puerto Montt" (On Behalf of Puerto Montt), Jara excoriates—and identifies by name—the government official who in 1969 ordered an attack on impoverished squatters in the Chilean city of Puerto Montt.

All the while, the United States government nervously watched the ascent of Allende's socialist government. The CIA decided to take covert action, which came to fruition on September 11, 1973, the "other September 11," as some scholars call that fateful day in Chilean history (Aguilera, Dorfman, and Fredes 2006). Under instructions from the Nixon administration, US fire bombers attacked the presidential palace in Santiago and General Pinochet seized power. (Allende committed suicide.) Pinochet set about torturing and "disappearing" his opponents. But he was also determined to kill nueva canción. So keenly did he and his forces feel its influence that days after the coup, Jara was tortured and executed. The kena and the charango were prohibited and DICAP was ordered to erase all its master tapes; later, the company itself was shut down and its archives were destroyed. Pinochet's goal was to create a cultural blackout *(apagón cultural),* which would erase any memory of the Allende era. Not surprisingly, many Chileans left the country, including several musicians.

Months before he was assassinated, Jara composed audio selection 7.4 "Aquí me quedo" (I'll Stay Here), setting a poem of the same title by the Chilean poet Pablo Neruda (1904–73), who believed in many of the same values as Jara.

Figure 7.5 The Chilean singer Víctor Jara with guitar in an undated photo by an unknown photographer.
APimages.com.

ACTIVITY 7.9

Research the Chilean ensemble Quilapayún. In what language is the word "Quilapayún" and what does it mean? Where did these musicians go after Pinochet came to power? Listen to the group perform Sergio Ortega's "¡El pueblo unido jamás será vencido!" (The People United Will Never Be Defeated!), a musical setting of the street chant mentioned in the introduction to this chapter. Listen several times so that you get the melody in your ear.

> ### Pablo Neruda, Poet and Activist
>
> Born in rural Chile, Neruda became one of Latin America's foremost poets. He was also a diplomat and a political activist, serving as a consul in Madrid in the 1930s. Because he was a communist and became involved in politics, however, he was dismissed from his post. He returned to Chile but at various intervals went into exile for his political activities. A prolific writer, Neruda published poetry, books, and essays and, in 1971, received the Nobel Prize for literature. He died on September 23, 1973, days after the coup. Neruda's language is simple (often deceptively so) and his poems appear in many anthologies of Spanish literature and in Spanish-language textbooks. They also lend themselves well to music and have been set by several composers. The classical composer Daniel Catán of Mexico (1949–2011) and the jazz artist Luciana Souza of Brazil (b. 1966) are just two musicians who have engaged with Neruda's poetry.

Unlike most of the songs on Jara's posthumously released album *Manifiesto*, "Aquí me quedo" was jointly written, with Patricio Castillo (b. 1946). When Jara and Castillo composed the song, tensions between Allende's government and the right-wing opposition were mounting. Still convinced that peaceful protest could effect change, however, in "Aquí me quedo" Jara sang of a united country in which Chileans are all of the same mind and in which all the "rich foreigners go back to Miami." With its poignant moments of silence and its prominent guitar interludes, "Aquí me quedo" is clearly a solo song, as shown in online audio guide 7.4. Jara's simple declaration "I'll stay" is as dramatic as any of his musical utterances. It also shows him at his most optimistic.

Chilean Protest Music over Time

In the mid-1970s, Chilean musicians still resident in Chile took the bold step of using indigenous instruments once more. They believed they could avoid difficulty with the authorities by using the kena or the charango to accompany metaphorical lyrics. For example, instead of railing against the dictatorship a singer might tell of endless winter. The result was a genre called *canto nuevo*, which sought to recapture some of the values of nueva canción but more subtly. Nonetheless, the government reacted. Although it did not explicitly prohibit musicians from performing canto nuevo, it took other steps, such as making it difficult to obtain permits for concert halls or maintaining a blacklist of musicians, individuals who were banned from performing on television or radio. In a curious intertwining of political ideology and musical style, the prohibited instruments came to be heard again when an ensemble called Barroco Andino began playing classical music on the kena, the charango, and other Andean

Figure 7.6 This photo from May 2013 shows the door leading to the locker room of the indoor stadium where the Chilean folk singer Víctor Jara was tortured and killed.

Brittany Peterson/APimages.com.

instruments. ("Barroco," or "baroque," is a style of classical music from the seventeenth and eighteenth centuries.) Since classical music was generally heard in churches and concert halls rather than in rallies, and since Barroco Andino's repertory had no words that could inflame opponents of the dictatorship, the regime decided that the group was harmless and Barroco Andino freely performed classical music by Johann Sebastian Bach (1685–1750) and Antonio Vivaldi (1678–1741), despite using instruments recently condemned as politically loaded.

CLASSICAL MUSIC AND POLITICS: SENSEMAYÁ

The story of Barroco Andino in Pinochet's Chile suggests that classical music enjoys a special status. For some people, it's the only type of music that deserves the designation "art." (As we noted in chapter 1, the terms "art music" and "classical music" are often used interchangeably.) According to proponents of this view, art occupies a plane elevated above ordinary life in which listeners are transported to a state of *transcendence*. Beyond mere entertainment or extramusical message, art exists for its own sake; therefore, they argue, classical composers should refrain from investing their works with political sentiment, which would sully the purity of art. Here, we'll discuss the music of the Mexican classical composer Silvestre Revueltas (1899–1940), who acted on a very different set of beliefs.

Silvestre Revueltas as Activist and Artist

Throughout his short and tempestuous life, Revueltas allied himself with various leftist causes. Although it is not clear that he ever joined the communist party, he did, however, sympathize with its values and was active in the leftist organization LEAR (Liga de Escritores y Artistas Revolucionarios, or League of Revolutionary Writers and Artists). Like his compatriots the poet Octavio Paz (1914–98) and the painter Fernando Gamboa (1909–90), both fellow LEAR members, Revueltas believed that art should speak directly to the social and political concerns of the common people rather than isolate itself in some ivory tower removed from the realities of life.

LEAR was especially active during the Spanish Civil War of 1936–39, an event that affected several Latin American countries, especially Mexico. In 1931, Spain elected a left-leaning republican government, which redistributed land and built hundreds of schools but also challenged the authority of the Spanish Catholic Church. In 1936, a group of insurgents led by General Francisco Franco (1892–1975) rose up against the Republic, sparking a bitter civil war that lasted three years. In the end, Franco prevailed and ruled Spain as a dictator for nearly four decades. Mexico was one of only two countries that lent support to the beleaguered Spanish Republic. (The Soviet Union was the other, while Hitler and Mussolini aided Franco. All other countries, including the United States, remained officially neutral even as many defied their governments to fight for the Republic.) Mexicans followed the war with interest and took in many Spanish refugees, among them several musicians. One group of Spanish expatriates founded a school in Mexico City, where the Republican anthem was sung daily.

In 1937, Revueltas toured Spain with LEAR, presenting his music, speaking on the radio, and trying to instill hope among those loyal to the Republic while Franco gained ground. One work performed on the tour was his *Homenaje a Federico García Lorca* (Homage to Federico García Lorca) for orchestra. Revueltas composed it in honor of Lorca (1898–1936), the Spanish poet and playwright murdered by Franco's troops for his controversial plays, leftist poli-

Figure 7.7 One of several variants of Spanish Republican flags. Mexico maintained an embassy for the Republic in Exile until 1976, a year after Franco died.
Marta Cobos/Shutterstock.com.

tics, and the fact that he was gay. Several other Latin American classical composers either have set Lorca's literary works to music or musically depicted his tragic death, including Juan José Castro (1895–1968) and Osvaldo Golijov (b. 1960) of Argentina, Marlos Nobre of Brazil (b. 1939), and Héctor Angulo (the Cuban composer who introduced "Guantanamera" to Pete Seeger). Clearly in composing *Homenaje,* Revueltas was attacking Lorca's assassins as much as he was honoring the slain poet.

"Chant for Killing a Snake"

In another work for orchestra, *Sensemayá: Chant for Killing a Snake,* Revueltas expressed a political point of view less directly, taking as his point of departure the eponymous poem by a contemporary, the Afro-Cuban poet Nicolás Guillén, and heard in audio selection 7.5.

In *Sensemayá: A Chant for Killing a Snake,* Guillén evokes a Santería ritual, one in which a snake is offered to an oricha as a sacrifice. Alternating the *alba,* a Spanish poetic form, with segments of an African chant on the words "¡Mayombe-bombe-mayombé!" Guillén combines European and Afro-Cuban influences. The end result resembles the call-and-response format of Santería

Nicolás Guillén and Afro-Cuban Culture

Although Nicolás Guillén (1902–89) began as a journalist, he eventually published his poetry in various magazines. In 1930, his *Motivos del son* appeared, eight poems that address racial inequality and which are loosely based on the Cuban *son*. Guillén was much impressed by the African American poet Langston Hughes (1902–67), whom he met personally in Havana and introduced to Afro-Cuban music. Like Revueltas, Guillén sympathized with the Spanish Republic and also traveled to Spain during the Civil War, mainly as a reporter. Several *nueva trova* artists have been drawn to Guillén's poetry and people of his era considered him the national poet of Cuba.

but for instruments. As for the meaning of the poem itself, several interpretations present themselves. Perhaps Guillén is simply being literal, depicting the ritual of snake-killing as a routine act to propitiate the oricha. On the other hand, killing the snake might refer to the long history of slavery in Cuba, which should be "killed." Alternatively, the snake could symbolize US imperialism.

When composers of instrumental music, classical or otherwise, are inspired by a given poem they generally take certain steps. First, they read the poem (or hear it recited). Next, they absorb its overall feeling, and then seek the best way of expressing this feeling musically. In composing *Sensemayá*, Revueltas departed from these procedures, engaging far more directly with the poem. He set each of Guillén's individual words to music, adhering to the natural speech rhythm of the text. Then, he deleted the words but retained the melody that had resulted. He also interspersed these poetry-generated notes with other musical ideas. Different ostinati (plural of ostinato) undergird whole sections of music. In one, for example (1:58), we can hear the rhythm of Guillén's poem, namely, the incantation "¡Mayombe-bombe-mayombé!" which dictates the timing of the musical notes so precisely such that listeners who know Guillén's poem may be aware of its "fingerprint" on the music. (As shown in online audio guide 7.5, a similar situation prevails with the word "Sensemayá.") Revueltas always considered it best to enhance his materials from the standpoint of timbre. He used several percussion instruments such as claves, maracas, rasping stick, gourd, small Indian drum, bass drum, high and low tom-toms, and more, requiring a total of three players. Dark timbres among the orchestral instruments include that of the tuba, a brass instrument rarely showcased in symphonic music, which introduces what some critics have called the "snake theme" seconds into the piece. A tremendous climax could suggest the actual killing of the snake, depending on one's interpretation.

ACTIVITY 7.10

Consider the idea that art should exist "for the sake of art," that is, for no purpose beyond its own beauty or expressiveness. Why might many people find this idea attractive? What objections, if any, could be raised? In the case of instrumental music, which has no words to make its meaning explicit, can a musical composition exist for its own sake?

Even if knowing Guillén's poem enhances our understanding of the music, one can also listen to *Sensemayá* without this awareness or, for that matter, without awareness of the composer's politics.

Politically Motivated Classical Music from Latin America over Time

Any number of Latin American classical composers have written music that expresses a political sentiment. Since the second half of the twentieth century, the life of Che Guevara has proved especially compelling to composers on the left, feelings that were only heightened after the revolutionary leader was captured by CIA operatives in the mountains of Bolivia and put to death. José Ardévol (1911–81), a Spanish-born composer who spent most of his career in Cuba, for example, wrote *Che comandante* for chorus and orchestra. A Cuban composer, Harold Gramatges (1918–2008), wrote *Muerte del guerillero* (Death of a Guerilla Fighter), for reciter and orchestra; *Ñancahuasú*, by César Bolaños (1931–2012) of Peru, also commemorates Che. *En memoria a Salvador Allende* by the Puerto Rican composer Rafael Aponte-Ledée (b. 1938) is one of several works that honor the fallen Chilean leader whereas . . . *después el silencio* by Hilda Dianda (b. 1925) of Argentina pays tribute to those disappeared during that country's dictatorship.

ACTIVITY 7.11

Listen to a performance of Sergio Ortega's "¡El pueblo unido jamás será vencido!" (The People United Will Never Be Defeated!) (see activity 7.9). Then, research the US composer Frederic Rzewski (b. 1930) and listen to his *36 Variations on "The People United Will Never Be Defeated!" by Sergio Ortega and Quilapayún* for solo piano, composed in the 1970s. What is a theme and variations? What is a cadenza? Does the piece contain a political message or can it be understood as music for its own sake?

CONCLUSIONS

In this chapter, we have explored several ways in which political sentiments can be expressed musically. In listening casually to the straightforward verse-and-refrain structure and simple harmonies of "Guantanamera," one could assume the song is about idealized country life, complete with mountain streams and palm trees where simple people live according to noble principles. Yet its twisted history tells a tale not only of authorship and intellectual property but of US-Cuban politics. The corrido "Tragedia de la Plaza de las Tres Culturas," with its literal account of facts, is much less poetic than "Guantanamera." Still, the reportage offered by this "musical newspaper" was for many years one of the few narratives of an event otherwise buried in collective forgetfulness. "Zelão" personalizes the problems of a nation from the viewpoint of a single, marginalized individual, set, perhaps ironically, to samba-like rhythms. In "Aquí me quedo," the listener experiences the calm before the storm uttered by a dramatic solo voice that would never be silenced, despite death at the hands of a dictator. *Sensemayá*, whose music is so closely married to a poetic text, can be heard as political statement or simply as a piece of orchestral music.

Music both responds to particular events and intensifies our understanding of them. It can also speak to a more generalized political attitude. It can be participatory, allowing ordinary people to raise their voices in song, or it can be for a solo voice or even a symphony orchestra, defying long-held beliefs about classical music. Just as multiple political persuasions exist, many questions present themselves regarding politics and music. Still, most would agree that aspects of the music itself—melody, rhythm, texture, harmony—are not in themselves political but that political meanings can arise from whatever significance the music's creators and its audiences attach to it.

STUDY GUIDE

Key Terms

Cold War

liberation theology

música guajira

bossa nova

Música Popular Brasileira (Brazilian Popular Music, or MPB)

Tropicália

funk carioca

Día del Estudiante Caído (Day of the Fallen Student)

ballad

corrido

nueva canción

nueva trova

charango

kena

canto nuevo

Spanish Civil War

For Further Study

General

Aharonián, Coriún. "Technology for the Resistance: A Latin American Case." *Latin American Music Review* 23, no. 2 (2002): 195–205.

Casey, Michael. *Che's Afterlife: The Legacy of an Image.* New York: Vintage, 2009.

Fulbright, J. William. *The Arrogance of Power.* New York: Random House, 1966.

Gilbert, Joseph M., and Daniela Spenser. *In From the Cold: Latin America's Encounter with the Cold War.* Durham and London: Duke University Press, 2008.

Gutiérrez, Gustavo. *A Theology of Liberation: History, Politics, and Salvation.* 15th anniversary ed. Translated by Caridad Inda. Maryknoll, NY: Orbis, 1988.

Holden, Robert H., and Eric Zolov, eds. *Latin America and the United States: A Documentary History.* New York: Oxford University Press, 2000.

Raymont, Henry. *Troubled Neighbors: The Story of U.S.–Latin American Relations from FDR to the Present.* Boulder: Westview, 2005.

Roy, William G. 2010. "How Social Movements Do Culture." In *Reds, Whites, and Blues: Social Movements, Folk Music, and Race in the United States*, 234–50. Princeton: Princeton University Press, 2010.

Schlesinger, Stephen C. *Bitter Fruit: The Story of the American Coup in Guatemala.* Cambridge, MA: Harvard University Press, 1982.

Guantanamera

Burns, E. Bradford. *Latin America: Conflict and Creation: A Historical Reader.* Englewood Cliffs, NJ: Prentice Hall, 1993.

Campbell, W. Joseph. *The Spanish-American War: American Wars and the Media in Primary Documents.* Santa Barbara: Greenwood, 2005.

Foner, Philip S. *The Spanish-Cuban-American War and the Birth of American Imperialism, 1895–1902.* Vols. 1 and 2. New York: Monthly Review Press, 1972.

Kobre, Sidney. *The Yellow Press and Gilded Age Journalism.* Tallahassee: Florida State University Press, 1964.

Manuel, Peter. "From Scarlatti to 'Guantanamera': Dual Tonicity in Spanish and Latin American Musics." *Journal of the American Musicological Society* 55, no. 2 (2002): 311–36.

———. "The Saga of a Song: Ownership and Authorship in the Case of 'Guantanamera.'" *Latin American Music Review* 27, no. 2 (2006): 121–47.

Corrido

Edberg, Mark C. "*Narcocorridos*: Narratives of a Cultural Persona and Power on the Border." In *Transnational Encounters: Music and Performance at the U.S.-Mexico Border*, edited by Alejandro L. Madrid, 67–82. New York: Oxford University Press, 2011.

Holden, Robert H., and Eric Zolov, eds. *Latin America and the United States: A Documentary History.* New York: Oxford University Press, 2000.

Paredes, Américo. "The Mexican Corrido: Its Rise and Fall." In *Folklore and Culture on the Texas-Mexican Border*, edited by Richard Bauman, 129–41. Austin: CMAS, 1993.

———. *With His Pistol in His Hand: A Border Ballad and its Hero.* Austin: University of Texas Press, 1958.

Shelemay, Kay Kaufman. *Soundscapes: Exploring Music in a Changing World.* 3rd ed. New York and London: Norton, 2015.

Brazil in the 1960s

Aidi, Hishaam. *Rebel Music: Race, Empire, and the New Muslim Youth Culture.* New York: Pantheon, 2014.

Béhague, Gerard. "Rap, Reggae, Rock, or Samba: The Local and the Global in Brazilian Popular Music (1985–1995)." *Latin American Music Review* 27, no. 1 (2006): 79–90.

Budasz, Rogerio. "Of Cannibals and the Recycling of Otherness." *Music & Letters* 87, no. 1 (2006): 1–15.

Dunn, Christopher. *Brutality Garden: Tropicalia and the Emergence of a Brazilian Counterculture.* Chapel Hill and London: University of North Carolina Press, 2001.

Freire, Paulo. *The Pedagogy of the Oppressed.* Thirtieth anniversary ed. Translated by Myra Bergman Ramos. New York and London: Bloomsbury Academic, 2000.

Hershberg, James G. "The United States, Brazil, and the Cuban Missile Crisis, 1962." *Journal of Cold War Studies* 6, no. 2 (2004): 1–20; 6, no. 3 (2004): 5–67.

May, Chris. "Stan Getz: The Bossa Nova Albums." *All about Jazz*, November 11, 2008. www.allaboutjazz.com/stan-getz-the-bossa-nova-albums-by-chris-may.php.

Moehn, Frederick. *Contemporary Carioca: Technologies of Mixing in a Brazilian Musical Scene.* Durham and London: Duke University Press, 2012.

Veloso, Caetano. *Tropical Truth: A Story of Music and Revolution in Brazil.* New York: Knopf, 2003.

Nueva Canción

Aguilera, Pilar, Ariel Dorfman, and Ricardo Fredes, eds. *Chile: The Other September 11: An Anthology of Reflections on the 1973 Coup.* Melbourne and New York: Ocean, 2006.

Jara, Joan. *An Unfinished Song: The Life of Victor Jara.* New York: Tickner & Fields, 1984.

Jara, Joan, and Adrian Mitchell. *Victor Jara: His Life and Songs.* Ottawa, Canada: Elm Tree, 1976.

Morris, Nancy. "'Canto porque es necesario cantar': The New Song Movement in Chile, 1973–1983." *Latin American Research Review* 21, no. 2 (1986): 117–36.

Party, Daniel. "Beyond 'Protest Song': Popular Music in Pinochet's Chile, 1973–1990." In *Music and Dictatorship in Europe and Latin America*, edited by Roberto Illiano and Massimiliano Sala. Turnhout: Brepols, 2009.

Taffet, Jeffrey F. "'My Guitar Is Not for the Rich': The New Chilean Song Movement and the Politics of Culture." *Journal of American Culture* 20, no. 2 (1997): 91–103.

Revueltas

Garland, Peter. In Search of Silvestre Revueltas: Essays, 1978–1990. Santa Fe: Sounding, 1991.

Hess, Carol. "Silvestre Revueltas in Republican Spain: Music as Political Utterance." Latin American Music Review 18, no. 2 (1997): 278–96.

Kubayanda, Joseph B. The Poet's Africa: Africanness in the Poetry of Nicolás Guillén and Aimé Césaire. Edited by Henry Louis Gates Jr. Contributions in Afro-American and African Studies 138. New York: Greenwood, 1991.

Williams, Lorna V. Self and Society in the Poetry of Nicolás Guillén. Baltimore: Johns Hopkins University Press, 1982.

Zohn-Muldoon, Ricardo. "The Song of the Snake: Silvestre Revueltas's Sensemayá." Latin American Music Review 19, no. 2 (1998): 133–59.

Reading for Pleasure

Alegría, Fernando. *Allende: A Novel.* Palo Alto, CA: Stanford University Press, 1993.

Allende, Isabel. *The House of the Spirits.* New York: Everyman's Library, 2005. Original: *La casa de los espíritus* (1982).

Asturias, Miguel Ángel. *The President.* Long Grove, IL: Waveland, 1997. Original: *El president* (1946).

Bejel, Emilio. *The Write Way Home: A Cuban-American Story.* Translated by Stephen A. Clark. Andover MA: Versal, 2003.

Greene, Graham. *Our Man in Havana.* 1958; New York: Penguin, 2007.

Guillén, Nicolás. *Yoruba from Cuba: Selected Poems of Nicolás Guillén.* Translated by Salvador Ortiz-Carboneres. Bilingual ed. Leeds, UK: Peepal Tree Press, 2005.

Heminway, Ernest. *For Whom the Bell Tolls.* 1940. New York: Scribner, 1995.

Jara, Joan. *An Unfinished Song: The Life of Victor Jara.* New York: Tickner & Fields, 1984.

Lorca, Federico García. *Three Plays: Blood Wedding; Yerma; The House of Bernarda Alba.* Translated by Michael Dewell and Carmen Zapata. New York: Farrar, Straus and Giroux, 1993. Originals: *Bodas de sangre* (1933); *Yerma* (1934); *La casa de Bernarda Alba* (1945).

Neruda, Pablo. *The Essential Neruda. Selected Poems.* Bilingual ed. San Francisco: City Lights, 2004.

————. *Spain in Our Hearts/España en el corazón.* Translated by Donald Walsh. New York: New Directions, 2005. Original: *España en el corazón* (1937).

Ribeiro, Edgard Telles. *His Own Man.* New York City: Other, 2014.

Sperber, Murray, ed. *And I Remember Spain: A Spanish Civil War Anthology.* New York: Macmillan, 1974.

But Is It Art? Experiencing Latin American Classical Music

8

What is your experience of Western European classical music? Perhaps you've attended a performance of *Messiah* by Georg Frideric Handel (1685–1759) and stood up during the "Hallelujah Chorus." Perhaps your piano teacher assigned you "Für Elise" by Ludwig van Beethoven (1770–1827), either the simplified version or the piece in its entirety. Perhaps you played "Minuet in G" by Johann Sebastian Bach (1685–1750) in your Suzuki violin class. In this book, we've not so much defined classical music as experienced it, discovering, for example, that Revueltas's *Sensemayá* and Ginastera's malambo sound very different from a polyphonic mass. We've also observed that many people attach special status to classical music. In this chapter, we consider questions that classical composers have confronted over history, concentrating mainly on aesthetics and style, and ways in which "art" has been defined. To do this, we'll focus on six classical music genres as realized by Latin Americans.

AESTHETICS AND STYLE

As we noted in chapter 3, *aesthetics* is the branch of philosophy dedicated to the arts. People interested in aesthetics determine whether a work of art is beautiful, ugly,

ACTIVITY 8.1

Partner with someone in the class and explain your experience of classical music in primary or secondary school. In what way did you participate? Did either you or your friends pursue classical music study because you thought it would help you get into college? If you have never been interested in classical music, why is this the case?

tragic, or comic. They also consider prior judgments about art, analyzing and often critiquing the principles on which these judgments are based. Since the time of the ancient Greeks, philosophers have linked questions of aesthetics to human behavior, as shown in the writings of Plato (c. 428–348 BCE), who set forth what he saw as the characteristics of different types of music and how these characteristics impacted human beings. In sum, aesthetics seeks to uncover the meaning of art.

Yet because aesthetic priorities change, artistic meanings are not fixed. Depending on the historical moment and the prevailing culture, some aesthetic positions will be more highly valued than others. Through this process of valuation, in which praxis and creativity converge, identifiable *styles* emerge. In Western European classical music, "style" simply means that enough composers have adopted certain techniques and have manipulated aspects of music (melody, rhythm, texture, harmony, and the like) within certain parameters. If most composers are writing conjunct, rather than disjunct, melodies, for example, this practice will come to be one attribute of a particular style. Aestheticians will evaluate the style, asking whether it is pleasing or whether it challenges listeners' expectations so much as to be unsettling. Of course, audiences react as well.

Many composers change styles several times over the course of their careers. Ginastera's earliest pieces expressed Argentine identity but as he became increasingly influenced by international trends, he stopped writing music that evoked the world of the gaucho and turned to other forms of expression. In other words, his aesthetic priorities changed. As composers test different styles over their careers, most will also seek to put their personal stamp on their works in whatever style they adopt. In other words, however much composers are influenced by the aesthetic trends of their time, they will generally cultivate an individual voice or musical personality.

The idea of a style (sometimes "school" is used) isn't confined to music. In Latin American literature, for example, naturalism was one style of writing, which lent itself especially well to grappling with questions of national identity during the nineteenth century. In the twentieth century, magical realist authors boldly juxtaposed the fantastic and the rational, ensuring that this style pushed the boundaries of perception. In the visual arts, the style of social realism confronted poverty and injustice head-on, often with near-photographic exactitude; surrealism, on the other hand, could depict the same subject matter but from the standpoint of the dream state. As you can see, many styles and aesthetic trends end with the suffix "-ism" ("-ismo" in Spanish and Portuguese). Sometimes an artist's style is so idiosyncratic that it occupies a category unto itself, as with *boterismo*, a term coined to describe the works of the Colombian painter Fernando Botero (b. 1932).

Western European classical music is often presented as a succession of chronological styles: medieval (c. 800–1400), Renaissance (1400–1600), baroque (1600–1750), classical (1750–1800), romantic (1800–1900), and modern (1900 to the present). The date ranges are only approximations, since stylistic change happens slowly. Within each, we also find many substyles, especially under the rubric "modern," as detailed below. These styles traveled from Europe to Latin America, where they acquired new traits and new meanings.

Figure 8.1 *Dancing in Colombia,* by Fernando Botero (1980). Metropolitan Museum of Art, New York/Art Resource, NY.

THE CANON AND LATIN AMERICA

In studying Western European classical music, you will often hear the term "canon," a collection of works that many people have considered "great" or authoritative over the years and that have withstood the test of time. Again, the concept extends beyond music: in Spanish literature, for example, Cervantes is a bedrock of the canon. Canonic works need not be from the distant past, as the works of García Márquez and Borges attest, both canonical authors of the twentieth century. In music, the canon comprises those works that are nowadays recorded, studied in colleges, universities, and schools of music, or performed at concerts, where people listen to them with no other activity to distract them. Over the centuries, the canon has wielded considerable influence, with many composers modeling their own music on it and absorbing what many believed are its timeless values.

Whatever our admiration for canonical works, the canon is not at all timeless. Rather, it is a relatively new concept. Its history is connected to the fact that what we now call "classical" music was not always such a serious affair, for during the seventeenth and eighteenth centuries audiences would sometimes eat or chat during concerts instead of listening in silence as they do today. Nor did the split between classical and popular music, which many people nowadays take for granted, exist. Over the course of the nineteenth century, several influential music critics and composers advanced a new aesthetic agenda, which held that classical music should edify the public, whether spiritually, intellectually, or aesthetically. The canon, which consists of works believed to possess these properties, was thus formed. The canon also became a litmus test for education: just as a cultivated person in the English-speaking world would be expected to know the works of Shakespeare (his or her Spanish-speaking counterpart would be equally familiar with Cervantes and Quevedo), that same person would have at least a passing knowledge of music by canonical classical composers, such as Beethoven and Bach. Some people opposed the canon to other kinds of music. Those favoring the canon came to believe that listening to it would elevate the mind and expose it to lofty ideals as expressed by geniuses, whereas popular music, directed to the mass audience, would merely entertain.

ACTIVITY 8.2

Consider the difference between "art" and "entertainment." How can one be distinguished from the other? Is such a distinction viable and, assuming we make it, is entertainment necessarily shallow? Does either position have a particular agenda to defend, and, if so, what is it?

Such attitudes have led some people to associate knowledge of the canon with elitism. (The term "elite music" is occasionally used.) Yet this notion is problematic, since nonelites may also enjoy classical music. Economics also complicates the matter, since elites are often wealthy. While it is true that classical music survives in part because affluent individuals help support symphony orchestras and opera companies, many people who enjoy classical music are far from wealthy, and many wealthy people have no interest in classical music. When we compare the price of a symphony ticket to the huge sums people may pay to see a rock or pop concert or a Broadway show such as Lin-Manuel Miranda's *Hamilton*, it becomes clear that neither elitism nor wealth is especially relevant to the appreciation of classical music.

The music of the Western European canon is beautiful, expressive, and inspiring. Many listeners respond to it on a gut level and no one can or should diminish this experience. Still, it is important to acknowledge certain questions regarding what scholars call *canon formation*. Who gets to decide which works deserve a place in the canon? Who determines which criteria should apply? Of interest here is how the canon has affected the music of Latin America. Given that the musical canon is a Western European creation, Latin America is clearly an outsider. As we've noted, some Latin American composers challenged the canon by asserting a non-European identity, writing music based on traditional idioms, national, regional, or traditional, whereas others have taken the canon as a point of reference. Several in this latter group, often considered worldly or sophisticated, gravitated toward a "Latin" sensibility, as detailed by the Uruguayan philosopher and essayist José Enrique Rodó (1871–1917), who saw such a sensibility as one of refinement and elegance.

As Rodó's ideas began to take hold in Latin America, a tug of war between nationalism and *cosmopolitanism* began. Whereas nationalism asserts identity, cosmopolitanism proposes that it is possible (indeed, desirable) to feel at home

Arielismo and Latin American Culture

Rodó set forth these ideas in a book called *Ariel*, published in 1900. Its title refers to a character in Shakespeare's *The Tempest*, known as a "New World drama" because it is set in the Americas. One character is Ariel, the sprite who comes to the aid of Prospero, a magician who is exiled on a remote island in the Americas. Ariel proffers enlightened advice and guards against Caliban, the monster who roams the island. Whereas Ariel is graceful and subtle, Caliban is inarticulate bulk. (Rodó actually equated the brutish Caliban with the United States, then bent on its mission of Manifest Destiny.) Accordingly, Latin American adherents of *arielismo* revered the European canon, especially as manifested in the art and music of France, Italy, and often Spain. Directly or indirectly, arielismo motivated much music and art.

ACTIVITY 8.3

Research the decades-long debate in Latin America that ensued over *arielismo*. After outlining as many sides of the debate as you can, take a position and defend it.

---

with cultures, perspectives, or forms of expression beyond the boundaries of one's own country. A cosmopolitan composer will choose international models, avoiding traditional idioms such as the malambo; similarly, a cosmopolitan composer will eschew Latin American instruments such as bongos or maracas so as to be considered a composer of the world. To be sure, that composer may occasionally wonder if his or her identity is being erased. Perhaps that individual will even try to write music that is both national and cosmopolitan. In all of these possibilities, an aesthetic position is at stake.

LATIN AMERICAN CLASSICAL MUSIC AND MARGINALIZATION

The Global North has long marginalized Latin American classical music, often pigeonholing it as folkloric, "colorful," or exotic. An episode from history underscores this point. In 1931, Theodore Roosevelt Jr. (son of President Theodore Roosevelt) was serving as governor of Puerto Rico. One day, he received a visit from some local musicians who wanted to establish a conservatory there so that Puerto Ricans could study classical music "according to the standards established in [other] countries" (Glasser 1995: 13). Governor Roosevelt was delighted to talk music with his visitors: he told them how much he enjoyed *música jíbara* and local instruments such as the cuatro and the güiro. Politely the musicians repeated their request. But the governor seemed not to hear them, and instead continued to enthuse over traditional Puerto Rican music. Frustrated, the musicians left, and ultimately Roosevelt vetoed the measure to build the conservatory even though both the Puerto Rican House of Representatives and the Senate had approved it.

In fact, Latin American classical music has rarely figured in the curricula of music conservatories in the Global North, its colleges and universities, or its primary- and secondary-school music programs. Latin America's contributions in other arts are often ignored as well. The Latino author Ray Suarez describes his conversation with Ricardo Jiménez, a Puerto Rican teenager who advocated for a Puerto Rican studies course at his overcrowded high school in the Midwestern United States. The young activist told Suarez, "I found out that we [Puerto Ricans] have authors, that we have painters, that we have poets; I mean, we have all these things that I didn't know, that I never knew were in existence" (Suarez 2013: 206). To that list, Jiménez could have added a solid roster of classical composers, which from the twentieth century alone would include Roberto Sierra (b. 1953), Rafael Aponte-Ledée (b. 1938), Luis M. Álvarez (b. 1939), Ernesto Cordero (b. 1946), William Ortiz (b. 1947), Raymond Torres Santos (b. 1958), and more.

Happily, this situation is changing and nowadays more educational institutions are teaching Latin American classical music. We'll sample some of this music by studying an opera, a character piece for solo piano, a symphony, a chamber music work, a concerto, and an electroacoustic piece, classical genres that various Latin American composers have approached in their own way. We'll take into account aesthetic questions while, as always, considering the music in its cultural and historical context.

OPERA

In 1701, over a century before the colonies of New Spain began agitating for independence, an opera was produced in the Americas for the first time. This landmark event took place not in New York, Boston, or Philadelphia, but in Lima. In studying this opera, we encounter several instruments unfamiliar to many listeners today and discover how they enhance a tale of love, jealousy, and intrigue.

Defining Opera

What comes to mind when you think of opera? A sumptuous hall filled with elegantly dressed ladies and gentlemen—most of them gray-haired—sipping expensive champagne in the red-carpeted lobby at intermission? Perhaps you have never attended an opera but have heard that it involves watching strangely costumed men and women screaming at one another for hours in a foreign language, usually Italian, French, or German. Opera can certainly be these things. But nowadays many people who would otherwise avoid this genre are lining up at their local movie theaters to watch *Live from the Met*, which broadcasts in real time the current season of the Metropolitan Opera in New York City. Viewers hear not only the opera but interviews with the singers; they also catch a glimpse of the dressing rooms and the engineering feats that go into the stage machinery. As in foreign-language films, these broadcasts are subtitled, which is also the case if you are attending a live performance, where supertitles are projected above the stage. These words are from the opera script, called a *libretto* (Italian for "booklet"). Usually someone other than the composer writes the libretto although occasionally an opera composer creates both score and libretto.

Nowadays operas are often staged anachronistically, in a time or place other than what the composer intended or even could have imagined. For example, *Don Giovanni* by Wolfgang Amadeus Mozart (1756–91) is an adaptation of a play by the Spanish author Tirso de Molina (1581?–1648), *El burlador de Sevilla* (The Trickster of Seville); in both play and the opera, the protagonist seduces women, defying social norms of the day. Although *Don Giovanni* is often staged with the sets and costumes of the eighteenth century, a production in 1990 set the opera in late twentieth-century Spanish Harlem, an environment that of course could never have occurred to Mozart. The music proceeds exactly as it would with traditional staging. Operagoers debate whether this practice mocks the composer's conception or whether such anachronistic settings affirm the enduring meaning of these canonical works.

Many versions of the essential idea of opera—a sung play—have existed through history. Unlike musicals, which contain spoken dialogue, in an opera every line is sung. Closer to the musical is *operetta,* which is called *zarzuela* in the Spanish-speaking world and which also combines sung numbers and spoken dialogue. As discussed in chapter 6, religious dramas were especially popular in Spain. So were secular plays such as the *comedia,* along with the *entremés,* a short play inserted between the acts of a longer drama, and the less formal *tonadilla,* which often amounted to little more than an improvised skit. All of these genres were enhanced with singing, instrumental music, and dance. Music played during scene changes or to set a mood before the dialogue begins is called *incidental music* and can cement the story line much the way a film score does.

Opera as an independent genre dates from around 1600. It originated not in Spain but in Florence, Italy, where a group of authors, musicians, scientists, and philosophers sought a genre that would clearly communicate the text, obviously an important element in any work that purports to tell a story. Rather than obscure the text with polyphonic textures and elaborate melismas, opera would observe the natural rhythms of speech. Further, these Florentine intellectuals reasoned, if the accompaniment were restricted to one or two unobtrusive plucked or bowed instruments, the text would meet with little interference. Most early operas took as their subject matter Greek and Roman mythology, a topic familiar to many listeners of the era. Nonetheless, the uniformity of texture—speech-like singing with sparse accompaniment—came to seem rather dull, and composers gradually sought other ways to bring the words to life. Sometimes they would offset the long stretches of solo singing with instrumental passages or use a more ample orchestra or insert a chorus for variety. To provide contrast to the speech-like text setting, they composed sections of metered music, which the vocal soloist could enhance with a few ornaments. These artistic decisions changed over time, according to the aesthetic of the era.

A First for the Americas

The opera produced in 1701 in Lima was *La púrpura de la rosa* (The Blood of the Rose). An adaptation, it's based on a play written several decades earlier by the Spanish author Pedro Calderón de la Barca (1660–81), a major figure of the *siglo de oro* (Golden Age), a period when literature, art, and music flourished in Spain. The play deals with Roman mythology, although the gods interact with humans. Calderón may have been inspired by a painting, *Venus and Adonis*, which hung in one of the Spanish royal family's residences and which depicts Adonis, the handsome mortal who falls for Venus, the goddess of love.

La púrpura de la rosa was first produced in 1660 (in Spain) as a theatrical pageant to celebrate the marriage of the Spanish princess María Teresa to Louis XIV, the powerful French king. Their union solidified several borders and helped end the War of the Spanish Succession, in which France and Spain had united against other European powers. The Spanish composer Juan Hidalgo (1641–85), then employed at the court, composed the music. The Lima

Figure 8.2 *Venus and Adonis* by Paulo Veronese (1528–88), an Italian painter known for his large-scale scenes and dazzling colors.

Photo credit: Erich Lessing/Art Resource, NY.

production came about thanks to the Viceroy of Peru and Count of Monclova, Don Melchor de la Vega (1636–1705). He cut a colorful figure: having lost his right arm in battle and replaced it with one of silver, Don Melchor displayed both his personal wealth and the wealth of Peru, whose riches were widely known. (The Spanish expression "vale un perú"—it's worth a Peru—indicated high value.) The Lima *La púrpura de la rosa* was performed in honor of the birthday of Felipe V, who had recently ascended to the Spanish throne and who was the grandson of Louis XIV and María Teresa, whose wedding forty-one years earlier occasioned the first performance of the opera.

In light of his prestige, it's not surprising that Don Melchor engaged one of the most important composers in the colonies for this "first." Tomás Torrejón y Velasco (1644–1728) was born in Spain and began his career as a page at the Spanish court, where he took dancing and music lessons and attended the theater regularly, as any gentleman of that period would. At age twenty-two, he went to Peru and became the *maestro de capilla* (chapel master or main composer) at the Lima cathedral, an unusual honor for anyone not a member of the clergy. With *La púrpura de la rosa*, Torrejón y Velasco probably did not compose the score in the modern sense of the word, however. Certainly he wrote some of the music, but given the existing score by Juan Hidalgo, the Lima performance may well have used portions of it, although exactly how much is by Hidalgo and how much is by Torrejón y Velasco remains an open question. Such a situation, not uncommon in this period, resembles the creative collaboration common in film music, where the principal composer may or may not do all the orchestration or even write every note of the score.

Going to the Opera in Lima in 1701

What would it have been like to see the first opera in the Americas? If you frequented theatrical performances in that era, you would have known that the performance would likely start with a *loa,* a prologue to orient the audience and common in Golden Age theater. In *La púrpura de la rosa,* the loa is declaimed in the temple of the god Apollo, with three of the nine muses, the goddesses who represent various branches of arts and sciences, onstage. When Urania, the muse of astronomy and music, notes a new star in the heavens, Calliope, the muse of epic poetry, and Terpsichore, the muse of dance, join the conversation. Another voice, that of Time, introduces the fifth planet, Mars, as a "cause for splendor," which the chorus affirms as a symbol of Felipe V's accession to the throne, becoming "ruler of two worlds" (i.e., Spain and Spanish America). Fanfares, drums, and shouts of "¡Viva!" help set the festive mood as the loa concludes.

Mythological characters, with all their intrigues and rivalries, may seem distant to us today. (In fact, they are not that different from the superheroes of contemporary film, comics, and science fiction.) In 1701, you would likely have been familiar with Venus and Adonis, whose love story is complicated by the fact that Venus is already claimed by Mars, the god of war, who, predictably enough, is jealous of Adonis. In several scenes, Mars comes off as petty rather than godlike, and his sister, Belona, helps conceal his personal weaknesses. Rustic characters, called *villanos* in Spanish Golden Age theater, include the couple Celfa and Chato, who wisecrack about marriage and love, thus parodying the feelings between Venus and Adonis. The villanos also add a degree of slapstick, with Chato getting roughed up by a soldier at one point. A bevy of nymphs, nature-spirits in the form of young women, attend to Venus. Although Mars engineers Adonis's death, love ultimately triumphs, for Adonis's blood turns a white rose bright red and he and Venus are elevated to the heavens, with Adonis taking the form of a flower and Venus of the evening star.

You would also notice the preponderance of women onstage. Two all-female acting troupes combined forces for the performance such that even male roles, including Mars and the solider who beats up Chato, were taken by women. (Only the role of the male villano, Chato, was sung by a man.) Consequently, the voice ranges are generally high throughout the opera. From your seat in the audience, you would also appreciate moments of sheer theatricality, as in the scene immediately following the loa when a wild boar frightens Venus and her nymphs scatter. We hear Venus's cries for help offstage, preparing Adonis's entrance, in which he carries Venus in his arms, a gesture that anticipates their eventual union, although, at this point, neither knows the other's identity—Venus believes Adonis is a simple hunter and he has no idea that he has just rescued a goddess. You, as a knowledgeable audience member, would delight in their confusion.

Surely you would also admire the music of *La púrpura de la rosa*, whether in the dance song with a strong downbeat (called a *jácara*), the solo singing, the conversations among characters, or the choruses, such as those of the four nymphs, Flora, Libia, Cintia, and Clori, who tenderly keep watch over Adonis and Venus in the goddess's garden, all set to music.

La Púrpura de la Rosa and Early Music

In audio selection 8.1, Venus wanders in the mountains so that she can decide if and how Adonis will fit into her life. Although her nymphs accompany her out into the wild, she sends them away so that she may have solitude, a moment that is set musically to suggest a conversation in which people interrupt one another. Throughout the scene (indeed, throughout *La púrpura de la rosa*) the harp figures prominently, an instrument that, as noted above, was brought to Latin America by Europeans and has remained popular since the Conquest. Other instruments featured in the opera were played regularly in the seventeenth century but fell into disuse, as instrument technology changed in Europe. At the beginning of the twentieth century, however, scholars and performers became interested in re-creating the sound world of the medieval, Renaissance, and baroque periods and began recovering these "early music" instruments. Many also learned to play them, largely by studying treatises and instruction manuals of earlier centuries or by recovering old manuscripts, which scholars edited for modern performance after deciphering the older notation systems. Often educated guesswork is involved, since older music manuscripts don't always indicate which instruments should be played.

One such instrument is the *theorbo*, which has a curved back and is plucked. Another is the *viola da gamba*, a bowed instrument with sloped "shoulders" held between the legs ("gamba" means "leg" in Italian). The *violone* is a bigger and lower-pitched version of the viola da gamba, approximately the size of a modern string bass and therefore played standing up. Whatever points in common might exist between these instruments and those used in classical music today, it is a grave error to consider the viola da gamba a mere "forerunner" or "prototype" of the cello, or the violone of the string bass. Once as common as the violin and the piano are today, these older instruments open our ears to sonic possibilities of earlier times. Like the jarana, the requinto, the cuatro, the tres, and the charango, each has its own timbre and performance style. As you follow along with online audio guide 8.1, notice not only these timbres but the changes in musical texture and the relationship between language and music.

ACTIVITY 8.4

Recall a conversation of at least eight lines that you've had at some point today and write it down. (Don't be surprised if you find this difficult.) Then, pretend that this conversation is part of an opera. Although you don't have to determine every twist and turn of the overall plot, map out at least a story outline so that you have a clear conception of the characters engaged in this dialogue, that is, what sort of people they are, in what era they live, and what motivates their behavior. Write an adjective next to each line of dialogue indicating the mood you will assign to each utterance. Then, make notes on how you would set each line of dialogue to music. Will the characters interrupt one another? Hear one another out? Is all of the dialogue you write in your initial draft absolutely necessary or may some of it be struck? Will a chorus enter at any point? Keep notes on how you arrive at your artistic decisions. Then determine the musical setting, indicating what instruments you will use. If you are able, set your dialogue to music.

Latin American Opera over Time

Like ballet, opera can be very expensive to produce and in countries that lack government or private support for the arts, composers have little incentive to write operas that have only a small chance of ever being performed. In 1870, Antônio Carlos Gomes (1836–96) of Brazil composed the opera *Il Guarany* (The Guaraní Indian), an adaptation of the novel *O Guarani* by a contemporary, the Brazilian author Jose de Alencar (1829–77). The title of the opera is in Italian rather than Portuguese, according to the practice of the day. (It was also performed in Italy.) French and Italian, not Latin American languages, were generally considered "proper" languages for opera, resulting in incongruities such as *Le roi poète* (French for "The Poet King") of 1901 by the Mexican composer Gustavo Campa (1863–1934), which takes as its subject matter the fifteenth-century poet-king Nezahualcoyotl.

Of course, some operas are in Spanish, increasingly so during the twentieth century. Ginastera, for example, wrote several operas with Spanish libretti, including *Don Rodrigo* (1962), chosen to inaugurate the New York State Theater in Lincoln Center (now the David H. Koch Theater) in 1966. His next opera, *Bomarzo*, is about a sixteenth-century duke with various neuroses and was banned in Buenos Aires because of its sexual content. Both Chávez and Villa-Lobos wrote operas as well. Daniel Catán (1949–2011), born in Mexico and of Sephardic Jewish descent, was the first Mexican composer to have his operas performed in major venues in the United States. His *Florencia en el Amazonas* (Florencia in the Amazon) was inspired by the magical-realist style of Gabriel García Márquez. Latin American composers have also treated contemporary topics in opera. In 2014, Gabriela Ortiz of Mexico (b. 1964) completed *Únicamente la verdad* (Only the Truth), which is about drug traffickers on the US-Mexican border. Ortiz received a prestigious Guggenheim Fellowship to complete it, and because *Únicamente la verdad* is a videopera, it was nominated for a Grammy award.

CHARACTER PIECE

The character piece became popular in the nineteenth century, a time of creative freedom, new musical styles, and rapid social change. We consider this genre here in relation to Teresa Carreño (1853–1917) of Venezuela, a brilliant musician whose multifaceted career reveals some of the challenges women in classical music face.

Classical Music in the Nineteenth Century: A Place for Women?

During the nineteenth century, the influence of the aristocracy waned and, as democratic movements spread throughout Europe and the Americas, a growing middle class ensured large audiences for public concerts. Many musical instruments were transformed. For example, the piano of the eighteenth century had a light frame and thin strings made of soft iron or brass, whereas its nineteenth-century counterpart boasted a metal frame and tightly strung steel strings, allowing for greater volume. In large concert halls, performers dazzled their public, with piano recitals becoming especially popular. Some touring pianists achieved rock-star status for their *virtuosity,* the ability to meet all sorts of physical challenges while delivering a performance marked by a strong personality. Audiences often responded with enthusiasm, if not outright delirium. As for composers, they began writing music that was much freer than that of earlier periods, rejecting formal templates and experimenting with more complex harmonies.

Yet even in this age of newfound freedom, women seeking careers in classical music were restricted, as has been the case throughout history. Musically talented women had to confront society's general expectation that they shun public exposure and avoid competing with men. They also encountered music-specific constraints. For example, some instruments were regarded as unfeminine, such as brass and percussion, long associated with the military; woodwind instruments, which require contorting the facial muscles, were equally unacceptable. Even in the twentieth century many a girl was discouraged from learning the cello because it requires sitting in an "unladylike" position. Happily, several world-famous female cellists have debunked this nonsensical notion.

Of course, certain musical responsibilities were regularly entrusted to women, such as singing soprano or alto. Several women pursued successful careers in the performing arts, although their sex was often mentioned in reviews of their concerts. For example, if a female instrumentalist played particularly authoritatively, a critic might comment, "she plays like a man." Such rhetoric may be well intentioned but it says little about the musical performance and objectifies the woman. More overt discrimination has also hindered musical women: one of Europe's most prestigious orchestras admitted women into its ranks only in 1997, and today fewer than a dozen women conduct major symphony orchestras, a job that requires telling the players (many of whom are men) what to do.

Ironically, music was nonetheless considered an essential part of a woman's life in the nineteenth century, provided she did not make it her career. Middle- and upper-class women were expected to instill an atmosphere of refinement in their homes, perhaps by singing or playing the piano in the parlor, often to complement a delicious dinner that the guests had just enjoyed. Such women saw to it that their daughters took piano or singing lessons so that they might attract suitable husbands and create gracious homes of their own someday. Of course, women of lower social classes had no such opportunities although they might have sung to accompany their often tedious work. Nuns maintained their centuries-old tradition of performing religious music within the walls of the convent.

What if a woman wanted to compose? At least she could do so at home. Just as women completed novels and poetry in the attic or in the parlor, sometimes after a long day of domestic duties, women could write music in these same environments. Like their literary counterparts, women composers sometimes used male pseudonyms to publish their works.

Women Classical Composers in Latin America through the Nineteenth Century

When we trace the history of women making music in Latin America, Sor Juana Inés de la Cruz (1651–95), a nun in colonial Mexico, stands out. She took advantage of the fact that, for Catholic women, convent life was an alternative to marriage and bearing numerous children, and that it could be rich in spiritual gratification and professional opportunities such as teaching, music, and leadership positions. For Sor Juana, convent life meant nurturing her formidable intellect, along with some of her musical skills.

At the time of Sor Juana's death, in 1695, the demands of colonial life would have proved challenging to any aspiring musician, male or female. Even though music flourished in religious institutions and viceregal courts, ordinary people had less opportunity to hear live music. Orchestras were practically nonexistent and pianos, which had to be shipped from Europe, began arriving in Latin America only in the nineteenth century. Nonetheless, in the decades after independence several Latin American women began writing music, among

Sor Juana Inés de La Cruz: The Tenth Muse

In her youth, Juana Ramírez de Asbaje (Sor Juana's name at birth) received a solid education, unusual in an era when schooling for girls consisted of reading, simple math, and needlework. She also taught herself music and began composing. At age eighteen, when she entered a Jeronimite convent, she became Sor Juana Inés de la Cruz (Sister Juana Inés of the Cross). Because of her brilliance, her superiors gave her a good deal of latitude. She wrote polemical essays and poetry, with "Hombres necios" (Small-Minded Men) one of her best-known poems. Of musical significance are her texts for numerous *villancicos,* which she did not set to music herself, although other composers have done so. Recent composers, such as Max Lifchitz of Mexico (b. 1947), have also set Sor Juana's poetry to music. She was so distinguished that she was known as the "tenth muse," an allusion to the nine muses of Greek mythology. Due to an outbreak of the plague, she died in her early forties.

Watch the movie *Yo, la peor de todas* (I, the Worst of All) by the Argentine director María Luisa Bemberg, released in 1990. From what angle does it depict the life of Sor Juana Inés de la Cruz? Early in the film, Fray Luis de León and Santa Teresa of Ávila are mentioned. Identify these two figures. Also, who was Descartes and why would Church authorities be concerned about a nun reading his works? Then comment on the music. How does the director balance diegetic and nondiegetic music in the film? What plot points or emotions are highlighted with music and what sort of music is used?

Figure 8.3 *Sor Juana Inés de la Cruz* by Miguel Cabrera (1695–1768), shown in religious garb alone in her study.

Photo credit: Schalkwijk/Art Resource, NY.

them Isadora Zegers of Chile (1803–69), Modesta Sanjinés of Bolivia (1832–87), Angela Peralta of Mexico (1845–83), and Chiquinha Gonzaga of Brazil (1847–1935). We can consider them the first generation of Latin American women composers.

Teresa Carreño: Virtuosity and Versatility

Knowing of the challenges women in classical music face makes Teresa Carreño's accomplishments all the more remarkable. She was born in Caracas and was a musical prodigy, the label given to a child so gifted that it almost seems that no instruction is necessary. In fact, Carreño did take lessons early on with her father, who was both a musician and a politician. But mainly she developed on her own, becoming a pianist, an opera singer, and a composer. Her three-pronged talent was (and still is) extremely rare in a field such as classical music, in which most artists specialize in a single area.

At age nine, Carreño and her family left Venezuela, since political instability there was making life difficult for her father. They went first to New York City, where she made her debut, and then to Boston, where she also performed. In both cities, music critics were most impressed with "little Miss Carreño," as they called her. In the fall of 1863, she even performed at the White House, where President Lincoln momentarily set aside his cares over the American Civil War to applaud the ten-year-old artist. After spending several years in Paris, Carreño, now an adult, made New York her home, although she constantly toured the Americas, Europe, Africa, Australia, and Russia. Most often she performed as a pianist but sometimes she appeared as an opera singer.

Carreño defied convention in other ways. Her personal life was complicated (she married four times) and she was also an entrepreneur, managing her own opera company, which she took to Venezuela in 1887. She composed around eighty works, many of which are in virtuosic style.

Defining the Character Piece

Audio selection 8.2, "Le printemps" (Spring), is a character piece. (At this time, many publishers believed that titles in French would sell better, given France's cultural capital worldwide.) In some ways, the genre exemplifies nineteenth-century music. The character piece was not confined by any particular form, thus allowing composers free rein for their imaginations. It could be extroverted, meditative, mercurial, passionate, or lyrical. Composers eager to show off their virtuosity would write character pieces that were brilliant and technically challenging, sure to please an audience.

We find several of these traits in "Le printemps." As shown in online audio guide 8.2, one section follows another, seemingly at the composer's whim. Its virtuosic requirements include wide leaps, which require the pianist to play in

Figure 8.4 Teresa Carreño, piano
prodigy, in 1861.
Wikimedia.com.

quick succession very high notes on the keyboard and then very low notes (or
vice versa). Another challenge is consecutive octaves, that is, playing one note
with the thumb and then the next instance of the same note with the fifth finger, difficult to do at top speed, as Carreño requires in "Le printemps." Also, the
rapid passagework has to be perfectly precise since stumbling onto the wrong
key can throw off an entire phrase. Carreño's piece, which is modeled on the
multisectional parlor waltz (see chapter 6), is marked "Allegro brillante," which
means "lively, brilliant." We can easily imagine her performing "Le printemps"
with great aplomb, perhaps as an encore after one of her demanding recitals.

In 1883, Carreño was commissioned to write a piece honoring Simon
Bolívar, which she then performed in Caracas. In 1973, over fifty years after her
death, construction began on the Teatro Teresa Carreño in Caracas, which was
inaugurated in 1985 and which welcomes artists from all over the world.

Latin American Women in Classical Music over Time

Among women active in classical music today are the composers Tania León of Cuba (b. 1943), Jocy de Oliveira of Brazil (b. 1936), Gabriela Lena Frank of US-Peruvian heritage (b. 1972), and Gabriela Ortíz of Mexico, whose video opera we discussed above. The late Graciela Paraskevaídis of Argentina (1940–2017) was an important and innovative composer in addition to being an incisive social critic. Several Latin American women enjoy international reputations as performers of classical music, although achieving recognition as a virtuoso is quite a different matter today than it was in Carreño's time. Performers aspiring to international careers achieve renown by winning international competitions, nerve-racking events comparable to the Olympics. Like Carreño, the pianist Martha Argerich of Argentina (b. 1941) was a piano prodigy, and at age sixteen she was winning prestigious international competitions. Known for her electric interpretations and awe-inspiring technique, Argerich has received several Grammy awards.

SYMPHONY

One of the monuments of classical music is the *symphony,* a composition for orchestra. (Note that in ordinary usage we sometimes say "symphony orchestra" to denote the ensemble; in colloquial English we also might say, "Let's go to the symphony," that is, a concert by a symphony orchestra.) The symphony we'll study here shows what a twentieth-century Mexican composer can do with this traditional Western European genre.

Defining the Symphony

Like all other genres we've studied, the symphony has changed over time. In the early eighteenth century, symphony and opera were linked. A short instrumental work would be played just before the opera began, largely to quiet down the audience. Usually consisting of three parts or *movements,* such a piece was called a *sinfonia,* Italian for "symphony." In hushing up the audience, it was less than effective—often everyone kept chattering—but by 1800, the symphony had become a longer and more serious affair, usually consisting of four movements. No longer mere background noise, the genre became a testing ground for all number of experiments in form and instrumentation.

The symphony orchestra includes representatives of all the instrument families—strings, woodwinds, brass, percussion—which perform in sections (i.e., the cello section or the clarinet section). Each section has a *principal,* a player who helps coordinate his or her section. To become a principal in a major symphony orchestra (indeed, to play in such an orchestra in any capacity) is a tremendous achievement, as hundreds of extremely talented players compete for a single position.

The strings, known as the "heart of the orchestra," are the most numerous. The violins are divided into two sections, first and second, each playing an independent but complementary part. The leader of the second violins is the *principal second* whereas the leader of the first violins is the *concertmaster.* (Women in this position are also called concertmaster.) There is nothing inferior about playing second violin, despite the colloquial expression "I won't play second fiddle," which means "I won't accept a second-rate position." Violas and cellos have twelve and ten players respectively, and string basses eight. The woodwind and brass sections have far fewer and, depending on the score, extra instruments may be necessary, such as special percussion, additional brass for especially loud pieces, or harp. Sometimes the piano is used in the percussion section, as in Ginastera's *Estancia.*

Rituals of the Modern Symphony

The modern symphony orchestra involves a series of rituals. Players and audiences take for granted the dress code, with most professional orchestra musicians wearing black (long, simple dresses or pants for women and tuxedos for men) since a variety of styles and colors would distract the audience from listening to the music. Another ritual concerns the concertmaster, who must fine-tune the different sections of the orchestra minutes before the performance begins. First, while the concertmaster is backstage, players warm up onstage, often making a tremendous cacophony since everyone is playing whatever they like. (This warm-up can be intriguing to listen to.) When the concertmaster walks onstage, the players fall silent. The concertmaster then signals to the oboist, who sounds the note "A," to which the various sections take turns tuning. (The oboe is a point of reference because it is among the more difficult instruments to tune.) After all are satisfied, the concertmaster sits down. Next the *conductor* or *music director* enters and proceeds to the podium. (The terms are often used interchangeably, although a music director tends to assume more administrative responsibility.) The players watch attentively as the conductor calls them to attention and readies them to play the first note. After a short silence, all begin, at the conductor's signal.

As the orchestra plays, the audience listens quietly, without whispering or flipping through the concert program. Cell phones should be turned off and put away, since even quietly looking at the screen can distract others in the darkened hall. Listeners refrain from clapping between movements, saving their applause for the end of a multimovement work. Perhaps observing these rules sounds utterly painful? In fact, any communal event sustains its own rituals. People used to waving their arms and shouting until they are hoarse at football games but who then decide to attend a tennis match find out soon

Figure 8.5 The Mexican conductor Alondra de la Parra acknowledges applause in this photo from 2014.

Steven Pisano/Wikimedia.com.

enough (perhaps with some embarrassment) that quiet is expected. Every collective human activity maintains unwritten rules that may seem arbitrary to outsiders but that the community takes for granted.

Although it might seem that the conductor does nothing but wave his or her arms, a skilled conductor must possess a working knowledge of every instrument in the orchestra and know the entire score so as to cue the players (indicate to them when it is time to play). The conductor must also arrive at a unifying conception of the piece—what the tempo and dynamics should be, how to delineate the musical form, which instruments to bring out and which to keep in the background—and convince the players of this conception in rehearsal. Nowadays, conductors are generally associated with a particular orchestra and those who direct major ensembles find themselves booked up years in advance for international guest-conducting, jet-setting superstars not unlike sought-after soccer players.

Latin Americans on the Podium

Among the many Latin Americans that have distinguished themselves as conductors is Guillermo Espinosa (1905–90) of Colombia, who began his career with the Colombian National Symphony but moved to Washington, DC, in the 1950s to direct the music division of the Organization of American States (OAS). Eduardo Mata (1942–95) of Mexico conducted various Mexican orchestras and also the Dallas Symphony. A conducting superstar is Gustavo Dudamel (b. 1981) of Venezuela (figure 1.5). He is a product of *El Sistema,* the network of symphony orchestras and music education programs in Venezuela that provides music instruction to disadvantaged children and turns out some world-class performers. Dudamel is music director of the prestigious Los Angeles Philharmonic and guest-conducts in Venezuela and worldwide. One of the few women to lead a major orchestra today is Alondra de la Parra (b. 1980), who was born in New York but moved to Mexico when she was two. In 2015, she was appointed the conductor of the Queensland Symphony Orchestra, one of Australia's most important orchestras. Another famous Latin American conductor was Carlos Chávez, discussed below.

ACTIVITY 8.6

Watch the DVD *Tocar y luchar* (To Play and to Fight). How did the Venezuelan Youth Orchestra and El Sistema come about? Who was José Antonio Abreu? How valid is the idea that an orchestra can bring about social change and interpersonal growth? Can the same argument be made on behalf of other activities?

Musical Infrastructure

A symphony orchestra depends on well-trained players, which in turn implies a solid music program in the community, including early training, in the absence of which musicians from other countries or regions will have to be enticed to relocate. Unless players are paid a decent salary, including benefits, they will need to hold other jobs to supplement their incomes, which may dilute their energies and play havoc with their personal lives given the long rehearsals, late hours, and weekend performances that are part of any symphony musician's professional commitments. A concert hall must be maintained and an administrative structure established for business-related matters. All these things are part of a *musical infrastructure.*

Over history, Latin American symphonic composers have faced significant challenges in infrastructure. Throughout much of the nineteenth and twentieth centuries, many conservatories were understaffed or dilapidated and a lack of government or private support made it difficult (if not impossible) to maintain orchestras. Likewise, the absence of a public able to purchase tickets threatens any aspiring ensemble. The fact that so many Latin American conductors, composers, and performers have overcome these obstacles is a tribute to their tenacity and creative powers. Indeed, a "golden age" occurred in the first half of the twentieth century, when a great many orchestral works were composed in Latin America.

Selected Latin American Symphony Composers

The composers below wrote pieces with the word "symphony" in the title. Many additional composers, from these and other Latin American countries, wrote other pieces for orchestra.

ARGENTINA

Alberto Williams (1862–1952)
Eduardo García Mansilla (1871–1930)
José María Castro (1892–1964)
Juan José Castro (1895–1968)
Washington Castro (1909–2004)
Alberto Ginastera (1916–83)

BRAZIL

Heitor Villa-Lobos (1887–1959)
Oscar Lorenzo Fernândez (1897–1948)
Mozart Camargo Guarnieri (1907–93)
Cláudio Santoro (1919–89)
César Guerra-Peixe (1914–93)

MEXICO

José Rolón (1876–1945)
Arnulfo Miramontes (1882–1960)
Candelario Huízar (1883–1970)
María Teresa Prieto (1896–1982)
Julián Carrillo (1875–1965)
Carlos Chávez (1899–1978)
Luis Sandi (1905–96)
Lan Adomián (1905–79)
Daniel Ayala (1908–75)
José Pablo Moncayo (1912–58)

Blas Galindo (1910–93)
Salvador Contreras (1910–82)

URUGUAY

Héctor Tosar (1923–2002)

PARAGUAY

Florentín Giménez (b. 1925)

PERU

Celso Garrido-Lecca (b. 1928)

COLOMBIA

José María Ponce de Léon (1846–82)
Guillermo Uribe Holguín (1880–1971)

CHILE

Enrique Soro (1884–1954)
Domingo Santa Cruz (1899–1987)
Juan Orrego-Salas (b. 1919)
Gustavo Becerra (1925–2010)

CUBA

Ignacio Cervantes (1847–1905)
José Ardévol (1911–81, born in Spain)
Argeliers León Pérez (1918–91)
Julián Orbón (1925–91, born in Spain)
Aurelio de la Vega (b. 1925)

PANAMA

Roque Cordero (1917–2008)

Carlos Chávez: International Mexican

One "golden age" composer was Carlos Chávez. Born in Aguascalientes, Mexico, at the turn of the twentieth century, he studied piano formally but never took lessons in musical composition, preferring instead to pore over the scores of other composers, past and present. As a young man, Chávez visited Europe with the idea of studying there but, after several months, he decided to return home. In Mexico, he taught at the conservatory, which he directed for a time, and also conducted the Orquesta Sinfónica de México (Symphonic Orchestra of Mexico, or OSM). He often visited the United States, where both his compositions and his conducting were enthusiastically applauded.

Chávez composed six symphonies, of which the second, his *Sinfonía India* (Indian Symphony), is the best known. Composed in 1935, it pays homage to the Mexican Indian heritage. Although it might seem inconsistent or misguided to honor indigenous peoples with a genre so rooted in the Western European canon, Chávez made three principal decisions in *Sinfonía India*. First, he modified the European tradition by writing a one-movement work, employing changes of texture and tempo in internal sections for variety. Next, he used indigenous melodies for some of his themes, which he could access either through fieldwork or from *transcriptions* of Indian music notated by scholars who had listened to native musicians. As you'll hear in audio selection 8.3, some of these themes, whether Chávez's own or native, consist of a few notes that are extended through repetition. The native themes in *Sinfonía India* represent the Cora and Seri peoples, of Nayarit and Sonora, respectively.

Finally, Chávez used native instruments. These included the *teponaztli* (a two-keyed xylophone), the *huehuetl* (a large drum), and the *grijutian* (a string of deer hooves). He also used the *tenebari*, the butterfly cocoon rattles discussed in chapter 6. A practical man, Chávez recognized that few orchestras would own indigenous instruments, so he devised several alternatives, such as using a normal xylophone instead of the teponaztli and a string of wooden beads for the deer hooves. As shown in online audio guide 8.3, other percussion instruments in *Sinfonía India* include a single maraca, claves, cymbal, various drums, and güiro (sound link 3.11). In all, four percussionists are required.

The *Sinfonía India* over Time

Chávez composed the *Sinfonía India* not in his native country but during one of his extended stays in New York City, where it also premiered in 1936. With any composition, the *premiere* (first performance) is critical. Will the public like the work and want to hear it again? What will the music critics have to say? In the 1930s and 1940s, many radio stations such as NBC (National Broadcast-

Figure 8.6 The Mexican composer Carlos Chávez in a photo taken in 1937 by
the US author and photographer Carl Van Vechten.
Wikimedia.com.

ing Company) and CBS (Columbia Broadcasting System) maintained symphony orchestra and, in January 1936, Chávez himself conducted the work
with the CBS Symphony on a radio broadcast, reaching thousands of listeners.
Critics and public were delighted and the *Sinfonía India* has occupied a place of
honor in Latin American symphonic music ever since. In 2010, it was performed by the Chicago Symphony Orchestra, one of the most prestigious
ensembles today, to celebrate the two hundredth anniversary of the beginning
of the war for Mexican independence.

CHAMBER MUSIC

Chamber music involves a small group of musicians, each playing a separate part. Because of its intimate nature, chamber music can resemble a conversation, a phenomenon we'll consider in the chamber work by Heitor Villa-Lobos discussed below.

Defining Chamber Music

Think again of the symphony orchestra and the distribution of instruments into sections. Now imagine just a few sections—say, clarinet, oboe, flute—with only one player per section. Then eliminate the conductor. The result will be a much reduced group of players, with each individual responsible solely for his or her part. In other words, no one can "hide" in the sounds produced by the section as a whole, but must play at the level of a virtuoso soloist while also listening carefully to the rest of the ensemble.

Any combination of instruments is possible in chamber music. The following standard formats have evolved over time:

- string quartet: first and second violin, viola, cello (four players total)
- woodwind quintet: flute, clarinet, oboe, French horn, bassoon (five players total)
- brass quintet: two trumpets, French horn, trombone, tuba (five players total)

Of these, the string quartet is perhaps the most common. Quartet players must find ways to blend the individual yet similar timbres of their instruments while also creating variety and playing precisely in tune. Composers who tackle this difficult medium often develop new and bold ideas about musical style, thanks to the challenges it presents.

The piano often figures in chamber music since it can provide harmonic support. Note that when the word "piano" is paired with the word "trio" or "quartet" it signifies participation with other instruments. Some common chamber-music genres with piano include:

- piano trio: violin, cello, and piano (three players total)
- piano quartet: violin, viola, cello, piano (four players total)
- piano quintet: first and second violin, viola, cello, piano (five players total)
- duo: any instrument with piano, including another piano (two players total)

In each of these formats, the most typical distribution for chamber music prevails (one player per part). One exception exists, however, namely, the chamber orchestra, which is simply a reduced orchestra. Composers also write chamber music for voices and small ensembles, a trend that was especially common during the twentieth century. Music scored for voice and piano has proved popular in many historical periods and in many contexts, as have ensembles of one

The String Quartet in Latin America

Revueltas, Ginastera, and Villa-Lobos all composed string quartets, as have several other Latin American composers. One well-known performing ensemble is Cuarteto Latinoamericano (Latin American Quartet), founded in Mexico City in 1981. The two violinists and the cellist are brothers. (Their names are Saúl, Arón, and Álvaro Bitrán; the violist is Javier Montiel.) For a time, they were the quartet-in-residence at the Carnegie Mellon University in Pittsburgh, Pennsylvania. Now the ensemble performs all over the world and has recorded on several labels. In 2012, it won the Latin Grammy for its recording of music by the Brazilian composer Francisco Mignone (1897–1986). The Cuarteto Latinoamericano has also commissioned guitar quintets (i.e., guitar + string quartet) from well-known composers such as Gabriela Lena Frank. Besides bringing Latin American chamber music to worldwide attention, the quartet is committed to teaching and organizes chamber music workshops throughout the Americas.

singer per part in vocal quartets (soprano, alto, tenor, bass), sextets, and other combinations.

Heitor Villa-Lobos: Brazilian Modernist

Born in Rio de Janeiro in 1887, Villa-Lobos studied the cello with his father. He then played in cinema orchestras for silent films, which, in the absence of a soundtrack, required live music. Villa-Lobos soon discovered his natural fluency in composition and eventually turned out approximately one thousand pieces. In 1915, in Rio de Janeiro, he organized a debut concert, which featured his own works. Critics excoriated his music, however, complaining that it was too dissonant and radical, breaking with past norms. In other words, Villa-Lobos was too closely tied to *modernism.*

What, exactly, did this attack mean? Although "modern" is a common enough word, it's rich in meaning and variants. For example, *modernity* and *modernism* are not the same thing. Modernity is usually understood as one of the fruits of industrialization, rooted in objectivity, rationality, and science. Many scholars take the mid-nineteenth century as a starting point for modernity, which saw the rise of technology, a break with rural life in favor of industrial urban societies, and a privileging of science over religion. Its origins were largely Western European. Modernism, on the other hand, is an aesthetic position. Modernist artists, musicians, writers, and dancers embraced conflict, upheaval, and change. They broke with the past, separating themselves from tradition. Composers rejected previously established forms, disrupted harmonic expectations of tension and resolution, and in some cases abandoned

Figure 8.7 Heitor Villa-Lobos during one of his many visits to New York City in March 1959, a few months before his death.

Jack Harris/APimages.com.

harmony altogether so that an entire composition might consist of nothing but *dissonances* (discordant combinations of sounds). Often a modernist composition lacks a melody that can be easily grasped, frustrating those in the public who appreciate a "good tune."

Notice that we have essentially defined modernism as an attitude rather than as a coherent style. After 1900, when this aesthetic ferment was beginning to intensify, so many artists started pursuing so many different directions at once that no one style was discernible. This was when a plethora of -isms arose—futurism, primitivism, serialism, and expressionism, to name just a few—evincing fragmentation rather than unity of purpose. As a result, it is rather simplistic to call modernism a "style" even if the label "modernist" is a convenient way of designating much of the music composed after 1900.

Also around 1900, numerous artists and musicians began to pen manifestos in which they would explain, sometimes quite vociferously, the premises of this or that new style, collectively justifying themselves with unprecedented verbiage and theoretical arguments. As artists and musicians experimented with ever-greater boldness, audiences increasingly expected to be shocked if they attended a concert or an art exhibit. To be sure, in previous periods artists and musicians had often felt misunderstood by the general public. But modernism created such an unprecedented rift between artist and the public that anything seemed possible. In 1913, at the Paris premiere of *The Rite of Spring,* a ballet by the Russian composer Igor Stravinsky (1882–1971), the audience was so incensed by the revolutionary choreography and the bizarre sounds emitted by the enormous orchestra that a riot broke out in the theater. This notoriety only helped Stravinsky, whose innovative style was admired by many Latin American classical composers.

Villa-Lobos's debut concert may not have caused a riot—critics simply said nasty things about his music—but it marked him as an aesthetic radical, and in 1922, he participated in the Semana de Arte Moderna (Week of Modern Art). This series of lectures, readings, concerts, and exhibits by Brazilians prominent in the arts took place in São Paulo, Brazil, and it sought nothing less than to define Brazilian art for the future. Historians consider it a turning point for the arts in Brazil. In true modernist spirit, the academics and artists who gathered in São Paulo preached no single aesthetic. They did, however, advocate upheaval and change. (Significantly, the event coincided with the centennial of Brazilian independence.) Throughout the week, canvasses by the Brazilian artists Anita Malfatti (1889–1964), Emiliano Di Cavalcanti (1897–1976), and Vicente de Rego Monteiro (1899–1970) hung in the Teatro Municipal. Many *paulistas* (residents of São Paulo) were scandalized by their bold colors and formal freedom. As for the musical portion of the Week of Modern Art, Villa-Lobos dominated, with many of his works performed, including several pieces of chamber music.

Villa-Lobos, Vargas, and Bach

After the Week of Modern Art ended, Villa-Lobos took off for Paris, where he spent most of the 1920s. Mainly, he secured performances of his music. Like Stravinsky's *Rite of Spring,* some of Villa-Lobos's orchestral works are noisy and dissonant, involving a gargantuan percussion section. But in 1930, the year Getúlio Vargas came to power in Brazil, Villa-Lobos returned to his native land, where he remained the rest of his life. Almost immediately, his style became less dissonant and more melodious. He also found that smaller numbers of traditional instruments suited his purposes. In changing his style, Villa-Lobos still explored a wide range of approaches, however. For example, during one of his many visits to the United States he composed a piano piece by sketching the New York City skyline on a piece of graph paper and then assigning pitches that corresponded to the heights of the different buildings. Not surprisingly, he called it *New York Skyline.* He also tried his hand at film music and even wrote a musical. Eventually he came to see that he did not have to shock all the time. Some scholars have linked this aesthetic shift to the position of prominence he suddenly enjoyed in the Vargas administration as superintendent of music, a job that required him to promote traditional Brazilian music.

During this period, Villa-Lobos began the series of works for which he is best known today. Like all classically trained musicians, he deeply admired the music of Johann Sebastian Bach, the eighteenth-century European composer who wrote in nearly all the genres of his day and who was especially known for his mastery of polyphonic texture. Villa-Lobos believed—rather fancifully— that Bach's music shared many traits with Brazilian traditional music. By highlighting Brazil, Villa-Lobos upheld Vargas's quest for cultural symbols that could unite Brazil; by weaving in hints of Bach's music, Villa-Lobos maintained his credibility as a cosmopolitan composer conversant with the Western European canon. He wrote a series of nine works for different combinations of instruments, which he titled *Bachianas brasileiras.* The Portuguese title is difficult to translate literally, but "Bach in Brazil" more or less suffices. (Musicians always refer to the piece by using the Portuguese title.) Some of the *Bachianas* are for orchestra, some are for solo instruments, and others are for various chamber ensembles.

In *Bachianas brasileiras* no. 5, audio selection 8.4 Villa-Lobos returned to his first instrument, the cello. He then multiplied it by eight and added a soprano, for a total of nine chamber musicians, an unusual combination that, moreover, presents several compositional challenges. Not the least of these was how to create timbral variety, given the homogeneous sound of the eight cellos. Villa-Lobos solved this problem by asking the cellists to alternate *arco* (playing with the bow) and *pizzicato* (plucking the string), the latter in imitation of a Brazilian guitar technique called *ponteio,* a picked style. The soprano soloist sings a wide range of pitches. Sometimes Villa-Lobos requires her to sing very softly on high notes, something that is extremely difficult to do. In the first part, she sings only the syllable "Ah," which is called *vocalise* style. In the middle section (B), however, she breaks into articulate speech to describe a beautiful sunset; then, when the A section returns, she returns to vocalise style but now hums, as if in a dream. Throughout, the gentle arcs of the melodic line and delicate pizzicato affirm that Villa-Lobos, the strident modernist, has been tamed. Follow along with online audio guide 8.4 to hear these details.

Vocal Chamber Music in Latin America over Time

Among twentieth-century composers in Latin America, Villa-Lobos is a leader in vocal chamber music. Besides *Bachianas brasileiras* no. 5, he composed *Choros* no. 3 for clarinet, bassoon, saxophone, three French horns, trombone, and male voices that sing indigenous texts, specifically from the Paresi of the Brazilian state of Mato Grosso. (In addition to the nine-work *Bachianas* series,

Villa-Lobos composed a series of *Choros,* which take as a point of departure the Brazilian urban genre *choro,* a serenade that traditionally emphasized flute and *cavaquinho,* the small ukulele-like instrument mentioned in chapter 3.) Another vocal chamber work by Villa-Lobos is his *Quarteto simbôlico* (Symbolic Quartet) for flute, saxophone, harp, celesta (a keyboard instrument), and female voices. Both date from the 1920s, as do Chávez's *Tres hexágonos* (Three Hexagons), for voice and piano on texts by Carlos Pellicer; a sequel called *Otros tres hexágonos* (Three Other Hexagons) followed. Ginastera tested the medium of vocal chamber music with his *Cantos del Tucumán* (Songs of Tucumán), scored for flute, violin, harp, percussion, and a soprano voice. (Tucumán is a province in northwest Argentina.) More recent composers include Roberto Sierra (b. 1953) born in Puerto Rico but living in the United States. In 1999, Sierra composed *Cancionero Sefardí* (Sephardic Songbook) for soprano (or tenor), flute, clarinet, violin, cello, and piano. Paul Desennes of Venezuela (b. 1959) wrote *Cantata Maqroll* for tenor, flute, soprano saxophone, violin, cello, and piano in 2003. In 2014, Pablo Ortiz of Argentina but resident in the United States (b. 1956) wrote *Garden Songs,* scored for soprano and string trio. As Ortiz's work shows, not all Latin Americans set Spanish or Portuguese texts. In 1973, the Brazilian composer Cláudio Santoro (1919–89) wrote a piece for vocal quartet and piano on a text by the German playwright Bertolt Brecht.

CONCERTO

In *Canciones de Jara* (Songs of Jara), the Venezuelan composer Ricardo Lorenz (b. 1961) combines the protest songs of the nueva canción artist Víctor Jara with a classical genre, the *concerto.* Although the full title of the piece is *Canciones de Jara: Concerto for Viola and Orchestra Inspired by Songs of Víctor Jara,* we'll refer to it here simply as *Canciones de Jara.*

Defining the Concerto

The word "concerto" can be understood in two ways: (1) to compete, in its Italian translation, or (2) to cohere, in its Latin translation. Since a concerto normally sets a solo instrument against a large ensemble, anyone composing in this genre will want to balance these parameters. When should the soloist stand out (compete) against the rest of the ensemble? When should he or she blend in (cohere)? Over history, composers have taken various approaches.

Composers began writing instrumental concertos in the early part of the eighteenth century, using a small orchestra mainly consisting of strings, which they offset with a group of three or four instrumentalists (instead of an individual soloist). By the late eighteenth century, it was more common for a concerto to feature a single soloist. A concerto generally contained three movements, with the two outer movements at a lively tempo and a slow second movement. During the nineteenth century, the age of the virtuoso, concertos showcased the performer's technical skills, although of course many composers and performers were equally interested in the music's expressive capacity. Composers of the twentieth and twenty-first centuries have continued to write concertos, some challenging existing forms and styles in true modernist fashion and others taking a more traditional approach.

The Viola as Soloist

In range and size, the viola is between the violin and the cello. When people try to describe the viola's timbre, they resort to adjectives such as "dark," "rich," or "velvety." Certainly its sound is unlike that of any other stringed instrument. Yet the viola is used as a solo instrument less frequently than the violin or the cello and is generally assigned one of the inner parts, whether in the symphony orchestra or in chamber music. This status has led to a number of jokes about the viola and violists. In one, a man goes to the doctor for a checkup, who pronounces him in reasonably good health. "You mean I'm as fit as a fiddle?" the man asks. "Not quite," replies the doctor. "You're as fit as a viola." Given the compelling timbre of their instrument, violists can easily laugh this kind of thing off. A handful of composers have written viola concertos to showcase these characteristics. Like other string players, violists have many expressive devices at their disposal, including sliding from one pitch to another or adjusting the speed of their *vibrato,* a slight shaking of the left hand that increases the intensity of a pitch, analogous to vibrations of the vocal cords.

Lorenz wrote *Canciones de Jara* in 2010, by then having moved from his native country to the United States. The work came about when Lorenz received a commission from one of the best violists in the world, the Chilean-born Roberto Díaz (b. 1965), then principal violist with the celebrated Philadelphia Orchestra. Delighted to fulfill Díaz's request, Lorenz considered various ways to approach the viola. He thought back to the 1970s, when, as a boy in Venezuela, he would listen to Jara's songs playing on his sister's turntable. Their beauty, variety, and inspiring social message all impressed the young Lorenz. But he was equally struck by Jara's performance style, his direct and dramatic delivery. Lorenz compared the intensity and nuance of Díaz's playing to Jara's singing and realized that Díaz and his viola could bridge the world of the classical concerto and Jara's protest songs. (Díaz, although Chilean, was unfamiliar with Jara's songs, since he was raised in Atlanta.)

Lorenz chose four of Jara's songs on which to base his concerto, planning a total of four movements. The songs include the hopeful "Aquí me quedo" and the desperate "Preguntas por Puerto Montt," in which Jara raged over the murder of squatters, both discussed in chapter 7. The other two songs are equally famous. "Te recuerdo Amanda" (I Remember You, Amanda) describes the experience of Amanda, a woman who loves a factory worker, Manuel, who is one day disappeared. "Canción del minero" (Song of the Miner) paints a dire picture of the miner's lot, which includes backbreaking labor in unsafe conditions while CEOs and multinational companies profit from his efforts.

Musical Quotation and *Canciones de Jara*

We might expect Lorenz to weave into his score the actual melodies of Jara's songs, since at least some listeners would recognize them. This practice, called *musical quotation,* has a long tradition. As we've seen, Chávez, in his *Sinfonía India,* quoted native melodies. Sometimes composers quoted national anthems in the midst of a symphony. Villa-Lobos took this approach in his Third Symphony, which he finished in 1919, just after World War I ended and in which the Brazilian navy participated. In the final movement, Villa-Lobos depicts a battle by quoting not only the Brazilian national anthem but the British and French national anthems as well. Musical quotation raises some interesting questions. Whereas the Brazilian national anthem might be entirely obvious to Brazilians, other listeners might not get it. Does failure to recognize the quoted material affect the listening experience? If the quoted material *is* recognized, what does it mean? In Villa-Lobos's symphony, the intention is clear: Brazil is on the side of the Allies in World War I, which included the British and the French, although, in other compositions, quotations are less clear. In short, by using musical quotation the composer adds a level of meaning that invites interpretation. As you might imagine, it can also spark lawsuits.

In three of the four movements of *Canciones de Jara,* Lorenz avoids direct quotation. Rather, he takes each song as a point of departure for mood, captured in the dialogue between the viola solo and the orchestra and in accordance with the premises of the classical concerto. As Lorenz himself notes, the songs "provide a general narrative framework and a particular melodic character" to each movement, such that the viola effectively acts as Jara's voice (Lorenz 2011). The viola conveys tenderness in "Te acuerdo Amanda" (movement 1), bitterness in "Preguntas por Pedro Montt" (movement 2), and hope in "Aquí me quedo" (movement 3). To be sure, in "Aqui me quedo," Lorenz highlights the "narrative framework" by conveying the political tension of the moment: he inserts a siren into the orchestral texture, a sound we associate with street demonstrations.

It is only in the final movement, "Canción del minero," that we hear a direct quotation. As the viola riffs on the basic materials of "Jara's song (audio selection 8.5a)," the music trudges along, descending into a state of resignation. Lorenz decided that an acoustic guitar—Jara's instrument and rarely part of a symphony orchestra—would directly quote the song. One challenge was to ensure that the guitar could be heard above the rest of the ensemble. An obvious solution would be a microphone. Lorenz, however, indicates in his score that the guitar be amplified through a megaphone, such as those used in political protests of the 1970s, clasped against the body of the instrument and thus offering a new perspective on the age-old question of whether the performing forces in a concerto should cohere or compete. The work concludes with only a dim echo of Jara, a musical ghost, as heard in audio selection 8.5b.

Besides the full symphony orchestra, *Canciones de Jara* calls for harp and a large percussion section, as shown in online audio guide 8.5. Lorenz divides the percussion into four groups, each containing five to ten instruments: bells, tambourine, crotales (tuned cymbals), and timpani. Among the pitched instruments is a crystal goblet. If you have access to fine glassware, rub the rim with your index finger. You'll hear a pitch, which will change if you put liquid in the glass. This unusual timbre can enhance the quality of an entire symphony orchestra.

Concertos by Latin Americans over Time

Several Latin American composers have written concertos. Some have followed traditional models, such as Ginastera, who wrote a violin concerto, a harp concerto, and three piano concertos. One of his piano concertos appealed to the progressive rock group Emerson, Lake & Palmer, who substantively quoted it in their album *Brain Salad Surgery*, released in 1973. Although Ginastera never would have imagined such a format for his musical ideas, he gave the end product his full endorsement. Chávez wrote concertos for piano and violin; he also wrote one for trombone, an instrument that appears as a soloist even less frequently than the viola. Another unusual format was his concerto for four French horns. (Chávez started a cello concerto but never finished it.) As noted in chapter 6, the once maligned guitar figures in several concertos by Santórsola (Uruguay) and Lauro (Venezuela); Sierra of Puerto Rico also wrote for guitar and orchestra. In addition to *Canciones de Jara,* Lorenz has composed a violin concerto, a piano concerto, a recorder concerto, and *Pataruco: Concerto for Venezuelan Maracas and Orchestra*.

ELECTROACOUSTIC MUSIC

Like their counterparts worldwide, many classical composers in Latin America are working in mixed media, combining music with video, dance, and spoken texts. At the center of many mixed media works are electronic instruments. For decades, composers have been seeking to expand the capabilities of traditional instruments. After all, a clarinet can play only so loud or soft and a soprano can sing only so high or so low. While urging performers to expand their approach to their instruments through what we call *extended techniques*—loudly tapping the keys of woodwind instruments, playing on the very edge of the bow for an airy sound, plucking the strings inside a grand piano, asking singers to whisper or scream—electronic instruments also arose to fill this need. Because they increase range and dynamics and expand the very nature of sound, electronic instruments effectively redefine music.

Defining Electroacoustic Music

Over the twentieth century, inventors, engineers, and musicians the world over collaborated to this end. In 1906, Thaddeus Cahill invented the telharmonium, an enhanced organ that enabled music to be piped into telephone lines. In 1920, the Russian inventor Leon Theremin devised the *theremin,* essentially a box with antennae that produces a wavy sound when the player moves his or her hands through the air. (If you know the last ten seconds of the Beach Boys song "Good Vibrations" then you've heard the theremin.) In 1928, the French inventor Maurice Martenot invented the *Ondes Martenot,* an instrument based on the same principle as the theremin but with a keyboard. "Ondes" is French for "waves."

Another new idea was *musique concrète,* which arose in France after World War II. A literal translation of this French term is "concrete music" although "found sounds" (the sounds of everyday life) is closer to actual practice. The first work of musique concrète, completed in 1948, used sounds from one of Paris's railroad stations. Although listeners used to traditional music were put off by these "noise collages," as they were sometimes called, composers became increasingly interested in challenging existing definitions of music. They were convinced that sounds previously considered noise had just as much aesthetic merit as the carefully calculated harmonies, timbres, and melodies of more traditional music.

Starting in the 1950s, sounds could be electronically generated with *synthesizers.* Several composers combined synthesized (created) sounds with natural sounds. Analog synthesis gave way to digital, and in 1982 the Roland Corporation created MIDI (Musical Instrument Digital Interface), a protocol that enables one synthesizer to communicate with another, sending messages about tempo, pitch, vibrato, and other parameters. It was only natural that computers would enter the world of classical music. In 1957, computers were programed to generate sound, giving rise to FM synthesis (frequency modulation) and AM synthesis (amplitude modulation). Computers could also be programmed to simulate the human voice, an idea rich in musical potential. Just as electronic instruments had done decades earlier, computers revolutionized musical creation.

Since the second half of the twentieth century, an ever-increasing range of new technologies has been available for musical composition. These include electronic tape (solo or with conventional instruments), real-time processing with instruments or hyperinstruments (conventional instruments that have been electronically modified, such as a hypercello), and real-time processing with electronics, in which a composer processes the sounds made by an instrument or instruments in real time, asking players to perform into a microphone, and then passes the resulting sound through filters that can be amplified on stage. As with any aesthetic revolution, old concepts are discarded as new ones arise. For example, some composers and critics find the notion of the musical phrase, with its connotations of completeness, obsolete. Consequently, the term "gesture" is often more appropriate.

Electroacoustic Music in Latin America

The first electronic music studio in Latin America was the Estudio de Fonología, founded in Buenos Aires in 1958. The following year, another was established in Córdoba (Argentina). During the 1960s, the Centro Latinoamericano de Altos Estudios Musicales (Latin American Center for Advanced Musical Studies) flourished. Founded in Buenos Aires and partly funded by the Ford Foundation and Rockefeller money, this important center for modern music, also known as the CLAEM, maintained an electronic music studio and presented Festivals of Contemporary Music. It was mostly geared to younger composers, who approached the new medium with optimism. As one young composer, Mariano Etkin (1943–2016) of Argentina, once recalled, at the CLAEM during the 1960s there was "a feeling that one could do anything" (Etkin 2010: 53). Composers elsewhere in Latin America also began writing electroacoustic music, including Mesías Maiguashca of Ecuador (b. 1938), Édgar Valcárcel of Peru (1932–2010), and Mario Kuri-Aldana of Mexico (1931–2013). Kuri-Aldana also composed a popular song, "Página blanca," which became a runaway hit.

The award-winning Nicaraguan-US composer Gabriel Bolaños Chamorro writes both electroacoustic music and music for traditional instruments. Born in Bogotá in 1981, he draws on his Latin American heritage in some works but not in others. References to Latin America are often quite subtle. For example, in one work, based on a poem by the Irish author James Joyce, Bolaños uses the Cuban chekere (figure 4.6). Like many composers today, he writes music shaped by areas of inquiry outside of music. His wide-ranging interests include linguistics, the physical properties of sound, geology, and psychoacoustics, the study of psychological and physiological responses to sound, and he incorpo-

ACTIVITY 8.7

Consider the history of electroacoustic music over the twentieth century. How do you envision musical instruments of the future? If you could invent a musical instrument, what would its capabilities be?

rates his knowledge of these subjects into his works. These sounds can range from acoustic instruments imitating vowel sounds or unvoiced fricatives (such as "s" or "sh" made without the vibration of the vocal cords) to ordinary objects, such as paper being torn. Sometimes he combines these sounds with Latin American instruments used in novel ways, such as bongos being scratched

Audio selection 8.6 shows the enduring links that connect various periods and styles of Latin American music. Bolaños combines a Nahuatl text with contemporary electroacoustic techniques, drawing on a work attributed to the philosopher, poet, and ruler Nezahualcoyotl (1402–72), mentioned above. The piece is in three movements and the vocal parts are taken by chorus and soprano and tenor soloists. The movement we'll study, the first one, is titled "Nic quetza tohuehueuh" (I Erect My Drum).

The work was commissioned by the Early Music Ensemble of the University of California, Davis, for a concert called "Hispanic Polyphony through the

NEZAHUALCOYOTL

Figure 8.8 Likeness of Nezahualcoyotl on the Mexican one-hundred-peso note.

Janusz Pienkowski/Shutterstock.com.

Centuries," presented in 2014. Bolaños wanted to complement other works on the program, several of which were in the style of the polyphonic mass by Gutiérrez de Padilla studied in chapter 4. At the same time, however, he wanted to question Eurocentrism, which, as you know, has often relegated Latin American classical music to a secondary position. Here, Bolaños saw as his biggest challenge the fact that he was working with singers trained in the Western European tradition. He decided to combine singing with vocal techniques such as whispering and shouting, perhaps suggesting the proximity between speech and music, discussed in relation to the Selk'nam shamans (chapter 4). He combines these strategies with electronics to create a twenty-first century sound. (Surprisingly, the piece ends on a traditional chord, a D-major triad.) In addition, Bolaños designed a novel type of musical notation to distinguish his music from that of Western Europe. Indeed, with this piece he honors a long-standing aspect of Latin American culture that you've already studied in various contexts. As Bolaños puts it,

> I wasn't thinking in terms of a rejection of the European tradition, nor a return to . . . the pre-Columbian era, but more in terms of *mestizaje*, a concept that many Nicaraguan artists embrace when discussing the mixing of old-world and new-world trends.

As detailed in online audio guide 8.6, clearly mestizaje has asserted itself in some surprising ways over the course of Latin American musical history.

Latin American Electroacoustic Music over Time

Electroacoustic composition has opened up numerous possibilities for Latin American classical composers. For many, it ultimately proved more attractive than nationalist music, with its reliance on traditional dance rhythms and folk melodies. This tendency to yield to more cosmopolitan models is borne out in the careers of several composers. For example, Blas Galindo of Mexico (1910–93) once composed music based on mariachi and the corrido but came to write electroacoustic music. Certain cosmopolitan composers never wrote nationalist music of any significance, such as Mauricio Kagel of Argentina (1931–08), who composed much of his electroacoustic music from Germany, where he made his home, or León Schidlowsky of Chile (b. 1931), who eventually settled in Israel. On the other hand, Joaquín Orellana of Guatemala (b. 1937) combines electroacoustic music with acoustic instruments of his own creation, sometimes transforming traditional instruments such as the marimba. Paul Desennes of Venezuela, mentioned above, mixes influences from Western Europe and Latin American indigenous musics. All add up to a healthy prognosis for Latin American classical music, now enjoying a global reach and embracing many perspectives.

CONCLUSIONS

In our survey of Latin American classical music we have considered aesthetics in relation to style, genre, and historical period. We have seen that, like composers elsewhere, Latin Americans reshaped classical music in accordance with tastes and circumstances, although the absence of musical infrastructure many have had to surmount has been considerably greater than similar problems faced by their European or US counterparts. We have also explored the norms and attitudes surrounding classical music and have seen that it is a vast and varied world, filled with possibilities for meaning and as relevant today as ever. Although once marginalized in the Global North, Latin American classical composers are finally beginning to receive the recognition they deserve.

STUDY GUIDE

Key Terms

aesthetics

style

style periods in classical music

canon, canon formation

nationalism

cosmopolitanism

opera

libretto

operetta

zarzuela

incidental music

siglo de oro

entremés

tonadilla

chapel master

loa

villano

theorbo

viola da gamba

violone

character piece

virtuoso

bravura

symphony

movement

principal

concertmaster

conductor

El Sistema

musical infrastructure

premiere

chamber music

modernism

dissonance

modernity

vocalise

arco

pizzicato

choro

cavaquinho

concerto

musical quotation

theremin

Ondes Martenot

electroacoustic music

musique concrète

psychoacoustics

For Further Study

General

Béhague, Gerard. *Music in Latin America: An Introduction.* Englewood Cliffs, NJ: Prentice Hall, 1978.

Glasser, Ruth. *My Music Is My Flag: Puerto Rican Musicians and Their New York Communities, 1917–1940.* Berkeley: University of California Press, 1995.

Goehr, Lydia. *The Imaginary Museum of Musical Works: An Essay in the Philosophy of Music.* Oxford: Clarendon, 1992.

Hoover, Maya. *A Guide to the Latin American Art Song Repertoire: An Annotated Catalog of Twentieth-Century Art Songs for Voice and Piano.* Bloomington and Indianapolis: Indiana University Press, 2010.

Labonville, Marie Elizabeth. *Juan Bautista Plaza and Musical Nationalism in Venezuela.* Bloomington and Indianapolis: Indiana University Press, 2007.

Rodó, José Enrique. *Ariel.* Translated by Margaret Sayers Peden. Austin: University of Texas Press, 1988.

Slonimsky, Nicolas. *Music of Latin America.* New York: Thomas Y. Crowell, 1945.

Tiemstra, Suzanne Spicer. *The Choral Music of Latin America: A Guide to Compositions and Research.* Westport, CT: Greenwood, 1992.

Opera

Lawrence-King, Andrew. Liner notes. *La púrpura de la rosa.* Deutsche Harmonia Mundi, CD 05472 773552, 1999.

LeGuin, Elisabeth. *The Tonadilla in Performance: Lyric Comedy in Enlightenment Spain.* Berkeley and Los Angeles: University of California Press, 2014.

Stein, Louise K. "'La Música a Dos Orbes': A Context for the First Opera of the Americas." *Opera Quarterly* 22, nos. 3–4 (2006): 433–58.

———. *Songs of Mortals, Dialogues of the Gods: Music and Theatre in Seventeenth-Century Spain.* Oxford: Clarendon, 1993.

Thomas, Susan. *Cuban Zarzuela: Performing Race and Gender on Havana's Lyric Stage.* Bloomington and Indianapolis: University of Illinois Press, 2008.

Women in Music

Cruz, Sor Juana Inés de la. *Sor Juana Inés de la Cruz: Selected Writings.* Edited and translated by Alfredo Mendez Plancarte and Alberto Salceda. Mahwah, NJ: Paulist, 2005.

Pendle, Karen. *Women in Music: A History.* 2nd ed. Bloomington: Indiana University Press, 2001.

Schonberg, Harold. *The Great Pianists: From Mozart to the Present.* New York: Simon and Schuster, 1963.

Stevenson, Robert M. "Carreño's 1875 California Appearances." *Inter-American Music Review* 5, no. 2 (1983): 9–15.

Symphony, Chávez

Belnap, Jeffrey "Diego Rivera's Greater America: Pan-American Patronage, Indigenism, and *H. P.*" *Cultural Critique* 63 (2008): 61–98.

Hess, Carol. "The Symphony in Latin America." In *The Symphonic Repertoire,* vol. 5, pt. B, *The Symphony in Europe and the Americas in the 20th Century.* Bloomington: Indiana University Press, 2018.

Parker, Robert L. *Carlos Chávez: Mexico's Modern-Day Orpheus.* Boston: Twayne, 1983.

Pedroza, Ludim R. "El Sistema: Orchestrating Venezuela's Youth." *Latin American Music Review* 37, no. 2 (2016): 246–49.

Saavedra, Leonora, ed. *Carlos Chávez and His World.* Princeton: Princeton University Press, 2015.

———. "Carlos Chávez's Polysemic Style." *Journal of the American Musicological Society* 68. no. 1 (2015): 99–150.

Torgovnick, Mariana. *Gone Primitive: Savage Intellects, Modern Lives.* Chicago and London: University of Chicago Press, 1990.

Tunstall, Tricia. *Changing Lives: Gustavo Dudamel, El Sistema, and the Transformative Power of Music.* New York: Norton, 2012.

Chamber Music, Villa-Lobos

Albright, Daniel, ed. *Modernism and Music: An Anthology of Sources.* Chicago and London: University of Chicago Press, 2004.

Appleby, David P. *Heitor Villa-Lobos: A Life, 1887–1959.* Lanham, Maryland and London: Scarecrow, 2002.

Béhague, Gerard. *Heitor Villa-Lobos: The Search for Brazil's Musical Soul.* Austin: Institute of Latin American Studies, University of Texas at Austin, 1994.

Caracas Garcia, Thomas George. "American Views of Brazilian Musical Culture: Villa-Lobos's *Magdalena* and Brazilian Popular Music." *Journal of Popular Culture* 37, no. 4 (2004): 634–47.

Hess, Carol A. *Representing the Good Neighbor: Music, Difference, and the Pan American Dream.* New York: Oxford University Press, 2013.

Radice, Mark A. *Chamber Music: An Essential History.* Ann Arbor: University of Michigan Press, 2012.

Concerto

Keefe, Simon P. *The Cambridge Companion to the Concerto.* Cambridge: Cambridge University Press, 2005.

Lorenz, Ricardo. *Canciones de Jara* (Jara Songs). Note, p. 4 of unpublished score, rev. 2011.

Electroacoustic Music

Etkin, Mariano. "Riesgo, dinero y heterodoxia." In *La Música en el Di Tella,* edited Rubio, Héctor et al., 52–53. Buenos Aires: Secretaria de la Cultura, 2011. This text is in Spanish.

Heile, B. *The Music of Mauricio Kagel.* Farnham, UK: Ashgate, 2006.

Moore, Adrian. *Sonic Art: An Introduction to Electroacoustic Music Composition.* New York: Routledge, 2016.

Reading for Pleasure

Carpentier, Alejo. *The Lost Steps.* Translated by Harriet de Onís. Minneapolis: University of Minnesota, 2001. Original: *Los pasos perdidos* (1953).
Note: few works of fiction on classical music in Latin America exist in English but for general reading on classical music the following are recommended.

Ross, Alex. *The Rest Is Noise: Listening to the Twentieth Century.* New York: Farrar, Straus and Giroux, 2007.
Schonberg, Harold. *The Great Conductors.* New York: Simon and Schuster, 1967.
———. *The Great Pianists from Mozart to the Present.* New York: Simon and Schuster, 1962.

Experiencing Latin American Music: Globalization and Transnationalism

Throughout this book, we've seen how musical genres change over time. Here we focus on musical change in relation to geographical fluidity, already introduced apropos several genres. For example, salsa arose outside of Latin America and then became popular worldwide, whereas cumbia and tango were enthusiastically taken up outside of their countries of origin. In this chapter we'll focus on this phenomenon mainly in relation to the global trends of the twenty-first century, studying several genres that aptly exemplify these tendencies. Then, instead of listening to preselected audio selections, you and your classmates will generate your own text by researching genres, artists, musical selections, or ensembles on your own. (See suggestions on pp. 335–339.)

First we need to have some concepts and definitions at our disposal. Those listed below will give you food for thought as you develop your independent research.

GLOBALIZATION

Globalization has been taking place in some form or other since the beginning of human history. As noted, the concept of "nation" took hold in the nineteenth century and became a powerful point of reference, which it remains for many people today, even despite the relative newness of the concept. It was in the 1980s that the notion of globalization gained currency, however, when politicians and policy makers began using expressions such as "global village" or "the global economy." These concepts signaled increased interactions among nations and communities, some aided by the rise of massive supranational entities such as the European Union, which took shape during the 1990s. In that decade, global exchanges both real and virtual became commonplace. Suddenly anyone in the world with internet access could acquire goods, capital, products (commodities), or ideas. As regions of the globe and regions in cyberspace became intertwined, national borders seemed increasingly porous. Concepts such as "nation" or "nation-state" came to strike many citizens of the world as outdated, if not meaningless. Yet others have become uneasy with this sensation of borderlessness, and in several countries the political right has recently begun to agitate for "stronger borders" (i.e., nationalism), fearing loss of identity and economic uncertainty.

Since the turn of the millennium, new technologies have developed at a dizzying pace. Border-defying exchanges range from ordinary communication between human beings to financial transactions relying on complex algorithms to terrorist propaganda. However ubiquitous such interactions, the processes through which they take place are often only vaguely understood. Who can say for sure why one seemingly innocuous YouTube video is watched by millions of people and another makes next to no impact? Why might we eagerly text an acquaintance but avoid an actual conversation with that person? These myriad processes, impactful as they are, remain mysterious. There is also the way in which information is transmitted. We are unlikely to objectively perceive current events or digest political debate if our news medium is a Twitter feed that provides essentially whatever we wish to know from a perspective that our prior internet behavior has shown to be either conservative or liberal.

As noted, many people feel ambivalent about globalization. Some believe that the impersonal forces of the global market are to blame for homogenizing or even erasing national identity. In 2015, the Starbucks coffee chain opened a store in Colombia, long famed for its coffee. Some Colombians welcomed the third largest exporter of coffee in the world to their country, praising the megacorporation for recognizing one of its main suppliers and for choosing Bogotá for its newest store. Colombians who sympathized with local growers feared that their already precarious circumstances would worsen, however, and mobilized the Movimiento por la Defensa y la Dignidad de los Cafeteros de Colombia (Movement for the Defense and Dignity of the Coffee-growers of Colombia). In 2015, Brazilian employees of the fast-food chain McDonald's took to the streets of São Paulo, Salvador, Goiania, and Brasilia to join the international protest on behalf of higher wages. Other Brazilians continue to order McFritas (fries) or NovoMcShake without much thinking about worker conditions or threats to traditional Brazilian cuisine. In the United States, some people believe too many jobs are being outsourced in the name of globalized "free trade" thanks to agreements such as NAFTA (North American Free Trade Agreement) of 1994 and its offspring CAFTA (Central American Free Trade Agreement) while others welcome the growth of a global market. Even as the Global North debates such matters, some of globalization's more positive aspects, such as internet access, still do not reach everyone in the world. In sum, globalization is an uneven process.

Two aspects of globalization that are often overlooked are time and space, so much a part of daily life that we often take them for granted. Thanks to instant communication, both time and space are being reconceptualized. At least in principle, we can all experience the same event at the same time—the Olympics, the Eurovision song contest, news of a terrorist attack—via the internet. Yet thanks to other technologies, we can also watch any television broadcast or major news event, such as a presidential inauguration, outside of "real time" (itself an increasingly ambiguous concept). How do such shifts in consciousness affect the way we make sense of the world around us, whether as individuals or as communities? The question of how future generations will mark time and how they will regard spatial distance remains open. Other concerns revolve around social media, which many people appreciate even as they fear that virtual friendships are replacing human interaction.

CULTURAL DYNAMICS

Sociologists, economists, historians, and political scientists were among the first to study the effects of globalization. Other scholars have tackled culture, which nowadays cuts across national and regional affiliations that were once taken for granted, but which is an important dimension of globalization. Anthropologists, sociologists, and specialists in media, cultural studies, and technocultural studies focus on *cultural dynamics,* the intricate circuitry of cultural exchanges in human systems that have been brought about by globalization. These scholars investigate the ways in which globalization, with its compressed time-space relationship, affects culture. Flipping the question, they also research culture's impact on globalization. Since music has been no stranger to globalization, it too is caught up in these rapidly multiplying systems.

One irony: although we may recognize the growing ambiguity of borders and national identities, we still habitually associate culture with a territory. Even in the second decade of the twenty-first century, we refer to "US culture" or "Andean culture" despite the reality that place-oriented cultures are being fragmented across the globe and recombined with other cultures, often in startling ways. Two scholars put this situation well, noting that "globalization has radically pulled culture apart from place," and adding that culture itself has become "unhinged" (Inda and Rosaldo 2001: 11).

ACTIVITY 9.1

The US poet Henry Wadsworth Longfellow (1807–82) once wrote that "music is the universal language." This well-worn phrase has since been repeated by music teachers, cultural diplomats, and all manner of performing musicians. Reflect on it by drawing on what you have learned about Latin American music.

TRANSNATIONALISM

The term "transnationalism" is often used in relation to these phenomena. Globalization and transnationalism do not mean the same thing, although they overlap. Thanks to globalization, national borders are often no longer points of reference. (For this reason, the term "global space" is often used to indicate a territory that cannot be found on a traditional map or that may be virtual.) With transnationalism, the nation does remain a point of reference but is only one among many. For example, we often refer to transnationalism to describe the migration of "nationals" from one country to another who either create new cultural expressions in their adopted environment or seek to protect their own traditions, as we saw, for example, with the Yaqui Deer Dance. So-called Mexamerica, the border region of the United States and Mexico, is one example of a transnational culture. If we want to study Mexamerica, we recognize that the two established nations of Mexico and the United States, although fundamental, are not the whole picture. Rather, they are only part of a complex of interactions, influences, and histories that combine under new conditions and yield a new culture with its own values and forms of expression. In short, transnationalism offers a model that is ampler than nationalism but with a more limited purview than globalization. Many people most affected by transnationalism, however, live in *liminal* (in between) conditions, where they find themselves unprotected by state governments. As we'll see, such individuals may forge a cultural path that challenges the status quo.

ACTIVITY 9.2

The so-called Mexamerica region is a site of much contentiousness in politics. It has also given rise to several musical genres. Research this region and report on at least three musical phenomena.

COSMOPOLITANISM

In chapter 8, we touched on *cosmopolitanism,* remarking that classical composers who consider themselves cosmopolitan generally avoid incorporating folk songs, dance rhythms, or other identifiably nationalist elements into their works. Cosmopolitanism should also be appreciated in its nonmusical context, however. A cosmopolitan rarely feels that nation or place is critical to his or her identity. Yet because most people identify with something beyond themselves, it is safe to say that the cosmopolitan sees him- or herself as tied to the world as it is in the present. The cosmopolitan hones the personal qualities necessary to adapt to this rapidly changing landscape, cultivating a perspective of receptivity, flexibility, and curiosity about other cultures, including those formerly considered "foreign." Cosmopolitanism also intertwines with the meaning of the word in everyday English, that is, sophistication or smartness (a synonym for "sophisticated" is "worldly"), embracing globalization and the way of being in the world that it presupposes. As one scholar puts it, in a global community "cosmopolitanism is *there*—not merely an abstract ideal like loving one's neighbor as oneself," but the reality of daily life (Robbins, in Cheah and Robbins 1998: 2).

To sum up:

- *Globalization* involves global trends. This may sound like a truism, but such trends, which are far reaching, can seem impersonal and random and, because they range over broad swaths of territory, are not necessarily controlled (or even comprehended) by human agents.
- *Transnationalism* emphasizes the fact that the nation-state is no longer the chief marker of identity but simply one point of reference among others. It often describes the experience of a particular group migrating to another nation and producing a new culture that blends the existing culture of that region with the group's previous culture.
- *Cosmopolitanism,* synonymous with "worldly" in ordinary English, is often used to describe the outlook of an individual (i.e., a cosmopolitan). Cosmopolitanism overlaps with globalization in that cosmopolitans believe national and regional affiliations once taken for granted have become increasingly irrelevant.

These phenomena imply social and economic inequities. After all, if a cosmopolitan is to embrace the world, that person will require the financial advantages needed to become acquainted with the world in the first place. One scholar sums up these asymmetrical power relations by arguing that such implications must be faced head-on and that there is no point in "pretending that our histories are not already overlapping, that the borders of each of our cultures are not porous." This position takes us back to history, an "official story" that now embraces the world instead of a nation. The same scholar cautions against racism, declaring that "'racism with a distance' ignores . . . the long waves of linkage that tie people together in ways we tend to forget" (Prashad 2003: 52).

The musical genres discussed below exemplify these concepts. We'll discuss the so-called *latune*, a term one scholar has recently coined to denote a faux Latin song engineered in the United States, mainly in the 1930s and 1940s (Pérez Firmat 2008). We then explore the Dominican *bachata*, which acquired one meaning in its country of origin before migrating to the United States, where it took on new significance. Latin American hip hop also crosses borders, intersecting with politics, just as its South Bronx prototype did. A song by a Peruvian *zarzuela* composer was appropriated by the global music market of the 1970s. As further confirmation that place is far less important to musical consumers than it once was, we'll consider Finnish tango, candombe in France, and salsa in Northern Ireland, all of which affirm that globalization, transnationalism, and cosmopolitanism are not something merely to theorize about but facts of life in a world that seems to be shrinking and expanding at the same time. Finally, we consider Brazilian *tecnobrega*, an example of a music routed not through the music industry but through an informal economy that upends conventional means of production and distribution.

Before we delve into specifics, one more broad concept is relevant, especially with regard to production and distribution. In the 1940s, the philosopher and composer Theodor Adorno (1903–69), along with his colleague Max Horkheimer (1895–1973), introduced the term "culture industry" to artistic and political discourse. Essentially, they proposed that the production of cultural goods in the twentieth century—film, music, novels, magazines, radio programs—was the same as any kind of factory production. Such cultural expressions were little more than products; moreover, as commodities, they could be used to manipulate the mass audience into conformity (Adorno 1991: 61–106). We have already hinted at the effects of the culture industry in considering how several genres with modest origins became commercially successful. This concept plays directly into the global economy of recent decades, whether through artists who work within the culture industry or those who have circumvented it.

ACTIVITY 9.3

Identify some genres that originated in humble environments but later catapulted to international fame. Then choose one and explain its trajectory, commenting on this process. Is this phenomenon a question of musical change or are other factors involved?

LATUNES AND THE CULTURE INDUSTRY

In the first half of the twentieth century, many popular music composers in the United States appropriated those traits of Latin American music they perceived as most salient—and marketable—and incorporated them into their own music. Mainly, they focused on rhythm and timbre, drawing on percussion instruments.

Legal Loopholes

With these cultural appropriations, such arrangers were simply responding to the voraciousness of the culture industry, a capitalist model of production and ownership that in the end protects certain individuals while dismantling any inherent democratization in music making. Some of these arrangers and lyricists had a twisted view of ownership: at the behest of publishers, they went so far as to take songs already written by Latin American composers and rewrite the words in English for consumption by the mass audience in the United States, often interjecting meanings having nothing to do with the original. The result of such manipulations was the latune, as noted, a term coined by a scholar and not part of the music industry's marketing strategy.

As latunes became increasingly commodified, Latin American composers sometimes got their due and their authorship was recognized. In other instances, unscrupulous publishers simply raided the works of unsuspecting composers. During the 1930s, the New York–based firm E. B. Marks, whose catalogue boasted some six hundred latunes, would periodically send one of their salesmen to Latin America to buy up whatever local sheet music he could amass so that it could be published in the United States. Due to the tangled state of copyright laws at that time and lack of country-to-country uniformity, this practice was not illegal. Latin American composers (as well as composers from other parts of the world) simply weren't protected.

As with "Guantanamera," some Latin American composers fought back. One famous case involves the vocal trio the Andrews Sisters, a singing sensation of the 1930s and 1940s, whose smooth, close-harmony style was beloved throughout the United States. In 1944, they recorded the song "Rum and Coca-Cola," an immediate hit. Three US Americans were credited as the composer and lyricists. A few years later, however, a judge ruled that the music had been plagiarized and that its real composer was a Trinidadian who had written it in 1906. Not only that, but in 1950, a Trinidadian singer known as Lord Invader brought a separate suit regarding the words, successfully arguing that he had written segments of them. The original words comment sarcastically on Trinidadian women prostituting themselves with US servicemen (who "pay a better price") whereas the cleaned-up version by the Andrews Sisters merely refers to the sunshine and romance of the tropics.

How Latunes Work

Three general approaches dominate in latunes:

- The singer describes a Latin American locale in enticing terms. Swaying palms and white sand beaches often figure prominently, such that Latin America assumes a generic vacationland atmosphere.
- The singer describes the music in the song itself, which is often a dance that marketers have hawked as a "new sensation from South of the Border." Sometimes these dances are invented and named by the US music industry, as was the case with a dance called the *carioca,* featured in the movie *Flying Down to Rio,* released in 1933. Alternatively, real Latin American music can be seen as so captivating as to be dangerous, as in the song by Barry Mann "Blame It on the Bossa Nova," released in 1963, in which the singer falls in love against her will, thanks to the bossa nova, "the dance of love." As you recall from chapter 7, bossa nova is generally music for listening rather than for dancing.
- The singer describes the personality of the typical Latin American, who is invariably sexy, lively, temperamental, and passionate.

Some people object to latunes, considering them diluted versions of the original with "feel-good" lyrics designed to please an undiscerning US public. Others consider them a harmless relic. Ultimately, the sheer consistency of the themes treated in latunes enabled the US music industry to feed into the stereotype of Latin American music discussed above: "'fun,' lightweight, and essentially trivial." As we've seen throughout this book, this description of Latin American music could hardly be further from the truth.

BACHATA AND TRANSNATIONALISM

In Dominican Spanish the word *bachata* can mean "patio party" (fiesta del patio). Yet in its earliest versions, as a song with guitar accompaniment, bachata was far from festive. Its mournful lyrics dealt so regularly with heartbreak and loss that it was originally called *amargue* (bitter music).

The Roots of Bachata

Like the tango, bachata was associated with the urban poor. (Unlike the tango, it was sung first and then danced.) Bachata derives from and overlaps with several existing Latin American genres, including the *bolero,* a Pan–Latin American song form. (It is unrelated to the Spanish dance in triple meter stylized by various European classical composers.) The Latin American bolero can be traced to the Caribbean, specifically to Cuba, where it acquired its characteristic rhythms. Its form is flexible, usually consisting of A and B sections combined in various ways (ABAB, AABB, ABA), and the words are often sentimental, with language many would find exaggerated today. The bolero was especially popular in Mexico, which in the mid-twentieth century boasted a powerful media industry. Eventually boleros were sung and recorded throughout Latin America.

Bachata has had to compete with *merengue,* a more traditional Dominican genre that dated from ballroom dances of the mid-nineteenth century. In the early 1930s, bachata came to be identified with the working classes thanks to the dictator Rafael Trujillo (1891–1961), who, like Vargas, Perón, and Pinochet, believed music could unify a nation. He promoted the merengue to solidify his working-class base and eventually the dance became such a popular national symbol that upper classes took it up as well.

It was not until the 1970s that bachata arose from these established genres in the shantytowns of Santo Domingo, the capital of the Dominican Republic. Immigrants from rural parts of the country had flocked there in search of better jobs and educational opportunities for their families, although often they were disappointed and forced to cobble together a precarious existence in the city, repeating a familiar pattern. *Bachateros* (bachata musicians) played mainly in bars and houses of prostitution, and although the new genre was seldom broadcast on the radio, inexpensive cassette tapes circulated so that people could listen freely to bachata. Thanks to artists such as Blas Durán, Leonardo Paniagua, and Marino (Esteban) Pérez, the genre became increasingly popular. Its music also changed: the tempo became somewhat quicker, and electric guitars and a drum set were often added. It was mainly as a couple dance, however, that bachata gained international fame, in part because it is easy to do. Partners keep a tight hold on each other, taking take three steps to one side and then three steps to the other, with a slight bounce. Throughout, the hips are quite active.

María Grever and the Bolero

Someone who helped propel the bolero onto the international stage was María Grever (1885–1951). She was born in Mexico, lived in Spain, and moved to New York in 1916 upon marrying a US oil executive. ("Grever" is her married name.) Grever became a global, if largely unrecognized, figure thanks to Hollywood, where she began working in the 1920s. Most of her over eight hundred songs are boleros. A famous latune is her "Cuando vuelva a tu lado," which translates as "When I Return to Your Side," but which was marketed and widely recorded under the title "What a Difference a Day Makes." Many of her boleros appear in films made by Paramount and 20th Century Fox, although she is not always credited, as was the practice with any number of film composers of that era.

Bachata in the United States

In 1961, Trujillo was assassinated and instability overtook the Dominican Republic. Shortly thereafter, President Johnson sent nearly twenty-three thousand troops and installed a former Trujillo aide as president and Dominican immigrants began arriving in the United States, most of them seeking political stability. Other waves of immigration took place in the 1980s and 1990s, when economic opportunity was the main draw. Today Dominicans are the fifth largest Latino population in the United States, living mainly in New York and New Jersey but with significant communities in Massachusetts and Florida.

The first Dominicans in the United States brought bachata with them, and subsequent generations, the *Dominicanyorks,* embraced it with the same fervor as their parents and grandparents. These immigrants worked at menial jobs and faced discrimination, the world into which the Dominican-US author Junot Díaz offers us a compelling glimpse.

Many interesting stories about bachata and transnationalization could be told. One ethnomusicologist researching ballroom dance competitions in the Midwestern United States made a surprising discovery when she judged a dance contest in the 1990s, in which a Dominican couple competed in the bachata section. Two of her fellow judges objected to the pronounced hip movement, not only for its "sexualized grinding" but because it prevented the dancers' feet from remaining on the floor at all times, which was a rule of the competition (Bosse 2015: 38). The ethnomusicologist protested that the dance should follow the form most authentic to Dominicans, who identify with it strongly and don't care to see it arbitrarily changed. Her arguments were in vain, for the Dominican dancers were eliminated in the first round. Merengue,

Junot Díaz

Born in Santo Domingo in 1968, Junot Díaz moved to the United States with his family when he was six. He grew up in New Jersey and worked his way through college at Rutgers University by washing dishes, pumping gas, and performing other decidedly unglamorous tasks. He earned an MFA (Masters of Fine Arts) at Cornell University and now teaches creative writing at MIT (Massachusetts Institute of Technology). Díaz is one of several US Latinos writing in English today, having publicly declared that his Spanish "sucks." Among his awards are a Pulitzer Prize and a MacArthur Fellowship. Díaz, who combines Spanglish, street slang, profanity, and literary quotations in rapid-fire style that sometimes leaves the reader breathless, also loves bachata, with "Hoja en blanco" by Monchy y Alexandra a particular favorite.

Figure 9.1 Junot Díaz during an interview in 2013 in New York.
Bebeto Matthews/APimages.com.

ACTIVITY 9.4

Listen to this interview with Junot Díaz: www.npr.org/player/v2/mediaPlayer
.html?action = 1&t = 1&islist = false&id = 160324187&m = 160623763&live = 1.
Then listen to the song "Hoja en blanco." Describe it in a few sentences, making
sure to refer to at least three aspects of the music (pitch, rhythm, melody, texture, and the like). Why do you suppose Díaz is drawn to it? Then listen to Omega
perform "Chambonea." Describe it in a few sentences as well, again making sure
to refer to at least three aspects of the music. How does Díaz evaluate Omega in
relation to bachata?

which also came to the United States during the various waves of Dominican
immigration, made the news in January 2017, when Adriano Espaillat (b. 1954)
became the first Dominican to serve in the US House of Representatives.
Brought to the United States as a child (he is also the first formerly undocumented immigrant to serve in the House), Espaillat represents New York's 13th
Congressional District, which consists of Harlem and parts of the Bronx. His
swearing-in ceremony featured merengue music by the Dominican artists Sergio Vargas and the accordionist Fefita La Grande.

Research *merengue*. What are its main musical characteristics and of what does the dance consist? Where was merengue first concentrated in the United States and how did it change in its new environment?

Figure 9.2 The annual Dominican Day in New York City has been celebrated on the second Sunday in August since 1982 with a parade on Sixth Avenue.

a katz/Shutterstock.com.

HIP HOP, LATIN AMERICA, AND THE WORLD

In the late 1970s, hip hop got its start in the South Bronx (New York City). Perhaps you know older people who remember their first experience of hip hop from this time, whether in the United States or Latin America. Maybe they read about—or were part of—DJing or breakdancing in hip hop's early days. If so, get as much detail out of them as you can, for they lived through a significant moment in music history. If they liked hip hop, ask them what exactly appealed to them. If they didn't warm up to it, ask them why not, again, soliciting as many concrete details as you can.

Also part of hip hop's early days were Puerto Ricans in New York. As discussed in chapters 5 and 6, Puerto Ricans had long participated in musical genres commonly associated with African Americans, including not only jazz but rhythm-and-blues (R & B) and so-called Latin soul. Yet in the 1970s and 1980s, young Puerto Ricans started making up rhymes in English, dancing along with African Americans. Some of these early Puerto Rican rappers rose to stardom, such as Big Pun (short for "Big Punisher"), born to Puerto Rican parents and the first Latino solo rap artist to enjoy platinum sales. (His real name was Christopher Lee Rios and he died in 2002, in his early thirties.) Yet some people decidedly resisted any notion of Puerto Rican rap, assuming that for such a thing to exist some overtly "Puerto Rican" feature would have to prevail, such as words in Spanish or Spanglish, to distinguish itself from rap by African Americans. Many of these attitudes are bound up in questions of race. Puerto Ricans who saw themselves as white didn't necessarily want to associate themselves with what some people crudely labeled "ghetto music" whereas other Puerto Ricans, who recognize that much Puerto Rican culture is part of the African diaspora, see themselves as Latino *and* black. This latter group would concur with the journalist Edward Sunez Rodríguez, who declared that hip hop is as much a part of the lives of Puerto Ricans in New York "as salsa and colonialism" (Rivera 2003: 1).

One additional detail: although the terms "rap" and "hip hop" are often used interchangeably this practice isn't quite correct. Rapping is rhythmical chanting, usually in common time. Adding a recording to the background, of either a popular song, an electronically manipulated mix of sounds drawn from other songs, ordinary speech, or the sounds of urban life, is called *sampling* and creates the rap song. (A handful of rappers sample classical music.) Generally this background music comments indirectly on the rhymed words and is often contemptuous of the establishment. A rap song may also be complemented by scratching, the technique of altering the sound on a turntable by moving the vinyl record and manipulating the cross-fader, a component of a DJ mixer. The rapper either writes or improvises the words, a practice in some of the genres we've already studied. In rap's early days, the words were often violent or misogynistic, thanks largely to the subgenre gangsta rap, and some people concluded that such lyrics encouraged young African Americans to commit crimes. In fact, as rap became increasingly popular, the crime rate in the United States dropped (Bump 2014). Another nuance is cultural: the figure of the "bad man" is part of African American storytelling (compare the malandro of Brazilian samba) but also extends to other cultural expressions we've considered, such as Mexican corridos that tell of outlaws. The "bad man" is master of his fate and the denizen of a universe in which social outcasts fight—and win—with the same weapons that have so long been used against them. Rap also calls attention to drug addiction, gun violence, police brutality, and other problems that mainstream society often avoids confronting.

"Hip hop," on the other hand, is a broader term that refers to the culture of which rap is a part. Hip hop includes music but many other behaviors too, such as breakdancing, graffiti, or certain fashions, such that some people consider hip hop a way of life. As noted, it was initially associated with African American and Puerto Rican youth in New York. But rap and hip hop soon became popular worldwide, including in Latin America. Here we mainly consider Cuba and Venezuela.

Hip Hop in Latin America

In the early 1990s, Fidel Castro had been at the helm of the Cuban government for over thirty years and his government had registered its disapproved of the US culture industry. Hip hop's message of aggression and violence was seen to characterize the great enemy, the fiercely capitalistic United States and, it was reasoned, if Cubans were seduced by rap, there was no telling where this cultural invasion from the United States might take the Cuban people. Anyone who wanted to listen to rap had to obtain a cassette tape, usually smuggled to the island from Miami, ninety miles away, or listened to radio broadcasts. As one scholar points out, they did not necessarily understand the English words but were "attracted to the sound and urgency of rap music" (Moore 2010: 170).

When the Soviet Union fell in 1991, Cubans were suddenly bereft of their most important trading partner. During what was known as the "Special Period," the Castro government imposed a series of austerity measures, making daily life extremely difficult for the average Cuban, who often suffered shortages of food, medicine, and other staples, in addition to frequent power outages. One way out of this problem was cultural tourism (see chapter 4, "Santería over Time"). But many Cubans also began rethinking their political and cultural values and the proper relationship between the values of the Revolution in 1959 and the international scene.

In this greater spirit of openness, hip hop culture gradually integrated itself into Cuban musical life and, in 1995, a rap festival took place in Havana with no opposition from the government. Thanks to this "about-face in state policy," it was now believed that rap could not only proclaim the values of the Cuban revolution but generate badly needed revenue by promoting Cuban culture abroad (Ramsdell 2012: 105–6). The duo Obsesión (Obsession) attacked racism and sexism, as in the song "Se Busca" ("Wanted," in the sense of a want ad), which exalts women's capabilities for a wide variety of careers. Another group, Los Aldeanos (The Villagers), claims to take its name from the fact that they are simple people from a small town who choose to pursue social justice. A group originally called Amenaza (Threat) was founded in Havana, but in 1998 relocated to Paris, becoming known as Orishas, the deities of Santería. Using instruments such as the chekere and some Yoruba words further identified them as part of an authentic Afro-Cuban tradition, as did their first major success, the album *A lo cubano* (Cubanness) of 1999. Throughout, Orishas managed to straddle the ideological demands of the Castro regime and the global market.

In 2002, hip hop and rap had been going strong for three decades, and in the final years of Fidel Castro's presidency (his brother Raúl Castro assumed the office in 2006, followed by miguel Díaz-Canel in 2018), the Cuban Ministry of Culture founded the Cuban Rap Agency (Agencia Cubana de Rap) to promote a "revolutionary" style of hip hop. It would give voice to the disenfranchised—the descendants of the poor people Martí defended over a century earlier in his *Versos sencillos*—in much the same spirit as the defiant young African Americans of the 1970s and 1980s. In December 2014, the administration of President Barack Obama announced that it would normalize relations with Cuba. The United States established an embassy in Havana and, in March 2016, Obama made a state visit there, the first US president to do so since 1928. After laying a wreath at the José Martí memorial in the Plaza de la Revolución, Obama made a speech in which he emphasized his desire to connect with the Cuban people rather than impose US values on them. In that speech, Obama referred to Pitbull (Armando Christian Pérez), the Cuban-American who raps about social and political issues such as global warming and globalization, issues of importance to the Obama administration. Thus, hip hop and Pitbull had become common points of reference for these erstwhile enemies.

Castro's political philosophy found a supporter in the Venezuelan president Hugo Chávez (1954–2013). Chávez also funded several hip hop schools in Venezuela and invited *raperos* (rappers) to his TV talk show, *Aló, Presidente*. Like Castro, Chávez considered the United States the great enemy. Yet in 2005, the Venezuelan leader paid a visit to the South Bronx, spending several hours at the

---

ACTIVITY 9.6

Research one of the following groups, artists, or phenomena related to rap and hip hop: Obsesión, Los Orishas, los Aldeanos, Calle 13, Pitbull, Andean rap. Write a short account of the group, including its origins, biographical detail of individual artists, and sociocultural background. Then choose one representative song that you can easily access and write a short description of it, making sure to refer to at least three aspects of the music (pitch, rhythm, melody, texture, and the like). Then, interpret the song in relation to the concepts discussed at the beginning of this chapter.

Rebel Diaz Arts Collective, a community-cultural center established in 2006 by two rapper brothers known as G1 and RodStarz. In their songs they not only advocated for immigrants and protested the wars in the Middle East, but praised Chávez in a rap tribute called "Work Like Chávez." Given the extreme precariousness of the Venezuelan economy under Nicolás Maduro (b. 1962), a member of Chávez's inner circle who assumed the presidency when Chávez died in office, many people would deem such a tribute both painful and laughable.

Indigenous rap made the news in October 2003, when the Bolivian president Gonzalo Sánchez de Lozada and his administration announced a plan to export natural gas through ports in Chile, which some Bolivians consider an enemy. When a plan for water privatization was also announced, a general strike was called, with marches by miners and peasants. In El Alto, the second largest city in Bolivia, Sánchez de Lozada imposed martial law, and a police crackdown resulted in many deaths. This so-called Gas War of 2003 galvanized rappers, some of whom rap in Aymara. During this period, rapper Abraham Bojorquez, a resident of El Alto, put his finger on rap's true nature. "The death and conflicts in the 2003 Gas War made a huge impact on El Alto," he explained, "and many of these songs reflect that. . . . We don't just sing things like 'I'm feeling bad, my girlfriend just left me and now I am going to get drunk.' It's more about trying to solve problems in society" (Dangl 2006).

Latin America, Rap, and Islam

Rap's global reach manifests itself in the group Outlandish, a trio formed in Copenhagen, Denmark, in 1997. Its members are three young men, all children of immigrants who met in Brøndby Strand, a housing project in the Danish capital. Isam Bachiri is of Moroccan descent, Waqas Ali Qadri is Pakistani, and Lenny Martínez is Honduran and a Catholic (the others are Muslims). Outlandish sings in Danish, English, Spanish, and Urdu and their tracks mix popular US styles such as R & B (itself a mixture of blues and up-tempo boogie-woogie), melodic motives from the Middle East, and rhythms borrowed from a variety of Latin genres. The three young men often show solidarity to *ummah*, the international Islamic community, and perform at rallies on behalf of the armed conflict in Sudan and for eradicating HIV among Muslim youth, among other causes. They promote what one scholar calls a "neo-Moorish identity" in that they suggest through the medium of hip hop the convivencia, the period prior to 1492 when Muslims, Jews, and Christians all coexisted in southern Spain (Aidi 2014: xxv). Because of globalization, no musical style is off limits in affirming the convivencia or any other issue on which Outlandish wishes to express itself.

Figure 9.3 The rap group Outlandish performing in Hamburg, Germany, in 2003.
Frank Rumpenhorst/picture-alliance/APimages.com.

ACTIVITY 9.7

Write a rap song in any language of the Americas. If you do not have access to or expertise in sampling, it is fine simply to write the words. Make sure, however, that your topic relates to a theme discussed in this book. Some possibilities include

- transnationalism and its effect on human beings
- loss of identity in an increasingly global culture
- new identities in an increasingly global culture
- the power of music

Depending on how thoroughly you pursue this project, you might turn it into a podcast or video and make it available to your classmates.

ANDEAN MUSIC AND THE CULTURE INDUSTRY: "EL CÓNDOR PASA/IF I COULD"

Sometimes a musical work lies dormant for many years but then explodes on the world stage, crossing stylistic, national, and genre borders. One early twentieth-century work by a Peruvian composer was ultimately transformed in ways its creator never would have imagined, all due to the impact of the culture industry.

Peruvian Zarzuela

Daniel Alomía Robles (1871–1942) was born in Huánuco, in central Peru. He was well educated in many areas, especially the sciences, and became a naturalist, traveling throughout the Andean region collecting plants. Also interested in folklore, he collected and transcribed hundreds of Andean songs, remaining a musical autodidact. Although most composers for the stage have years of formal training, Alomía Robles nonetheless wrote the zarzuela *El cóndor pasa* (The Condor Flies By), which dates from 1913.

The condor, a potent symbol in the Andean countries, dates from pre-Conquest times, when it figured in religious ceremonies. In Alomía Robles's zarzuela, the bird symbolizes freedom and triumph over evil forces. As one musicologist explains, Alomía Robles composed *El cóndor pasa* to assert regional identity, taking as his subject a theme much on the minds of Peruvians in 1913: the exploitation of indigenous mine workers by US business, a great source of conflict. The Indians in *El cóndor pasa* successfully stage a rebellion against "Anglos," and at the end, the condor flies overhead. Alomía Robles was probably surprised that as a musical amateur he managed to write a zarzuela that was performed over three thousand times in Lima. Yet he did not feel that *El cóndor pasa* was quite finished, and never published the full score, which contains some traditional Andean music. After moving to New York in 1919, he released a piano arrangement of one section of the opera, one based on a *yaraví*, "a slow, romantic mestizo song form" (Ritter, in Moore and Clark 2012: 363–64).

Andean Music and Cosmopolitanism

In 1942, Alomía Robles died, as did his zarzuela, with its modest performance history. Meanwhile, Andean folk styles were becoming popular in various parts of non-Andean Latin America, especially Buenos Aires. This so-called Andean music also made quite a hit in Europe, especially in the Paris club scene, where it was performed by professional musicians. To what extent was it Andean? Certainly it featured the kena, the charango, the bombo, and the panpipes, along with ordinary guitars of various dimensions. Instead of repeating the same melody many times, however, as is common in Andean participatory music, some of these groups varied the melodic structure, or incorporated changes of timbre. The genre was attractive to cosmopolitan audiences largely because it hinted at a rural life that city dwellers often idealize. As a commercially successful brand, Andean music was performed throughout the world on concert stages, in parks, and on street corners by brown-skinned individuals in colorful ponchos. To further this brand, these musicians sometimes performed popular songs from the United States on Andean instruments.

In 1965, Paul Simon of the folk duo Simon and Garfunkel was in Paris. There he heard a group called Los Inca perform the song "El cóndor pasa." (The group later changed its name to Urubamba.) Much taken with the song, Simon became acquainted with the group. He also decided to write his own words to "El cóndor pasa," although, before he and his collaborator Art Garfunkel recorded it, they consulted Los Inca, who gave the duo permission to use it, believing the song was traditional music and therefore not copyrighted. Their recording appeared on Simon and Garfunkel's album *Bridge over Troubled Water,* released in 1970, under the title "El Cóndor Pasa/If I Could." Simon and Garfunkel's version was superimposed on a recording that Los Inca had given them, one that showed off the timbres of Andean instruments.

Alomía Robles's son saw the matter differently, however, and sued the musicians. Ultimately, the parties agreed that all had been a misunderstanding and, ever since, the song has been extremely popular, with translations into Hebrew, Croatian, Czech, and Mandarin, among other languages. It is important to note that it was neither Alomía Robles, Los Inca (Urubamba), nor Simon and

Figure 9.4 Andean musicians at the Northwest Folklife Festival in front of the Fisher Pavillion in Seattle in 2007.

Joe Mabel/Wikimedia.com.

Garfunkel who made this song a hit. Rather, a musical composition inspired by the altiplano was performed according to the norms of globalized Andean music many decades after its initial creation and refashioned for international consumption, thanks to the often circuitous pathways carved out by globalization and the culture industry. Individual listeners will have to decide for themselves if this trend is positive or deleterious.

LATIN AMERICAN MUSIC, EUROPE, AND GLOBALIZATION

Paul Simon first heard "El cóndor pasa" in Europe, the part of the world that Latin American musicians have alternately rejected or embraced. We have already discussed Latin American dance genres that made their way back to Europe during the colonial period. In the following section, we consider recent examples of this phenomenon.

Tango in Finland

It may seem surprising that a dance so associated with Argentina would become popular in Finland. In the early twentieth century, Finns visiting Argentina became enamored of the tango and took it back to Finland with them. For example, there is a Finnish-language version of "El choclo," the tango we studied in chapter 6. It's called "Tulisuudelma," which means "Kiss of Fire," also the title of the English latunes version.

By the 1930s, several Finns were composing tangos, such as Toivo Kärki (1915–92). Others, such as the singer Olavi Virta (1915–72), specialized in performance; Virta himself was known as the "king of Finnish tango." Finns made a few adjustments to the Argentine model. For example, they use a regular accordion instead of bandoneón and also add drums. Unlike "Adios Muchachos," Finnish tangos are invariably in minor keys, although like many of their Argentine counterparts they are likely about sorrow, unrequited love, or nostalgia. The words may refer to Finland's often harsh climate, with descriptions of inclement weather or long nights often symbolizing despair or loneliness. Because such metaphors can easily be realized visually, any number of Finnish films use tangos for the soundtrack, such as those directed by Aki Kaurismaki (b. 1957).

The choreography of the Finnish tango resembles the Argentine version in that couples maintain close contact. Feet stay close to the floor, however, and steps such as the *gancho* (hooking your leg around your partner's) are infrequent. Some observers claim that when a Finnish couple dances the tango, the pair requires far more space between themselves and their fellow dancers than Argentine couples do. Since 1985, a Tangomarkkinat (Festival) is held every summer in Seinäjoki, in southeastern Finland. In 1999, over 130,000 people attended;

Figure 9.5 A stamp from Finland issued in 1997 shows a couple dancing the tango.
Boris15/Shutterstock.com.

a more typical figure is 100,000. The festival gets plenty of television coverage and a tango-singing contest is held, which is open to both men and women. Winners receive the title "Tango King and Queen," with runners-up holding the rank of prince and princess. The public votes in both the finals and the semifinals.

The Finnish tango has also influenced classical music. For example, the Argentine-US composer Pablo Ortiz, mentioned in chapter 8, has written a Finnish tango for symphony orchestra. The piece came about when the National Orchestra of Catalonia (Spain) commissioned Ortiz to write a composition that could be programmed alongside *Tangazo*, an orchestral work by Piazzolla, the Argentine composer and tango pioneer mentioned in chapter 6, and Symphony No. 7 by the Finnish classical composer Jean Sibelius (1865–1957). The result was *Suomalainen Tango* ("Suomi" is Finnish for Finland). In it, Ortiz cleverly uses musical quotation, inserting a trombone theme from the symphony along with familiar tango motifs, all of which combine with his own creative voice to great effect.

Candombe in France

For the past fifteen years, a special dance festival has taken place every fall near Lyon, the third largest city in France, about one hundred miles from Geneva,

> **ACTIVITY 9.8**
>
> We have discussed many genres from various perspectives. Choose one that we have explored in terms of one dimension of human experience and relate it to a different experience. For example, instead of considering the son jarocho in relation to the body, consider it in terms of identity. Alternatively, choose a genre from the list of topics at the end of this chapter and discuss it from as many angles as you can.

Switzerland. Historically, Lyon has been known for industry, especially textile production. Today, tech industries such as software development and biotechnology have taken hold. The festival itself is held in neighboring Décines, a town of around twenty-seven thousand inhabitants and with a similar economy. Normally around two hundred thousand spectators attend, with roughly forty-five hundred participants, who include choreographers, dancers, visual artists, musicians, and consultants.

The festival of September 2002 was devoted to Latin America, with the spotlight on Uruguayan candombe. Festival organizers contacted members of the French-Uruguayan community in nearby Lyon, along with two Uruguayans, Mirtha Pozzi and Pablo Cueco. These Latin Americans assembled a comparsa of fifty drums, played by the French-Uruguayans of Lyon and by others in the area. Pozzi and Cueco also invited candombe specialists from Montevideo. Drums were sent from Uruguay to Décinnes and it was decided to use the "Cuareim" style, which is named after a street in Montevideo.

The newly established group, which went by the name Comparsa Lionesa (Comparsa of Lyon), was extremely dedicated. Since scarcely any of its members were familiar with drumming, much less candombe style, they practiced regularly for about five months. Many could read music but wanted to absorb candombe as Afro-Uruguayan street musicians do, playing by ear rather than learning their parts from a score. The instructors invented a special method, using French words to replicate the rhythms of the various toques to develop the comparsa members' aural retention, the skill on which traditional candombe players rely to such an impressive degree. In all, the Décinnes festival shows the power of globalization to educate, in this instance to make the case that Western notation is less than adequate to represent this Latin American genre.

Salsa in Northern Ireland

New York City may be the birthplace of salsa but the genre has spread to many other new contexts in which the local and the international confront each other. One such place is Belfast, the capital of Northern Ireland. Northern Ireland shares a border with the Republic of Ireland but is part of the United Kingdom. Its history is a traumatic one: Starting in the sixteenth century, England controlled all of Ireland, although pockets of Irish resistance grew over the years, coming to a head during the Easter Uprising of 1916. The rebellion failed but five years later Ireland was partitioned, with the Republic of Ireland independent from the United Kingdom and Northern Ireland under British rule.

Northern Ireland today is inhabited mainly by Protestants (unionists) along with a significant Catholic minority (nationalists). The latter complain of discrimination in housing, employment, and voting rights. In the 1960s a period of intense violence known as "The Troubles" began, during which the nationalist IRA (Irish Republican Army) rebelled against the British constabulary (police force). Acts of terrorism and provocation were committed on both sides, with Belfast particularly affected. In 1999, on the Christian holiday Good Friday, a peace agreement was signed, according to which Northern Ireland would remain a part of the United Kingdom until a majority decides otherwise.

What does it mean to dance salsa in this environment? One researcher decided to find out, asking why salsa became so popular in Belfast in the early 2000s, which is when many salsa classes and clubs were established. Most participants are Catholic and most are women, since men in Northern Ireland are a bit wary about dancing, some believing it effeminate and others conditioned to strike a macho, warlike—or at least confident—pose in the face of ongoing political strife. To be sure, some men dance, but women dominate the scene at salsa clubs, often dancing together. Salsa in Belfast confirms the performative element of dance among nonprofessional dancers. One devotee is Debbie, a single Catholic (names were changed to protect anonymity) who dances in clubs to advertise her attractiveness and availability for marriage and childbearing. Her way of performing salsa underscores this desire. As a Catholic, Debbie claims to be less reticent about sexualized dancing than Protestants, whom she considers repressed. (Whether these generalizations are true or not is beside the point.) Christina, a Protestant, is a salsa instructor but likes to go to clubs for a night off from teaching. On the dance floor, she feels attractive because other people in the club admire her coordination, but then she goes home to her husband, whom she deeply loves. Another Protestant, Annabel, is a widow in her fifties and will only visit salsa clubs in a group because she is convinced that going out to dance alone makes her look desperate.

For each of these women, salsa dancing is an authentic performance experience. Unlike acting in a play, in which the emotions and values expressed are those of a character created by a dramatist, female salsa dancers of Belfast, separated from their daily routine of home or office, perform their own values, emotions, and culture. They are aided by the fact that dancing is done at night, with the dark spaces of the dance floor enabling their emotions and fantasies to roam, just as sitting in a darkened movie theater does. Unlike going to the movies, however, salsa dancing involves contact with other human beings, behaviors that reflect the culture. Whereas unattached women in the United States station themselves at the edge of the dance floor and move to the music to encourage male interest, Belfast women do not take the initiative but wait for a man to invite them (or simply dance with women). Dancers touch hands and shoulders, rather than engage in torso-to-torso contact. Some women find the hip movement, which involves switching direction on the clave and is a normal part of the step, to be overly sexual and minimize it, again a performance of their own cultural norms.

LATIN AMERICAN MUSIC, TECHNOLOGY, AND THE TWENTY-FIRST-CENTURY ECONOMY

What happens if the post–Cold War vision of a shared "global village" doesn't come to pass? However optimistically such ideals were advanced during the 1990s, for many, especially in the Global South, *neoliberalism* put an end to such dreams. Neoliberalism, rooted in free-market capitalism, was seen as the salvation for many former communist countries and was promoted by leaders as diverse as Ronald Reagan (United States), Margaret Thatcher (Great Britain), and Pinochet. Today many discredit neoliberalism in light of calamities such as the economic meltdown in Argentina (2001) and the so-called Great Recession in the United States (2008).

Tecnobrega

Musicians have sought alternatives to neoliberalism, the spirit of which has long nourished the culture industry. A telling example of this resistance is found in Belém, a city of about 1.5 million in the eastern part of the Brazilian Amazon. The population is a mixture of European, Indian, and African peoples and, throughout the second half of the twentieth century, rural immigrants arrived there seeking economic opportunity. A recently created musical genre is *tecnobrega,* an electronic version of a local type of dance music called *brega,* which combined elements of rock with the bolero, discussed above. ("Brega" is colloquial Portuguese for something outdated or, as we might say in colloquial English, "cheesy" or "tacky.") Tecnobrega is produced in low-tech home studios by digital artists using software, often pirated, in place of acoustic instruments; indeed, many of these artists don't play acoustic instruments. Tecnobrega may contain echoes of the bolero rhythm but ordinarily this rhythm is transformed into a synthesized loop with any number of digital alterations. The result is a huge quantity of CDs and MP3s, which are sold by street vendors for under the equivalent of one US dollar each. None of the producers expects to turn a profit from sales or receive royalties but instead they hope that the CDs will entice sponsors of electronic dance parties to offer gigs to the digital artists or commissions for more songs. These sound-system parties take place in dance-halls and empty lots and can last all night.

The combination of all these factors—the digital artists, the cheap or pirated software, the street vendors, the massively attended dance parties—is a central part of the musical scene in Belém. The *tecnobrega* economy has employed over six thousand people and has brought in the equivalent of approximately 1.6 million US dollars in monthly revenue from these shows. Participants in this scene have effectively circumvented the culture industry, with tecnobrega's production model bypassing the mainstream media and creating an informal economy not dissimilar to the so-called gig economy or shared economy that permits Uber and lyft drivers to circumvent norms that a taxi company would impose on its drivers. Just as that economy raises questions over ownership, exploitation, and production, those who hawk tecnobrega sometimes find themselves in confrontations with more conventional sectors of the economy, such as shop owners in the downtown area.

Mixing

Tecnobrega also signals the confused relationship between technology, race and ethnicity, and the economy. Is it unusual that this area of Brazil, histori-cally seen as "primitive," should be the site of innovation? As one song defiantly notes, "It's no joke, it's no joke, Indians like sound systems too." One scholar has commented on an image associated with tecnobrega, a Cyborg Indian that is depicted in several murals throughout the city and stares at passers-by with an "inscrutable, backlit gaze" (Lamen 2014: 39). The same scholar suggests that this image also captures the mixed-race inhabitants of Belém, who are not yet full partners in global modernity.

We cannot be certain if the informal musical economy will help liberate inhabitants of cities such as Belém by encouraging new forms of cultural production and upsetting the complacency of the historical center. Nor is it clear that such practices are a viable model for global citizenship or a way of injecting democratization into music making. A bleaker possibility looms: it may be that the sound-system parties are little more than an escape from the oppression of daily life. This "collective sublimation of violence and abuse" that is endured daily includes "hour-long bus rides into the center from the outlying neighborhoods . . . cling[ing] to hand rails, pressed up against other bodies squeezed into high-heel shoes, body-shaping underwear, or long pants ill-suited to the equatorial climate—to the stifling heat, the haze of diesel exhaust, . . . the cacophony of distorted *tecnobrega* songs played from a hundred bus, radio, and cellphone speakers" (Lamen 2014: 41–42). This cautionary note should warn those who optimistically hail "gig econo-mies" as a form of liberation; indeed, such systems may be little more than a replay of the centuries-old domination of the center over the periphery, with its ongoing saga of boom and bust that has left so many marginalized peoples in its wake.

CONCLUSIONS

As is clear from each of the snapshots just discussed, the global Latin American musical scene is richer and more diverse than ever before. One ethnomusicologist maintained at the turn of the twenty-first century that at no point in the history of artistic creation had the environment in which musical utterances emerged ever been so all encompassing (Monson 1999: 48). This trend, which has only intensified, is affirmed in Latin America. Surely we will continue to debate the role of globalization: whether vast, impersonal forces will prevail over human agency, whether the shared global village will win out or what some scholars call the "global ghetto."

Again, we return to questions of self and other. Abstract theories have great value and must be addressed, since they stimulate our thinking and sharpen the vocabulary we need to further constructive conversation on these points. Ultimately, however, it will be human behavior that determines the future. If we recognize, as we have done throughout this book, that decentering the self is the first step to becoming receptive to unfamiliar ways, to appreciating perspectives that point us to new awareness, then that willingness will enable us to shed habits of mind that entrap rather than enlighten. We do not have ready-made solutions for what is not yet fathomable. Only through a spirit of openness can we hope to make sense of the future and all its unknowns.

Music and our experience of it, along with our constant effort to comprehend as deeply as we can the musical experiences of others, can highlight our spiritual or religious beliefs; our national, regional, racial, ethnic, or gender identity; our sense of place; our awareness of our own bodies; political convictions; and our relationship to art. In each, we negotiate relationships, construct community, and extract meaning. As we consider Latin America as a site for these relationships, we can bear in mind that some people nowadays go so far as to argue that there is no longer any such entity—that in effect, Latin America no longer exists—given the sweeping trends of globalization, transnationalism, and cosmopolitanism just discussed. As we have seen over the course of this book, the label "Latin America" not only is a misnomer but has never accurately described the plethora of regions, nations, cultures, languages, and peoples within the territory's geographic borders. Amid demographic shifts and in the face of time- and space-bending technological innovations, we continue to nurture at least for the foreseeable future a concept of Latin America that prods us toward cultural openness. In honing our ability to know this region through music and music's meanings, we sensitize our ears, our minds, and our spirits, and thus enrich the experience of being human.

STUDY GUIDE

Key Terms

globalization

cultural dynamics

transnationalism

cosmopolitanism

culture industry

neoliberalism

informal economy

latune

bachata

bolero

merengue

hip hop

rap, rapero

sampling

Andean music (as marketing category)

Finnish tango

Tangomarkkinat

tecnobrega

For Further Study

Globalization, Cultural Dynamics, Transnationalism, Cosmopolitanism

Adorno, Theodor W. *The Culture Industry: Selected Essays on Mass Culture.* Edited by J. M. Bernstein. London and New York: Routledge, 1991.

Appadurai, Arjun. *Modernity at Large: Cultural Dimensions of Globalization.* Minneapolis: University of Minnesota Press, 1996.

Béhague, Gerard. "Rap, Reggae, Rock, or Samba: The Local and the Global in Brazilian Popular Music (1985–1995)." *Latin American Music Review* 27, no. 1 (2006): 79–90.

Cheah, Pheng, and Bruce Robbins, eds. *Cosmopolitics: Thinking and Feeling beyond the Nation.* Minneapolis: University of Minnesota Press, 1998.

Erlmann, Veit. "The Politics and Aesthetics of Transnational Musics." *World of Music* 35, no. 2 (1993): 3–15.

Fojas, Camilla. *Cosmopolitanism in the Americas.* West Lafayette, IN: Purdue University Press, 2005.

Gupta, Akhil, and James Ferguson, eds. *Culture, Power, and Place: Explorations in Critical Anthropology.* Durham: Duke University Press, 1997.

Inda, Jonathan Xavier, and Renato Rosaldo, eds. *The Anthropology of Globalization: A Reader.* Malden and Oxford: Blackwell, 2001.

Madrid, Alejandro L. *Transnational Encounters: Music and Performance at the U.S.–Mexican Border.* New York: Oxford University Press, 2008.

Mignolo, Walter. *Local Histories/Global Designs: Coloniality, Subaltern Knowledges, and Border Thinking.* Princeton: Princeton University Press, 2000.

Monson, Ingrid. "Riffs, Repetition, and Theories of Globalization." *Ethnomusicology* 43, no. 1 (1999): 31–65.

Ong, Aihwa, ed. *Flexible Citizenship: The Cultural Logics of Transnationality.* Durham: Duke University Press, 1999.

Prashad, Vijay. "Bruce Lee and the Anti-Imperialism of Kung-Fu: A Polycultural Adventure." *positions* 11, no. 1 (2003): 51–90.

Tomlinson, John. *Globalization and Culture.* Chicago: University of Chicago Press, 1999.

Zolov, Eric. *Refried Elvis: The Rise of the Mexican Counterculture.* Berkeley: University of California Press, 1999.

Latunes and the Culture Industry

Adorno, Theodor W. *The Culture Industry: Selected Essays on Mass Culture.* Edited by J. M. Bernstein. London and New York: Routledge, 1991.

Madrid, Alejandro L. *Music in Mexico.* Experiencing Music, Expressing Culture. New York: Oxford University Press, 2013.

Pérez Firmat, Gustavo. "Latunes: An Introduction." *Latin American Research Review* 43, no. 2 (2008): 180–203.

Roberts, John Storm. *The Latin Tinge: The Impact of Latin American Music on the United States.* 2nd ed. New York and Oxford: Oxford University Press, 1999.

Bachata and Transnationalism

Bosse, Joanna. *Becoming Beautiful: Ballroom Dancing in the American Heartland.* Urbana, Chicago, and Springfield: University of Illinois Press, 2015.

Moore, Robin D. *Music in the Hispanic Caribbean.* Experiencing Music, Expressing Culture. New York: Oxford University Press, 2010.

Pacini Hernández, Deborah. *Bachata: A Social History of a Dominican Popular Music.* Philadelphia: Temple University Press, 1995.

———. *¡Oye como va! Hybridity and Identity in Latino Popular Music.* Philadelphia: Temple University Press, 2010.

Hip Hop, Latin America, and the World

Aidi, Hishaam. "The Grand (Hip-Hop) Chessboard: Race, Rap, and Raison d'État." *Middle East Report* 260 (2011): 25–39.

———. *Rebel Music: Race, Empire, and the New Muslim Youth Culture.* New York: Pantheon, 2014.

Bodenheimer, Rebecca M. "National Symbol or a 'Black Thing': Rumba and Race Politics in Cuba in the Era of Cultural Tourism." *Black Music Research Journal* 33, no. 2 (2013): 177–205.

Bump, Philip. "As Hip-Hop Became Popular, Crime Dropped." *Wire,* January 7, 2014.

Dangl, Benjamin. "Rapping in Aymara: Bolivian Hip Hop as an Instrument of Struggle." 2006. http://upsidedownworld.org/archives/bolivia/rapping-in-aymara-bolivian-hip-hop-as-an-instrument-of-struggle/.

Flores, Juan. *Divided Borders: Essays on Puerto Rican Identity.* Houston: Arte Público, 1993.

McFarland, Pancho. *Chicano Rap: Gender and Violence in the Postindustrial Barrio.* Austin: University of Texas Press, 2008.

Moore, Robin D. *Music in the Hispanic Caribbean.* Experiencing Music, Expressing Culture. New York: Oxford University Press, 2010.

Perry, Imani. *Prophets of the Hood: Politics and Poetics in Hip Hop.* Chapel Hill and London: Duke University Press, 2004.

Ramsdell, Lea. "Cuban Hip Hop Goes Global: Orishas' *A lo cubano.*" *Latin American Music Review* 33, no. 1 (2012): 102–23.

Rivera, Raquel Z. *New York Ricans from the Hip Hop Zone.* New York: Palgrave Macmillan, 2003.

Andean Music and the Culture Industry: "El Cóndor Pasa/If I Could"

Bennighof, James. *The Words and Music of Paul Simon.* Westport, CT: Praeger, 2007.

Moore, Robin D., and Walter A. Clark, eds. *Musics of Latin America.* New York: Norton, 2012. See especially the essay by Ritter.

Turino, Thomas. *Music in the Andes.* Experiencing Music, Expressing Culture. New York: Oxford University Press, 2008.

Latin American Music, Europe, and Globalization

Hess, Carol. "The Symphony in Latin America." In *The Symphonic Repertoire*, vol. 5, pt. B, *The Symphony in Europe and the Americas in the 20th Century.* Bloomington: Indiana University Press, 2018.

Skinner, Jonathan. "Women Dancing Back—and Forth: Resistance and Self-Regulation in Belfast Salsa." *Dance Research Journal* 40, no. 1 (2008): 65–77.

Latin American Music, Technology, and the Twenty-First-Century Economy

Davis, Mike. *Planet of Slums.* London: Verso, 2007.

Holston, James. *Insurgent Citizenship: Disjunctions of Democracy and Modernity in Brazil.* Princeton: Princeton University Press, 2008.

Lamen, Darien. "Amazonian Sound Systems, Cyborg Indians, and the Future of the Future, Or, the Renewed Search for El Dorado under Late Capitalism." *Global South* 8, no. 1 (2014): 24–50.

Reading for Pleasure

Alvarez, Julia. *How the Garcia Girls Lost Their Accents.* New York: Workman, 1991.

———. *In the Time of the Butterflies.* New York: Workman, 1994.

Cisneros, Sandra. *The House on Mango Street.* New York: Vintage, 1984.

Diaz, Junot. *The Brief, Wondrous Life of Oscar Wao.* New York: Riverhead, 2007.

———. *Drown.* New York: Riverhead, 1996.

———. *This is How You Lose Her.* New York: Riverhead, 2012.

García, Cristina. *Dreaming in Cuban.* New York: Knopf, 1992.

MacIntosh, Fiona M. *Rosa of the Wild Grass: A Nicaraguan Family.* Shropshire: Practical Action, 2016.

Independent Research

Choose one or more topics from the following list and research it using the skills you've learned in this class. What type of music (classical, popular, traditional) will you explore? Once you decide, figure out which musical characteristics catch your ear. How so? How else does the music cohere? From what perspectives—identity, politics, the body, globalization, etc.—can your topic be most fruitfully considered? Your investigations can culminate in a class presentation, a podcast, a research paper, or a video. See also the interview option at the end of the list, in which you discuss music with an immigrant, perhaps from your own family. Alternatively, you could create a simulation or a listening guide, such as those that appear in this book.

For some topics, it will be highly advantageous to know a Latin American language. If you do not know that language, choose a different topic. You'll see once you begin to peruse the list that the categories below are not always fixed. For example, some of the artists are also composers. Topics not on this list may also occur to you. Feel free to propose them to your instructor.

Genres, Styles, and Rituals

nueva trova

marinera

Brazilian funk

Candomblé

timba

banda

música norteña

tecnobanda

tecnocumbia

Latin jazz

conjunto
aguinaldo
habanera
choro
frevo
seis
jaraví (yaraví, harawi)
rock nacional
history of rock in Mexico
zamba
samba reggae
axé
rumba
guaguancó
lundú
banda sinaloense
bumba-meu-boi
afoxé
bossa nova
albazo
forró
reggaetón
palo
festijo
landó
tinku
caporales
Los Kjarkas
bambuco
baguala
pasito duranguense
payada, payador
rock en español
chamamé
vidala
balada
gato
música caipira
nor-tec vidala

villancico de negros
Los Angeles Azules
musical traditions surrounding the Virgin of Guadalupe
sandunga
fandango
jarabe
cumbé
ch'unchu
chicha
danzón
música jíbara
chacarera
marinera
jácara
maxixe
pasillo
milonga
tonada
sanjuánito
salve (Dominican)
champeta
charanga
música tropical (Colombia)
huapango
corrido
narcocorrido
quebradita
Afro-Colombian hip hop

Performers, Including Ensembles

Shakira
Lydia Mendoza
Mario Gutiérrez
Jenni Rivera
Frankie Negrón
Juanes
Patricio "Toribio" Rijos
Havana Cuba All-Stars
Ismael Rivera

Linda Ronstadt
Dorival Caymmi
Pastorita Huaracina (María Alvarado)
Domini-Can
Pixinguinha
Suni Paz
Expresión Joven
Edgardo A. Franco ("El General")
Azúcar Negra
Klímax
Grupo Aymara
Eddie Palmieri
Jilguero del Huascarán
Los Tigres del Norte
Los Lobos
Agustín Mendieta
Rubén Blades
Convite
Vania Borges
Haila Mompié
Trio Ayacucho
Celia Cruz
Arturo Sandoval
Tito Puente
Los Errantes
Buena Vista Social Club
Elidio "Pródigo" Claudio
Arsenio Rodríguez
Omara Portuondo
Zenaida Romeu (Camerata Romeu)
Carlos Santana
Don Dinero
Tony Vicioso
Lira Paucina
Vico C. (Luis Armando Lozada Cruz)
Los Pleneros de la 21
Chuchumbe
Jennifer López
Flor de Hyancayo
Silvio Rodríguez

Jesús "Chucho" Valdés
Wilfrido Vargas
Los Parientes
Bahia Orchestra Project
Eddy-K
Julio Iglesias
Enrique Iglesias
Christopher "Big Pun" Rios
Johnny Pacheco
Ivy Queen
Los Cojolites
DJ Blass
Selena Quintanilla
Agustín Lara
Cubanos en la Red
Francisco Saldaña
Eleazar de Carvalho
Son de Madera
Blas Durán
Sérgio Assad
Odair Assad
Víctor Cabrera
Quilipayún
Johnny Ventura
Inti-Illimani
Abraham Laboriel, Johnny Laboriel
Teri Gender Bender
Gloria Estefan
Luis Miguel
Chicano Batman
Fher Olivera, Maná
Marino (Esteban) Pérez
Leonardo Paniagua
ContraTiempo
Omar Rodríguez López
Ricky Martin
Carmen Miranda
César Amaro
Los Amigos Invisibles
Héctor Lavoe

Laurindo Almeida
Los Panchos
Jesús María Sanromá
João Gilberto
Astrud Gilberto
Max Lifchitz
Don Omar (William Omar Landrón)
Claudio Arrau
Nelson Freire
Cristina Ortiz
Berta Rojas
Los Macopejes
Daddy Yankee
Tego Calderón (Tegui Calderón Rosario)
Andrea Echeverri
Abel Carlevaro
Rafael Hernández
Xavier Cugat
Luis Herrera de la Fuente
Luis Díaz
Antonio Cabán Vale
Daniel Viglietti
Marc Anthony
Alex Bueno
Baby Ranks
Arthur Moreira Lima
N. O. R. E. (Víctor Santiago)
Sylvia Rexach
Banda Didá
Andrés ("El Jíbaro") Jiménez
Sonia Silvestre

Classical and Film Composers
Sonia Possetti
Gerardo Gandini
alcides lanza
Ignacio Cervantes
Coriún Aharonián
Mozart Camargo Guarnieri

José Ardévol
Blas Galindo
Jacobo Ficher
Manuel Ponce
Celso Garrido-Lecca
Manuel Saumell
Sergio Ortega
Miguel Ángel Estrella
Gustavo Becerra
Juan José Castro
Julio Alberto Hernández
Alfonso Leng
Lalo Schifrin
Domingo Santa Cruz
José Asuar
Luis Advis
Luis Antonio Escobar
Edgar Valcárcel
Mario Davidovsky
Mauricio Kagel
Alberto Nepomuceno
Eduardo Fabini
Héctor Tosar
Roque Cordero
José Serebrier
Felipe Boero
Arturo Márquez
Andrés Sas
Amadeo Roldán
Juan Carlos Paz
Francisco Mignone
Marlos Nobre
Juan Bautista Plaza
Juan Morel Campos
Héctor Campos Parsi
Rafael Aponte-Ledée
Enrique Iturriaga
José Pablo Moncayo
Roberto Sierra

Mario Lavista
Paulo Chagas
Paul Desenne
Corián Aharonían

Interview-Research Essay

Interview an immigrant from Latin America to the United States. Mainly, concentrate on what sort of music meant most to this person over the course of this experience. Interviewing a member of your family can prove most gratifying. Be sure to read the interviewing strategies below and apply them to your project. Note that by modifying the questions below you can also interview a musician or a participant in whatever musical style or genre you decide to explore.

Interviewing Strategies

You will want to ascertain in a few words relevant details of your subject's biography (country of origin, experience of the United States, salient memories). The focus of your interview, however, should be why

certain music has sustained this person. How did listening to this music enhance the experience of immigrating? What associations and memories does the interviewee have with this music? Does it mean something different in the United States than it did in the interviewee's country of origin? You will undoubtedly arrive at additional questions, depending on the music under discussion. When you write up the interview you can use Q & A style.

Then, research the music your interviewee specifies. In your project, you can either discuss it by way of introduction or weave it into your interview. Use outside sources and cite them in whatever citation format is most common in your discipline.

Warning: Not everyone wants to discuss the experience of leaving one's native country, which may have been due to traumatic circumstances. If the subject of music and immigration proves too painful, choose another topic.

Research tip: In Shelemay 2015, read the chapter "Music and Migration," pp. 163–201, listed in the bibliography; see also Titon 2009: 457–74 and Wade 2004: 152–157.

Glossary of Musical Terms

Note: Several of the terms listed below can be defined in more than one way. Those given here reinforce the definitions discussed in the text.

a cappella. Singing unaccompanied by instruments. Italian for "as in a chapel."

ABA form. A musical form in which two identical (or nearly identical) sections, each called "A," are separated by contrasting material ("B").

abanico. Spanish for "fan." On the timbales, a roll that suggests the sound of an old-fashioned fan being snapped open and that often leads from one section into another of genres such salsa.

accelerando. An increase in speed (tempo).

accompaniment. Music that is subservient to a melody.

accordion. A portable, box-shaped musical instrument that relies on a bellows and freely beating reeds for sound, often with a piano keyboard.

aerophone. An instrument that generates sound through a vibrating column of air, whether blown directly or through a reed or mouthpiece. Example: flute, gaita.

aesthetics. The branch of philosophy that concerns itself with the significance of art.

agogô. A double cowbell, used in Afro-Brazilian music. See also batucada.

aiyam. A gourd rattle used in the Yaqui Deer Dance.

alto. The range that lies between soprano and tenor. Applies to the female voice and also to certain instruments (saxophone, flute).

antara. Quechua for panpipes. See also panpipes.

antiphonal singing. The practice of singing in alternating choruses, which are often stationed at different areas of the performance space.

apito. A whistle used in Brazilian drumming. Serves as a conductor, signaling to the rest of the ensemble and keeping the players together. See also batucada.

arco. The Italian word for "bow"; also a performance instruction directing the player to use the bow.

aria. A solo song, often in an opera, with instrumental accompaniment. Generally longer and more complex than a song.

arpa jarocha. The variety of harp used in the son jarocho, usually about five feet tall and with thirty-odd strings. See also son jarocho.

arpeggiation. See broken chords.

arpero. Harpist.

atabaque. A tall, wooden hand drum with calfskin heads often used in capoeira. See also capoeira.

attitude. A posture in dance; in classical ballet, the dancer lifts one leg, bends the lifted knee, and maintains a straight back.

augmented second. An interval consisting of three half steps.

authentic cadence. A cadence that progresses from dominant to tonic. See also cadence.

bachata. A style of dance from the Dominican Republic derived in part from the Latin American bolero. Originally a marginalized, rural genre, it became very popular among Dominicans in the United States.

baile de la marimba. A generic name for a series of dances accompanied by marimba in Nicaragua, often involving processions and special costumes.

Ba kubahe. See water drum.

ballad. A song, usually in strophic form, that narrates a story. See also corrido.

ballet suite. Several sections from a ballet selected by the composer for orchestral performance in the concert hall, that is, without dancers.

bandola. A pear-shaped chordophone that resembles the mandolin, common in Venezuela and Colombia.

bandoneón. An accordion-like instrument in which the player presses buttons while managing the bellows (i.e., not a piano-keyboard accordion). Of German origin, the bandoneón is often featured in tango and is much associated with Argentina.

bar. A group of beats with emphasis on the first, constituting a metrical unit. Also called a measure.

baritone. The range that lies between tenor and bass. Applies to the male voice and also to certain instruments (saxophone, horn).

baroque period. In music, the period from c. 1600–1750.

bass. The range that lies below the tenor, that is, the lowest voice. Applies to the male voice and also to certain instruments (clarinet, string bass).

bass line. The line of music that has the lowest range.

batá drums. Double-headed drums with an hourglass shape. Played in sets of three for some Santería ceremonies and considered sacred.

bateria. The ensemble of capoeira instruments. See berimbau, caxixi, agogô, atabaque, berimbau, pandeiro, reco-reco.

batería. Spanish for percussion ensemble.

batucada. A subgenre of Brazilian samba characterized by fast, intense drumming. See also repinique, surdo, tamborim, agogô, chocalho, timbal, pandeiro, reco-reco, apito.

beat. Pulse. A temporal unit of music.

bembe. A variety of Santería observance in which the three drums used are not consecrated. See also cachimbo, mula, and caja.

berimbau. A musical instrument used in capoeira made of a hollowed-out gourd and a stick that supports a wire, which the player strikes with a stick, using also a small stone, or a coin. See also capoeira.

big band. A jazz term meaning (**1**) a style of music popular during the 1930s and 1940s featuring twelve to fifteen players with various combinations of brass, woodwinds, and percussion and (**2**) the ensemble that plays in this style.

blocked chords. The label used when all the notes of a chord are sounded simultaneously. See also broken chords.

bolero. A pan–Latin American song form that originated in the Caribbean, was then taken up in Mexico, and then spread to other countries. Boleros usually tell of some affair of the heart, often dwelling on frustrated love. In duple meter.

bombo. A large drum with two heads, typically played in the Andean region.

bongo. A pair of small, open-bottomed drums of Afro-Cuban origin.

bongocero. The percussionist who plays the bongos.

bossa nova. A genre of Brazilian song popular from the 1950s with relatively complex harmonies, often jazz-based, and syncopation, characterized by an intimate singing style.

brass quintet. A chamber music ensemble consisting of two trumpets, French horn, trombone, and tuba. Also applies to a composition for such an ensemble.

bravura. Virtuosic style, designed to show off the player's skill.

break. An improvisatory section inserted between the phrases of a jazz composition.

broken chords. The label used when all the notes of a chord are played individually. Often called arppeggiation. See also blocked chords.

cabasa. A percussion instrument of African origin that consists of a wide cylinder covered in steel-ball chain and fastened to a stick. The player agitates the instrument with one hand and strikes it with the other.

cachimbo. The highest-pitched drum of the bembe ensemble in Afro-Cuban Santería.

cadence. A point of conclusion created by a short chord progression. See also authentic cadence, half cadence, and deceptive cadence.

caixa. A Brazilian drum similar to the snare drum (i.e., a shallow drum with two heads) but deeper and often of a smaller diameter. See also snare.

caja. (**1**) A single-headed, conical drum used in música vallenata, (**2**), an Andean frame drum, and (**3**) the lowest-pitched drum of the bembe ensemble in Afro-Cuban Santería.

call-and-response form. An African-derived musical practice in which a leader sings a vocal line that is answered by a group. The group may repeat what the leader sings or introduce variants.

canción ranchera. See música ranchera.

candombe. An Afro-Uruguayan genre that combines song, dance, and sometimes theater, traditionally emphasizing percussion. See also tamboril, chico, repique, piano.

canon. A collection of works (literary, musical, or from the visual arts) that many people have considered "great" or authoritative over the years and that have been studied from this perspective.

cantante recia. A female música llanera singer. See also canto recio.

canto. A verse or narrative portion in salsa music. See also montuno.

cantor. The principal singer in Jewish worship.

canto recio. The "rough" or robust singing associated with male performers of música llanera.

cantorial. Musical settings of prayers and other texts in the Jewish worship service.

capoeira. An Afro-Brazilian martial art or dance accompanied by music. See also agogô, atabaque, bateria, berimbau, caxixi, ginga, pandeiro, roda de capoeira, ladainha, chula, corrido.

cathedral. The site of ecclesiastical authority.

cavaquinho. A small, ukulele-like instrument with wire strings.

caxixi. A rattle used in capoeira that is essentially a small, closed basket that contains seeds. See also capoeira.

chacarera. A couple dance from the central region of Argentina that alternates duple and triple metric patterns.

chamame. A couple dance from Argentina influenced by the polka.

chamber music. A type of classical music involving a small group of players, often with only one player per part. See also string quartet, woodwind quintet, piano trio, piano quartet, piano quintet.

chapel master (maestro de capilla). The person in charge of music at a church or cathedral. Often responsible for directing the choir, playing or supervising instrumentalists, and at one time, for composing music for the religious services.

character piece. A piece without formal requirements that often portrays some sentiment or pictorial idea. Common during the romantic period (i.e., the nineteenth century).

charango. An Andean instrument in the lute family traditionally made from the shell of an armadillo or a gourd that can be either plucked or strummed.

charleo. The buzzing sound that results from the presence of pig intestines inserted into the resonating chamber under the key of a marimba.

chekere. An Afro-Latin American idiophone. A dried gourd wrapped in a net made of beads or seeds. Alternate spellings: chéquere, shekere.

chico. A high-pitched drum used in candombe. See also candombe.

chocalho. An idiophone consisting of rows of jingles used in Brazilian music. See also batucada.

chord. Three or more pitches played simultaneously or as a unit. See also harmony.

chordophone. An instrument in which a string is stretched over a support and that generates sound when the string is plucked, bowed, strummed, or struck. Example: guitar, berimbau.

chord progression. A series of chords. See also chord, harmony.

choreographer. The person who determines the movements of the dancers in a ballet or other dance performance.

choro. A Brazilian urban genre often used in serenades and that showcases cavaquinho and flute.

chromatic scale. A scale that consists solely of half steps. See also scale, diatonic, half step.

chula. A call-and-response portion of a capoeira song.

cinquillo. A five-note rhythmic pattern common in Caribbean music.

classical music. Music of the Western European canon.

classical period. In music, the period from c. 1750–1800.

clave. A rhythmic pattern common in Afro-Latin American music that consists of a five-stroke pattern. Spanish for "key," clave is the rhythmic foundation for the rest of the percussion section.

claves. A percussion instrument consisting of two thick wooden sticks eight to eleven inches long, usually of rosewood or ebony.

coda. The concluding section of a musical composition, usually confirming a sense of finality.

codex. A book, usually bound, with a handwritten text. It may include drawings or musical notation.

communion. The focal point of the Roman Catholic mass, which commemorates Christ's last supper before he sacrificed himself on the cross. The priest serves worshipers a sip of wine, which becomes Christ's blood, and a small amount of bread, which becomes Christ's body.

comparsa. The candombe ensemble; more generally, a group of carnival performers. See also candombe.

compás. A fragment of melody and harmony, consistently repeated, as the basis for a son jarocho.

composer. An individual who conceives of and preserves, often in writing, a musical work.

compound meter. A temporal organization of music in which beats fall into three divisions. See also meter.

computer music. Developed from the 1950s, it draws on computer technology in the process of composition or is created by a computer program.

concertmaster. The leader of the first violin section in a symphony orchestra.

concerto. A genre of classical music that features a soloist (or sometimes a small group of soloists) and a symphony or chamber orchestra.

conductor. The individual who leads a symphony orchestra by learning and interpreting a musical score.

conga. A tall, narrow drum with a single head used in Afro-Cuban music.

conguero. A percussionist who plays the conga drums.

conjunct melody. A melody consisting of stepwise intervallic motion. See also interval.

cool jazz. A type of jazz with complex rhythms and harmonies that was popular in the 1950s and 1960s and that did not involve dancing.

corpophone. A human body used to generate sounds, as in finger snapping, hand clapping, or thigh slapping.

Corpus Christi. The Roman Catholic celebration of the sacrament of communion. See also communion.

corrido. (**1**) A ballad, often strophic, that tells a story. Most often associated with Mexico. Can also refer to (**2**) the section in Brazilian capoeira that signals that the dance is about to begin.

countermelody. A melody that is played or sung simultaneously with the main melody.

course. In certain types of guitars, two strings that are closely placed in comparison with other strings and tuned at the unison or the octave. A course is typically played as one string and amplifies the sound.

cowbell. A clapperless bell struck with a stick and used as percussion instrument.

crotales. A small, tuned cymbal.

cuatro. A small, four-stringed member of the guitar family used in música llanera. Another type of cuatro has five metal strings and is used in traditional Puerto Rican music.

cueca. The national dance of Chile, associated with rural traditions. Danced in couples and accompanied by guitar, accordion, harp, and percussion. See also cueca brava, cueca nortina, cueca sola.

cueca brava. The urban variety of the cueca, dating from the 1960s. Accompanied by instruments such as accordion or piano.

cueca nortina. A cueca from the northern part of Chile, which uses some Andean instruments, such as the bombo and panpipes.

cueca sola. A variant of this traditional couple dance in which a woman dances alone because her husband or her partner was "disappeared" by the regime of Augusto Pinochet (1973–90).

cumbia. A couple dance initially associated with Colombia that combines African, Spanish, and indigenous influences. In its traditional versions, either party would hold lit candles while dancing.

See also gaita, tambora, tambor llamador, tambor alegre.

deceptive cadence. A chord progression in which the dominant harmony moves to a chord other than the tonic, often creating an element of surprise. See also cadence.

Deer Dance. A dance performed at religious ceremonies in Yaqui communities.

diatonic. Music is said to be diatonic if its pitches are confined to those of a given scale in the Western music system, that is, excluding chromatic pitches. An instrument lacking chromatic pitches is also said to be diatonic. See also chromatic.

diegetic music. A film music term denoting music whose source (a radio, for example) is part of the plot. Also called source music.

diegetic sound. Sound in film that is also of the plot.

disjunct melody. A melody consisting of intervals further away than the next successive note of the scale. See also interval.

dissonance. The effect of combining intervals and chords so as to defy established rules of scale, key, and harmony.

downbeat. The first beat of a measure, usually emphasized.

drone. A sustained note, usually the lowest part, that serves as an accompaniment to a melody.

duple meter. A regularly recurring pattern of two beats per bar.

duration. The time in which something elapses. In music, determined by pulse, meter, and rhythm.

dynamics. Volume. In classical music, Italian terminology is generally used, that is, *piano, forte, mezzo forte,* etc.

electroacoustic music. Music that uses technologies such as the synthesizer, magnetic tape, and the computer to generate electronic sounds.

electrophone. An instrument that generates sound via electronics. Examples: synthesizer, electric guitar.

elements of music. The building blocks of music, that is, the musical ingredients used in a musical creation. See also timbre, pitch, beat, rhythm, meter, tempo, melody, harmony, texture, form, performing forces.

end credits. The portion at the very end of a film or television program in which all the collaborators are listed, and which normally involves music.

entremés. One of several varieties of short, nonreligious dramatic works with music often inserted between the acts of a religious drama during the Spanish Golden Age. See also tonadilla.

equal temperament. A system in which a given range of pitches is divided into equal parts, that is, adjacent pitches that are the same distance apart.

escola de samba. See samba school.

ethnomusicology. The discipline in musical scholarship that concentrates on traditional and popular music outside of the Western European classical canon, often from an anthropological perspective. See also fieldwork.

etude. French for "study." A piece of music composed to tackle some technical, performance-related problem, such as how to play successive loud chords on the piano, or how to move the bow of a stringed instruments swiftly and without tension.

fieldwork. A type of research traditionally undertaken by ethnomusicologists that involves going to the country or region where a certain type of music is performed, learning how to play from local teachers, and interviewing performers and listeners. To carry out this research, scholars generally learn the local language.

film score. The music composed or selected to enhance a film. Generally notated, unless written with a sequencing program on a computer. See also hummer.

Finnish tango. A variant of the Argentine tango. Calls for a regular accordion (instead of bandoneón) and adds drums. See also tango.

folk music. A variety of traditional music associated with rural environments, either learned by ear or written down. In Latin America, often influenced by Spanish and Portuguese traditions. See also traditional music.

folksong. A category of music popularized by singers who performed, mainly with guitar accompaniment, sometimes to advance a social message or highlight some aspect of rural or working-class culture. See also traditional music.

foreshadowing. In film music, preparing the viewer for the next scene through music.

form. The organization of the various sections of a musical creation; the way music unfolds through time. See also elements of music.

frequency. In acoustics, the number of vibrations per second in a sound wave.

fuga. The final section of a wayno, usually at a quicker tempo.

fundamental. In acoustics, the lowest frequency in a composite tone, which consists of multiple and simultaneously produced frequencies. Since the fundamental is the loudest of these, it is the fundamental that determines the pitch of the composite tone. See also overtone series.

funk carioca. A type of dance music popular in Rio de Janeiro that involves sampled songs and repeated patterns or grooves.

gaita. A type of Latin American flute made from bamboo cane or wood and of variable length. Long gaitas are played in pairs, called male and female (macho, hembra).

genre. A category of music, a label that refers to the type of instruments or voices used (viola concerto) or denotes the general parameters of a given type of music (wayno). See also style.

ginga. The basic movement in capoeira in which the player drags one leg behind the other and then reverses legs. See also capoeira.

glissando. A series of notes played so rapidly as to sound like a sweep or a slide. Possible on many instruments.

Golden Age, Spain *(siglo de oro)*. A period of intense creativity in literature, art, and music in Spain (overlaps sixteenth and seventeenth centuries).

golpe. In Latin American music, can refer to (1) the percussive strummed patterns played in joropo or (2) a subcategory of joropo, which has a quick tempo and driving character. In Spanish, the verb "golpear" means to strike or hit and is thus also a term in flamenco guitar playing. See also joropo, pasaje.

golpe con leco. A long, wailing sound made by the singer at the beginning of a sung joropo ("leco" meaning "cry" or "wail").

Grammy, Latin Grammy. The award given to the best recording in a given category of music. Originally called the Gramophone Award, the gramophone being an early device for playing recorded sound. The Latin Grammy honors music sung in Spanish or Portuguese. The first Latin Grammy awards ceremony was held in 2000.

Gregorian chant. Another term for plainchant. See also plainchant.

grijutian. A string of deer hooves, used as a percussion instrument.

guacharaca. In música vallenata, a scraper made from a dried gourd or of metal that presumably resembles the raspy call of the guacharaca bird.

guache. An African-derived percussion instrument used in traditional cumbia consisting of a tube of either metal or cane filled with seeds.

guaguancó. A type of traditional Cuban music and couple dance characterized by a lively tempo and elaborate percussion.

guarimba. A genre in Central American marimba music characterized by frequent sesquiáltera.

güiro. A percussion instrument consisting of a notched gourd, held in one hand, that the player scrapes with a stick held in the other hand. Common in many Latin American genres.

guitarrón. A large guitar-like instrument tuned a fifth lower than most standard guitars. See also mariachi.

half cadence. A cadence that progresses from tonic to dominant. See also cadence.

half step. In traditional Western music, the smallest interval. The distance between any two keys on the piano. See also interval, whole step, chromatic scale.

haraví. An indigenous Andean genre sung by women in rituals that mark the agricultural and life cycle.

harmonium. A reed organ operated by foot pedals.

harmony. In contrast to the horizontal nature of melody, harmony is the vertical dimension of music, that is, notes grouped in chords or other groups of pitches.

heptatonic scale. A scale consisting of seven pitches.

hip hop. A term that refers to a culture in which rap music plays an important part. Includes music, break dancing, graffiti, fashion. Sometimes used interchangeably with rap. Initially associated with the African American community. See also rap.

hocket. The practice of dividing the pitches in a given melodic line between two musicians (or groups of musicians) who alternate in playing successive pitches.

homophonic texture. A musical texture that results when one melody predominates over an accompaniment. See also texture.

homorhythm. A style of music in which the melody and the accompaniment all have the same rhythm.

huayno. See wayno.

huayñu. See wayno.

hummer. An individual without much musical training who arrives at an idea for a film score but must dictate it to a scribe. See also film score.

hymn. A song designed for worship. Depending on the period in which a hymn was created, it may be in plainchant, homorhythmic style, or in some other format.

idiophone. An instrument made of a substance that will produce sound when struck. Examples: claves, caxixi.

improvisation. The art of spontaneous musical performance, either by creating an entirely new creation or by embellishing existing music.

incidental music. Music played to enhance a live drama, either during the scene changes, between acts, or to set a mood.

instrumentation. The process by which a composer selects those instruments that will form part of the performing forces in a composition. See also orchestration.

instrument families. In Western music, the collective name for four groups of commonly used instruments, namely, string, woodwind, brass, and percussion.

interlocking rhythm. A situation common in percussion-rich ensembles in which players perform various rhythms that overlap among the players. See also polyrhythm, polymeter.

interpretation. In music, the attempt to discern the significance and guide the performance of a musical creation.

interval. The distance between two pitches ("inter" meaning "between").

irregular meter. A type of meter that combines even- and odd-numbered patterns of beats, such as groups of twos and threes.

jarabe. A set of several related pieces dating from the colonial period in Latin America, each of which would be danced to a different step.

jarabe tapatío. A variant of the jarabe associated with the Mexican state of Jalisco, sometimes known in English as the "Mexican Hat Dance."

jarana. A small, shallow instrument in the guitar family used in son jarocho. See also son jarocho.

jíbaro. In music, a genre associated with rural Puerto Rican farmers consisting of improvised verses.

joropero. Performers of the joropo.

joropo. The principal subgenre in música llanera. A lively dance, it features the cuatro, maracas, and harp. See also cuatro, golpe, pasaje, música llanera.

kena. Vertical Andean flute. May be made of wood, bone, bamboo, or, more recently, plastic. Spanish: quena.

key. In Western music, the scale on which the melodies and harmonies of a musical creation are based. See also scale, resolution.

ladainha. In capoeira, a litany, in which a solo singer tells a story, sometimes improvising music, words, or both.

latune. A popular Latin American song altered by the music industry for consumption by US audiences.

libretto. The story of an opera, usually written by someone other than the composer. Italian for "booklet."

liturgy. A religious ritual associated with a certain purpose, approved by religious authorities, and recognized as such by congregants. Music is an important liturgical element.

loa. A spoken prologue in a Golden Age theater work in which the audience is oriented to the subject matter and broader questions the play will seek to address and which may involve music.

louvação. A salutation, or type of capoeira song in which the singers greet their master and which precedes the actual play.

lute. A plucked stringed instrument with a curved back. See also charango, theorbo.

major scale. See scale.

malambo. An Argentine dance associated with the gauchos, the horsemen of the pampas, that features coordination and endurance, often performed competitively.

maqam. A system in Arab music that determines pitch and melody.

maracas. A small percussion instrument made from either wood or leather with seeds inside that sound when the instrument is shaken.

mariachi. (1) A style of music that was initially associated with the Mexican state of Jalisco but that is now widely imported. Instrumentation includes violins, trumpets, six-stringed guitar, guitarrón, and vihuela. (2) A performer of mariachi music.

Marian worship. The Roman Catholic tradition of worshiping the Virgin Mary, including numerous musical traditions.

marimba. A xylophone with wooden keys, often with resonance chambers beneath the keys and much associated with Central America, especially Guatemala and Nicaragua. See also baile de la marimba, simple marimba, charleo.

marimbero. A marimba player.

maso bwikam. The song that accompanies the Yaqui Deer Dance.

mass. The principal Roman Catholic worship ritual with multiple sections, which can be either spoken or sung. Over centuries, hundreds of composers have set portions of the mass to music.

mbira. An African thumb "piano" consisting of a wooden board to which metal tongues have been attached.

measure. A group of beats with emphasis on the first, constituting a metrical unit. Also called a bar.

medieval period. In music, the period from c. 800 to 1400.

melismatic setting. An approach to setting words to music in which a single syllable can receive many notes. See also syllabic setting.

melody. A series of pitches. A tune.

membranophone. An instrument that produces sound through a membrane stretched over a support, which is then struck. Examples: bombo, surdo, other kinds of drums.

merengue. A dance genre from the Dominican Republic.

meter. A regularly recurring pattern of weak and strong beats. See also duple, triple, quadruple, compound meter, rhythm.

microtone. An interval smaller than the half step found in the chromatic scale of European music, used widely in musical cultures throughout the world.

MIDI (Musical Instrument Digital Interface). A protocol that enables one synthesizer to communicate with another, sending messages about tempo, pitch, vibrato, and other parameters.

miniature. In classical music, a composition that is very short, generally only a few minutes.

minor scale. See scale.

modernism. An aesthetic movement in the arts that, in music, is principally associated with the first half of the twentieth century. Among other attributes is the tendency of modernists to break with traditions of the past.

monophonic texture. A musical texture that results when one melody stands alone, without accompaniment or other pitches. See also texture.

montage. In film music, a set of short scenes connected by one piece of music.

montuno. The refrain section in salsa music, generally in some form of call-and-response style. See also canto.

motive. A fragment of a few notes that often recurs in a musical composition. See also theme, thematic recall.

movement. A part of a classical composition. At the conclusion of a movement, it is customary at concerts of classical music to withhold applause until the entire composition (i.e., all the movements) has been played.

mula. The medium-pitched drum of the bembe ensemble in Afro-Cuban Santería.

multisectional form. A musical form in which contrasting sections are freely juxtaposed.

música criolla. Refers to a musical genre of European origins but reimagined in Latin America. From "criollo," which refers to a person of European descent born in Latin America.

música guajira. The music of rural Cuba, often accompanied by the guitar or other instruments in the guitar family and involving sung improvisations.

música jarocha. Music of the jarochos of Veracruz, Mexico. See also son jarocho.

musical. Noun: a theater work involving musical numbers and spoken dialogue, frequently incorporating dance as well. See also operetta.

musical infrastructure. A network of musicians, instruments, audiences, organizations, media, and material support that permit a musical community to exist.

música llanera. A collective term for music from the Orinoco plains of Colombia and Venezuela. See also cuatro, joropo, golpe, pasaje.

musical nationalism. The representation of national (or regional) sentiment through music whether through compositional means (i.e., incorporating folk songs, dance rhythms, or subject matter into a work) or because an audience comes to attach nationalist meanings to a given musical creation.

musical quotation. The practice of borrowing preexisting music into a new musical work, often by weaving a melody into the musical texture.

música ranchera. A type of music associated with mariachis that treats the circumstances and emotions of ordinary people, often rural.

música vallenata. A collective term for music from the Caribbean coastal region of Colombia, known as La Costa, encompassing several subcategories and types and commonly using gaitas, caja, guacharaca, and button accordion. A lead singer is joined by another who harmonizes. Often involves verse-and-refrain form. See also paseo.

musicology. The study of music history and criticism. Traditionally, musicologists have focused on the Western European canon.

music therapy. A discipline that seeks to understand the effects of music on health.

musique concrète. Music that incorporates recordings of the sounds of everyday life into a musical creation, conceived in France during the post–World War II period.

narcocorrido. A subcategory of the corrido, which tells of the exploits of drug smugglers.

nondiegetic music. A film music term indicating music used to enhance the plot and characterization but whose source is not identified in the plot and is thus heard without the characters being aware of it. See also diegetic music.

note. A pitched sound that is either high or low depending on frequency, the number of vibrations per second in the sound wave. See also pitch.

nueva canción. Spanish for "new song," here, music of social and political involvement, often for solo voice. Subject to national and regional variants, such as nueva canción chilena (Chilean new song).

octave. The interval between a given pitch and another pitch with half or double the first pitch's frequency. (A note an octave lower will have half the initial frequency; a note an octave higher will have double.) The two notes of the octave will always have the same name, e.g., A to A.

Ondes Martenot. An electronic instrument dating from the 1920s and invented by a Frenchman, Maurice Martenot. Sound is produced through vacuum tubes with variable frequency of oscillation.

opening credits. The section at the very beginning of a film or television program in which the most important collaborators are listed, which often involves music.

opera. A play in which every word is set to music, usually involving orchestra, scenery, costumes.

operetta. A play that features musical numbers, spoken dialogue, and sometimes dance. See also opera, musical.

orchestration. The process by which a composer, once having selected those instruments that will form part of the performing forces in a composition, decides how best to combine them. See also instrumentation.

organology. The study of musical instruments, including their histories, acoustic properties, and social function.

oricha. Spanish term for a divinity associated with Cuban Santería, often representing some natural force.

ornament. A series of notes, sometimes improvised, that embellish an existing melody.

ostinato. A repeated pattern that serves as the basis for a musical creation or a section thereof. Can consist of rhythmic or melodic elements or a combination of both.

overtone series. An ordered series of pitches that sound when a note is played. The loudest of these is the fundamental. See also fundamental.

pandeiro. A shallow drum with one head and jingles. Held with one hand and struck with the other. Similar in appearance to a tambourine. See also batucada, capoeira.

pandereta. A round, handheld frame drum borrowed by Latin Americans from Spanish and Arab cultures.

Pan-Latinamerican. In music, a genre is said to be Pan-Latinamerican if it has crossed national boundaries and enjoys a wide audience throughout Latin America.

panpipes. A series of double-ranked pipes of graduated lengths, generally of cane, and associated with the Andean region. See also siku, antara.

pasaje. A subcategory of joropo. More melodious than the golpe. See also golpe.

paseo. A subcategory of música vallenata. In common (4/4) time. See also música vallenata.

performing forces. The instruments or voices used in a musical creation.

phrase. A unit of musical thought, comparable to a clause in a sentence.

Phrygian mode. A scale in the Western European system (i.e., pattern of half and whole steps) that features a half step for its initial interval.

piano. (1) The lowest-pitched drum in the candombe ensemble. (2) keyboard instrument.

piano quartet. A chamber music ensemble consisting of violin, viola, cello, and piano. This name also applies to a composition for such an ensemble.

piano quintet. A chamber music ensemble consisting of two violins, viola, cello, and piano. This name also applies to a composition for such an ensemble.

piano trio. A chamber music ensemble consisting of violin, cello, and piano. This name also applies to a composition for such an ensemble.

pinkillu. See pinkullu.

pinkuyllu. The Quechua term for a pre-Conquest vertical flute, usually with five to six holes with a mouthpiece. The Aymara term is "pinkillu."

pitch. A note. A pitch or note will be high or low depending on frequency.

pizzicato. The practice of plucking a stringed instrument rather than using the bow.

plainchant. Monophonic, Latin-texted music of Roman Catholicism. Also known as Gregorian chant.

plainchant mass. A setting of the entire mass in plainchant. See also mass, plainchant.

plena. An African-influenced Puerto Rican genre that involves call-and-response singing, pandereta (seguidor, segundo, requinto), and güiro.

polca. A lively dance in duple meter of European origin, especially popular in Mexico from the nineteenth century but also in other regions of Latin America. See also polca paraguaya.

polca paraguaya. Spanish for "Paraguayan polka." Unlike the European polca, uses sesquiáltera and may contain syncopation. See also polca.

polyphonic mass. A setting of the entire mass in plainchant. See also mass, polyphony.

polyphonic texture. A musical texture that results when several independent melodies sound at once. See also texture.

polyphony. The presence of many independent parts or melodies sounding at once.

polyrhythm. Several independent rhythms heard simultaneously. See also rhythm.

popular music. A type of music generally associated with the mass audience.

premiere. The first performance of a musical composition, play, or other production.

primera drum. A type of drum used in Garífuna religious observance. See also segunda drum.

principal. In music, the section leader in a symphony orchestra.

principal second. The leader of the second violin section in a symphony orchestra.

protest song. A song that directly or indirectly advances some political or social point of view.

psychoacoustics. The study of psychological and physiological responses to sound.

public domain. In music, a legal category indicating that the creative rights of the composer have expired.

pulse. In music, another word for beat. See also rhythm, meter.

quadruple meter. A regularly recurring pattern of four beats per bar.

ranchera. See música ranchera.

range. The span of pitches that a given instrument can play or that a human voice can sing.

rap. A musical genre that involves rhythmical chanting, usually in duple meter, and often with another recording playing in the background on which the rapper may comment, directly or indirectly. See also hip hop.

rapero. Spanish for "rapper."

rasping stick. A percussion instrument consisting of two notched wooden sticks that are scraped together.

recital. A concert, often by a single performer (or a small number of performers), of classical music.

reco-reco. A percussion instrument used in Brazilian music and consisting of a metal scraper and a stick. See also batucada.

reggaeton. A contemporary dance style with rapped or sung vocals and Caribbean rhythms.

register. The overall pitch of a musical passage.

Renaissance period. In classical music, the period from c. 1400 to 1600.

repinique. A two-headed drum used in Brazilian drumming ensembles, the function of which is to cue the other instruments. See also batucada.

repique. The medium-pitched drum in the candombe ensemble. See also candombe.

requinto. (1) An instrument in the guitar family used in son jarocho with four single strings that are picked rather than strummed or **(2)** a pandereta used in plena. See also son jarocho, plena.

resolution. A chord progression in the Western European system in which harmonic tension is followed with a note or a chord that suggests stability or completion.

rest. A moment of silence in a musical creation.

rhumba. A ballroom dance popular in the United States during the 1930 and 1940s. Not related to the Afro-Cuban rumba. See also rumba.

rhythm. The way in which music is organized in time. See also beat, meter.

rim shot. In percussion playing, the sharply accented sound produced when the player strikes the head and the rim simultaneously.

ritard, ritardando. A gradual slowing down of tempo.

roda de capoeira. The circle of participants in capoeira. See also capoeira.

romantic period. In music, the period from c. 1800 to 1900.

rumba. An Afro-Cuban dance-song genre performed with conga drums, claves, and wooden sticks. "Rumba" can also refer to the event at which this music is performed.

Sachs-Hornbostel system. A classification scheme for musical instruments devised in 1914 by two European scholars, Curt Sachs and Erich Moritz von Hornbostel. See also idiophone, aerophone, chordophone, membranophone.

salsa. Spanish for "sauce." A pan–Latin American style that emerged in the Latino immigrant community in the 1970s in New York that blends Cuban son jazz, and Puerto Rican influences.

salsa dura. Spanish for "hard salsa." A subgenre of salsa normally with hard-driving rhythms See also salsa.

salsa romántica. Spanish for "romantic salsa." A subgenre of salsa that is usually at a more relaxed tempo than salsa dura and that often involves studio manipulation, such as reverb. See also salsa.

Salve Regina. One of four medieval chants sung in Roman Catholic worship to honor the Virgin Mary. See also Marian worship.

samba. A song or dance in duple meter associated with Brazilian Carnaval in which African influences endure in rhythm and percussion.

samba canção. A sung samba, generally at a slower tempo than the more standard samba. See also samba.

samba school. A neighborhood institution in Brazil that prepares for the yearly Carnaval celebration.

sampling. Using a portion of an existing recording in a new context, often in rap music.

Santería. An Afro-Cuban religion, mainly of Yoruban origins, that combines music and dance. Some rituals also draw on imagery from Roman Catholicism.

sardana. A circle dance emblematic of Catalonia, a region of northeast Spain with its own language and culture.

scale. A pattern of pitches on which all or part of a musical creation may be based. See also key, interval, half step, whole step.

segunda drum. A type of drum used in Garífuna religious observance. See also primera drum.

sequence. The repetition of melody or a chord progression at a different pitch level than at which it initially sounded.

sesquiáltera. A metrical pattern in which two groups of three beats alternate with three groups of two beats. Common in much Spanish and Spanish-influenced Latin American music.

siku. Aymara for panpipes. See also panpipes.

simple marimba (marimba sencilla). A diatonic marimba with a single row of keys and played by several musicians at once.

snare. A length of wire, gut, or hide stretched across the top of a drum to increase volume or produce a buzzing sound.

social dance. A category of dance in which interacting with others is a primary focus.

son. A Spanish cognate for "song." A collective term in the music of Mexico and Cuba that refers to several stylistic transformations.

son huasteco. A son from the Huastec region of northeast Mexico. See also son.

son jaliscience. A son from the Mexican state of Jalisco and important in mariachi music. See also son, mariachi.

son jarocho. A son from the Mexican state of Veracruz, which relies on certain instruments. See also jarana, requinto, and arpa jarocha.

soprano. The range that lies above the alto. Applies to the female voice and also to certain instruments (saxophone).

string quartet. A chamber music ensemble consisting of two violins, viola, and cello. This name also applies to a composition for such an ensemble.

strophe. A verse of a poem. See also strophic form.

strophic form. In music, the practice of setting each verse of a poem or other text to the same music.

style (music). A mode of performance or expression by performers or composers, including the manipulation by the latter of the elements of music within a range of parameters common to a given style or trend. See also genre.

stylization. An approach to traditional music that involves enhancements or adjustments to its original form.

surdo. A bass drum used in Brazilian percussion music. See also batucada.

syllabic setting. An approach to setting words to music in which a single syllable receives only one note. See also melismatic setting.

symphony. (1) A composition for symphony orchestra, the style and form of which vary according to era and (2) the ensemble that plays such music, that is, a symphony orchestra.

synesthesia. A neurological phenomenon in which stimulation of one sense leads simultaneously to the stimulation of another. In music, people affected by synesthesia see colors when they listen to music, a phenomenon known informally as "colored hearing."

synthesizer. An electronic musical instrument that generates electronic signals that are converted to sound. See also electrophone.

tambora. The lowest-pitched drum in the cumbia ensemble. See also cumbia.

tambor alegre. Spanish for "happy drum." The drum in the cumbia ensemble that generally improvises rhythmic patterns. See also cumbia.

tamboril. A tubular and single-headed drum in the candombe ensemble. See also candombe.

tamborim. A small, hand-held, tambourine-like instrument used in Brazilian percussion. See also batucada.

tambor llamador. Spanish for "caller drum." In the cumbia ensemble, smaller and higher-pitched than the tambora, generally providing an ostinato. See also cumbia.

tam-tam. A gong used in the percussion section of symphony orchestras.

tango. An Argentine and Uruguayan dance in duple meter popular both in Latin America and abroad in the early decades of the twentieth century. See also Finnish tango, tango canción.

tango canción. A sung tango, usually on some tragic topic.

tarima. A wooden platform used for dancing in son jarocho. See also zapateado.

technique. In music, (1) the ability of a performer to control his or her instrument or vocal cords with optimal efficiency and (2) the ability of a composer to write in a variety of forms and styles.

teleology. In music, the progression toward a goal.

tempo. The speed at which a musical creation unfolds.

tenebari. Rattles made from butterfly cocoons.

tenor. The range that lies between alto and bass. Applies to the male voice and also to certain instruments (saxophone).

teponaztli. A Nahautl word indicating the two-keyed xylophone used by various indigenous communities in pre-Conquest Mexico.

texture. (1) The distribution of the horizontal (melodic) and vertical (harmonic) elements of music. See also monophonic, homophonic, polyphonic. (2) In a more general sense, overall distribution of sounds, that is, light (transparent) or heavy (dense) depending on the number of instruments used.

thematic recall. A procedure in which a composer states a theme and then restates it later in the composition, sometimes more than once.

theme. In Western music, an extended musical idea. See also motive.

theme-and-variations form. A procedure in which a composer or performer takes a melody, either preexisting or newly composed, as a point of departure and varies it by reimagining selected elements of music.

theorbo. A large lute common in the seventeenth century and played in early music ensembles today.

theremin. An electronic instrument dating from the 1920s and invented by a Russian, Leon Theremin. Sound is produced through two oscillators operating at fixed and variable frequencies and activated by the proximity of the performer's hands.

timbal. A tall, narrow drum from northeast Brazil. See also batucada.

timbalero. The percussionist who plays the timbales. See also timbales.

timbales. A percussion instrument consisting of a pair of drums with plastic heads on a stand that are struck with a stick. Often used in salsa.

timbre. The quality of sound that is peculiar to a given instrument or voice. Used interchangeably with the term "tone color."

time signature. In the Western European system, the numbers at the beginning of a piece, displayed in the format of a fraction, that indicate the meter.

tlapnhuehuetl. A Nahuatl word signifying a large drum.

tonadilla. One of several varieties of short, nonreligious dramatic works with music often inserted between the acts of a religious drama or opera during the Spanish Golden Age. See also entremés.

tonal center. The note to which other pitches gravitate.

tone color. The quality of sound that is peculiar to a given instrument or voice. Used interchangeably with the term "timbre."

toque. (1) The rhythmic-melodic pattern used in capoeira and (2) the rhythmic pattern used in candombe.

traditional music. A type of music generally associated with rural communities.

transcription. In music, (1) the score that results when an ethnomusicologist or other researcher writes down the music of an oral tradition or (2) an arrangement of an existing piece of music for performing forces other than those originally used.

tres. A small instrument in the guitar family with three courses of double strings that are often tuned to a major or minor triad. Used in Cuban son.

triad. In the Western European system, a chord consisting of three notes, each separated by the interval of a third.

triple meter. A regularly recurring pattern of three beats per bar.

tritonic scale. A scale consisting of three pitches.

unmetered. A descriptor for a musical creation that lacks meter.

unpitched sound. A pitch with an irregular waveform. See also pitched sound.

upbeat. An unaccented beat preceding an accented beat.

vals de salón. A subgenre of the triple-meter vals (waltz) and Spanish for "parlor waltz." Performed in the salons (parlors) of the bourgeoisie, often on the piano rather than actually danced. See also waltz.

vals popular. A subgenre of the triple-meter vals (waltz) and Spanish for "popular waltz." Performed in rural settings. See also waltz.

vals venezolano. A subgenre of the triple-meter vals (waltz) and Spanish for "Venezuelan waltz." Generally at a quick tempo and rhythmically intricate. See also waltz.

vernacular. The spoken language of the people of a given country or region.

verse-and-refrain form. A musical form in which one set of words is sung to one melody (A, the verse) and another is set to a different melody (B, the refrain). The verse repeats, often several times, with different words and is answered by the refrain, which generally maintains the same words.

vibrato. In stringed instruments, refers to a slight shaking back and forth on the fingerboard, which can be intensified for expressive purposes and which causes a slight oscillation in pitch. The technique can be applied to other instruments and to the voice.

vihuela. A five-stringed member of the guitar family. See also mariachi.

villancico. In Latin American music, a religious but nonliturgical composition in the vernacular, including indigenous languages such as Nahuatl and Quechua. Sometimes translated as "Christmas carol."

viola da gamba. One of a family of bowed instruments with flat backs and sloping "shoulders," common in the sixteenth and seventeenth centuries and played in early music ensembles today. Held between the legs, "gamba" being Italian for "leg."

violone. The biggest member of the family to which the viola da gamba belongs, approximately the size of an upright bass. Common in the sixteenth and seventeenth centuries and played in early music ensembles today. See also viola da gamba.

virtuoso. An individual who has mastered all the resources of his or her voice or instrument and whose technique is equal to any technical challenge.

vocable. A syllable (often a series of syllables) lacking meaning but employed for expressive or other reasons.

vocalise. A type of singing in which the performer sings a single syllable, such as "ah" or "oo," without declaiming any words.

waltz. A couple dance in triple meter of European origin, especially popular in Vienna from the early nineteenth century and initially controversial because of the tight embrace it required. See also vals popular, vals de salón, vals venezolano.

water drum. A pitched percussion instrument consisting of half a gourd placed in a wooden bowl of water (or half of a larger gourd) with the open side downward.

wayno. A centuries-old musical genre associated with the Andean region that has been modified in numerous ways over time. Also spelled huayno, huayñu, wayñu.

whole step. In traditional Western music, two half steps, that is, the distance between two keys on the piano with one key in between. See also interval, half step, conjunct melody.

woodwind quintet. A chamber music ensemble consisting of flute, clarinet, oboe, French horn, and bassoon. This name also applies to a composition for such an ensemble.

word painting. A strategy composers use to highlight musically the meaning of the words being set, such as writing the Latin word "descendit" at lower pitch.

yanantin. A fundamental precept of Q'eros cosmology that privileges the union of two interdependent but different elements.

yaraví. A mestizo song from the Andes, sung at a slow tempo.

zapateado. Spanish for "energetic footwork" in dance. See also tarima, son jarocho.

zarzuela. Spanish for "operetta." See also opera, operetta.

Selected Bibliography (English)

The following are readable, English-language sources. Occasionally I've cited and translated a Spanish-language source in the text, indicated as such here. Of course, students who read Spanish, Portuguese, or other languages besides English will have a much wider array of sources from which to choose.

Abreu, Christina D. "Celebrity, 'Crossover,' and Cubanidad: Celia Cruz as 'La Reina de Salsa,' 1971–2003." *Latin American Music Review* 28, no. 1 (2007): 94–124.

Acevedo-Muñoz, Ernesto. *West Side Story as Cinema: The Making and Impact of an American Masterpiece.* Lawrence: University Press of Kansas, 2013.

Adorno, Theodor W. *The Culture Industry: Selected Essays on Mass Culture.* Edited by J. M. Bernstein. London and New York: Routledge, 1991.

Aguilera, Pilar, Ariel Dorfman, and Ricardo Fredes, eds. *Chile: The Other September 11: An Anthology of Reflections on the 1973 Coup.* Melbourne and New York: Ocean, 2006.

Aharonián, Coriún. "Technology for the Resistance: A Latin American Case." *Latin American Music Review* 23, no. 2 (2002): 195–205.

Aidi, Hishaam. "The Grand (Hip-Hop) Chessboard: Race, Rap, and Raison d'État." *Middle East Report* 260 (2011): 25–39.

———. *Rebel Music: Race, Empire, and the New Muslim Youth Culture.* New York: Pantheon, 2014.

Albright, Daniel, ed. *Modernism and Music: An Anthology of Sources.* Chicago and London: University of Chicago Press, 2004.

Almeida, Bira. *Capoeira: Brazilian Art Form.* Berkeley: North Atlantic, 1986.

Amado, Andrés. "The Foxtrot in Guatemala: Cosmopolitan Nationalism among Ladinos." *Ethnomusicology Review* 16 (2011): 1–19.

Ana Veydó: Colombian Joropo Vocalist. Artist Spotlight. Smithsonian Folkways. www.folkways.si.edu/ana-veydo-colombian-joropo-vocalist/latin-world/music/article/smithsonian.

Andermann, Jens, and William Rowe, eds. *Images of Power: Iconography, Culture and the State in Latin America.* New York and Oxford: Berghahn, 2005.

Anderson, Benedict. *Imagined Communities: Reflections on the Origin and Spread of Nationalism.* Rev ed. London: Verso, 2006.

Andrews, George Reid. *Blackness in the White Nation: A History of Afro-Uruguay.* Chapel Hill: University of North Carolina Press, 2010.

Anzaldúa, Gloria. *Borderlands La Frontera: The New Mestiza.* 2nd ed. San Francisco: Aunt Lute, 1999.

Aparicio, Frances R. *Listening to Salsa: Gender, Latin Popular Music, and Puerto Rican Cultures.* Hanover, NH: Wesleyan University Press, 1998.

Appadurai, Arjun. *Modernity at Large: Cultural Dimensions of Globalization.* Minneapolis: University of Minnesota Press, 1996.

Appleby, David P. *Heitor Villa-Lobos: A Life, 1887–1959.* Lanham, Maryland and London: Scarecrow, 2002.

Avila Hernández, Juan A. "Yoeme (Yaqui) Deer Dance." In *American Indian Religious Traditions: An Encyclopedia,* edited by Suzanne J. Crawford and Dennis F. Kelley, vol. 3, 1165–68. Santa Barbara: ABC-CLIO: 2005.

Baim, Jo. *Tango: Creation of a Cultural Icon.* Bloomington: Indiana University Press, 2007.

Baker, Geoffrey. *Imposing Harmony: Music and Society in Colonial Cuzco.* Durham and London: Duke University Press, 2008.

Bakota, Carlos Steven. "Getúlio Vargas and the Estado Novo: An Inquiry into Ideology and Opportunism." *Latin American Research Review* 14, no. 1 (1979): 205–10.

Beauschene, Kim, and Alessandra Santos, eds. *The Utopian Impulse in Latin America.* New York: Palgrave Macmillan, 2011.

Béhague, Gerard. *Heitor Villa-Lobos: The Search for Brazil's Musical Soul.* Austin: Institute of Latin American Studies, University of Texas at Austin, 1994.

———. *Music in Latin America: An Introduction.* Englewood Cliffs, NJ: Prentice Hall, 1978.

———. "Rap, Reggae, Rock, or Samba: The Local and the Global in Brazilian Popular Music (1985–1995)." *Latin American Music Review* 27, no. 1 (2006): 79–90.

Beliso-De Jesús, Aisha M. "Contentious Diasporas: Gender, Sexuality, and Heteronationalisms in the Cuban Iyanifa Debate." *Signs: Journal of Women in Culture and Society,* 40, no. 4 (2015): 817–40.

Belnap, Jeffrey "Diego Rivera's Greater America: Pan-American Patronage, Indigenism, and *H. P.*" *Cultural Critique* 63 (2008): 61–98.

Bendix, Regina. *In Search of Authenticity: The Formation of Folklore Studies.* Madison: University of Wisconsin Press, 1997.

Bennighof, James. *The Words and Music of Paul Simon.* Westport, CT: Praeger, 2007.

Bergeron, Katherine. "The Virtual Sacred: Finding God at Tower Records." *New Republic* 212 (February 27, 1995): 29–34.

Bermúdez, Esmeralda. "Exhibit Highlights Women Who Made Mariachi History." *Los Angeles Times.* March 5, 2014. http://articles.latimes.com/2014/mar/05/local/la-me-mariachi-women-20140306.

Bernstein, Leonard. *The Joy of Music.* New York: Simon and Schuster, 1954.

Bethell, Leslie. *A Cultural History of Latin America: Literature, Music, and the Visual Arts in the Nineteenth and Twentieth Centuries.* New York: Cambridge University Press, 1998.

Blacking, John. *The Anthropology of the Body.* London: Academic, 1977.

———. *How Musical Is Man?* Seattle: University of Washington Press, 1973.

Bodenheimer, Rebecca M. "National Symbol or a 'Black Thing': Rumba and Race Politics in Cuba in the Era of Cultural Tourism." *Black Music Research Journal* 33, no. 2 (2013): 177–205.

Bor, Daniel. *The Ravenous Brain: How the New Science of Consciousness Explains Our Insatiable Search for Meaning.* New York: Basic, 2012.

Borges, Jorge Luis. "Oyendo un tango viejo." www.clarin.com /sociedad/borges-vision-particular-tango_0_BJRx5ufswml .html.

Born, Georgina, and David Hesmondhalgh, ed. *Western Music and Its Others: Difference, Representation, and Appropriation in Music.* Berkeley: University of California Press, 2000.

Bosse, Joanna. *Becoming Beautiful: Ballroom Dancing in the American Heartland.* Urbana, Chicago, and Springfield: University of Illinois Press, 2015.

Brandes, Stanley. "The Sardana: Catalan Dance and Catalan National Identity." *Journal of American Folklore* 103, no. 407 (1990): 24–41.

Brill, Mark. *Music of Latin America and the Caribbean.* Boston, Columbus: Pearson/Prentice Hall, 2011.

———. "The Oaxaca Cathedral 'Examen de oposición': The Quest for a Modern Style." *Latin American Music Review* 26, no. 1 (2005): 1–22.

Broad, William J. "Complex Whistles Found to Play Key Role in Maya and Inca Life." *New York Times,* March 29, 1988.

Brown, David H. *Santería Enthroned: Art, Ritual, and Innovation in an Afro-Cuban Religion.* Chicago and London: University of Chicago Press, 2003.

Browning, Barbara. *Salsa: Resistance in Motion.* Bloomington: Indiana University Press, 1995.

Budasz, Rogerio. "The Blessed and the Sinner: Two Foundational Myths of Brazilian Music Historiography." In *Treasures of a Golden Age: Essays in Honor of Robert M. Stevenson,* edited by Walter Aaron Clark and Michael O'Connor, 167–80. New York: Pendragon, 2012.

———. "Of Cannibals and the Recycling of Otherness." *Music & Letters* 87, no. 1 (2006): 1–15.

Bump, Philip. "As Hip-Hop Became Popular, Crime Dropped." *Wire,* January 7, 2014.

Burns, E. Bradford. *Latin America: Conflict and Creation: A Historical Reader.* Englewood Cliffs, NJ: Prentice Hall, 1993.

Burton, Cyndy. "Reflections on Segovia's Guitars at the Metropolitan Museum of Art, New York." *American Lutherie: The Quarterly Journal of the Guild of American Luthiers* 21 (1990): 32–34.

Campbell, W. Joseph. *The Spanish-American War: American Wars and the Media in Primary Documents.* Santa Barbara: Greenwood, 2005.

Candelaria, Cordelia, Peter J. García, and Arturo J. Aldama, eds. *Encyclopedia of Latino Popular Culture.* Vol. 2. Westport, CT; Greenwood, 2004.

Capoeira, Nestor. *Capoeira: Roots of the Dance-Fight-Game.* Berkeley: North Atlantic, 2002.

Cara, Ana C. "Entangled Tangos: Passionate Displays, Intimate Dialogues." *Journal of American Folklore* 122 (2009): 438–65.

Caracas Garcia, Thomas George. "American Views of Brazilian Musical Culture: Villa-Lobos's *Magdalena* and Brazilian Popular Music." *Journal of Popular Culture* 37, no. 4 (2004): 634–47.

Cardoso, Fernando Enrique, and Enzo Faletto. *Dependency and Development in Latin America: Dependencia y desarrollo en América Latina.* Expanded and emended ed. Translated by Marjory Mattingly Urquidi. Berkeley, Los Angeles, and London: University of California Press, 1979. Originally published in 1971.

Carlson, Marvin. *Performance: A Critical Introduction.* 1996; New York and London: Routledge, 2013.

Casey, Michael. *Che's Afterlife: The Legacy of an Image.* New York: Vintage, 2009.

Cashner, Andrew A. "Playing Cards at the Eucharistic Table: Music, Theology, and Society in a Corpus Christi Villancico From Colonial Mexico, 1628." *Journal of Early Modern History* 18 (2014): 383–419.

Chanda, Mona Lisa, and Dan Levitin. "The Neurochemistry of Music." *Trends in Cognitive Sciences* 17, no. 4 (2013): 179–93.

Chapman, Anne. *Drama and Power in a Hunting Society: The Selk'nam of Tierra del Fuego.* Cambridge: Cambridge University Press, 1982.

———. "Selk'nam (Ona) Chants of Tierra del Fuego, Argentina." Liner notes. *Selk'nam Chants of Tierra del Fuego, Argentina.* Smithsonian Folkways, FE 4176, 1976. Reissued in 2007.

Chasteen, John Charles. *National Rhythms, African Roots: The Deep History of Latin American Popular Dances.* Albuquerque: University of New Mexico Press, 2004.

Cheah, Pheng, and Bruce Robbins, eds. *Cosmopolitics: Thinking and Feeling beyond the Nation.* Minneapolis: University of Minnesota Press, 1998.

Chernoff, John Miller. *African Rhythm and African Sensibility: Aesthetics and Social Action in African Music.* Chicago: University of Chicago Press, 1979.

Chestnut, Andrew. *Born Again in Brazil: The Pentecostal Boom and the Pathogens of Poverty.* New Brunswick, NJ: Rutgers University Press, 1997.

Clark, Walter A. "Doing the Samba on Sunset Boulevard: Carmen Miranda and the Hollywoodization of Latin American Music." In *From Tejano to Tango: Latin American Popular Music,* edited by Walter Aaron Clark, 252–76. New York and London: Routledge, 2002.

———. "The Music of Latin America." *Latin America: An Interdisciplinary Approach.* Edited by Gladys Varona-Lacey and Julio López-Arias. New York: Peter Lang, 1998.

Clarke, David, and Eric Clarke. *Music and Consciousness: Philosophical, Psychological, and Cultural Perspectives.* Oxford: Oxford University Press, 2011.

Claxton, Guy. *Intelligence in the Flesh: Why Your Mind Needs Your Body Much More Than It Thinks.* New Haven and London: Yale University Press, 2015.

Cleary, Edward L., and Timothy Steinenga. *Resurgent Voices in Latin America: Indigenous Peoples, Mobilization, and Religious Change.* New Brunswick and London: Rutgers University Press, 2004.

Cohen, John. "Huayno Music of Peru, vol. 1 (1949–1989)." Liner notes. *Huayno Music of Peru,* vol. 1. Arhoolie, CD 320, 1991.

———. "Mountain Music of Peru." Liner notes. *Mountain Music of Peru,* vol. 1. Smithsonian Folkways, SFW CD 40020, 1989.

Collier, Simon. *Tango! The Dance, the Song, the Story.* New York: Thames and Hudson, 1995.

Collier, Simon, and María Susana Azzi. *Le Grand Tango: The Life and Music of Astor Piazzolla*. New York: Oxford University Press, 2000.

Colman, Alfredo C. *The Paraguayan Harp: From Colonial Transplant to National Emblem*. Lanham, MD: Lexington, 2015.

———. "The Paraguayan Harp and Its Music." Liner notes. *Maiteí América: Harps of Paraguay*. Smithsonian Folkways, SFW CD 40548, 2009.

Comaroff, Jean, and John L. Comaroff. *Theory from the South: How Euro-America Is Evolving Toward Africa*. Stellenbosch, South Africa: Sun, 2014.

Cook, Susan. "Passionless Dancing and Passionate Reform: Respectability, Modernism, and the Social Dancing of Irene and Vernon Castle." In *The Passion of Music and Dance: Body, Gender, and Sexuality*, edited by William Washabaugh, 133–50. Oxford: Oxford University Press, 1998.

Cope, Douglas. *The Limits of Racial Domination: Plebian Society in Colonial Mexico City, 1660–1720*. Madison: University of Wisconsin Press, 1994.

Copland, Aaron. *What to Listen for in Music*. Rev. ed. New York: McGraw-Hill, 1999.

Cornelius, Steven. "Encapsulating Power: Meaning and Taxonomy of the Musical Instruments of Santería in New York City." *Selected Reports in Ethnomusicology* 8 (1990): 125–41.

Cornelius, Steven, and John Amira. *The Music of Santería: Traditional Rhythms of the Batá Drums*. Crown Point, IN: White Cliffs Media, 1992.

Cornelius, Steven, and Mary Natvig. *Music: A Social Experience*. Boston: Pearson, 2012.

Crook, Larry. *Black Brazil: Culture, Identity, and Social Mobilization*. Los Angeles: UCLA Latin American Center Publications, University of California, Los Angeles, 1999.

———. *Brazilian Music: Northeastern Traditions and the Heartbeat of a Modern Nation*. Santa Barbara: ABC-CLIO, 2005.

———. "The Form and Formation of the Rumba in Cuba." In *Salsiology: Afro-Cuban Music and the Evolution of Salsa in New York City*, edited by Vernon Boggs. Westport, CT: Greenwood, 1992.

Crumrine, N. Ross. *The Mayo Indians of Sonora: A People Who Refuse to Die*. Tucson: University of Arizona Press, 1977.

———. "A New Mayo Indian Religious Movement in Northwest Mexico." *Journal of Latin American Lore* 1, no. 2 (1975): 127–45.

Cruz, Sor Juana Inés de la. *Sor Juana Inés de la Cruz: Selected Writings*. Edited and translated by Alfredo Mendez Plancarte and Alberto Salceda. Mahwah, NJ: Paulist, 2005.

Damásio, António. *Descartes' Error: Emotion, Reason, and the Human Brain*. New York: HarperCollins, 1994.

———. *The Feeling of What Happens: Body and Emotion in the Making of Consciousness*. New York: Harcourt, 1999.

Damrosch, David. *What Is World Literature?* Princeton and Oxford: Princeton University Press, 2003.

Dangl, Benjamin. "Rapping in Aymara: Bolivian Hip Hop as an Instrument of Struggle." 2006. http://upsidedownworld.org/archives/bolivia/rapping-in-aymara-bolivian-hip-hop-as-an-instrument-of-struggle/.

Davis, Mike. *Planet of Slums*. London: Verso, 2007.

Dean, Carolyn. *Inka Bodies and the Body of Christ: Corpus Christi in Colonial Cuzco, Peru*. Durham and London: Duke University Press, 1999.

De Buenosaires, Oscar. *Tango: A Bibliography*. Albuquerque: FOG, 1991.

Delano, Jack. *Puerto Rico Mío: Four Decades of Change*. Washington: Smithsonian Institution Press, 1990.

Dent, Alexander Sebastian. *River of Tears: Country Music, Memory, and Modernity in Brazil*. Chapel Hill and London: Duke University Press, 2009.

Díaz, Juan Diego. "Between Repetition and Variation: A Musical Performance of *Malícia* in Capoeira." *Ethnomusicology Forum* 26, no. 1 (2017): 46–68.

Domingo, Plácido. *My First Forty Years and More*. 2nd ed. Sussex, UK: Gardners, 2010.

Domínguez, Alberto, and Nancy de los Santos, directors. *The Bronze Screen: One Hundred Years of the Latino Image in Hollywood*. Questar, 2002.

Dorfman, Ariel, and Armand Mattelart. *How to Read Donald Duck: Imperialist Ideology in the Disney Comic*. Translated by David Kunzle. New York: International General, 1975.

Downey, Greg. "Introduction." Liner notes. *Capoeira Angola*. Smithsonian Folkways. Smithsonian Folkways, SFW CD 40465, 1996.

———. *Learning Capoeira: Lessons in Cunning from an Afro-Brazilian Art*. Oxford and New York: Oxford University Press, 2005.

———. "Listening to Capoeira: Phenomenology, Embodiment, and the Materiality of Music." *Ethnomusicology* 46, no. 3 (2002): 487–509.

Downing, Mary Katherine. "Yaqui Cultural Continuity: A Question of Balance." *Wicazo Sa Review* 8, no. 1 (1992): 91–98.

Duany, Jorge. "Popular Music in Puerto Rico: Toward an Anthropology of 'Salsa.'" *Latin American Music Review* 5, no. 2 (1984): 186–216.

———. "Review: 'Salsa,' 'Danza,' and 'Plena': Recent Materials on Puerto Rican Popular Music." *Latin American Music Review* 11, no. 2 (1990): 286–96.

Dunn, Christopher. *Brutality Garden: Tropicalia and the Emergence of a Brazilian Counterculture*. Chapel Hill and London: University of North Carolina Press, 2001.

Edberg, Mark C. "*Narcocorridos*: Narratives of a Cultural Persona and Power on the Border." In *Transnational Encounters: Music and Performance at the U.S.-Mexico Border*, edited by Alejandro L. Madrid, 67–82. New York: Oxford University Press, 2011.

Edelman, Gerald. *Wider Than the Sky: The Phenomenal Gift of Consciousness*. New Haven, CT: Yale University Press, 2004.

Efraín, Kristal, ed. *Cambridge Companion to the Latin American Novel*. Cambridge: Cambridge University Press, 2005.

Eliade, Mircea. *Shamanism: Archaic Techniques of Ecstasy*. Princeton: Princeton University Press, 1964.

Erlmann, Veit. "The Politics and Aesthetics of Transnational Musics." *World of Music* 35, no. 2 (1993): 3–15.

Espinosa, Christian Spencer. "Imagining Traditions: Performance and Social Imagination in the Urban Cueca Scene in Santiago de Chile (2000–2010)." In *Made in Latin America: Studies in Popular Music*, 64–75. Routledge Global Popular Music Series. New York: Routledge, 2016.

Etkin, Mariano. "Riesgo, dinero y heterodoxia." In *La Música en el Di Tella*, edited Rubio, Héctor et al., 52–53. Buenos Aires: Secretaria de la Cultura, 2011. This text is in Spanish.

Evers, Larry, and Felipe S. Molina. *Yaqui Deer Songs Maso Bwikam: A Native American Poetry*. Tucson: Sun Tracks and the University of Arizona Press, 1987.

Faulkner, Anne Shaw (aka Mrs. Marx E. Oberndorfer). "Does Jazz Put the Sin in Syncopation?" In *Keeping Time: Readings in Jazz History*, edited by Robert Walser, 32–36. New York and Oxford: Oxford University Press, 1999.

Fernández-Armesto, Felipe. *Our America: A Hispanic History of the United States.* New York: Norton, 2014.

Finkel, Jori. "What's in a Name? Some Say Inclusion." www.nytimes.com/2017/09/11/arts/design/pacific-standard-time-getty-latino.html?mcubz = 3.

Flores, Juan. *Divided Borders: Essays on Puerto Rican Identity.* Houston: Arte Público, 1993.

———. *From Bomba to Hip-Hop: Puerto Rican Culture and Latino Identity.* New York: Columbia University Press, 2000.

———. *Salsa Rising: New York Latin Music of the Sixties Generation.* New York: Oxford University Press, 2014.

———. *Viento de Agua: Materia Prima Unplugged.* Liner Notes. Smithsonian Folkways, CD 40513, 2004.

Fojas, Camilla. *Cosmopolitanism in the Americas.* West Lafayette, IN: Purdue University Press, 2005.

Foner, Philip S. *The Spanish-Cuban-American War and the Birth of American Imperialism, 1895–1902.* Vols. 1 and 2. New York: Monthly Review Press, 1972.

Forbes, Jack D. *Black Africans and Native Americans: Color, Race and Caste in the Evolution of Red-Black Peoples.* Oxford: Basil Blackwell, 1988.

Fosler-Lussier, Danielle. *Music in America's Cold War Cultural Diplomacy.* Oakland, CA: University of California Press, 2015.

Freire, Paulo. *The Pedagogy of the Oppressed.* Thirtieth anniversary ed. Translated by Myra Bergman Ramos. New York and London: Bloomsbury Academic, 2000.

Freud, Sigmund. "Remembering, Repeating, and Working-Through." In *The Standard Edition of the Complete Psychological Works of Sigmund Freud,* edited and translated by James Strachey, vol. 12, 147–56. London: Hogarth, 1958.

Fuentes, Carlos. *The Buried Mirror: Reflections on Spain and the New World.* Boston and New York: Houghton Mifflin, 1992.

Fulbright, J. William. *The Arrogance of Power.* New York: Random House, 1966.

García Canclini, Néstor. *Hybrid Cultures: Strategies for Entering and Leaving Modernity.* Translated by Christopher L. Chiappari and Silvia L. López. Minneapolis: University of Minnesota Press, 1995. Originally published in Mexico City in 1989.

Gardner, Nathanial. *Como agua para chocolate: The Novel and Film Version.* Critical Guides to Spanish & Latin American Texts and Films. London: Grant & Cutler, 2009.

Garfias, Robert. "The Marimba of Mexico and Central America." *Latin American Music Review* 4, no. 2 (1983): 203–28.

Garland, Peter. *In Search of Silvestre Revueltas: Essays, 1978–1990.* Santa Fe: Sounding, 1991.

Garrard-Burnett, Virginia, Paul Freston, and Stephen C. Dove, eds. *The Cambridge History of Religions in Latin America.* Cambridge: Cambridge University Press, 2016.

Geertz, Clifford. "Art as a Cultural System." *Modern Language Notes* 91 (1978): 1473–99.

Gibson, James Jerome. *The Senses Considered as Perceptual Systems.* Westport, CT: Greenwood, 1983.

Gidal, Marc. "Contemporary 'Latin American' Composers of Art Music in the United States: Cosmopolitans Navigating Multiculturalism and Universalism." *Latin American Music Review* 31, no. 1 (2010): 40–78.

Gilbert, Joseph M., and Daniela Spenser. *In From the Cold: Latin America's Encounter with the Cold War.* Durham and London: Duke University Press, 2008.

Gilly, Adolfo. *The Mexican Revolution.* New Press People's History. New York: New Press, 2006.

Glasser, Ruth. *My Music Is My Flag: Puerto Rican Musicians and Their New York Communities, 1917–1940.* Berkeley: University of California Press, 1995.

Gleason, Philip. "Identifying Identity: A Semantic History." In *Theories of Ethnicity: A Classical Reader.* Edited by Werner Sollors. New York: New York University Press, 1996.

Glocer, Silvia. "Judaísmo y exilio: las palabras ausentes." *Latin American Music Review* 33, no. 1 (2012): 65–101. This text is in Spanish.

Goehr, Lydia. *The Imaginary Museum of Musical Works: An Essay in the Philosophy of Music.* Oxford: Clarendon, 1992.

Goertzen, Chris, and María Susana Azzi. "Globalization and the Tango." *Yearbook for Traditional Music* 31 (1999): 67–76.

Goldin, C., and Rouse, C. "Orchestrating Impartiality: The Impact of 'Blind' Auditions on Female Musicians." *American Economic Review* 90, no. 4 (2000): 715–41.

Goldman, Gustavo. *Uruguay: Tambores del Camdombe.* Musique du monde. Buda Records, 1999 (92745–2).

Gómez, Laura. *Manifest Destinies: The Making of the Mexican American Race.* 2nd ed. New York and London: New York University Press, 2018.

Gonzalez, Juan Pablo. "The Making of a Social History of Popular Music in Chile: Problems, Methods, and Results." *Latin American Music Review* 26, no. 2 (2005): 248–72.

Graham, Richard. "Technology and Culture Change: the Development of the 'Berimbau' in Colonial Brazil." *Latin American Music Review* 12, no. 1 (1991): 1–20.

Graham, Richard, and N. Scott Robinson, eds. "Berimbau." In *Continuum Encyclopedia of Popular Music of the World,* edited by John Shepherd et al., vol. 2, 344–45. New York and London: Continuum, 2003.

Green, Thomas A., and Joseph R. Svinth, eds. *Martial Arts in the Modern World.* London: Praeger, 2003.

Greenberg, Amy S. *A Wicked War: Polk, Clay, Lincoln, and the 1846 Invasion of Mexico.* New York: Vintage, 2013.

Gregory, Steven. *Santería in New York City: A Study in Cultural Resistance.* New York: Garland, 2000.

Griffin, Martin. "Narrative, Culture, and Diplomacy." *Journal of Arts Management, Law, and Society* 38, no. 4 (2009) 258–69.

Gupta, Akhil, and James Ferguson, eds. *Culture, Power, and Place: Explorations in Critical Anthropology.* Durham: Duke University Press, 1997.

Gutiérrez, Gustavo. *A Theology of Liberation: History, Politics, and Salvation.* 15th anniversary ed. Translated by Caridad Inda. Maryknoll, NY: Orbis, 1988.

Hagedorn, Katherine. *Divine Utterances: The Performance of Afro-Cuban Santería.* Washington, DC: Smithsonian Institution Press, 2001.

———. "Resorting to Spiritual Tourism: Sacred Spectacle in Afro-Cuban Regla de Ocha." In *Sun, Sound, and Sand: Music Tourism in the Circum-Caribbean,* edited by Timothy Rommen and Daniel Neely. New York: Oxford University Press, 2014.

Hamilton, John Maxwell, *Journalism's Roving Eye: A History of American Foreign Reporting.* Baton Rouge: Louisiana State University Press, 2009.

Hanna, Judith Lynn. "Dance." In *Ethnomusicology: An Introduction,* edited by Helen Meyers, 315–26. London and New York: Macmillan and Norton, 1992.

———. *Dance, Sex, and Gender.* Chicago: University of Chicago Press, 1988.

Hart, Stephen. *Como agua: A Companion to Latin American Film.* Rochester: Tamesis, 2014.

Hearn, Adrian H. *Cuba: Religion, Social Capital, and Development.* Durham and London: Duke University Press, 2008.

Heile, B. *The Music of Mauricio Kagel.* Farnham, UK: Ashgate, 2006.

Hernández, Alexandro. "The Son Jarocho and Fandango Amidst Struggle and Social Movements: Migratory Transformation and Reinterpretation of the Son Jarocho in La Nueva España, México, and the United States." PhD diss., University of California, Los Angeles, 2014.

Hernández, Alexandro, and Micaela Díaz-Sánchez. "The Son Jarocho as Afro-Mexican Resistance Music." *Journal of Pan African Studies: Africans in México: History, Race and Place,* edited by Itibari M. Zulu, 6, no. 1 (2013): 187–209.

Herndon, Marcia, and Susanne Ziegler, eds. *Music, Gender, and Culture.* Wilhelmshaven: Florian Noetzel, 1990.

Hershberg, James G. "The United States, Brazil, and the Cuban Missile Crisis, 1962." *Journal of Cold War Studies* 6, no. 2 (2004): 1–20; 6, no. 3 (2004): 5–67.

Hess, Carol A. *Representing the Good Neighbor: Music, Difference, and the Pan American Dream.* New York: Oxford University Press, 2013.

———. "Score and Word: Writing about Music." In *Teaching Music History,* edited by Mary Natvig, 193–204. London: Ashgate, 2002.

———. "Silvestre Revueltas in Republican Spain: Music as Political Utterance." *Latin American Music Review* 18, no. 2 (1997): 278–96.

———. "The Symphony in Latin America." In *The Symphonic Repertoire,* vol. 5, pt. B, *The Symphony in Europe and the Americas in the 20th Century.* Bloomington: Indiana University Press, 2018.

———. "Walt Disney's *Saludos Amigos:* Hollywood and the Propaganda of Authenticity." In *The Tide Was Always High: The Music of Latin America in Los Angeles,* edited by Josh Kun, 105–23. Oakland: University of California Press, 2017.

Hilley, David. *Introduction to Gregorian Chant.* Cambridge Introductions to Music. Cambridge: Cambridge University Press, 2009.

"The Hispanicisation of America: The Law of Large Numbers." *Economist* 396, no. 8699 (September 11–17, 2010): 35–36.

Hobsbawm, Eric, and Terence Ranger. *The Invention of Tradition.* Cambridge: Cambridge University Press, 1983.

Hochschild, Adam. *Spain in Our Hearts: Americans in the Spanish Civil War, 1936–39.* New York: Houghton Mifflin Harcourt, 2016.

Holden, Robert H., and Eric Zolov, eds. *Latin America and the United States: A Documentary History.* New York: Oxford University Press, 2000.

Holmes, Thom. *Electronic and Experimental Music: Technology, Music, and Culture.* 5th ed. New York and London: Routledge, 2015.

Holston, James. *Insurgent Citizenship: Disjunctions of Democracy and Modernity in Brazil.* Princeton: Princeton University Press, 2008.

Hood, Mantle. *The Ethnomusicologist.* New ed. Kent: Kent State University Press, 1982.

Hoover, Maya. *A Guide to the Latin American Art Song Repertoire: An Annotated Catalog of Twentieth-Century Art Songs for Voice and Piano.* Bloomington and Indianapolis: Indiana University Press, 2010.

Hoyos, Héctor. *Beyond Bolaño: The Global Latin American Novel.* New York: Columbia University Press, 2015.

Hutchinson, Sydney. "The Ballet Folklórico de México and the Construction of the Mexican Nation through Dance." In *Dancing across Borders: Danzas y Bailes Mexicanos,* edited by Olga Nájera-Ramírez, Norma E. Cantú, and Brenda M. Romero, 206–25. Urbana and Chicago: University of Illinois Press, 2009.

———. "Breaking Borders/*Quebrando fronteras:* Dancing in the Borderscape." In *Transnational Encounters: Music and Performance at the U.S.–Mexico Border,* edited by Alejandro L. Madrid, 41–66. New York: Oxford University Press, 2011.

Huxley, Michael, and Noel Witts, eds. *The Twentieth-Century Performance Reader.* 2nd ed. New York and London: Routledge, 2002.

Inda, Jonathan Xavier, and Renato Rosaldo, eds. *The Anthropology of Globalization: A Reader.* Malden and Oxford: Blackwell, 2001.

Iyanaga, Michael. "Why Saints Love Samba: A Historical Perspective on Black Agency and the Rearticulation of Catholicism in Bahia, Brazil." *Black Music Research Journal* 35, no. 1 (2015): 119–47.

Jara, Joan. *An Unfinished Song: The Life of Victor Jara.* New York: Tickner & Fields, 1984.

Jara, Joan, and Adrian Mitchell. *Victor Jara: His Life and Songs.* Ottawa, Canada: Elm Tree, 1976.

Jenkins, Carol, and Travis Jenkins. Liner notes. *Dabuyabarugu: Inside the Temple. Sacred Music of the Garífuna of Belize,* Smithsonian Folkways Archival, FE 4032, 1982. Reissued in 2007.

Jones, LeRoi. "The Changing Same (R & B and New Black Music)." In *The Black Aesthetic,* edited by Addison Gayle Jr., 112–25. New York: Anchor, 1972.

Josel, Seth F., and Ming Tsao. *The Techniques of Guitar Playing.* Kassel: Barenreiter-Verlag Karl Kotterle, 2014.

Joseph, Gilbert M., and Daniela Spenser. *In From the Cold: Latin America's New Encounter with the Cold War.* Durham and London: Duke University Press, 2008.

Katzew, Ilona. *Casta Painting: Images of Race in Eighteenth-Century Mexico.* New Haven and London: Yale University Press, 2004.

Keefe, Simon P. *The Cambridge Companion to the Concerto.* Cambridge: Cambridge University Press, 2005.

Kennedy, Merrit. "'Game Changer': Maya Cities Unearthed in Guatemala Forest Using Lasers." National Public Radio, 2018. www.npr.org/sections/thetwo-way/2018/02/02/582664327/game-changer-maya-cities-unearthed-in-guatemala-forest-using-lasers.

Klein, Herbert S., and Francisco Vidal Luna. *Slavery in Brazil.* Cambridge: Cambridge University Press, 2010.

Klich, Ignacio, and Jeffrey Lesser, eds. *Arab and Jewish Immigrants in Latin American Images and Realities.* New York and London: Routledge, 2013.

Knapp, Ray. *The American Musical and the Formation of National Identity.* Princeton: Princeton University Press, 2005.

Knauer, Lisa Maya. "Babalu Ayé in the Bronx." http://etnocuba.ucr .edu/?p = 3974. December 19, 2010.

Kobre, Sidney. *The Yellow Press and Gilded Age Journalism.* Tallahassee: Florida State University Press, 1964.

Koegel, John. "Music and Christianization on the Northern Frontier of New Spain." In *Conversion to Christianity from Late Antiquity to the Modern Age: Considering the Process in Europe, Asia, and the Americas,* edited by Calvin B. Kendall et al., 293–332. Minneapolis: Center for Early Modern History, University of Minnesota, 2008.

Koetting, James, and Roderic Knight. "What Do We Know about African Rhythm?" *Ethnomusicology* 30, no. 1 (1986): 57–63.

Koskoff, Ellen, *A Feminist Ethnomusicology: Writings on Music and Gender.* Urbana, Chicago, and Springfield: University of Illinois Press, 2014.

———, ed. *Women and Music in Cross-Cultural Perspective.* Urbana and Chicago: University of Illinois Press, 1989.

Kubayanda, Joseph B. *The Poet's Africa: Africanness in the Poetry of Nicolás Guillén and Aimé Césaire.* Edited by Henry Louis Gates Jr. Contributions in Afro-American and African Studies 138. New York: Greenwood, 1991.

Kuss, Malena. *Music of Latin America and the Caribbean: An Encyclopedic History.* Austin: University of Texas Press, 2004.

Labonville, Marie Elizabeth. *Juan Bautista Plaza and Musical Nationalism in Venezuela.* Bloomington and Indianapolis: Indiana University Press, 2007.

Laird, Paul. *Leonard Bernstein: A Guide to Research.* New York: Routledge, 2001.

Lamen, Darien. "Amazonian Sound Systems, Cyborg Indians, and the Future of the Future, Or, the Renewed Search for El Dorado under Late Capitalism." *Global South* 8, no. 1 (2014): 24–50.

Lawrence-King, Andrew. Liner notes. *La púrpura de la rosa.* Deutsche Harmonia Mundi, CD 05472 773552, 1999.

LeGuin, Elisabeth. *The Tonadilla in Performance: Lyric Comedy in Enlightenment Spain.* Berkeley and Los Angeles: University of California Press, 2014.

Lehnhoff, Dieter. "Introduction." Argentina. Liner notes. *Chapinlandia: Marimba Music of Guatemala.* Smithsonian Folkways, CD 40542, 2007.

León-Portilla, Miguel. *Bernardino de Sahagún: The First Anthropologist.* Norman: University of Oklahoma Press, 2002.

Levitin, Daniel. *This Is Your Brain on Music.* New York: Dutton Penguin, 2006.

Lewis, J. Lowell. *Ring of Liberation: Deceptive Discourse in Brazilian Capoeira.* Chicago: University of Chicago Press, 1992.

List, George. *Music and Poetry in a Colombian Village: A Tri-Cultural Heritage.* Bloomington: Indiana University Press, 1983.

Llewellyn, Howell. "Meet the Monks: EMI's Next Hit?" *Billboard* 106 (January 29, 1994): 1.

Loesser, Arthur. *Men, Women, and Pianos: A Social History.* New York: Simon and Schuster, 1954.

López-Rodríguez, Miriam. "Cooking Mexicanness: Shaping National Identity in Alfonso Arau's *Como Agua.*" In *Reel Food: Essays on Food and Film,* edited by Anne L. Bower, 61–74. London: Routledge, 2004.

Lorenz, Ricardo. *Canciones de Jara* (Jara Songs). Note. Revised, unpublished score. 2011.

Lornell, Kip, and Anne K. Rasmussen, eds. *Musics of Multicultural America.* New York: Schirmer, 1997.

Loza, Steven. *Barrio Rhythm: Mexican American Music in Los Angeles.* Urbana: University of Illinois Press, 1993.

———. *Essay on Chicano/Latino Music.* Los Angeles: UCLA Chicano Studies Research Center Press, 2017.

———. "From Veracruz to Los Angeles: The Reinterpretation of the 'Son Jarocho.'" *Latin American Music Review* 13, no. 2 (1992): 179–94.

———, ed. *Music of Latin America, Mexico, and the Caribbean.* San Diego: Cognella, 2013.

Madrid, Alejandro L. "Dancing with Desire: Cultural Embodiment in Tijuana's Nor-Tec Music and Dance." *Popular Music* 25, no. 3 (1996): 383–99.

———. *In Search of Julián Carrillo & Sonido 13.* New York: Oxford University Press, 2015.

———. *Music in Mexico.* Experiencing Music, Expressing Culture. New York: Oxford University Press, 2013.

———. *Nor-tec Rifa! Electronic Dance Music from Tijuana to the World.* New York: Oxford University Press, 2008.

———. *Transnational Encounters: Music and Performance at the U.S.–Mexican Border.* New York: Oxford University Press, 2008.

Madrid, Alejandro L., and Robin Moore. *Danzón: Circum-Caribbean Dialogues in Music and Dance.* New York: Oxford University Press, 2013.

Magaldi, Cristina. *Music in Imperial Rio de Janeiro: European Culture in a Tropical Milieu.* Lanham, MD: Rowman and Littlefield, 2004.

Magrini, Tullia, ed. *Music and Gender: Perspectives from the Mediterranean.* Chicago and London: University of Chicago Press, 2003.

Manuel, Peter. "The Anticipated Bass in Cuban Popular Music." *Latin American Music Review* 6, no. 2 (1985): 249–61.

———. *Essays on Cuban Music: North American and Cuban Perspectives.* Lanham, MD: University Press of America, 1991.

———. "From Scarlatti to 'Guantanamera': Dual Tonicity in Spanish and Latin American Musics." *Journal of the American Musicological Society* 55, no. 2 (2002): 311–36.

———. "The Saga of a Song: Ownership and Authorship in the Case of 'Guantanamera.'" *Latin American Music Review* 27, no. 2 (2006): 121–47.

Manuel, Peter, Michael Largey, and Kenneth M. Bilby. *Caribbean Currents: Caribbean Music from Rumba to Reggae.* Philadelphia: Temple University Press, 1995.

Martínez, María Elena. *Genealogical Fictions: Limpieza de Sangre, Religion, and Gender in Colonial Mexico.* Stanford: Stanford University Press, 2008.

Mason, John. *Orin Òrìṣà: Songs for Selected Heads.* New York: Yoruba Theological Archministry, 1992.

May, Chris. "Stan Getz: The Bossa Nova Albums." *All about Jazz,* November 11, 2008. www.allaboutjazz.com/stan-getz-the-bossa-nova-albums-by-chris-may.php.

McDonnell, Patrick J., and Tracie Wilkinson. "In a Mass in Chiapas, Pope Francis Denounces the Exclusion of Mexico's Native Peoples." *Los Angeles Times,* February 15, 2016. www.latimes.com/world/mexico-americas/la-na-pope-mexico-20160215-story.html.

McFarland, Pancho. *Chicano Rap: Gender and Violence in the Postindustrial Barrio.* Austin: University of Texas Press, 2008.

McGowan, Chris, and Ricardo Pessanha. "Samba: The Heartbeat of Rio." In *The Brazilian Sound: Samba, Bossa Nova and the Popular Music of Brazil.* Philadelphia: Temple University Press, 1991.

McGuire, Thomas R. "Ritual, Theater, and the Persistence of the Ethnic Groups: Interpreting Yaqui Semana Santa." *Journal of the Southwest* 31, no. 2 (1989): 159–78.

McNapsy, Clement J., S. J. "Conquest or Inculturation: Ways of Ministry in Early Jesuit Missions." In *Critical Moments in Religious History,* edited by Kenneth Keulman, 77–94. Macon: Mercer University Press, 1993.

McRobbie, Angela. "Dance and Social Fantasy." In *Gender and Generation,* edited by Angela McRobbie and Mica Nava, 130–61. London: Macmillan, 1984.

Mendoza, Zoila. *Shaping Society through Dance: Mestizo Ritual Performance in the Peruvian Andes.* Chicago: University of Chicago Press, 2000.

Menkart, Deborah, ed. *Caribbean Connections: Puerto Rico.* Washington, DC: Network of Educators of the Americas, 1992.

Mignolo, Walter. *The Idea of Latin America.* Malden, MA: Blackwell, 2005.

———. *Local Histories/Global Designs: Coloniality, Subaltern Knowledges, and Border Thinking.* Princeton: Princeton University Press, 2000.

Mintz, Sidney W., and Richard Price. *An Anthropological Approach to the Afro-American Past: A Caribbean Perspective.* Philadelphia: Institute for the Study of Human Issues, 1976.

Moehn, Frederick. *Contemporary Carioca: Technologies of Mixing in a Brazilian Musical Scene.* Durham and London: Duke University Press, 2012.

Monson, Ingrid. "Riffs, Repetition, and Theories of Globalization." *Ethnomusicology* 43, no. 1 (1999): 31–65.

Moore, Adrian. *Sonic Art: An Introduction to Electroacoustic Music Composition.* New York: Routledge, 2016.

Moore, Robin D. *Music and Revolution: Cultural Change in Socialist Cuba.* Berkeley: University of California Press, 2006.

———. *Music in the Hispanic Caribbean.* Experiencing Music, Expressing Culture. New York: Oxford University Press, 2010.

———. *Nationalizing Blackness: Afrocubanismo and Artistic Revolution in Havana.* Pittsburgh: University of Pittsburgh, 1995.

Moore, Robin D., and Walter A. Clark, eds. *Musics of Latin America.* New York: Norton, 2012.

Morales, Ed. *Latinx: A New Force in American Politics and Culture.* New York: Verso, 2018.

Morris, Nancy. "'Canto Porque Es Necesario Cantar': The New Song Movement in Chile, 1973–1983." *Latin American Research Review* 21, no. 2 (1986): 117–36.

Murphy, Annie. "The History of Modern Chile, Mirrored in Dance." National Public Radio, 2009. www.npr.org/templates/story /story.php?storyId = 120619384.

Murphy, John P. *Music in Brazil.* Experiencing Music, Expressing Culture. New York: Oxford University Press, 2006.

Nash, Manning. *The Cauldron of Ethnicity in the Modern World.* Chicago: University of Chicago Press, 1989.

Nettl, Bruno. *The Study of Ethnomusicology: Thirty-One Issues and Concepts.* Urbana: University of Illinois Press, 2005.

Nettl, Bruno, and Ruth Stone, Timothy Rice, and James Porter, eds. *The Garland Encyclopedia of World Music.* New York: Garland, 1998–2002; *Garland Encyclopedia of World Music Online.* Alexandria, VA: Alexander Street, 2008.

Niebylski, Dianna. "Passion or Heartburn? The Uses of Humor in Esquivel's and Arau's *Like Water for Chocolate.*" In *Literature and Film: A Guide to the Theory and Practice of Film Adaptation,* edited by Robert Stam and Alessandra Raengo. Oxford: Blackwell, 2005.

Noë, Alva. *Out of Our Heads: Why You Are Not Your Brain, and Other Lessons from the Biology of Consciousness.* New York: Hill and Wang, 2009.

Novak, David, and Matt Sakakeeny, eds. *Keywords in Sound.* Durham and London: Duke University Press, 2015.

Nye, Joseph S., Jr. "Soft Power and American Foreign Policy." *Political Science Quarterly* 119, no. 2 (2004): 255–70.

Ochoa Gautier, Ana María. *Aurality: Listening and Knowledge in Nineteenth-Century Colombia.* Durham and London: Duke University Press, 2014.

———. "García Márquez, *Macondismo,* and the Soundscapes of Vallenato." *Popular Music* 24, no. 2 (2005): 207–22.

———. "Introduction." Liner Notes. *Un fuego de sangre pura,* Smithsonian Folkways Recordings, SFW CD 40531, 2006.

Oja, Carol J. "*West Side Story* and *The Music Man:* Whiteness, Immigration, and Race in the U.S. in the 1950s." *Studies in Musical Theatre* 3, no. 1 (2009): 13–30.

Olsen, Dale A. "Music-Induced Altered States of Consciousness among Warao Shamans." *Journal of Latin American Lore* 1, no. 1 (1975): 19–33.

———. *Music of Eldorado: The Ethnomusicology of Ancient South American Cultures.* Gainesville: University of Florida Press, 2002.

Olsen, Dale A., and Daniel E. Sheehy, eds. *The Garland Encyclopedia of World Music: South America, Mexico, Central America, and the Caribbean.* New York and London: Garland Publishing, 1998.

———, eds. *The Garland Handbook of Latin American Music.* 2nd ed. New York and London: Routledge, 2008.

Ong, Aihwa, ed. *Flexible Citizenship: The Cultural Logics of Transnationality.* Durham: Duke University Press, 1999.

Ortega y Gasset, José. *The Dehumanization of Art and Notes on the Novel.* Translated by Helene Weyl. Princeton: Princeton University Press, 1948.

Pacini Hernández, Deborah. *Bachata: A Social History of a Dominican Popular Music.* Philadelphia: Temple University Press, 1995.

———. *¡Oye como va! Hybridity and Identity in Latino Popular Music.* Philadelphia: Temple University Press, 2010.

Palmié, Stephan. *The Cooking of History: How Not to Study Afro-Cuban Religion.* Chicago and London: University of Chicago Press, 2013.

Paredes, Américo. "The Mexican Corrido: Its Rise and Fall." In *Folklore and Culture on the Texas-Mexican Border,* edited by Richard Bauman, 129–41. Austin: CMAS, 1993.

———. *With His Pistol in His Hand: A Border Ballad and Its Hero.* Austin: University of Texas Press, 1958.

Parker, Robert L. *Carlos Chávez: Mexico's Modern-Day Orpheus.* Boston: Twayne, 1983.

Party, Daniel. "Beyond 'Protest Song': Popular Music in Pinochet's Chile, 1973–1990." In *Music and Dictatorship in Europe and Latin America,* edited by Roberto Illiano and Massimiliano Sala. Turnhout: Brephols, 2009.

Pedelty, Mark. *Musical Ritual in Mexico City from the Aztec to NAFTA.* Austin: University of Texas Press, 2004.

Pedroza, Ludim R. "El Sistema: Orchestrating Venezuela's Youth." *Latin American Music Review* 37, no. 2 (2016): 246–49.

Peña, Elaine A. *Performing Piety: Making Space Sacred with the Virgin of Guadalupe.* Berkeley, Los Angeles, and London: University of California Press, 2011.

Peña, Manuel. *The Texas-Mexican Conjunto: History of a Working-Class Music.* Austin: University of Texas Press, 1985.

Pendle, Karen. *Women in Music: A History.* 2nd ed. Bloomington: Indiana University Press, 2001.

Penyak, Lee M., and Walter J. Petry, eds. *Religion in Latin America: A Documentary History.* Maryknoll: Orbis, 2006.

Pérez Firmat, Gustavo. "Latunes: An Introduction." *Latin American Research Review* 43, no. 2 (2008): 180–203.

Pérez-Torres, Rafael. "Mestizaje in the Mix: Chicano Identity, Cultural Politics, and Postmodern Music." In *Music and the Racial Imagination,* edited by Ronald Radano and Philip V. Bohlman, 206–30. Chicago and London: University of Chicago Press, 2000.

Pernet, Corinne A. "'For the Genuine Culture of the Americas.'" In *Decentering America,* edited by Jessica C. E. Gienow-Hecht, 132–68. New York and Oxford: Berghahn, 2007.

Perone, Charles A., and Christopher Dunn. *Brazilian Popular Music & Globalization.* New York and London: Routlegde, 2001.

Perry, Imani. *Prophets of the Hood: Politics and Poetics in Hip Hop.* Chapel Hill and London: Duke University Press, 2004.

Powell, John. *Why You Love Music: From Mozart to Metallica.* New York, Boston, and London: Little, Brown, 2016.

Prashad, Vijay. "Bruce Lee and the Anti-Imperialism of Kung-Fu: A Polycultural Adventure." *positions* 11, no. 1 (2003): 51–90.

Prendergast, Roy M. *Film Music: A Neglected Art.* 2nd ed. New York and London: Norton, 1992.

Pressing, Jeff. "Black Atlantic Rhythm: its Computational and Transcultural Foundations." *Music Perception: An Interdisciplinary Journal* 19, no. 3 (2002): 285–310.

Querol, Miguel. "La Chacona en la época de Cervantes." *Anuario Musical* 25 (1970): 49–65. This text is in Spanish.

Quintero-Rivera, Ángel G., and Roberto Márquez. "Migration and Worldview in Salsa Music." *Latin American Music Review* 24, no. 2 (2003): 210–32.

"Race in Brazil: Affirming a Divide." *Economist,* 2012. www.economist.com/node/21543494.

Radano, Ronald M. "Interpreting Muzak: Speculations on Musical Experience in Everyday Life." *American Music* 7 (1989): 448–60.

Radice, Mark A. *Chamber Music: An Essential History.* Ann Arbor: University of Michigan Press, 2012.

Ragland, Cathy. *Música Norteña: Mexican Migrants Creating a Nation between Nations.* Philadelphia: Temple University Press, 2009.

Ramirez Berg, Charles. "Stereotyping and Resistance: A Crash Course on Hollywood's Latino Imagery." In *The Future of Latino Independent Media: A NALIP Sourcebook,* edited by Chon A. Noriega, 3–14. Los Angeles: UCLA Chicano Studies Research Center, 2000.

Ramos-Kitrell, Jesús. "Transnational Cultural Constructions: Cumbia Music and the Making of Locality in Monterrey." In *Transnational Encounters: Music and Performance at the U.S.–Mexico Border,* edited by Alejandro L. Madrid, 191–206. New York: Oxford University Press, 2011.

Ramsdell, Lea. "Cuban Hip Hop Goes Global: Orishas' *A lo cubano.*" *Latin American Music Review* 33, no. 1 (2012): 102–23.

Ramsey, Guthrie P., Jr. *Race Music: Black Culture from Bebop to Hip-Hop.* Berkeley: University of California Press, 1973.

Raymont, Henry. *Troubled Neighbors: The Story of U.S.–Latin American Relations from FDR to the Present.* Boulder: Westview, 2005.

Reily, Suzel Ana. "Remembering the Baroque Era: Historical Consciousness, Local Identity, and the Holy Week Celebrations in a Former Mining Town in Brazil." *Ethnomusicology Forum* 15, no. 1 (2006): 39–62.

Rein, Raanan. *Argentine Jews or Jewish Argentines? Essays on Identity, Ethnicity, and Diaspora.* Leiden: Brill, 2010.

Reis, João José. *Death Is a Festival: Funeral Rites and Rebellion in Nineteenth-Century Brazil.* Chapel Hill: University of North Carolina, 2003.

Reséndez, Andrés. *The Other Slavery: The Uncovered Story of Indian Enslavement in America.* New York: Houghton Mifflin Harcourt, 2016.

Reyes, Adelaida. *Music in America.* Experiencing Music, Expressing Culture. New York: Oxford University Press, 2004.

Reyes, David. *Land of a Thousand Dances: Chicano Rock 'n' Roll from Southern California.* Albuquerque: University of New Mexico Press, 1998.

Rivera, Raquel Z. *New York Ricans from the Hip Hop Zone.* New York: Palgrave Macmillan, 2003.

Rizzolatti, Giacomo, and Corrado Sinigaglia. *Mirrors in the Brain: How Our Minds Share Actions and Emotions.* New York: Oxford University Press, 2008.

Roberts, John Storm. *The Latin Tinge: The Impact of Latin American Music on the United States.* 2nd ed. New York and Oxford: Oxford University Press, 1999.

Robertson, Carol E. "Power and Gender in the Musical Experiences of Women." In *Women and Music in Cross-Cultural Perspectives,* edited by Ellen Koskoff. Westport, CT: Greenwood, 1987.

Rodó, José Enrique. *Ariel.* Translated by Margaret Sayers Peden. Austin: University of Texas Press, 1988.

Rodríguez, Clara E., ed. *Changing Race: Latinos, the Census, and the History of Ethnicity in the United States.* New York and London: New York University Press, 2000.

———. *Latin Looks: Images of Latinos and Latinas in the U.S. Media.* Boulder: Westview, 1997.

Rodríguez, Jeanette. *Our Lady of Guadalupe: Faith and Empowerment among Mexican-American Women.* Austin: University of Texas Press, 1994.

Röhrig Assunção, Matthias. *Capoeira: The History of an Afro-Brazilian Martial Art.* London and New York: Routlegde, 2005.

Rojas, Ricardo. *Los Gauchescos.* Buenos Aires: Losada, 1948. This text is in Spanish.

Romero, Brenda M. "*Matachines Danza* as Intercultural Discourse." In *Dancing across Borders: Danzas y Bailes Mexicanos,* edited by Olga Nájera-Ramírez, Norma E. Cantú, and Brenda M. Romero, 185–205. Urbana and Chicago: University of Illinois Press, 2009.

Romero, Raúl R. *Debating the Past: Music, Memory, and Identity in the Andes.* New York and Oxford: Oxford University Press, 2001.

Rondón, César Miguel. *The Book of Salsa: A Chronicle of Urban Music from the Caribbean to New York City.* Chapel Hill: University of North Carolina Press, 2008.

Roosevelt, Theodore. *Theodor Roosevelt: An Autobiography with Illustrations.* 1913; New York: Scribner's, 1920.

Rothman, Joshua. "The Meaning of Culture." *New Yorker,* December 26, 2014.

Rowe, William, and Vivian Schelling. *Memory and Modernity: Popular Culture in Latin America.* London: Verso, 1991.

Roy, William G. 2010. "How Social Movements Do Culture." In *Reds, Whites, and Blues: Social Movements, Folk Music, and Race in the United States,* 234–50. Princeton: Princeton University Press, 2010.

Ruiz, Ramón Eduardo. *Triumphs and Tragedy: A History of the Mexican People.* New York and London: Norton, 1992. See especially chapters 16–18.

Russell, Craig H. *From Serra to Sancho: Music and Pageantry in the California Missions.* Currents in Latin American & Iberian Music. New York: Oxford University Press, 2009.

Russell, Melinda. "'Give Your Body Joy, Macarena.'" In *From Tejano to Tango: Latin American Popular Music,* edited by Walter Aaron Clark, 172–92. New York and London: Routledge, 2002.

Saavedra, Leonora, ed. *Carlos Chávez and His World.* Princeton: Princeton University Press, 2015.

———. "Carlos Chávez's Polysemic Style." *Journal of the American Musicological Society* 68. no. 1 (2015): 99–150.

Sachs, Curt. *World History of the Dance.* New York: Norton, 1963.

Sacks, Oliver. *Musicophilia.* New York: Knopf, 2007.

Sadie, Julie Anne. *The Norton/Grove Dictionary of Women Composers.* London and New York: Macmillan, 1995.

Sadlier, Darlene J. *Americans All: Good Neighbor Cultural Diplomacy in World War II.* Austin: University of Texas Press, 2012.

Savigliano, Marta E. *Tango and the Political Economy of Passion.* Boulder: Westview, 1995.

Schechter, John. *The Indispensable Harp: Historical Development, Modern Roles, Configurations and Performance Practices in Ecuador and Latin America.* Kent and London: Kent State University Press, 1992.

———, ed. *Music in Latin American Culture: Regional Traditions.* New York: Schirmer-Thomson, 1999.

Schlesinger, Stephen C. *Bitter Fruit: The Story of the American Coup in Guatemala.* Cambridge, MA: Harvard University Press, 1982.

Schonberg, Harold. *The Great Pianists: From Mozart to the Present.* New York: Simon and Schuster, 1963.

Schwartz-Kates, Deborah. *Alberto Ginastera: A Research and Information Guide.* New York and London: Routledge, 2010.

———. "Alberto Ginastera, Argentine Cultural Construction, and the Gauchesco Tradition." *Musical Quarterly* 86, no. 2 (2002): 248–81.

———. "The *Gauchesco* Tradition as a Source of National Identity in Argentine Art Music (ca. 1890–1955)." PhD diss. University of Texas at Austin, 1997.

Shapiro, Daniel. *Negotiating the Nonnegotiable: How to Resolve Your Most Emotionally Charged Conflicts.* New York: Viking, 2016.

Shaw, Lisa. *The Social History of Brazilian Samba.* Aldershot, UK: Ashgate, 1999.

Sheehy, Daniel. *¡Ayombe! The Heart of Colombia's Música Vallenata.* Liner notes. Smithsonian Folkways CD 40546, 2008.

———. *La Bamba: Sones Jarochos from Veracruz.* Liner notes. Smithsonian Folkways CD 40505, 2003.

———. *Mariachi Music in America.* Experiencing Music, Expressing Culture. New York: Oxford University Press, 2006.

———. "Mexico." In *The Garland Encyclopedia of World Music,* vol. 2, 600–25. New York: Garland, 1998.

———. "Popular Mexican Musical Traditions: The Mariachi of West Mexico and the *Conjunto Jarocho* of Veracruz." In *Music in Latin American Culture: Regional Traditions,* edited by John M. Schechter, 34–79. New York: Schirmer-Thomson, 1999.

Shelemay, Kay Kaufman. *Soundscapes: Exploring Music in a Changing World.* 3rd ed. New York and London: Norton, 2015.

Shepherd, John, ed. *Continuum Encyclopedia of Popular Music of the World.* London: Continuum, 2003.

Sheridan, Thomas E. "How to Tell the Story of 'A People without History': Narrative versus Ethnohistorical Approaches to the Study of the Yaqui Indians through Time." *Journal of the Southwest* 30, no. 2 (1988): 168–89.

Simon, Alissa. "The Costeño Hip Movement: A Conceptual Framework for Understanding Sexuality in Afro-Colombian Folklore Music and Dance." PhD diss. University of California, Los Angeles, 2012.

Simonett, Helena. *Banda: Mexican Musical Life Across Borders.* Middletown, CT: Wesleyan University Press, 2001.

Skidmore, Thomas E., and Peter H. Smith. *Modern Latin America.* 5th ed. New York and Oxford: Oxford University Press, 2001.

Skinner, Jonathan. "Women Dancing Back—and Forth: Resistance and Self-Regulation in Belfast Salsa." *Dance Research Journal* 40, no. 1 (2008): 65–77.

Skinner, Thomas E. *Black into White: Race and Nationality in Brazilian Thought.* New York: Oxford University Press, 1974.

Slatta, Richard. *Gauchos and the Vanishing Frontier.* Lincoln: University of Nebraska Press, 1983.

Slayton, Michael. *Women of Influence in Contemporary Music: Nine American Composers.* Lanham, MD: Scarecrow, 2011.

Slonimsky, Nicolas. *Music of Latin America.* New York: Thomas Y. Crowell, 1945.

Small, Christopher. *Musicking: The Meanings of Performing and Listening.* Hanover: University Press of New England, 1998.

Smith, Christian, and Joshua Prokopy, eds. *Latin American Religion in Motion.* New York and London: Routledge, 1999.

Sollors, Werner. "Foreword: Theories of Ethnicity." In *Theories of Ethnicity: A Classical Reader.* New York: New York University Press, 1996.

Spicer, Edward H. "Contrasting Forms of Nativism among the Mayos and Yaquis of Sonora, Mexico." In *The Social Anthropology of Latin America: Essays in Honor of Ralph Leon Beals,* edited by Water Goldschmidt and Harry Hoijer, 104–25. Los Angeles: University of California Press, 1970.

———. *The Yaquis: A Cultural History.* Tucson: University of Arizona Press, 1980.

Spicer, Rosamond B., and N. Ross Crumrine. *Performing the Renewal of Community: Indigenous Easter Rituals in North Mexico and Southwest United States.* Lanham, MD: University Press of America, 1997.

Stallings, Stephanie N. "Collective Difference: The Pan American Association of Composers and Pan American Ideology in Music, 1925–1945." PhD diss., Florida State University, 2008.

Starkloff, Carl F. *A Theology of the In-Between: The Value of Syncretic Process.* Milwaukee: Marquette University Press, 2002.

Stein, Louise K. "'La Música de Dos Orbes': A Context for the First Opera of the Americas." *Opera Quarterly* 22, nos. 3–4 (2006): 433–58.

———. *Songs of Mortals, Dialogues of the Gods: Music and Theatre in Seventeenth-Century Spain.* Oxford: Clarendon, 1993.

Stevenson, Robert M. "Carreño's 1875 California Appearances." *Inter-American Music Review* 5, no. 2 (1983): 9–15.

———. *Music in Inca and Aztec Territory.* Berkeley and Los Angeles: University of California Press, 1968.

———. *Music in Mexico: A Historical Survey.* New York: Thomas Y. Crowell, 1952.

Stone, Ruth. *Music in West Africa.* Experiencing Music, Expressing Culture. New York: Oxford University Press, 2005.

Suarez, Ray. *Latino-Americans: The 500-Year Legacy That Shaped a Nation.* New York: Penguin, 2013.

Taffet, Jeffrey F. "'My Guitar Is Not for the Rich': The New Chilean Song Movement and the Politics of Culture." *Journal of American Culture* 20, no. 2 (1997): 91–103.

Taylor, Julie. "Tango: Theme of Class and Nation." *Ethnomusicology* 20, no. 2 (1976): 273–91.

Terry, Don. "Mariachi Musicians Sustaining Their Traditions." *New York Times,* October 31, 1997.

Thomas, Helen, ed. *Dance, Gender, and Culture.* Basingstoke, UK: Macmillan, 1993.

Thomas, Susan. *Cuban Zarzuela: Performing Race and Gender on Havana's Lyric Stage.* Bloomington and Indianapolis: University of Illinois Press, 2008.

———. "Ibero-American Music and the Music History Curriculum: Reform, Revolution and the Pragmatics of Change." *Journal of Music History Pedagogy* 7, no. 2 (2017): 94–98.

Tiemstra, Suzanne Spicer. *The Choral Music of Latin America: A Guide to Compositions and Research.* Westport, CT: Greenwood, 1992.

Timerman, Jacobo. *Prisoner without a Name, Cell without a Number.* Translated by Tony Talbot. New York: Knopf, 1981.

Titon, Jeff Todd. *Worlds of Music: An Introduction to the Music of the World's Peoples.* 5th ed. Boston: Cengage Learning, 2009.

Tobin, Jeffrey. "Tango and the Scandal of Homosocial Desire." In *The Passion of Music and Dance: Body, Gender, and Sexuality,* edited by William Washabaugh, 79–102. Oxford: Oxford University Press, 1998.

Tomlinson, Gary. *The Singing of the New World: Indigenous Voice in the Era of European Contact.* Cambridge: Cambridge University Press, 2007.

Tomlinson, John. *Globalization and Culture.* Chicago: University of Chicago Press, 1999.

Torgovnick, Mariana. *Gone Primitive: Savage Intellects, Modern Lives.* Chicago and London: University of Chicago Press, 1990.

Tunstall, Tricia. *Changing Lives: Gustavo Dudamel, El Sistema, and the Transformative Power of Music.* New York: Norton, 2012.

Turino, Thomas. *Music in the Andes.* Experiencing Music, Expressing Culture. New York: Oxford University Press, 2008.

Urfé, Odiolio. "Music and Dance in Cuba." In *Africa in Latin America: Essays on History, Culture, and Socialization,* edited by Manuel Moreno Fraginals, translated by Leonor Blum. New York: Holms and Meier, 1977.

Vargas, Deborah L. *Dissonant Divas in Chicana Music: The Limits of La Onda.* Minneapolis: University of Minnesota Press, 2012.

Vega Seña, Marcos Fidel. *Vallenato: Cultura y sentimiento.* Bogotá: Universidad Cooperativa de Colombia, 2005. This text is in Spanish.

Veloso, Caetano. *Tropical Truth: A Story of Music and Revolution in Brazil.* New York: Knopf, 2003.

Vila, Pablo, ed. *The Militant Song Movement in Latin America: Chile, Uruguay, and Argentina.* Lanham, MD: Lexington, 2014.

Wade, Bonnie. *Thinking Musically.* Experiencing Music, Expressing Culture. New York: Oxford University Press, 2004.

Wade, Peter. "Music, Blackness, and National Identity: Three Moments in Colombian History." *Popular Music* 17, no. 1 (1998): 1–20.

———. *Music, Race, and Nation: Música Tropical in Colombia.* Chicago and London: University of Chicago Press, 2000.

Wagstaff, Grayson. "Franciscan Mission Music in California, c. 1770–1830: Chant, Liturgical, and Polyphonic Traditions." *Journal of the Royal Musical Association* 126, no. 1 (2001): 54–82.

Washburne, Christopher. "Play It 'Con Filin!': The Swing and Expression of Salsa." *Latin American Music Review* 19, no. 2 (1998): 160–85.

———. *Sounding Salsa: Performing Latin Music in New York City.* Philadelphia: Temple University Press, 2008.

Waxer, Lise. "'En Conga, Bonga, y Campana': The Rise of Colombian Salsa." *Latin American Music Review* 21, no. 2 (2000): 118–68.

———. *Situating Salsa: Global Markets and Local Meanings in Latin Popular Music.* London: Routledge, 2002.

Weiss, Piero, and Richard Taruskin. "Music in Temple and Synagogue: The Judaic Heritage." In *Music in the Western World: A History in Documents,* 15–21. New York: Schirmer-Thomson, 1984.

Wells, Elizabeth. *West Side Story: Cultural Perspectives on an American Musical.* Lanham, MD: Scarecrow, 2011.

Wendland, Kristin F. *Tracing Tangueros: Argentine Tango Instrumental Music.* Oxford University Press, 2016.

Wieschiolek, Hieke. "'Ladies, Just Follow His Lead!': Salsa, Gender and Identity." In *Sport, Dance and Embodied Identities,* edited by Eduardo Archetti and Noel Dyck, 115–38. Oxford: Berg, 2003.

Williams, Alistair. *Constructing Musicology.* New York and London: Routledge, 2001.

Williams, Daryle. *Culture Wars in Brazil: The First Vargas Regime, 1930–1945.* Durham and London: Duke University Press, 2001.

Williams, Lorna V. *Self and Society in the Poetry of Nicolás Guillén.* Baltimore: Johns Hopkins University Press, 1982.

Wirtz, Kristina. *Performing Afro-Cuba: Image, Voice, Spectacle in the Making of Race and History.* Chicago and London: University of Chicago Press. 2014.

Wissler, Holly. "From Grief and Joy We Sing: Social and Cosmic Regenerative Processes in the Songs of Q'eros, Peru." PhD diss., Florida State University, 2009.

Woll, Allen L. *The Latin Image in American Film.* Rev. ed. Los Angeles: UCLA Latin American Center Publications, University of California, 1997.

Wright, Simon. *Villa-Lobos.* Oxford and New York: Oxford University Press, 1992.

Young, James O. *Cultural Appropriation and the Arts.* Sussex: Wiley, 2008.

Zea, Luis. "'I Thought of It in Terms of Pure Music': An Interview with Antonio Lauro." *Classical Guitar* 21, no. 1 (2002): 11–16.

———. "The Works for Solo Guitar by Antonio Lauro: Analysis and Interpretation." *Classical Guitar* 21, no. 11 (2003): 51–53.

Zinn, Howard. *A People's History of the United States.* New York: HarperCollins, 2003.

Zohn-Muldoon, Ricardo. "The Song of the Snake: Silvestre Revueltas's *Sensemayá*." *Latin American Music Review* 19, no. 2 (1998): 133–59.

Zolov, Eric. *Refried Elvis: The Rise of the Mexican Counterculture.* Berkeley: University of California Press, 1999.

FILMS (IN ADDITION TO THOSE DISCUSSED IN TEXT)

Afro-Uruguayan Rhythms: Candombe. Surmeanges, 2006.

Beyond Ipanema: Brazilian Waves in Global Music. Beyond Ipanema Films, 2009.

Chulas Fronteras. Arhoolie Records, 2003 (originally released in 1976).

Cidade de Deus. General distribution, 2002.

Favelas on Blast. Mad Decent, 2008.

"The Latin American Spirit." Broadcast of March 8, 1961. *Leonard Bernstein's Young Peoples Concerts.* Doubleday, 1993.

Latin Music USA. PBS Distribution, 2009.

Plena is Work, Plena is Song, directed by Pedro A. Rivera, Susan Zeig. PBS. www.youtube.com/watch?v = iAsX3qi0Kg8.

La Quinceañera, directed by Adam Taub, 2007.

Salsa: Latin Music of New York and Puerto Rico. Shanachie, 1973.

Shotguns and Accordions: Music of the Marijuana Regions of Colombia. Shanachie, 2001.

Index